P9-ASL-958

Education in American History

Theodore Lownik Library
Illinois Benedictine College
Lisle, Illinois 60532

Education in American History

Readings on the Social Issues

edited by
Michael B. Katz

Praeger Publishers
New York · Washington · London

370
.973
K19e

PRAEGER PUBLISHERS
111 Fourth Avenue, New York, N.Y. 10003, U.S.A.
5, Cromwell Place, London SW7 2JL, England

Published in the United States of America in 1973
by Praeger Publishers, Inc.

Almost all of the footnotes have been deleted from the articles in this book. We faced a choice of deleting footnotes or chapters since the book turned out to be substantially longer than anticipated. It seemed best in the circumstances to preserve as much of the substance as possible. Readers interested in pursuing the topics treated in the articles will find full documentation in sources listed in the acknowledgements, all of which should be available in most college and university libraries.

© 1973 by Praeger Publishers, Inc.
"The Integration of Higher Education into
the Wage-Labor System" © 1973 by Samuel Bowles

All rights reserved

Library of Congress Cataloging in Publication Data

Katz, Michael B. comp.
  Education in American history.

  CONTENTS: Education and early American society: Cremin, L. A. Educational configurations in colonial America. Rothman, D. J. A note on the study of the colonial family. Zuckerman, M. [etc.]
  1. Education—United States—History—Addresses, essays, lectures. 2. Educational sociology—United States history—Addresses, essays, lectures. 1. Title.
LA205.K33   370'.973   72-79541

Printed in the United States of America

Contents

Introduction

The history of education has not been a popular subject. It is frequently a compulsory part of teacher training in which students enroll with reluctance and from which they emerge neither enlightened nor interested. The responsibility for this unhappy situation rests with the people who have taught and written on the subject. In the hope of inspiring prospective educators with the glory of their calling, professors of education early in the twentieth century turned the history of education into a celebration of the glorious evolution of the public school and its triumph over reactionary foes. This was bad history, and bad pedagogy as well. It transformed a potentially exciting subject into an insipid mythology. As they sensed what had happened, serious historians increasingly avoided the study of education, which, in the eyes of the academic world, acquired an anti-intellectual taint from which it still suffers.

For a variety of reasons, historians began to show a vastly heightened interest in education in the late 1950's. A committee of distinguished historians published a pamphlet calling for renewed effort in the field and sponsored some research; schools of education looked for professional historians to hire; scholarship money became available for students in history of education; and the U.S. Office of Education even began to give a few research grants in the area. However, the new essays and books were slow in coming. It took about a decade, in fact, for the history of education to catch a foothold in the world of serious scholarship, and only in the last five or six years has serious scholarly work begun to appear with any regularity. Even so, the amount might better be described as a steady stream than a flood. The progress of the field can most easily be gauged by means of a cursory examination of the *History of Education Quarterly,* which, in the last few years, has developed from a mediocre publication struggling for survival into an important academic journal.

The work of the last several years has transformed conventional interpretations of the history of education. Historians have asked new questions, used new methods, and approached the past with a less reverential attitude toward contemporary schooling. The result is a vital and dynamic field of study whose boundaries, approaches, and conceptual bases are still far from settled. Recent scholarship in the area is of great significance both to students of history in general and to people concerned with current educational issues. The role of education in American history has been immense, and the attempt to illuminate it forms an integral part of the larger effort to understand social and intellectual development. At the same time, the reinterpretations of the history of education are immensely suggestive for people critical of contemporary schooling, for these reinterpretations replace myths with a realistic and usable educational past—one that shows how the current situation, with all its faults, came to be.

The purpose of this collection is very simply to make some of this recent work available to students and teachers in a form suitable for use in an introductory course. Much of the best recent writing is to be found in journals or specialized books and hence is somewhat inaccessible to students. This book, it is hoped, will serve to bring students together with a number of historians who are interpreting the educational past.

The book is organized into six sections. Four of them are chronological, corresponding to the time periods into which courses are often divided. The other two—dealing with higher education and the education of blacks—are topical, though each section is itself roughly chronological. Any selection of articles—indeed, any division of history into periods and topics—is partially arbitrary. There are many fine articles that considerations of space, regrettably, made it necessary to omit. There are also other ways into which the material here could have been organized and other emphases that it could have been given. I hope that the decisions reflected in the book present a compromise that can be accepted and found useful by people of differing views.

The articles themselves have been chosen to emphasize new interpretations and new methods of study. A number of them, it should be pointed out, deal primarily with the family. The history of education must consider the constellation of educational influences within a society, and the family is an educational setting at least as influential as the school. The history of the family in America has even less of a tradition as a subject of study than the history of education. However, it, too, has begun to receive serious consideration in recent years. Some of the early results of that work are of immediate interest to historians of education, and I have included selections that contribute to understanding the process of socialization and the relations among the family, the school, and other social institutions.

Each section of the book begins with an introduction explaining the choice of the articles that follow and presenting some of the major interpretive and methodological issues with which they deal. My intent in these introductions is to provide the student with a framework into which to fit the selections and to provide the teacher with a springboard for provocative and useful discussion.

Indeed, "provocative" and "useful" describe my hopes for this book. For I want to supply material that will help to change the image of educational history in students' minds. There is no excuse for boredom with a subject that can contribute so significantly to both historical understanding and contemporary reform.

Education in American History

1. Education and Early American Society

The search for origins is inherently fascinating. In American history it has concentrated traditionally on the colonial period, at times neglecting the European culture and society that settlers brought with them to the New World. Thus, colonial history sometimes has overemphasized the uniqueness of early American thought, activity, and institutions. As well as obscuring America's European beginnings, the preoccupation with origins has led on occasion to an inaccurate notion of historical development as a simple process through which institutions such as schools gradually evolved into their current form, much as a seed becomes a flower. Contemporary scholarship has shown the inadequacy of both the idea of American uniqueness and simple, evolutionary conceptions of change. Colonial settlers adapted European patterns to the New World, and the institutions they created underwent profound alterations before they assumed their current form.

But the study of colonial history remains a topic of great interest and importance. Indeed, in the last few years it has become perhaps the most vital and exciting area in American historical research. Part of the fascination of colonial history lies in its story: the establishment of societies in the wilderness. Colonial history also provides an opportunity to examine the way in which a society takes shape. The relative simplicity and newness of colonial society make it possible to analyze the relations among important social features—such as population, family structure, education, and political organization—more directly than is possible in more complex and highly developed societies. Thus, the questions that concern colonial historians are of broad interest to scholars of all periods, for they involve the fundamental organization of society. In their attempt to answer these questions, colonial historians have been among the first American scholars to use some of the newest techniques of historical research and sophisticated concepts from the behavioral sciences. Their work, therefore, has broad methodological significance.

One of the most influential works in stimulating the development of colonial social history also has been one of the seminal books in sparking recent interest in the history of education as a field of study. Bernard Bailyn's *Education in the Forming of American Society*, discussed in the selection by David J. Rothman, calls attention to the central place of the family in the social and educational experiences of colonial Americans. By doing so, it forcefully highlights the need for educational historians to extend their concerns beyond schooling. In the past, formal institutions played a much smaller role in the education of young people than they do today. In fact, the equation of education and schooling is largely a modern development. Thus, to understand the process of education in earlier times it is critical to consider the range and interrelationships of the various settings in which people learned—family, school, apprenticeship, church, community. Even for a relatively simple society like colonial America, historians disagree about the nature of these relationships. Indeed, determining the relative roles of different social agencies in the formation of personality and society is one of the liveliest and most controversial occupations in American history today. The selections that follow illustrate some of these concerns, and each exemplifies the attempt to extend the definition of education to include family and community.

In the first selection, Lawrence A. Cremin describes the distinctive configurations of educational and social institutions that characterized the diverse regions of colonial America. At the same time, he points to the common elements in educational development throughout the colonies and assesses their significance in shaping the experience of young people. David J. Rothman, in the second selection, contrasts two seminal books on the colonial family, by Edmund Morgan and Bernard Bailyn, and evaluates their conflicting interpretations in light of recent European scholarship on the history of the family. In the process, Rothman points to a number of significant and intriguing questions that must be attacked by historians trying to understand the relations among education, the family, and colonial society. In the third selection, Michael Zuckerman argues that the goal of socialization in colonial America was to bring young people to internalize the dominant social values: concord and consensus. Viewed in this way, Zuckerman maintains, the phases of the socialization process from infancy through marriage can be understood as part of a well-regulated cycle designed to perpetuate a very special type of social order.

Educational Configurations in Colonial America

Lawrence A. Cremin

Diversity . . . also flourished among the communities of provincial America, as the interaction of ethnic and religious traditions, settlement patterns, internal and external migration, and economic circumstances produced fundamental differences in modes of life and thought. The result was a considerable variety of contexts in which Americans grew up and were educated to maturity. The New England town was no longer a frontier experiment preoccupied with problems of subsistence and defense but a fully developed institution, firmly rooted in the countryside and solidly established in its ways. The relatively isolated farmsteads of the seventeenth-century Chesapeake region had become by the eighteenth a series of more settled counties, with connecting roads and waterways and occasional hamlets marking diminutive crossroads of trade and communication, though it should be noted that there were persistent efforts throughout the century to develop additional centers of commerce and industry. And the market towns of the seventeenth century, Boston, New York, Philadelphia, and Charleston, had become the thriving cities of the eighteenth, with New York having achieved an unprecedented population of twenty thousand by 1770. Moreover, as settlers pushed out from the initial centers of population, there arose a second and third generation of communities, frontier, back-country settlements that wrestled with many of the same problems that had beset the original pioneers—many, that is, but significantly not all, for what had been learned in the crucible of seventeenth-century experience, from the Indians, from trial and error, and from one another, had been passed along via education to the eighteenth-century frontiersman.

The religious and ethnic composition of these communities varied considerably, according to the fortunes of migration, the receptiveness of the original settlers, and the character and productivity of the regional economy. But at the very least the external immigration and internal migration of the eighteenth century brought increasingly diverse subcommunities into physical and social contiguity, strengthening, on the one hand, the determination of particular groups to preserve their cultural purity through guarded education (thus the schools maintained by Quaker meetings throughout the colonies) and, on the other hand, the need and opportunity

Abridged from Chapter 17, "Configurations," in *American Education: The Colonial Experience, 1607–1783* by Lawrence A. Cremin. Copyright © 1970 by Lawrence A. Cremin. By permission of Harper & Row, Publishers, Inc.

to mount common educational ventures toward agreed upon but limited ends (thus the neighborhood schools established under multidenominational auspices in the province of Pennsylvania).

* * *

Yet, granted the coexistence of communities at different stages of development and granted the contrasts in education deriving from variations in life-style from community to community and from group to group within the same community, there remain certain significant changes in the general configuration of provincial educational institutions that are worthy of note. In the first place, there is considerable evidence of a redifferentiation—to employ a neologism—of educational functions that had, in the seventeenth-century colonies, commonly been carried by the family simply because of the paucity or absence of alternative institutions. Thus, as schools and churches became more readily accessible, certain aspects of the nurture of piety and literacy moved outside the household to the agencies that had borne them in England at the time the colonies were originally settled. And, by 1773, the Reverend Jonathan Boucher, who had been a schoolmaster in his youth, was arguing that Americans had generally failed in the execution of parental responsibility for education, and that the least they could do was to support decent schools and colleges for their children.

Second, with the proliferation of types of schooling, the concomitant increase in the variety of printed textual materials for instruction and self-instruction, and the development of libraries for the collection and dissemination of such materials, the range of possible life-styles open to a given individual beyond the particular version proffered by his family, his church, or even his neighboring school or surrounding community, was vastly enlarged. A particular school might or might not have been liberating for a particular individual, but the institution of schooling in general, when coupled with the flow of didactic material from the press, was indeed liberating, in that it provided genuine life alternatives. And, in an expanding economy with a persistent labor shortage and a consequent dearth of certificatory requirements for entry into careers, the access to alternative life-styles provided by education was confirmed by the access to alternative careers afforded by the economy. The legal career of Patrick Henry, built as it was upon a brief attendance at an English school, the tutelage of his father, John Henry, who had attended King's College at Aberdeen, the preaching of the Reverend Samuel Davies, and some self-instruction in Coke on Littleton and the Virginia code, is a splendid case in point.

Third, there was the emergence of the voluntary association as an instrument of informal education—the young people's societies organized by New England preachers; the neighborhood groups that gathered around the coffeehouses, taverns, and inns of the towns and cities; the salons of Boston and Charleston; the innumerable ministers' organizations, merchant associations, professional societies, Masonic lodges, and Committees of Correspondence through which Americans gathered information, exchanged ideas, debated policy, and in the process formed character and world view. These, too, liberated, in that they afforded opportunity for the creation and development of alternative modes of life and thought.

Finally, though London remained the hub of the empire, growing in size and influence throughout the eighteenth century, and though the colonies remained part of the network of communities that spread out from London to constitute the political, economic, and intellectual empire, it is important to recognize that there was a decided increase in the extent and variety of intercolonial and interprovincial communication, and hence education. London styles of thought, taste, and conduct continued to exert profound influence, especially on the emerging colonial merchant and gentry class that was aware of them and eager and able to imitate them. But equally important were the influence of Scottish styles throughout the colonies, and the influence of particular colonial styles, both imported and indigenous, beyond the bounds of particular colonies. The improvement of the post, the facilitation and increase of travel, the enlargement of trade, the multiplication of newspapers—all enhanced and extended this process of mutual education among the colonists, and in so doing served as a countervailing force to the inherent localism that dominated the culture of provincial America.

* * *

New England towns varied significantly, of course, in their particular character and traditions, the remote fishing communities of Barnstable and Nantucket bearing at best minimal resemblance to the western agricultural communities of Westfield and Hadley. Yet, it is interesting to examine the educational development of a particular township during the eighteenth century, not so much for any generalizations that might be drawn from the data as for the light they shed upon the changing educational configurations of the provincial era. And for this purpose the history of Dedham is instructive.

Dedham was the very model of the seventeenth-century inland agricultural town, even though it was situated only nine miles from the hubbub of commercial Boston. Planted in 1636 by about thirty families "being come together by divine providence from several parts of England: few of them known to one another before," the town grew in population to some 650 inhabitants in 1689, to some 1,200 by 1710, and to 1,919 by 1765 (organized into 309 families living in 239 houses). In the classic New England pattern, the first church was gathered late in 1638, growing out of a series of meetings of "all the inhabitants who affected church communion . . . lovingly to discourse and consult together such questions as might further tend to establish a peaceable and comfortable civil society, and prepare for spiritual communion," and with the Reverend John Allin, a graduate of Caius College, Cambridge, as minister. In the early decades, most families had at least one member within the church and several had two, though the problems that led eventually to the adoption of the halfway covenant began to afflict Dedham in the later 1650's, with a consequent decline in baptisms and church affiliations. The proportion of freemen was also high, with 75 per cent of the adult males eligible to vote in provincial elections. The first school was authorized by unanimous action of the town meeting on January 2, 1643, and put on a stable financial basis two years later by another unanimous decision to raise twenty pounds annually to maintain a schoolmaster (the first, Ralph Wheelock, was an alumnus of Clare College, Cambridge). Whether in testimony to household or church or school instruction, Dedham's literacy rate, at least among adult males (as measured by the ability to sign their names), remained high: Of forty-four settlers in the first generation, signatures have been located for twenty-five, of whom eight made marks; of forty townsmen in the second generation, signatures have been located for at least thirty-six, of whom only two made marks, and at least one of these, John MacKintosh, had come to the town as an adult from Scotland.

Throughout the seventeenth century, Dedham was a stable, close-knit community, increasing in wealth and enjoying a substantial measure of internal democracy—at least among admitted townsmen. In the early decades of the eighteenth century, however, population pressures began to exert a perceptible effect. During the 1720's and 1730's, the town found it necessary to take various actions setting new boundaries, annexing surrounding territory, and establishing well-defined precincts. At the same time, the easy prosperity of the first years began to wane: Most of the best land had been taken; the number of poor rose; and many sons whose fathers were having difficulty providing for them found themselves forced to leave. An early—and, in retrospect, idyllic—simplicity began to give way to internal conflicts and social complexities.

* * *

Probably the most important outcome of the town's growing size and diversity was the partial breakdown of older communal ties. Before the division into precincts, the town meeting had maintained a pervasive influence over all aspects of life, and the selectmen had exercised considerable power. Sharpening internal conflicts, however, slowly disrupted the older functioning of town government. The town meeting was frequently captured by one faction or another for partisan purposes, and appeals were increasingly made over the meeting and selectmen to the provincial authorities and the justices of the peace. Out of the growing impasse came a decentralized system that divided the town's powers between town and precincts. The latter began to hold their own meetings with their own clerks to deal with religious affairs and other local problems; the former continued to handle the administration of town property and finance, the maintenance of roads, and the care of the poor. In one respect, decentralization made possible a new form of political community, one increasingly freed from the assumption that stability depended upon town-wide conformity. In effect, the inability of the town to enforce conformity, coupled with the emergence of alternative agencies for contending with day-by-day problems on the local level, placed the stability of the town on a new basis, leaving greater latitude for individuals to differ and to initiate alternative policies without appearing to threaten the very foundations of social order.

In 1692, the general court enacted a new province law, requiring that grammar schools be "constantly kept" by all towns of a hundred families or more. The law was stringently enforced by the courts of session, and, in 1701, its terms were strengthened by the requirement that each grammar school be staffed with a full-time, certified Latinist. Although Dedham had not been wholly remiss—the town, incidentally, had been indicted in 1690 for failing to maintain a grammar school under the mandate laid down in 1647—it was inevitably affected by the higher standards implicit in the new legislation. In effect, the town could no longer employ a minister or other person to teach part time as an adjunct to his regular occupation; and so, like other towns throughout the province, it was forced to turn to the interim schoolmaster, the college graduate awaiting a call to a church. And, because the laws also demanded that grammar masters be suitably paid, Dedham was forced, in addition, to pay higher salaries, the figure reaching twenty-eight pounds per annum in 1708 and sixty pounds by 1730.

The difficulties created by rising standards were compounded, too, by the spread of families outward from the center of the town. In 1684, a flexible rate scale was adopted, exempting those living more than two and a half miles from the school from the traditional school assessment upon each householder of five shillings annually for every male child or servant between the ages of four and fourteen. In 1693, the outer limit was extended to three miles, and the following year the assessment was abandoned entirely. Presumably, the willingness of the town to release such revenues during a period of economic stringency was testimony to the strength of the assumption that assessments for town services demanded at least their availability to the assessed.

The creation of precincts, which were coterminous with the parishes, only exacerbated the problems of dispersion, for the outlying families now had formal governmental agencies through which to voice their grievances. The town tried to cope initially with the difficulty by having the master teach for a few months in the schoolhouse and then for six- to twelve-week periods in private houses in the several precincts; but the arrangement was inevitably disruptive, since some persons objected to the use of their houses, others disagreed as to which houses ought to be used, and still others refused to be satisfied with anything less than separate money for their own precinct schools. Such disputes, interestingly enough, were indicative of the extent to which the school was looked upon as integral to an ordered community, and the right to maintain one essential to community integrity. Indeed, petitions to the general court for the right to form new towns during this period often based their appeal on the need for better educational services, an appeal, incidentally, which seemed to carry considerable weight with the magistrates.

By 1755, the rotating master arrangement—or the moving school, as it has been called—was abandoned in favor of a new system under which each of Dedham's four precincts (a fourth, the Springfield precinct, had been created contemporaneously with the Springfield Parish in 1748) maintained its own schools, interestingly enough, with those of the first and third (Clapboardtrees) precincts remaining under direct town control and those of the second (South) and fourth (Springfield) precincts coming under local precinct control. The arrangements for 1759–60 are indicative of the new system at work. Three of the schools, at First Parish, South Parish, and Clapboardtrees Parish, had as masters Harvard graduates capable of teaching Latin, and it is probable that the master of the fourth, at Springfield Parish, was at least a certified Latinist. All four of the parishes also had teachers (of whom three were women) offering instruction in reading, writing, and ciphering during the summer term. The number of known teachers after 1755 and the regularity with which both the winter and summer sessions were taught in all four parishes strongly suggest that

Signatures on Dedham Wills, Deeds, and Other Documents 1760–75

	Men		Women	
	Signature	Mark	Signature	Mark
Wills of adult males who died between 1760 and 1775	12	1	0	0
Administrations of wills of adult males who died between 1760 and 1775	5	0	5	1
Deeds (including divisions or transfers of land), 1760–75	31	1	8	4
Other documents (including official receipts for estates, bonds for loans, etc.), 1760–75	23	0	16	4
Total wills, administrations, deeds, and other documents	71	2	29	9

Configuration of Educational Institutions: Dedham

	1700	1765	
Population	750	1,919	First Parish—813 Second Parish—441 Third Parish—313 Fourth Parish—352
Households	111	309	
Churches	1	4	
English schools (summer)		4	
Latin and English schools (winter)	1	4	

instruction in reading and writing had moved almost wholly into the schools; and, as the statistics [therein] suggest, literacy, which had long been virtually universal among men in Dedham, was coming also to prevail among women. Moreover, the steady flow of Dedhamites through Harvard —there were thirty-six alumni from Dedham during the colonial period, of whom eighteen were graduated between 1760 and 1783—indicates that it was quite possible to obtain a competent Latin education as well, though there is evidence that some boys at least had to supplement the instruction obtained in school with tutoring from the parish minister.

* * *

Like Massachusetts townships, Virginia counties varied considerably in their character and traditions, such tidewater communities as James City and King and Queen differing significantly among themselves and even more sharply from back-country areas like Albemarle and Amherst. Yet, as in the case of Massachusetts, it is useful to examine the educational development of a particular county during the provincial era for the light it sheds upon the changing educational patterns of the eighteenth century. And for this purpose the history of Elizabeth City County is particularly instructive.

Founded by the London company in 1609 as Kecoughtan, after the Indian name for the area, Elizabeth City County was one of the eight original shires of the Virginia plantation. During the early years, the settlement existed under the constant threat of Indian attack, but by 1623 a series of military expeditions had driven all hostile Indians from the region. Meanwhile, local government gradually replaced military rule, a church was built, several mills and taverns appeared, and the "savage name," Kecoughtan, was duly changed to Elizabeth City, in honor of the daughter of James I. By 1634, with 859 inhabitants, Elizabeth City was the second most populous county in Virginia, even though it remained the smallest in area.

Originally settled in small scattered plots, the county did not develop a genuine nuclear village until late in the seventeenth century. The rich soil of the "back-river district," comprising about a third of the area, ensured that agriculture would remain, for an initial period at least, the principal element in the county's economy. In 1680, however, in an effort to create trade centers for the colony, the assembly passed an Act for Encouraging Towns, setting aside fifty acres for this purpose in each county; and, in Elizabeth City, the Jarvis plantation on the west side of the Hampton River, with its fine harbor and easy access to the hinterland via waterway, was chosen as the natural site for such a community. Despite initial resistance from the local farmers, the town of Hampton slowly took root and soon became, with nearby Norfolk, one of the foremost commercial centers of the region.

During the first half of the eighteenth century, relentless tobacco-farming soon depleted the rich soil of the back-river district, and agriculture began to decline. But commerce flourished, and by mid-century the total tonnage of ships arriving in Hampton harbor was nearly equal to that of New York's. Not surprisingly, the town began to take on urban characteristics: Streets multiplied; hogs were ordered penned (by act of the general assembly); ferries were built; and the number and variety of craftsmen increased steadily. White and black servants were present in roughly equal numbers during the early eighteenth century, but, as indentures decreased, Negro slavery became basic to the local economy.

Not surprisingly, too, population rose markedly. During most of the seventeenth century, the number of inhabitants had grown slowly, from 859 in 1634 to about 1,000 in 1693. During the [1690's], however, coincident with the rise of the town, the population appears to have jumped almost 10 per cent, to approximately 1,100 in 1698. Thereafter, the rate of growth remained fairly high, with the number of inhabitants doubling to 2,250 by 1747 and standing at 3,100 in 1782.

Church records for Elizabeth City are virtually nonexistent for the initial decades, the earliest extant vestry book covering the years from 1751 through 1784. Various other sources reveal the names of at least fourteen different clergymen who served the parish during the seventeenth century; and, although the backgrounds of many remain obscure, it is known that the minister who settled in 1687, the Reverend Cope D'Oyley, was a graduate of Merton College, and that his successor, the Reverend James Wallace, served the county simultaneously as physician and pastor during his incumbency between 1691 and 1712.

According to the Reverend James Falconer in his 1724 report to the bishop of London, the parish was "about fifty miles in circumference"; and, although it was smaller than many in Virginia, a family living at the perimeter would have found the trip to church long, uncomfortable, and occasionally dangerous. For obvious reasons, church attendance throughout the century was scant and sporadic, with one estimate for the 1720's placing the figure as low as one out of seven families. Yet, given the overlap of civil and ecclesiastical government in provincial Virginia, church attendance is at best only one index of ecclesiastical effectiveness; and the vestry book for 1751–84 reveals a number of other things about the Elizabeth City church and its place in the community. First, the vestry was exceedingly active in caring for the large number of charity cases within the parish. During a sample twelve-year period, 1751–63, the vestry administered and paid for the boarding of at least seventy individuals (roughly thirty of whom were children), assuming the costs of food, clothing, and medicine and, occasionally, meeting funeral and burial expenses as well. The vestry also protected itself from assuming unnecessary burdens by paying representatives from time to time to escort unwanted vagabonds to the parish edge. Second, the vestry appears to have given Elizabeth City's ministers considerable security in office during the eighteenth century, engaging only nine during the entire period between 1691 and 1783, and at least three of these for more than a decade each. And, third, it is clear that this particular vestry was fairly tightly controlled by a small group of well-to-do parishioners. Of the thirty-four vestrymen from 1751 through 1784, at least half served for ten years or more, nearly a third for fifteen years or more, and almost a fourth for twenty years or more. Nine of these men were also members of the House of Burgesses at some time during their careers, and almost all held one or more county offices at some time or other. Indeed, the control of public offices by a relatively small number of leading families appears to have been generally more pronounced in Elizabeth City than it was, for example, in contemporary Dedham, or even, for that matter, in some of the inland counties of contemporary Virginia.

* * *

In 1753, the Syms free school and, in 1759, the Eaton charity school were incorporated by formal acts of the assembly, the Syms school remaining free to all its students, the Eaton school remaining free only to poor children. The legal trustees were identical for both institutions and included the county justice, the two churchwardens, and the minister; but, actually, the vestry seems to have been the most consistently active agency in administering the two schools. Rogers D. Whichard, the historian of lower tidewater Virginia, has remarked that this was natural, if extralegal, owing to the traditional connection between church and school. It was especially natural in Elizabeth City, given the overlap of civil and ecclesiastical functions and the control of both by a fairly small number of families.

The county also had a continuing tradition of official concern for the maintenance of minimal educational standards, and from the beginning the authorities consistently held parents and masters responsible for the education of their children and servants. Thus, the court, in 1688, ordered a family to put its apprentice to school "and learn him to read a chapter in the Bible," and, in 1725, upheld the claim of a boy's mother that his master "has not learned her son, Armistead House, to read, write, and cipher" as agreed in the boy's indenture. And, in the years between 1756 and 1762, the court called at least four Elizabeth City fathers before it "to show cause why they have neglected the education of their children." There is no way of ascertaining whether these last cases represented special attempts to enforce laws that were being widely flouted or routine actions against occasional instances of parental neglect. What is clear, however, is that instruction in basic literacy by parents and masters was as acceptable, and possibly as ordinary, as formal schooling in Elizabeth City, even given the presence of Syms and Eaton.

Some light is thrown upon education in eighteenth-century Elizabeth City by the existence in the county records of a guardians' account book covering the twelve-year period between 1737 and 1749. Bearing in mind that the children listed were orphans with estates, that is, the children of well-to-do families, and that their education was for that reason scarcely representative, one can draw a number of inferences. First, over half of the orphans listed are recorded as having received some kind of formal education. From a total of twenty-four accounts, fourteen included schooling costs, as compared with ten that failed to mention schooling at all. Such payments may have gone either to private teachers or to one of the local free schools. And those children whose accounts did not include payments for schooling might nevertheless have received instruction from the families of their guardians, or they might have attended one of the free schools without cost—a practice sufficiently prevalent to have elicited complaints from the Eaton school's trustees in the 1750's. It would also seem a valid surmise that other families with means were probably providing for their children in much the same way as the guardians of the orphans.

Second, the records indicate a substantial number of persons in the community apparently capable of teaching. Ten persons (possibly eleven) appear in the account book as teachers during the twelve-year period, and three additional names are cited in a separate account for John Tabb covering the years 1762–64. These teachers may have included persons recruited from within the county as private tutors, persons brought in from outside specifically for the purpose, or local schoolmasters paid to take the orphans into their classes or instruct them privately.

Third, the records include payments for Latin books in at least two of the accounts, indicating that some of these teachers, if not all, were instructing in grammar-school subjects. Whether these same teachers taught English as well as Latin is not known; but, given the character of the local economy, which would place no special premium on a classical education, most teachers who taught Latin probably also taught English, the extent of instruction received by a particular pupil doubtless being a function of family taste and aspiration. In any case, some twenty Elizabeth City youths are known to have attended the College of William and Mary during the eighteenth century, a number that is certainly significant in its own right, though not particularly high in light of the special attributes of Elizabeth City County.

Using the guardians' account book along with other sources, one can identify the names of twenty-two different persons—and possibly as many as twenty-four—who taught in the county at one time or another from 1690 through 1770. This list includes teachers in the Syms and Eaton schools, teachers named in the guardians' accounts and in deeds and wills, and at least one private schoolmaster. Taking the year 1745 as a base, it is possible to construct a rough estimate of the minimum number of teachers in the community around mid-century. In that year, three names appear in the guardians' accounts as teachers, a Mrs. Parker, a Mr. Booth, and a Captain Wallace, and one person, Mr. Hunter, is known to have been a schoolmaster at either Syms or Eaton. To these the rector of the church, the Reverend William Fyfe, can be added as, in all probability, the instructor of some youngsters. This would indicate a minimum of five teachers in the community during 1745, probably covering the full range of English and grammar-school subjects. And, by way of gross result, a sampling of signature counts from records in the county reveals a substantial measure of literacy among women as well as men.

Signatures on Elizabethan City Deeds and Depositions 1693–99

Men		Women	
Signature	Mark	Signature	Mark
142	48	16	29

Signatures on Wills, Deeds and Mortgages, and Other Depositions 1763–71

	Men		Women	
	Signature	Mark	Signature	Mark
Wills	15	5	7	1
Deeds and mortgages	111	11	35	18
Other depositions	35	0	0	0
Total	161	16	42	19

There is scant evidence concerning the education of Elizabeth City's blacks. The Reverend James Falconer remarked, in his 1724 report, that slaveowners "are generally careful to instruct those capable of instruction, and to bring them to baptism, but it is impossible to instruct th[o]se that are grown up before they are carried from their own country, they never being able either to speak or understand our language perfectly." Of course, there remains the central question of what such instruction comprised even when it was given; and, in any case, one may doubt whether too much energy was expended, since there were more expedient ways of keeping slaves docile. A few blacks must have learned to read, however, for, in 1739, a slave named Ned, convicted of stealing, managed to escape execution by successfully pleading benefit of clergy. And, given the attitude toward slaves who stole, Ned at the very least must have read fluently and well.

Configuration of Education Institutions: Elizabeth City

	1700	1782
Population	1,200	3,100
Households	170	248
Churches	1	1
Schools	2	5

* * *

. . . [T]wo cities . . . flourishing in the eighteenth century served as foundries for the richest variety of character types produced in provincial America. Situated in the greatest natural harbor on the eastern coast of North America, New York grew from a respectable-sized market town of 4,300 in 1690 to a bustling city of 21,863 by 1771; while Philadelphia, serving as the chief port of entry for immigrants from the Palatinate and Ulster, expanded from a nascent trading center of 1,444 in 1693 to a thriving city of 13,708 by 1779—or, if one prefers to include the population for Philadelphia County as a whole, an astronomical 41,144. Both cities continued to display the phenomenal range of ethnic, religious, and racial types that marked seventeenth-century New York: A dozen languages and dialects might be heard at any given time, particularly in the market and wharf sections of the two cities; whites, Indians, and blacks, and every conceivable combination of the three, mingled in the houses and streets; and one could worship in any of a dozen liturgies. An English visitor to New York in 1768 enumerated eighteen principal churches in the city, including three Anglican congregations, three Dutch Reformed, three Presbyterian, two Lutheran, and single congregations of German Reformed, French Reformed, Baptists, Moravians, Quakers, Methodists, and Jews. And this obviously did not include the smaller congregations and splinter groups that worshipped in households or in temporary quarters. Similarly, Philadelphia could boast twenty churches at the time of the Revolution, spanning the same range of denominations, with the exception of the Dutch and French Reformed, but including two of Roman Catholic profession.

This same striking diversity that marked the households and churches of the two cities also appeared in their schools. Recall that most formal schooling during the seventeenth century had been carried out under the joint auspices of the ecclesiastical and civil authorities. The initial town school in New Amsterdam, begun in 1638, became, after the accession of the English, essentially a parochial school of the Dutch Reformed church, which continued to teach in the Dutch language until 1773, when English became an optional vehicle of instruction. On the English side, official provision for schooling was desultory, at best. In 1702, the assembly voted to provide a free school for the city. Two years later, George Muirson was employed as master; but Muirson served only a few months and was succeeded by Andrew Clarke in 1705. A few years thereafter, the school seems to have expired. Another effort by the assembly in 1732 appears to have lasted about as long. Meanwhile, in 1702, William Huddleston, a private schoolmaster, began to conduct a charity school at Trinity Church, and, in 1709, the S.P.G. made him its official schoolmaster in New York. Aside from the catechetical schools maintained for Negroes by the Society and the Bray Associates and the preparatory school begun by King's College in 1763, these exhaust New York's official efforts at schooling. The dissenting congregations doubtless carried on some formal instruction for their children, in the fashion of the day, but, aside from the efforts of Congregation Shearith Israel to teach Hebrew, the indications of such ventures are, at best, ephemeral. Little wonder that, in 1757, William Smith leveled a blistering indictment of the educational efforts of his countrymen: "Our schools are in the lowest order—the instructors want instruction; and, through a long shameful neglect of all arts and sciences, our common speech is extremely corrupt, and the evidences of a bad taste, both as to thought and language, are visible in all our proceedings, public and private."

In Philadelphia, the Friends, of course, were active from the start. . . .
[I]n 1683, the provincial council appointed Enoch Flower to instruct children in reading, writing, and ciphering, and, six years later, the monthly meeting employed George Keith to conduct public Latin classes for rich and poor alike, the latter work subsequently evolving into the William Penn Charter School. The 1760's and 1770's also saw the establishment of schools for Negroes under the auspices of the Friends and the Bray Associates, while there is direct evidence that the Anglican, Lutheran, German Reformed, Moravian, and Baptist churches conducted schools for greater or lesser periods of time, depending on the needs of their congregations and the availability of alternative institutions. And, as in New York, there were doubtless other such ventures that simply failed to appear in the records.

Even in the seventeenth century, however, it was the private entrepreneurial schoolmaster who carried an increasing share of the formal education in New York City; and, during the eighteenth, it was entrepreneurial schooling that expanded most impressively in the two cities. Several factors may have contributed, including the general restrictiveness of the congregational schools and their tendency to favor Latin or Hebrew instruction over English; but easily the most important was the concentration of artisans, tradesmen, and shopkeepers in the two cities (Bridenbaugh has estimated that between a third and two-thirds of the population of the two cities was made up of such men and their families) and the considerable mobility into and within their ranks—a mobility, incidentally, to which many a private schoolmaster made subtle and indirect appeal in his advertising. In any case, for the period to 1783, it is possible to identify by the name at least 260 teachers in New York and 283 teachers in Philadelphia; and, upon grouping them, the following patterns emerge:

New York City Schoolmasters 1638–1783

	1638–88	1689–1783
Parochial and town schoolmasters	11	27
Private schoolmasters	16	206
Total	27	233

Philadelphia Schoolmasters 1689–1783

Parochial and town schoolmasters	76	(includes Philadelphia Academy)
Private schoolmasters	207	
Total	283	

In addition, if one averages the population figures of the two cities for five-year periods, derives the number of households and school-aged children, and averages the number of teachers for five-year periods to soften

New York City Households and Teachers
(*Five-Year Averages*)

Years	Population	Households	Children	Teachers	Children per Teacher	
1700–4	4,587	829	1,241	5	248.2	
1705–9	5,060	888	1,378	5.6	246.1	
1710–14	5,862	1,028	1,586	2.8	566.4	
1715–19	6,805	1,194	1,789	4.2	426.0	
1720–24	9,670	1,696	1,991	6.4	311.1	Average 357.5
1725–29	8,635	1,515	2,197	7.2	305.1	
1730–34	9,600	1,684	2,388	7.2	331.7	
1735–39	10,619	1,862	2,592	6.2	418.1	
1740–44	11,249	1,974	2,704	7.4	365.4	
1745–49	11,852	2,079	2,799	9.8	280.0	
1750–54	12,511	2,195	2,960	15.8	187.3	
1755–59	13,719	2,407	3,246	15.6	208.1	Average 253.7
1760–64	16,569	2,907	3,882	16.6	233.9	
1765–69	19,510	3,423	4,528	13.6	332.9	
1770–74	21,885	3,822	5,184	18.5	280.2	

Philadelphia Households and Teachers
(*Five-Year Averages*)

Years	Population	Households	Children	Teachers	Children per Teacher	
1700–4	2,132	374	581	3.0	193.7	
1705–9	2,514	441	684	2.8	244.3	
1710–14	2,896	508	775	2.0	387.5	
1715–19	3,278	576	861	2.2	391.4	
1720–24	3,877	680	1,001	2.4	417.1	Average 297.2
1725–29	4,803	843	1,218	5.0	243.6	
1730–34	5,728	1,005	1,425	6.2	229.8	
1735–39	6,948	1,219	1,696	5.8	292.4	
1740–44	8,529	1,496	2,029	5.4	375.7	
1745–49	9,991	1,753	2,359	8.4	280.8	
1750–54	11,298	1,982	2,675	15.2	176.0	
1755–59	12,140	2,130	2,868	20.0	143.4	Average 175.3
1760–64	12,710	2,230	2,979	16.8	177.3	
1765–69	12,913	2,262	2,997	23.4	128.1	
1770–74	13,115	2,301	3,106	21.2	146.5	

the impact of fortuitous shifts, the striking change in the availability of formal schooling after mid-century becomes readily apparent.

In assessing these data, several cautions must be borne in mind. First, the listing of teachers gleaned from advertisements and other records probably provides fairly reliable information with respect to minimum numbers, though there were almost certainly teachers who advertised but never actually taught and teachers who taught but never appeared in any records. Second, there is no way of estimating the number of children from surrounding areas, or even from distant colonies, who came to New York and Philadelphia for their schooling, but it is almost certain that there were such children, especially from the populous suburbs of Philadelphia. And, third, since there is evidence that some private teachers offered basic instruction in reading, writing, and ciphering even when their advertised specialties lay elsewhere, all teachers of all subjects have been included—there being only the most ephemeral evidence in most instances as to which students actually studied which subjects under which teachers. Yet, even if one were to remove the specialized teachers of sewing, dancing, fencing, art, and music from the tables, it would not significantly affect the trend, since the number of such teachers totaled only 27 for New York (out of 260 for the period) and 14 for Philadelphia (out of 283). The conclusion seems valid, then, that the availability of schooling of various sorts increased markedly in New York and Philadelphia during the eighteenth century, and not merely as a function of population growth. One outcome, as elsewhere, was a continuing high rate of literacy among men, and a perceptibly rising rate among women. Another, in effect, was the same institutionalized extension of alternative possibilities that had appeared in the households and churches of the two cities.

That extension of possibilities appeared elsewhere as well, in the colleges and subscription libraries that grew up in both cities during the 1740's and 1750's, in the enlarged range of apprenticeships made possible by the greater variety of craftsmen, in the increased opportunity for informal association afforded by coffeehouses, taverns, clubs, and scientific societies, and in the mounting flow of printed materials that issued from a steadily rising

Signatures on New York City Wills 1692–1775

	Men		Women	
	Signature	Mark	Signature	Mark
1692–1703	40	4	10	3
1760–75 (City proper)	91	12	13	5
1760–75 (Harlem and Bloomingdale)	5	2	1	2
1760–75 (Combined)	96	14	14	7

Signatures on Philadelphia Wills 1699–1775

	Men		Women	
	Signature	Mark	Signature	Mark
1699–1706	32	8	6	4
1773–75 (City proper)	66	12	26	7
1773–75 (Northern liberties)	14	6	4	1
1773–75 (Combined)	80	18	30	8

number of printers. One need not live in the city of publication, of course, to enjoy the benefits of literature, a fact that was amply demonstrated by the spirited circulation of English and French books in both communities. But to live in the city of publication is to have easier, more immediate, and more assured access to those benefits. And that is what the residents of New York and Philadelphia had in increasing measure during the provincial era, to the inevitable enhancement of their knowledge, taste, and most important, perhaps, imagination.

New York City and Philadelphia Printers and Newspapers

	1700	1710	1720	1730	1740	1750	1760	1770	1780
New York City printers	1	2	1	2	2	3	4	7	9
New York City newspapers				1	2	2	3	3	5
Philadelphia printers	1	1	1	5	4	8	8	16	14
Philadelphia newspapers			1	2	3	3	4	6	7

There is less to be said about the back country, not because it was less significant during the provincial era, but only because there are fewer reliable data from which to draw generalizations. Certainly no simple evolutionism will suffice, for the communities of the frontier were not merely nascent replicas of tidewater communities a century earlier. For one thing, they were founded by men and women from quite different circumstances—on the one hand, emigrants from the Palatinate or Ulster rather than from England or Holland; on the other hand, emigrants from the older settled communities of New England, New York, and the Chesapeake region. For another, they were founded by men and women bearing the fruits of a hundred years of colonial experience. The elements and the Indians were still there and often still hostile. But the farm family bearing the Bible, a primer, Franklin's almanacs, Jared Eliot's *Essays upon Field-Husbandry in New-England* (1760), and *The American Instructor*, [as well as] an oral tradition based on a century of New England or Chesapeake lore, was simply in a better position to survive and multiply than its progenitors, who [had] arrived with the Bible, Tusser, Bayly, and dreams of earthly or heavenly glory. The frontier may have been the crucible of the American experience, but it was education that filtered, synthesized, and transmitted what was learned and enabled men to profit from the testing.

The early history of Kent, Connecticut, a town founded in 1738 in the westernmost part of that colony, lends impressive documentation to this thesis. Of the forty original families who settled Kent, sixteen had moved west from such river towns as Colchester, Tolland, Mansfield, and Windham, and twenty-four, north from such Long Island Sound towns as Danbury, Fairfield, and Norwalk. A majority were fourth-generation descendants of "first-comers" to the earlier communities; and a majority came to Kent in groups of three or more families. The first cabin was erected early in 1738; the first school is mentioned in the minutes of the proprietors' meeting in May, 1739; the town was formally settled by act of the general assembly on October 13, 1739; and the covenant formally gathering the Congregational church was made on April 29, 1741. Within three years, all the formal institutions of education had been initially constituted. Most of the town's inhabitants appear to have joined the new church, and all the town's children appear to have received an English education at school—and, indeed, as the settlers dispersed in the 1740's, additional schools were built to serve the several localities. So far as can be determined, no member of a Kent family ever had to sign with a mark during the eighteenth century, and at least two young men, Samuel Mills and Edmund Mills, the sons of John Mills, one of the original proprietors, were prepared for Yale by the Reverend Joel Bordwell, who acceded to the pulpit of the town church in 1758.

The settlement of the South Carolina back country, which began in earnest about the same time Kent was founded, proceeded quite differently. There, the story is one of rapid population by emigrants from Europe, the British Isles, Africa, the tidewater communities of South Carolina, and the older frontier communities of Pennsylvania and Virginia. Arriving in groups, in families, and as individuals, these men and women settled in townships, hamlets, and dispersed farmsteads. The established religion being Anglican, parishes were laid out in Charleston, but the back country was so poorly served that, as late as 1767, the Reverend Charles Woodmason, the itinerant rector of St. Mark's Parish, traveled some four thousand miles in caring for some twenty congregations numbering over three thousand individuals. Equally important, perhaps, the various communities of Dissenters started their own churches, and within Woodmason's parish alone there were knots and clusters of Regular Baptists, Seventh Day Baptists, New Light Baptists, Presbyterians, Huguenots, Quakers, Lutherans, and German Reformed. "It is very few families whom I can bring to join in prayer," Woodmason lamented in his journal, "because most of them are of various opinions: the husband a Churchman: wife, a Dissenter; children, nothing at all."

It was essentially within these churches, as well as within the households of the settlers, that most formal education took place. True, Woodmason himself conducted a school for some twenty poor children in the hope that, through them, he could "make impression on their relations," and there is also occasional indication of a schoolhouse on maps of the parish and surveyors' records. But, in the main, the settlers were forced to depend on their pastors and themselves. Yet, surprisingly perhaps, literacy rates remained relatively high, as indicated by signatures on deeds, wills, and mortgages, not falling much below 80 per cent for any substantial group of white male settlers and running around 90 per cent among the Germans. Given the isolation of particular families and the persistent difficulties of obtaining and retaining pastors, these rates are extraordinary, and stand as eloquent testimony to the power [that] the tradition of learning had acquired in the minds of provincial Americans.

A Note on the Study
of the Colonial Family

David J. Rothman

Contemporary studies of the American colonial family have infused a new methodology and fresh interpretation into a traditional subject of inquiry. Rather than cram their texts with random details of dress and diet, historians now eagerly place their materials in the broadest contexts. Far from compiling irrelevant snatches of information, they often locate within the family the basic determinants of historical change. Perhaps the two most important contributions to this field are Edmund Morgan's *The Puritan Family* and Bernard Bailyn's *Education in the Forming of American Society*. Morgan and Bailyn persuasively contend that economic, political, as well as social alterations cannot be understood apart from the story of the family in the New World. But, as is often the case with pioneer efforts, these works raise and leave unsettled issues of paramount significance. A review of their approaches and findings, especially in the light of the work of such European historians as Philippe Ariès, may help to frame the sorts of questions future researchers will have to resolve.

Two general difficulties characterize the arguments in *The Puritan Family* and *Education in the Forming of American Society*. First, they tend to ascribe a uniqueness and distinction to the American experience that may well be untenable. While both authors do, of course, recognize that the colonists often carried European customs into the wilderness, the comparisons they draw between Old and New World practices must confront the findings of recent European scholarship. Secondly, both volumes offer sweeping interpretations, albeit conflicting ones, of the history of the colonial family. For Morgan, the rise of the family describes the Puritan experience; for Bailyn, its decline is of prime significance. On the basis of the evidence presented, however, there is little to confirm one position or the other.

Morgan emphasizes the overwhelming importance of the Puritan family to the ordering of society. Vital connections linked it to the economic as well as religious structure of the settlement. Apprenticeship, for example, was not simply a rational method for bringing laborers to the artisan's bench; rather, this widespread practice indicated a basic distrust of the family as a socializing agent. Although no New England writer indicated the purpose for these economically unnecessary removals from the home, Morgan suggests [that] Puritan families placed their sons and daughters in other households because "they did not trust themselves with their own

From *William and Mary Quarterly*, Volume 23, Number 4 (October, 1966), pp. 627–34. Used by permission.

children . . . they were afraid of spoiling them by too great affection. . . . A child learned better manners when he was brought up in another home than his own." Where fathers indulged, a neighbor would discipline. Moreover, Morgan asserts that the history of the family can help to account for the Puritans' diplomatic and political failures. Granted that "forces beyond their power" led to the Crown's revocation of the Massachusetts charter in 1684, still, Morgan asks, "would they have given up, if they had not already lost their strength?" A failure of nerve toppled the Puritan government, and its cause was to be found in the "family tribalism" that dominated the second and third generations. In the privacy of their homes, the children of the founders lost their vision of the world. Household relationships became so encompassing that parents, obsessed with the salvation of their children, lost sight of "the universal significance of the Christian gospel." They fled the world rather than revolutionize it. "Love thy Neighbor" became "Love thy Family."

Bailyn's study of education in the colonial period also relates the history of the family to broad social changes. The seventeenth-century European family, he notes, was "the most important agency in the transfer of culture," a role reflecting its medieval heritage. In America, however, it could not fulfill its traditional function. The stress of life in the wilderness, the availability of land, and the scarcity of labor conspired to weaken the patriarchal family; sons left their fathers' homes to establish their own households, which, under these conditions, "would never grow to the old proportions." As the extended family became nuclear, education was "wrenched loose from the automatic, instinctive workings of society," and formal institutions, the schools, were forced to assume "cultural burdens they had not borne before." Bailyn, too, sees even wider implications in the fate of the colonial family. As "the once elaborate interpenetration of the family and the community dissolved," as "the passage of the child from the family to the society lost its ease," successive generations experienced an acute sense of separateness. They came to view society "from without rather than from within," and henceforth alienation would distinguish the American national character.

Although both studies contend that changes in the family were of great consequence to colonial society, their particular arguments do not correspond. The family in Morgan's presentation was so engrossing that parents distrusted it; throughout the seventeenth century, here as in England, apprenticeship reflected the fear that the family could not properly socialize its offspring. He also argues, somewhat inconsistently, that, by the end of the seventeenth century, the Puritan family had grown so absorbing that tribalism overtook the community. His evidence is the weakened efforts to convert the sinners, the Half-Way Covenant, and the prevalence of marriage metaphors in Puritan sermons. Yet, oddly enough, he makes no attempt to explain why apprenticeship remained a typical Puritan practice even when tribalism reached its apogee. Surely parents then would have stopped exiling their children from the household. On the other hand,

Bailyn's explanation for the rise of the school rests on the notion that the colonial family decreased in importance. His documentation, in turn, assumes that the American wilderness led to a nuclearization of the family and a decline in the father's authority that *per se* weakened it as an agency of acculturalization.

The differences here are not semantic ones. Morgan and Bailyn measure the strength of the family on a scale that is sensitive to the institution's ability to socialize the child and stabilize the community—that is, to serve as a focus for the emotional life of parent and child, to transmit appropriate knowledge and skills, and to maintain social order. Both volumes employ common standards of judgment, but this coincidence mainly serves to clarify the divergences that mark their respective interpretations.

The story of the American family is better understood when it is placed in broader perspective. European scholars have been busily and fruitfully at work in this field, and their research has revised many standard notions. Perhaps the most stimulating investigation has been performed by Philippe Ariès, the results of which have been published in English under the title *Centuries of Childhood.*

Traditionally, students have assumed that the family in Western society constituted the ancient basis of civilization; that it achieved maximum significance in the medieval era, began a decline in the Renaissance, and lost most of its importance with the advent of industrialism. Ariès, to the contrary, presents the development of the family in precisely the opposite direction. It was far less important than other community institutions in the Middle Ages, and its role expanded only with the coming of the Renaissance. By the seventeenth century, it occupied a foremost position, and industrialism assured its triumph. It never before "exercised so much influence over the human condition."

New attitudes toward the child account for this change. As the family recognized his singularity, it assumed its modern position. "There was no place for childhood in the medieval world," explains Ariès. The period between birth and adulthood was simply a time of transition of no interest or reality to the man of the tenth or eleventh century. But slowly, from the thirteenth century onward, the family began to discover childhood, that is, to protect and distinguish the preadolescent from the adult environment. To document this transition, Ariès turns, first, to the world of art. Tenth-century canvases rarely included children among their subjects; by the seventeenth century, however, parents rushed to preserve a permanent record of their youngsters' early stages of growth, and the painting of children flourished. Similarly, between the thirteenth and seventeenth centuries, children's costumes became unique, no longer a replica in miniature of their parents' dress. Their reading material grew distinct, for adult fare was considered inappropriate without careful expurgation. Concomitantly, parents stopped speaking freely and openly, especially [o]n sexual matters, before their children; authors with varying credentials began to produce pedagogical literature. And the church, sensitive to nuances of change, started to emphasize the importance of First Communion. "As the attitude toward the child changed," Ariès notes, "so did the family itself." To serve the nursery better, it assumed unprecedented responsibilities.

The family's new prominence altered the balance of functions among social institutions and compelled readjustments. The apprenticeship system was one casualty. By the seventeenth century, parents preferred to keep their children at home, finding it undesirable to dispatch them to a neighboring household to learn a trade. The school, once intended as a training place for Latin clerics, stepped in to fill the gap. It transmitted technical and intellectual knowledge in an arrangement that at once satisfied the pedagogue's desire to keep the child separate from the adult world and the parent's wish to retain him in his own home. Still, the family's altered significance did not immediately disrupt the community. In the seventeenth century, concludes Ariès, there existed an equilibrium between the demands of the family and the needs of the community. The "centripetal or family forces" did not yet conflict with the "centrifugal or social forces." The balance, however, did not last, for the forces of domesticity proved too powerful. The family, in the course of the next generations, turned more and more inward, leaving the community to fare as it could. In short order private needs triumphed over the public good.

The implications of Ariès's work are of great importance to the history of the colonial family. In the first instance, his findings force a reappraisal of the links American writers have tried to establish between apprenticeship, schooling, and the development of the family. The European family's increasing significance was accompanied by a growth in schools and a decline in apprenticeship. When parents devoted particular attention to the child, they also provided neutral institutions to transmit necessary skills. In this light, Morgan's hypothesis that the Puritans' reliance on apprenticeship was symptomatic of a fear of spoiling children "with too great affection" seems ill-founded. More likely, the survival of the practice indicates that Puritan families were not doting, that the family in early Massachusetts had not yet become the key institution of socialization. Similarly, Bailyn's assumption that the multiplication of schools is a function of the breakdown of the family is challenged by events in Europe. There, an increase in schools signaled the rise of the family, not its decline. While it is possible that Old and New World developments did not coincide, still American historians have advanced as axiomatic, formulas that are contradicted by the European experience. It is not *a priori* true that apprenticeship reveals the distrust of the family, or that schools increase when the family declines.

Ariès's research also prompts a reconsideration of the broad trends that have marked the histories of the American family. Most current writing on the subject follows Bailyn's approach: In the American wilderness, the traditional European family broke down. This sort of explanation generally opens with a description of an extended, secure, and father-dominated European household, medieval in origin, that performed religious, economic, and social functions. When the family confronted the New World, however, vital transformations occurred. The household shrank in size and became nuclear in an environment where land was as abundant as labor was scarce. At the same time the father-husband lost his authority; sons, daughters, even wives could leave his home to establish, with facility, their own households. Under these circumstances, the American family underwent a unique development. Its various functions were taken over by the community, and, in this sense, it declined in significance.

There are serious weaknesses, however, to this analysis. First, it is based on a distorted model of the European household. The American image of a stable and ongoing Old World family—a convenient backdrop against which to portray the dynamic elements of the New World situation—is inaccurate. Ariès convincingly demonstrates that vital changes altered the institution between the medieval and early modern period. Moreover, the stereotype notwithstanding, it was not the extended medieval family but the smaller, more nuclear one that came to dominate other community institutions. It was parents, not kinfolk, who promoted the social significance of the family. And it is worth noting that the work of such historians as Lawrence Stone and Peter Laslett lends credence to the Ariès argument, for they demonstrate that seventeenth-century families in England, for example, were far smaller in size than we have hitherto suspected. Thus, the notion that the American family was conjugal rather than extended, and hence of more limited importance to the society than its European counterpart, is invalid on two grounds. Probably households on both sides of the Atlantic were more nuclear than extended by the seventeenth century; and there is every reason to suspect that this change increased rather than lessened the family's importance.

Other claims for the uniqueness of the American family must also be qualified by recent European scholarship. Geographical mobility may have been as common in English villages as in Massachusetts settlements in the seventeenth century; physical movement neither distinguishes the American story nor points to a decline in the institution's influence. It appears that, during these same years, English Peers, like Puritan fathers, faced great difficulties when they attempted to dictate their children's marriage. And it is by no means certain that, as children's considerations of love began to replace their parents' notions of property as the proper base for marriage, . . . there would necessarily follow a decline of the influence of the family in society.

The changing position and function of the family ha[ve] occupied the sociologist as well as the historian, and a cross-disciplinary approach is particularly useful here. Ariès himself, for example, was first trained in demography. In general, current sociological writings also clarify the weaknesses characterizing the histories of the American family. Investigations of the contemporary family point not to a decline but rather, as Talcott Parsons puts it, to the conclusion that "the society is dependent more exclusively on it for the performance of certain of its vital functions," the primary socialization of the child and the stabilization of the adult. William Goode, exploring the "fit" between the modern family and the industrial system, concludes that the institution has suffered no loss of importance in a technological and bureaucratic society. The household may not be the basic economic unit of production, but its social importance has not been thereby diminished. These sorts of findings, on the one hand, make it awkward to describe a colonial family in a state of decline; yet, perhaps even more important, they reveal the inadequacies of the assumptions that have led historians to their conclusions. The size of a household, sociological research indicates, is not related to the strength of the family. The emancipation of women and children is not identical with the disintegration of the family. The strength or solidarity of the family is not a function of the authority of the father or husband.

Whatever shortcomings weaken existing formulations of the history of the colonial family, the subject clearly warrants greater attention. If broad generalizations of questionable validity still characterize the state of our knowledge, it is because the details of the story have yet to be sorted. It may turn out that Morgan's notion of a settlement transformed by tribalism was a brilliant hunch. Parsons, for example, suggests that the reduction in size of the modern household has exaggerated the distinction between members and nonmembers of the family. "The modern child has 'farther to go' in his socialization than his predecessors," and the extension of the journey may not work to the benefit of the community. Ariès also alludes to this tension, concluding that the seventeenth-century balance of family and social forces was only temporary. Still, before any description of the colonial family's development becomes persuasive, it must rest on a foundation of fact. It may well be that the New World family, facing the wilderness, expanded its functions. Migration to a country where other social institutions were either weak or absent perhaps strengthened the primary ties between members of a household. Fathers in frontier communities did not necessarily lose or abdicate authority over their children's lives. In the absence of alternative organizations, the family filled a vacuum, and tribalism became an American trait before becoming a European one. But, at the moment, we simply do not have the evidence to support this judgment.

What kinds of research will provide the necessary underpinnings? To begin with, we must have more demographic knowledge of the colonial family. What was the size of the household, [what were] the rates of birth, the ages at marriage, at different points in time? Was there a decline in the practice of apprenticeship? Did social status become less important in the choice of mates? Were there regional differences that might help to account for particular developments? Were urban families different in size and habits from rural ones; did Massachusetts and Virginia develop along similar lines? We need more information on the types of social duties that the family and community performed, and on the division of labor between them. Was the care of dependents and deviants a family or community responsibility? Did philanthropic practices reflect judgments on their respective roles? Was the American solution radically different from the European? We should also want to know . . . whether family structure influenced social mobility; did household relationships permit or encourage sons to follow occupations different from their fathers'? Did the position of women reflect changes in the family? . . . Were there also alterations in the concept of privacy that are relevant to this study; did changes in home architecture or in concepts of civil liberty reveal shifts in the family's position? The materials for answering these inquiries, from church records, wills, and sermons to the reports of charitable institutions and child-rearing literature, are readily available. When they have been more fully utilized, it should be possible to describe with greater assurance the history of the American colonial family.

Socialization in Colonial New England

Michael Zuckerman

Children who grew up in provincial Massachusetts grew up in a society that insisted on concord and consensus; as they grew they became, subtly, almost irresistibly, people who could live in such a society.

In this, of course, there was nothing singular. Every society attempts to impress its values upon the young, so that they may assume the postures and positions of their parents and perpetuate the social order that seems only right and decent to all around them. But, for that very reason, the education of children is an extremely useful index to the values of the society of adults. Such values must be transmitted in terms so simple that even a child can understand them, and so they stand out even more plainly, quite often, than the attitudes and assumptions of the elders in addressing each other.

Yet, they do not stand out as starkly as they might; for, in eighteenth-century Massachusetts, there was no clear distinction between child and adult. Portraits of Puritan children show only scaled-down adults, not children as the romantic nineteenth century would have recognized them. Age is evident in the wigs on their heads, in the "premature sadness" of their faces, and in the very clothes that they wore, the same clothes that their parents wore, simply smaller. If clothes do not make the man, they do mark social differentiations; a distinctive mode of dress for children never developed before the Revolution. As Monica Kiefer explained, since children

From *Peaceable Kingdom: New England in the Eighteenth Century* (New York: Knopf, 1970), pp. 72–83. Used by permission.

"were expected to behave like adults, they quite logically wore clothes appropriate for the role."

The limners of provincial Massachusetts painted as they saw, and they saw as their society saw. Which is to say that they scarcely saw the child at all. Indeed, by subsequent standards, there were no children in eighteenth-century New England. The culture had no conception of the child as a being with distinctive needs and desires, and it accorded the child no distinctive places or roles. Massachusetts children, two centuries ago, did not live separated from the society in a protected preserve of carefree innocence; they were part of a single undifferentiated community. Even very small boys and girls were brought to church services and compelled to stay there for the duration, well before they were capable of comprehension or proper conduct. And on the child's small shoulders rested the same momentous responsibility for his own everlasting fate that his parents assumed for theirs. "Wilt thou tarry any longer, my dear Child," asked one book for the young, "before thou run into thy Chamber, and beg of God to give thee a Christ for thy Soul, that thou mayest not be undone forever?" Massachusetts children appeared in their portraits as, to their elders and so to themselves, they appeared in life: responsible people wrestling with the defects of their nature.

Original sin was the heart of the matter, because it was believed to be "bound up in the heart of a child." "You are all of you naturally the children of God's wrath," Jonathan Edwards denounced the children of Northampton in a sermon to them in 1740. "If you are not converted, God is angry with you every day; if you should die in the condition you are now in, you would surely go to hell." Others were less stern than Edwards, but few went further than the well-known lines of Wigglesworth's *Day of Doom*, written in 1662 but reproduced in New England primers through the eighteenth century, which merely reserved to children "the easiest room in hell." Thus, if the "natural" child was "a poor, wicked, miserable, hateful creature," indulgence was absurd. No provincial parent could reasonably envision childhood as a privileged preserve, an interlude of irresponsibility and innocence, for children who were obviously not innocent, who were, in fact, innately depraved. It was contrary to common sense to trust any impulses from within, or to authorize their expression. Socialization in New England, in the family, in religious training, and in education, was a preparation for sainthood and citizenship by a suppression of the "natural" child.

The premise of Puritan education was precisely this conviction of corruption and the consequent necessity to pour in good things from without. As Edmund Morgan wrote of the colonial era, there was "no question of developing the child's personality, of drawing out or nourishing any desirable inherent qualities which he might possess, for no child could by nature possess any desirable qualities." Since any impulse of the child was certain to be sinful, little else was often required of a teacher than a strong right arm; and, even if not all teachers relied so crudely on might to make right, the distrust of inner urges was endemic in the education of provincial Massachusetts.

The pre-eminent function of education, whether in religion or the three R's, was restraint: direct restraint in the case of discipline, indirect restraint in the case of instruction. The former was clear to all concerned. Samuel Willard explained the latter in a sermon from which one of his listeners took these notes:

> 1. they are all born in Ignorance rom. 3.17. Without the knowledge and fear of god they must have it by doctrine and institution 2^{ly} this ignorance layeth them open to satan to lead them wither he will. 3^{ly} holdeth them under the Power [and] efficacy of sin a blind mind and dead conscience are companions. hence they sin without shame ignorance stopps the activity of all the faculties. 4^{ly} as long as they remain in their naturall ignorance there is no hope of being freed from everlasting misery. if you have any Compassion for them take Pains that they may know god. 5^{ly} Hardness of heart allienation from god Springs from ignorance and 6^{ly} they hence are inclined to fulfill their owne evil will.

In Willard's conclusion was the beginning of it all: The child's sinning was due to his "evill will" and the inclination to fulfill it. Education had to be bent to overcoming that will. Or, put more precisely, ignorance was not the cause of evil action—evil nature was—but ignorance did prevent *restraint* of evil action. Instruction was aimed at the elimination of this hindrance to restraint.

From the early days of the colony, instruction had been heavily inclined to the inculcation of obedience "in point of good manners, and dutiful behavior towards all," but, even in its other academic aspects, Massachusetts education served to suppress self-expression and promote uniformity. The intimate connection of instruction to discipline was explicit in the injunction of the *New England Primer* to the child about to enter upon spelling—"Let him learn these and such like sentences by Heart, whereby he will be both instructed in his Duty and encouraged in his Learning"—and it was also apparent in other subjects. Reading and arithmetic were taught through techniques of rote memorization, and all education in provincial Massachusetts was subtly shaped by the pervasive influence of the catechism.

The catechism was a summary, cast in the form of questions and answers, of orthodox beliefs. As such, it was the conventional method of religious instruction in most branches of Christianity at the time, but the men of Massachusetts did not cling to it on that account alone. They had, after all, cast off other Christian conventions. Rather, they retained it because it was congenial to them; as Edmund Morgan maintained, "This method of instruction was well adapted to the purposes of Puritan education. It was not designed to give play to the development of individual initiative, because individual initiative in religion usually meant heresy." Children were introduced to the catechism "before they could possibly know the meaning of what they said," and thereafter it was used not only for religious instruction but also in reading and writing drills in school and in regular rehearsals with parents and pastors. And, even as a child came to learn the meaning of the words he repeated, he also came to understand that that meaning was fixed forever. The catechistic method assumed that there were "right" answers. The most the student could hope was to comprehend them; he could not amend them. And many did not even comprehend them, for clergymen themselves admitted that the Shorter Catechism had never been "designed or fitted for Babes." In fact, the largest volume published in all New England prior to the nineteenth century, Willard's *Complete Body of Divinity*, was based upon the very same catechism the children studied. The Shorter Catechism was aimed at adults; children had to tag along, managing as well as they could.

Children's books, with their effort to provide a sequestered simplicity commensurate with a child's capacities, were an innovation that awaited the nineteenth century in Massachusetts. "Read no ballads and romances and foolish books" went the ordinary injunction before the Revolution. One student of the subject has concluded that no period in all American juvenile literature was "so bleak and uninspiring as the first seventy-five years of the eighteenth century." Children were seen only as ignorant adults, and "nothing was written especially for the needs of the immature mind." Indeed, "the note of fear and repression, which dominated every phase of Colonial childhood, is clearly apparent to the most casual reader of the literature of the young."

Certainly it is apparent in the *New England Primer*, the most widely read item in all that provincial literature and one of the most celebrated schoolbooks in American history. In the *Primer*, education was plainly placed in the service of securing uniformity and restraining the Puritan potential for the release of individual expression. The book's center of gravity was the catechism, which no eighteenth-century printing was without; its presence was invariably proclaimed on the title page itself. The second page was filled with quotations that set the tone of what was to follow: It was studded with injunctions and inducements to fear and obedience. Then came devices for the teaching of reading and spelling, including the rhymed alphabet with the immortal opening couplet "In Adam's Fall/We Sinned all." Then a series of precepts in various forms, under such titles as "The Dutiful Child Promises" and including such "Choice Sentences" as "Praying will make thee leave sinning, or sinning will make thee leave praying." Then the names of the books of the Bible, and then the numbers up to one hundred ("for the ready finding of any Chapter, Psalm, and Verse in the Bible"). Then the story of the burning of John Rogers, his wife, and nine small children at the stake, and, finally, the Shorter Catechism. Nowhere in all this was any concession made to the child simply for the child's pleasure, never did the *Primer* cater to what the child might enjoy. The only "story" in the *Primer* was the martyrdom of John Rogers, an exceedingly earnest tale even by the standards of the *Primer*. For the standards were adult standards, and what went into the *Primer* was determined entirely by an adult judgment of suitability.

Accordingly, almost no allowance at all was made for childhood. Damnation, death, and depravity—the facts of Puritan life—were impressed upon the youth of New England from such an early age that there developed an entire genre of Puritan literature, the narratives of "precocious conversions." In the *Primer*, death was flaunted before young readers repeatedly, and more than merely as an inescapable eventuality. The *Primer* insisted on death as a very present danger even to children, and consequently it urged them to direct their youthful energies into an appropriate preparation for it. One of the "Verses" was typical:

> I in the Burying Place may see
> Graves shorter there than I;
> From Death's Arrest no Age is free,
> Young Children too may die;
> My God, may such an awful Sight,
> Awakening be to me!
> Oh! that by early Grace I might
> For Death prepared be.

In the *Primer*, a young lad was "constantly impressed with the fact" that he "was born not to live but to dy," and that his time and talents were to be focused on the proper fulfillment of this eternal end. In such popular works as Janeway's *Token for Children*, those were still stronger preoccupations; typical of its exemplary youth was one New England lass of five who fell sick of consumption and "would not by any sports be diverted from the Tho'ts of *Death*, wherein she took such Pleasure, that she did not care to hear of any Thing else." And the exposure of children to their own mortality went beyond the literature. It was in their universal presence at funerals, in the sermons addressed to them, and in the common conversation of a family such as Samuel Sewall's. "Sabbath, Jan. 12," one of the judge's diary entries was dated. "Richard Dummer, a flourishing youth of 9 years old, dies of Small Pocks. I tell Sam. [his young son] of it and what need he had to prepare for Death. . . ."

Depravity, too, was something that was held before children constantly. And from death and depravity, the prospect of damnation followed easily enough; yet no chances were taken that children might miss the logical development. As Janeway's preface promised, bad children would "go to their Father the Devil, into everlasting burning; . . . and when they beg and pray in Hell Fire, God will not forgive them; but there they must lie forever." The same promise of an infernal future was also made by proper Puritan parents in the home. A revealing entry in Sewall's diary recorded the terror of his little daughter Betty, who "burst into tears," one winter day in 1696, "when she came to fear that she 'was like Spira, not Elected.' " Edmund Morgan found the significance of the episode in the fact that her father wept, too. "The above descriptions were not fairy stories with which to frighten little children; to the Puritans they were unpleasant but inescapable facts, and the sooner children became aware of them the better." But, actually, the significance of the story may be carried a bit further. Mortality, original sin, and damnation may have been "unpleasant and inescapable facts" of Puritan life, but facts do not dictate the attitude men adopt toward them or the use men make of them. New Englanders of the provincial period unblinkingly informed their children of unpleasant facts of life because they thought of their children as little adults. They never established separate standards of awareness for children because they were only able to conceive of a single standard for the whole community.

Accordingly, there was a constant condition of earnestness enjoined upon children. One of the girls approvingly offered for emulation by Janeway spent days and nights in tears and prayers, "desiring with all her Soul to escape from everlasting Flame." Another model child was said to be in "Horror," "Anguish," and "trouble of his Spirit," and those were extolled as exemplary states of mind for the young; and, indeed, all of New England's children were described as "remarkably grave, devout, and serious." There was no age necessarily too young to impose such weights of responsibility and induced intensity, either. Janeway offered one boy who was "admirably affected with the Things of GOD, when he was between two and three Years old," and a girl who was fearful for her "corrupt Nature" before she left the cradle. The adult attitude toward youthful frivolity was epitomized in the common parental injunction to children to "let thy Recreation be Lawful, Brief, and Seldom."

Not every child was as compliant as a Janeway model, of course, but, for the disobedient, the culture quite approved whatever discipline was necessary to secure their submission. The child's will was to be broken if he would not surrender it of his own accord, and an early start in that affair was essential, since "will" was defined as "any defiance of the parents' wishes, at any age." None of the medical advice available to New England parents before the second half of the eighteenth century advocated permissiveness in aggression-training, and the "note of fear and repression" was "clearly apparent" in juvenile literature. The model schoolgirl was "eminent for her Diligence, Teachableness, Meekness, and Modesty, speaking little"; and, in still more important situations, not merely "speaking little" but "silence" was extolled. In the *New England Primer* almost all of "The Dutiful Child's Promises"—

I Will fear GOD, and honour the KING
I will honour my Father & Mother
I will Obey my Superiours
I will Submit to my Elders
I will Love my Friends
I will hate no man
I will forgive my Enemies, and pray to God for them

—were injunctions to fear, obedience, submission, and control of enmity. They were, in other words, injunctions to community harmony by the control of aggressive and any other self-expressive impulses.

Socialization did not cease when a child came to a degree of competence.

Such competence came early to the youngsters of provincial Massachusetts —Ben Franklin was sent to work at the age of ten, and he was the pampered scholar of his father's brood—but in no way did it exempt them from the exaction of obedience. Apprenticeship, into which most of them went, was a relationship of servitude, and the Puritans were quite clear on the obligations of servants.

Law and religion alike, to say nothing of the neighbors, ordained obedience for the servant or apprentice. A standard apprenticeship contract called for a term of seven years, "During all which term, the said Apprentice his said Master faithfully shall serve, his secrets keep, his lawful commandments everywhere obey." Religion similarly supported, by divine sanction, an almost limitless obedience of servants, and the courts, too, provided for the fulfillment of servile obligation, affirming the master's right to chastise his servants if it was necessary to secure their obedience and respect. Even the complementary responsibilities laid upon masters served only to add a further dimension of authoritarianism to their relations with such subordinates. "God, according to the Puritans, gave masters authority in order that they might use it 'in furthering their Servants in a blameless behavior; and in restraining them from sin.'" Inevitably, that injunction meant that the servant was caught coming and going. His obligations to his master and his master's obligations to him amounted to one and the same thing: a demand for self-abasement rather than self-assertion.

Indeed, such discipline may well have been the very essence of apprenticeship, since apprenticeship was not only an economic and educational necessity in provincial Massachusetts, as it was across much of early modern Europe, but also a part of a larger system for which there was no such necessity. Children of the Bay settlement were put out not only to master craftsmen, as was common in many Western societies, but also to schoolmasters or even, in the case of girls, to other mothers, to learn housekeeping. Moreover, and still more revealing, boys were often put out to learn nothing at all, simply being sent for "long visits in the homes of friends, and not always at their own desire." The reason that has been suggested for these removals is that the children were actually put out to learn good behavior, on the assumption that "a child learned better manners when he was brought up in another home than his own"; and Morgan has speculated that control could thereby be continued at an otherwise difficult age, since any potential for renewed self-assertion by the young man could be curbed, in his new milieu, "by someone who would not forgive him any mischief out of affection for his person." But, whether or not the removal to another family placed youths in a psychologically more auspicious setting for the application of strict discipline, it certainly placed them in social roles—servant or student—guided by norms of obedience, where sharp correction was the standard penalty for any expression of their own will.

The final phase of the socialization cycle occurred when young men and women established their own families and thus became agents of education for the next generation. That phase, too, until its very consummation, was subject to canons of control that were considerably more rationalized, more consistently formal, and more public than those of old England. Indeed, the Puritans attempted to contain the attractions of love much as they sought to govern that other potentially passionate disruption of the social peace, the conversion experience. The choice of a marriage partner was not notably unfree in Massachusetts, any more than men were to be coerced to Christ; but, for matrimony no less than for regeneration, the emotions that were aroused had then to be harnessed to a rigid and formal pattern proceeding through specified stages that were to be passed one at a time in the prescribed order.

2. Class, Culture, and Family in the Origins of Public Education

Conventional wisdom about the origins of public education holds that public schools emerged in the nineteenth century as democratic inventions. Born of struggle, opposed by the rich and by sectarian bigots, public schools triumphed through the efforts of a coalition of dedicated humanitarian reformers and workingmen. The school systems that resulted represented the finest achievement of democracy: open to all, free, avenues to social mobility, guarantors of political stability, and instruments of social harmony.

Recent historical writing indicates quite clearly that this traditional account is false. The alignment of forces in debates about public education was very different and vastly more complex. In such a situation it is impossible to identify heroes and villains; human motivation is far too intricate and tangled, and the "right" stand on issues is far from clear. Nor, as in the colonial period, will simple evolutionary explanations do; history does not move in a straight and narrow path. Finally, it would seem that the assumption of the success of public education, on which the traditional account rests, must be reconsidered. Present-day educational criticism makes it difficult to offer glowing appraisals of the results of public schooling, and a more sober evaluation calls for a different history.

Nonetheless, it is true that, between roughly the first and third quarters of the nineteenth century, systems of public education were established in the more urban and densely populated parts of the country and, furthermore, that these systems were similar in many ways to educational systems today: They were universal, tax-supported, free, and bureaucratic. The problem of explaining their creation remains; it is only the traditional answer that must be rejected. The task is an extraordinarily complex one. For one thing, it involves sorting out the relationships between new educational practices and changes in the social, demographic, and economic contexts in which they happened. The period in which public educational systems developed in America was the time when industrialization and urbanization began to spread. School systems, railroads, factories, and cities developed at about the same time. The problem is to determine how and why this happened, to move beyond a simple association in time to a convincing and sophisticated explanation of relationships.

Part of any explanation must involve the family. Major social change registers profoundly on the domestic relations of people, and alterations within the family always affect education. As the functions that the family can and does perform shift, people come to want new and different things from schools. The problem for the historian is that it is far more difficult to identify changes in the composition and role of the family than in the nature of work, in the magnitude and density of population, or even in schools. Thus, any attempt to relate family and school historically must include not only an explanation of developments but also an effort to find out precisely what those developments were.

Any explanation of educational change in America must also take into account the fact that innovation occurs primarily within individual cities and towns, as a result, usually, of decisions made locally. Thus, the history of education must be partly a branch of local history. It must show how a sequence of developments fits within the broad history of individual communities. Somewhat paradoxically, the impact of broad forces on education often can best be seen by studying individual places, for an analysis of local history reveals most clearly the impact of technological change, urban problems, political processes, and demographic shifts.

Taken together, the selections that follow reflect all of these issues. My opening essay conceptualizes leading schemes for the organization of public education in terms of models that are related to social values, social stratification, and social change. It provides, as well, a less linear and less evolutionary description than is found in conventional accounts. In the next selection, Joseph F. Kett assesses the causes and consequences of profound alterations in the perception of childhood and youth, which he finds in the period when public education began. William E. Bridges's essay complements Ketts's by arguing that the concept and role of the family were also shifting at the same time. Bridges points to tensions within the family that, in this period, assumed contradictory goals, not unlike those given to the schools by the people I have described in my opening essay as incipient bureaucrats. Finally, my essay on Quincy illustrates how local history can help in understanding broad historical processes. It shows how widespread social forces, local problems, and educational concerns interacted to produce one of the most prominent local reform movements of the nineteenth century.

From Voluntarism to Bureaucracy in American Education

Michael B. Katz

The creation of institutions preoccupied early-nineteenth-century Americans. Whether they were building banks or railroads, political parties or factories, hospitals or schools, Americans confronted the inappropriateness of traditional organizational arrangements, and their attempts to find a suitable fit between the form and context of social life stimulated a prolonged national debate. For the most part, the public record of the controversy rests in massively tedious proposals for the introduction or alteration of particular organizational details; it appears to be the prosaic and even trivial record of practical men solving everyday problems. Yet, the arguments of these practical men over the external features of institutions frequently represented a fundamental clash of social values. For the task of appropriately arranging public activities formed an intimate part of the problem of building a nation, and alternative proposals embodied different priorities and dissimilar aspirations for the shape of American society.

It is my hypothesis that four major models of organization conflicted in the first half of the nineteenth century. The four models I shall term paternalistic voluntarism, corporate voluntarism, democratic localism, and incipient bureaucracy.

For the most part, the debate centered on objective questions—that is, definite structural characteristics on which organizations may be said to differ. The primary dimensions in the controversy were: scale (or size), control, professionalism, and finance. Each proposal concerning one of these organizational characteristics rested on social values, which, though often remaining implicit, had enormous emotional significance. (We have only to recall the decentralization controversy in New York City today to realize the emotion-laden value content of issues of control and professionalism in education.) At the same time, issues of value often explicitly enveloped the debate, especially when proponents raised questions of organizational purpose. And here the issue most frequently at odds became the degree of standardization desirable in American institutional forms, behavior, and cultural values.

I

The New York Public School Society, established as the New York Free School Society in 1805, represents the paradigm case of paternalistic voluntarism in educational organization. Its purpose was to provide rudimentary training in literacy and morals for lower-class children not catered to by existing denominational schools. However, the Society expanded its scope and ambition until, in the early 1820's, it became the agency that dispersed virtually the entire public grant for elementary education in the city of New York. By its use of the term "free school," it should be noted, the Society did not advocate free, tax-supported education in our contemporary sense. Rather, it promoted free schooling only for the very poor. In fact, voluntarism underlay the organization of the Society, which was administered by an unpaid, self-perpetuating board of first citizens. It was precisely this fact—the unrewarded and disinterested dedication of able men, the enlistment of the energy of that class of distinguished citizens who would not stoop to practice democratic politics—that gave this form of organization its distinctive virtues in the view of its champions. In this conception, voluntarism was a variety of *noblesse oblige*; it rested on faith in the individual talented amateur and, at an over-all administrative level, scorned the need for elaborate organization, state control, or professional staff. From one perspective, paternalistic voluntarism worked extremely well. With a minimum of administrative expense and scrupulous financial integrity, with commendable efficiency and unpaid administrators, the Society maintained an extensive network of schools that for decades taught thousands of children annually.

But have no doubt about it: This was a class system of education. It provided a vehicle for the efforts of one class to civilize another and thereby ensure that society would remain tolerable, orderly, and safe. The Society offered mass education on the cheapest possible plan—the monitorial, or Lancasterian, system, which counterbalanced the lack of central organization with rigid internal arrangements for each school. Aside from its minuscule per pupil cost, this mechanistic form of pedagogy, which reduced education to drill, seemed appropriate because the schools served lower-class children who were likened to unfinished products needing efficient inculcation with norms of docility, cleanliness, sobriety, and obedience. The zealous amateurs of the New York Public School Society did not design their system for their own children or for the children of their friends. Rather, they attempted to ensure social order through the socialization of the poor in cheap, mass schooling factories.

Critics of paternalistic voluntarism stressed three defects. First, it was undemocratic. Under this system, education remained a monopoly of self-perpetuating trustees unresponsive and unaccountable to the public. As such, it violated the basis of the democratic theory of public organizations and perverted the notion of voluntarism, which had shifted its meaning and by then, in the American context, found expression most favorably through willingly offered participation in the conduct of institutions owned and managed by elected public representatives. In one sense, the repudiation of paternalistic voluntarism participated in the general attack on monopolies that characterized public discourse in Jacksonian America.

To its critics, paternalistic voluntarism ignored the variety of American life and reflected an unacceptable cultural bias by imposing uniform services upon a diverse clientele. Though often couched in religious terms, this criticism revealed a perception of important cultural differences, of which religious doctrines served as symptoms. An educational system that ignored, or tried to stamp out, these variations clearly appeared to violate the criteria for free and democratic institutions.

Animosity to upper-class benevolence underscored both religious and political denunciations of paternalistic voluntarism. A Catholic spokesman, Bishop Hughes, argued that the class bias inherent in the schools of the New York Public School Society alienated poor Catholic children and their parents. In this view, irregular attendance—a problem of which the Society complained—reflected the insensitivity of the schools to working-class children, not an ignorant lower-class rejection of education as the Society's sponsors maintained. Bourgeois hostility to paternalistic voluntarism forms a related theme. Through the existence of organizations like the Public School Society, free education, public education, and the monitorial system had all become identified with lower-class education. Only a radical reorganization, a rejection of paternalistic voluntarism, could divorce the concepts of public and pauper and thereby provide institutions acceptable to proud and enterprising parents of limited means.

The first alternative proposed was democratic localism. Its sponsors sought to adapt to the city an organizational form current in rural areas, the district or community school. They asked for an absolute minimum of state or city supervision and the conduct of schools through elected neighborhood boards, which would permit local variation. They assumed that emulation between schools and local pride would promote educational progress more effectively than any central body. Democratic localism subordinated considerations of efficiency and organizational rationality to an emphasis on responsiveness, close public control, and local involvement.

Democratic localists fought, actually, on two fronts, against paternalistic voluntarism and against bureaucracy or centralization as well. Their stress on variety, local adaptability, and the symbiotic relation of school and community permeated both conflicts. In the latter, however, the resistance to bureaucracy, two other aspects of their attitude emerged most strongly. One was antiprofessionalism. They were not, as had been the sponsors of the

New York Public Society, vaguely indifferent to the concept of the professional educator; they were, instead, hostile and suspicious. They saw little reason why school teaching should become a career or profession, or why, even more, it required special training centers or, above all, a special administrative class and state apparatus. The state apparatus, represented to the democrats the essence of the centralizing viewpoint: the imposition of social change and the attempt to force attitudes on the people. Neither of these, argued the democratic localists, would work; changes in society, in habits, and in attitudes came only from within a people themselves as they slowly, haltingly, but surely exercised their innate common sense and intelligence. By leaving them to their own devices, by perhaps encouraging, cajoling, and softly educating, but not by forcing, one would rouse the people to the importance of universal education and of the regular school attendance of their children.

As a proposal for the organization of urban education (for instance, the scheme put forward by the New York Secretary of State to replace the Public School Society), democratic localism flourished for only a short time. Its failure was predictable from the start, for it rested on a distinctively rural point of view. The propounders of democratic localism did not adapt their viewpoint to the city, and hence ignored critical differences between rural and urban contexts and the particular problems that the latter posed for the conduct of education. Nor did its sponsors—for instance, Berkshire Congregationalists in Massachusetts—see the ironically undemocratic possibilities inherent in giving free rein to local majorities.

Indeed, at its worst, democratic localism was the expression of tyrannical local majorities whose ambition was control and the dominance of their own narrow sectarianism or political bias in the schoolroom. But, at its best, democratic localism embraced a broad and humanistic conception of education as uncharacteristic of nineteenth- as of twentieth-century schools and schoolmen. Consider, for example, the exhortation of one democratic localist (probably Orestes Brownson) who eschewed the specially utilitarian in education in terms of a distinctively American social structure:

> Here professions and pursuits are merely the accidents of individual life. Behind them we recognize Humanity, as paramount to them all. Here man, in theory at least, is professor. Professions and pursuits may be changed according to judgment, will, or caprice, as circumstances permit, or render necessary or advisable. Consequently, here we want an education for that which is permanent in man, which contemplates him as back of all the accidents of life, and which shall be equally valuable to him whatever be the mutations which go on around him, the means he may choose or be compelled to adopt to obtain a livelihood.

The education of importance thus was "general education," or the "education of Humanity," the education that "fits us for our destiny, to attain our end as simple human beings."

A third model coexisted with paternalistic voluntarism and democratic localism. This was corporate voluntarism, the conduct of *single* institutions as individual corporations operated by self-perpetuating boards of trustees and financed through endowment and tuition. Corporate voluntarism characterized primarily secondary and higher education, academies and colleges. Because it would place each institution under a different administrative authority, corporate voluntarism seemed to combine the virtues of the other two models. Without the stigma of lower-class affiliation, it offered disinterested, enlightened, and continuous management that kept the operation of education out of the rough and unpredictable field of politics. At the same time, it retained the limited scope essential to institutional variety, flexibility, and adaptation to local circumstances. Moreover, this corporate mode of control was congruent with contemporary arrangements for managing other forms of public business. As states turned from mercantilist regulation of the economy, they adopted a liberal stance that identified public interest with unrestricted privileges of incorporation and the removal of regulations governing economic activity. The argument that autonomous, competing corporations, aided but not controlled by the state, best served the public interest extended easily from finance, transportation, and manufacturing to education. Academies, for instance, were educational corporations.

In the late eighteenth and early nineteenth centuries, states promoted corporate voluntarism as public policy by giving legislative and financial assistance to academies, which were supposed to fulfill an evident need for institutions of secondary education. Academies represented the quintessence of voluntarism as *noblesse oblige* because they rapidly diffused throughout the country a combination of public goals and private control wrapped in the mantle of disinterested service. Academies shared a fate similar to that of the New York Public School Society when popular attitudes began to exclude from the public domain institutions managed and owned by self-perpetuating boards of trustees. As it became apparent that only institutions financed by the community or state and directly controlled by its officers merited definition as public, both paternalistic and corporate voluntarism were doomed.

Among the competing organizational models, incipient bureaucracy triumphed. The promoters of bureaucracy, including the great figures of the "educational revival," concentrated on attacking democratic localism, which was the chief hindrance to their schemes. They struck first at the notion that democratic localism was, in fact, democratic, by pointing out that it would permit 51 per cent of local parents to dictate the religious, moral, or political ideas taught to the children of the remainder. The proponents of democratic localism erred by assuming the widespread existence of homogeneous potential units of school administration. In actuality, the variety within most communities, city wards, or neighborhoods would foster intensely political competition for control of the local school in order to ensure the propagation of particular points of view or, at the least, the exclusion of rival ones. Aside from the debilitating effect of political struggle upon education, the result could easily abridge the liberties of parents by forcing them to choose between submitting their children to alien points of view and expensive private schooling.

The second defect of democratic localism was its rural bias, which overlooked the special educational problems posed by cities. Population growth and heterogeneity made extremely decentralized administration inefficient in an urban setting, because it permitted duplication of facilities and the maintenance of uneconomical units that squandered financial resources. As well, democratic localism within a city encouraged an inequitable situation, for it allowed a lack of parity in educational facilities and standards within a relatively small geographical area. Nor did democratic localism permit the schools to undertake the distinctive tasks assigned them in urban settings. For a complex set of reasons that we cannot consider here, schools came to be perceived as key agencies for uplifting the quality of city life by stemming the diffusion of poverty, crime, and immorality, which were thought to accompany urban and industrial development. A demand for the regular attendance of all children upon a prolonged, systematic, and carefully structured formal education followed obviously from the heightened conception of the importance of schooling to urban social order. This demand, in turn, required capacities for coordination and supervision lacking in democratic localism.

Thus, the first generation of professional urban schoolmen rejected democratic localism. Fully developed plans for systems of schools and elaborate architecture, curricula, and pedagogy mark the reports and appeals of Mann, Barnard, and their counterparts. Their goal was to uplift the quality of public education by standardizing and systematizing its structure and content. All their plans had certain characteristics in common, most importantly centralization. Centralization had two principal components: first, the modification and eventual elimination of the bastion of democratic localism, the district system, whereby each section of a town or city managed its own schools with a great deal of autonomy. Public high schools were to reduce the powers and scope of the district committees by siphoning off the older scholars into central institutions. Revitalized central school committees or boards were to manage the high schools and encroach gradually upon the prerogatives of the districts, thus preparing the way for their abolition. The second and related component of centralization was the grading of schools. Careful gradation between and within schools was to provide the hallmark of a properly centralized system.

An emphasis on supervision accompanied centralization. The opponents of democratic localism argued eloquently for state boards of education with paid secretaries and, at the local level, for superintendents of schools. The stress on paid, full-time supervision spilled over into arguments for professional expertise. Arguments both for the appointment of superintendents and for upgrading teaching through the creation of normal schools shared an important assumption: Education had become a difficult and complex undertaking whose conduct and administration demanded the attention of individuals with specialized talents, knowledge, and experience.

The content of education presented a twofold problem: honoring minority sensibilities while inculcating the norms requisite for upright and orderly urban social living. The official response to the problem of minority sensibility was to proclaim the schools religiously and politically neutral, though, in practice, they represented a chauvinistic, pan-Protestant point of view that remained particularly offensive to Catholics. The class bias of educational content was even more pervasive than its tepid Protestant tone. A configuration of moral and cultural values best described as mid-Victorian permeated school textbooks and statements of educational objectives. It was apparent that the traits of character deemed necessary to fit the working class for upright urban living represented a Victorian middle-class portrait of itself.

Herein lies an irony: Schoolmen who thought they were promoting a neutral and classless, indeed a *common*, school education remained unwilling to perceive the extent of cultural bias and imposition inherent in their own writing and activity. However, the bias was central and not incidental to the standardization and administrative rationalization of public education. For, in the last analysis, the rejection of democratic localism rested only partly on inefficiency and violation of parental prerogative. It stemmed equally from a gut fear of the cultural divisiveness inherent in the increasing religious and ethnic variety of American life. Cultural homogenization played counterpoint to administrative rationality. Bureaucracy was intended to standardize far more than the conduct of public business.

Yet, the movement of the bureaucrats was not entirely toward order and rigid system. Their proposals for the actual conduct of the classroom and the reform of pedagogy moved in precisely the opposite direction. In this, they represented the reverse of the paternalistic voluntarists, who accompanied a relative lack of external order with a rigid internal system of teaching. To the common-school revivalists, "mechanical," as applied to pedagogy, was a thoroughly pejorative term. As they systematized the administration and grading of schools, these schoolmen, for a very complex variety of reasons, argued for a softening of pedagogy, marked by an emphasis on the motivating of students through the arousal of interest, the abandonment of interpersonal competition, and the virtual elimination of corporal punishment. The model for the teacher-pupil relation became the relation of parent and child at its finest, firm and affectionate.

In one other crucial way the leading figures of the educational revival did not behave like traditional bureaucrats: They did not adopt the bureaucratic ideal of personality. Neither their ideal teacher nor their ideal administrator was to be a colorless public servant efficiently and quietly executing the public will. Quite to the contrary: The model for the educational administrator came from neither business nor the military but, instead, from evangelical religion. It was not by accident that the period of midcentury reform was called, even at the time, the educational revival. It was to be a secular evangelicalism. Often reared in religious orthodoxy, from which they had fled, as in Mann's case, to Unitarianism, these schoolmen retained the evangelical ideal of a moral and spiritual regeneration of American society through the moral and spiritual regeneration of individual personalities. It is this goal that lay at the center of the new, soft, child-centered pedagogy. It was to be a pedagogy that recognized the sterility and even danger of purely cold and intellectual education. Education had, as well, to be moral, which meant that schools had to awaken and shape the affective side of personality by delicately stimulating and cultivating the emotions. Evangelical models inspired, as well, the campaigns of these educational promoters, who saw their mission as converting the populace—if need be, town by town—to the cause of salvation through the common school.

Compulsory education followed inexorably upon the demise of democratic localism. Abridgment of the freedom of property owners by compulsory taxation for school support forecast the elimination of the freedom to be unschooled. Proponents of bureaucracy argued that the heightened importance of education in urban society required a vast increase in the proportion of community resources devoted to schooling. Furthermore, part of the price of removing the stigma of pauperism from free schooling became the universal distribution of the burden of school finance through general property taxation. Clearly, for the schools to work, everyone had to attend, but schoolmen did not anticipate that this would pose a problem. Educational promoters expected an overwhelming voluntary response, even from the working class, to the excellence and transparent utility of their new institutions. But only the middle classes responded with enthusiasm and regularity. At first, school promoters tried a number of expedients to improve attendance, the most notable of which was the creation of reform schools, special compulsory institutions to mop up the residue left by the regular public schools. But the residue proved larger and more intractable than anyone had anticipated. Thus, a number of strands came together and pointed in only one direction. If everyone was taxed for school support, if this was justified by the necessity of schooling for the preservation of urban social order, if the beneficial impact of schooling required the regular and prolonged attendance of *all* children, and, finally, if persuasion and a variety of experiments had failed to bring all the children into school, then, clearly, education had to be compulsory. In the crunch, social change would be imposed.

Bureaucracy retained a legacy from the organizational models that it superseded. It bowed in the direction of the democrats by accepting their redefinition of voluntarism and consequently placing educational institutions under boards that were publicly elected rather than self-perpetuating. It innovated in its rejection of a loose, personalistic style of operation for organizational rationality, impersonality, and professionalism. Nevertheless, in two respects the path from paternalistic voluntarism to bureaucracy is direct. First, bureaucracy retained the notion of a central monopoly and systematized its operation through the creation of elaborately structured schools and school systems. Second, bureaucracy continued, and even strengthened, the notion that education was something the better part of the community did to the others to make them orderly, moral, and tractable. Unfortunately, the embodiment of that idea in compulsory, bureaucratic monopolies has continued to characterize American education.

II

One can make the precise differences between models emerge more distinctly by focusing on the four objective dimensions—scale, control, professionalism, and finance—and comparing the positions of the models on each. As for scale, both the democrats and the corporate voluntarists advocated smallness and viewed the proper administrative unit as the individual institution or, at most, a section of a town. Both of the others, of course, stressed size in their definition of administrative area, and recommended the entire town or city at the least, the whole state desirably, and, in some cases, the nation. On the other hand, the two varieties of voluntarists united on the question of control and sponsored essentially amateur self-management by boards removed from direct public control. Here, at one level, the democrats and bureaucrats united in stressing the importance of management assigned to bodies directly responsible to, and representative of, the public. However, the bureaucrats extended this position to advocate the delegation by these public bodies of executive responsibility to public professionals—a proposal the democrats treated with horror.

Neither variety of voluntarist was particularly concerned with the question of professionalism. Both assumed that, as talented, educated amateurs, they were fit to manage educational institutions. Thus, when they were in control, the question of professionalism simply did not arise. Where the democrats were indifferent, interestingly, was on the question of finance. They did not especially care whether schools were absolutely free and tax-supported or whether they were partly supported by rates. In fact, if free schools meant the imposition of state authority against community will, they were positively opposed. The point is that free schools, while ultimately desirable, remained subordinate on their scale of priorities to community self-determination. The bureaucrats, with a few notable exceptions, most ardently championed free schools, which were logically necessary to their ideal of universal education. The voluntarists supported tuition for those who could pay, free education for the poor, and endowment wherever possible.

On the question of the social role of education, the corporate voluntarists and democrats retained a pluralistic and libertarian vision. As one democrat put the matter, government had as a "right no control over our opinions, literary, moral, political, philosophical, or religious." To the contrary, its task was "to reflect, not to lead, nor to create the general will." Government thus "must not be installed as the educator of the people." The democrats could see no particular virtue in uniformity. It was, after all, the same writer who said that it was the idiosyncratic character of community schools, shaped by local parents, that gave the common school its "charm."

The paternalistic voluntarists and the bureaucrats, of course, saw education precisely *as* the educator of the people, leading, not reflecting, the general will and, at the least, shaping moral opinions. The "charm" of the common school did not especially concern them, if, indeed, they ever noticed it. They hoped for, basically, an increasing standardization of institutions, practices, and culture in American society. Safety of property, upright behavior, a reduction in crime and welfare expense—these values marked both as the advocates of law and order of their day. As an acute critic of the Massachusetts Board of Education pointed out, with unmerciful clarity, the Board viewed education as "merely a branch of general police" and "schoolmasters" as only a "better sort of constables." The "respectable" members of the Board promoted universal education "because they esteem it the most effectual means possible of checking pauperism and crime, and making the rich secure in their possession." Education thus had "a certain utility," whose measure was "solid cash saved to the Commonwealth."

III

With the exception of the bureaucrats, whose love for system led them to expound their point of view repeatedly and at the slightest excuse, the best source for highlighting the difference between models is the analysis of moments of conflict. The controversy between the New York Public School Society and its antagonists—first, the Catholic Church and, later, the State of New York—brings dramatically into play the confrontation between paternalistic voluntarism and democratic localism, and highlights the poignancy of the paternalists, men of good will who worked hard and honestly only to find themselves suddenly rejected and condemned. The same note of poignancy permeates another classic, and even more complex, controversy, namely, that over the abolition of the Boston Primary School Committee, which could not understand why, suddenly, it had become to all the world (and this is the word used by one of its apologists) an "anachronism."

The literature of the academy–high school controversy throughout the United States reveals the conflict between corporate voluntarists and centralizers, for the high school was the favorite institutional innovation of the latter. Of all the controversial literature that I have seen on this issue, by far the most interesting involves the Norwich Free Grammar School, an endowed secondary school founded in the early 1850's to serve as the high school for Norwich, Connecticut, but owned and managed by a board of trustees in the same manner as the academies. The proponents of the school clearly saw in it a desirable alternative to the public high school, and their controversy with the public school men of Massachusetts over this point is an important document in educational history.

The conflicts between the democratic localists and the bureaucrats often assumed the atmosphere of an undeclared guerrilla war of sabotage and resistance, as local school districts refused to comply with state regulations and parents refused to cooperate with the state's representative, the teacher. Insofar as most of this resistance came from inarticulate people, it is the hardest and most maddening aspect of nineteenth-century educational history to document. That it existed is, however, beyond doubt, as the frustrated testimony of local and state reformers testifies in almost every document they wrote.

Still, excellent examples of democratic localism can be found. The proposals of New York State Secretary John C. Spencer have already been mentioned. Excellent, too, on this score is the controversy over free schools in both New York and Pennsylvania, particularly the extensive debates on education in the latter during the constitutional convention of 1837–38. There, most explicitly, the democrats and centralizers confronted each other and, using the issue of language, debated the problem of cultural uniformity; then, turning to free schools, they explicitly clashed over the source and pace of social change. The other major collision between democrats and centralizers happened in Massachusetts, when the former mounted a concerted attack on the newly formed Massachusetts Board of Education. The statement of the committee of the legislature that advocated the abolition of the Board is in many ways the classic statement of the democrats. More reflective, more philosophical, and one of the finest educational statements of the mid-nineteenth century is the attack on the Board in the *Boston Quarterly Review,* from which the earlier quotations have been taken. For the viewpoint of the bureaucrats, in addition to their replies in conflict, the standard sources of educational history suffice: state and local school reports; Henry Barnard on school attendance, linking up the various strands in the argument I have described; George Boutwell putting the case for the high school with devastating directness; Horace Mann rhetorically linking crime, poverty, disorder, and education; and so it goes. For these were the most articulate of the proponents. They were also victorious.

IV

Even if the specific models proposed in this paper are rejected, it is my hope that the underlying argument has been persuasive. That argument is that the analysis of organizational models provides direct insight into the key value conflicts within nineteenth-century society. In their arguments over the details of organizations, nineteenth-century Americans revealed most clearly their aspirations and, as well, their anxieties concerning the society they would build and bequeath. However, if we accept the centrality of organizational form to nineteenth-century people, we are left with an important general question: Why has the nature of organization been of such primary importance? From one direction, the question points to a comparative inquiry. Was the nature of organization as passionate and value-laden a subject of controversy in other countries during the same period? I suspect the answer, at least insofar as England and Canada are concerned (although I may well be wrong), is no; Americans made organization uniquely their own national problem. And they did so precisely because they lacked fixed traditions and the security of ancient forms. The search for the distinctively American in art, architecture, and government, to name but three aspects of American culture, is too well known a subject to belabor. This nervous self-consciousness knew few boundaries; it made the creation of organizations—their forms and characteristics—an intellectual and even nationalistic issue. It thus assumed special importance in the American context.

But the question of the centrality of organization can be put in a more general context as well. Even if not quite so emotionally charged, it nevertheless was important elsewhere during the nineteenth century. In both England and Canada, for instance, problems of devising or revising institutions to cope with poverty, ignorance, and other forms of social distress enlisted enormous amounts of thought and energy in precisely the same period. The explanation of that fact requires the formulation of relationships between organizations and other key aspects of nineteenth-century society—a task clearly outside my scope here in any detailed sense. However, it is important to speculate, even briefly, on the nature of that relationship and hence the direction the inquiry into its delineation might assume. Tentatively, therefore, I should like to advance the proposition that the importance of organization derived from its mediating position between social structure and social change.

The mediating position of organizations becomes evident from a consideration of the three broad areas that must be included in any comprehensive analysis of the nineteenth century: First is social change, perhaps best described as industrialization and urbanization. Of the three areas, this is the one about which we know most. Second are changes in social structure and demographic characteristics. We have some idea of the change in the ethnic composition of the population, of its physical distribution, of the white birth rate. We know very little, in an empirical sense, about changes in structure, particularly the family or patterns of stratification and mobility, though a number of scholars are working on these topics. However, we can be generally certain that there were some changes of a fairly substantial nature, whatever they may turn out to be precisely. The third area of the change is organizational, which I have sketched here with regard to education.

We can observe some relations between these major areas of change already. Paternalistic voluntarism was the form of organization characteristic of education in the preindustrial, mercantile city. Corporate voluntarism and democratic localism characterized rural areas and were proposed for urban places precisely at times of transition between mercantile and industrial stages of development. Incipient bureaucracy spread with incipient industrialization. In terms of social structure, one might suggest that paternalistic voluntarism characterized a society in which stratification was based on traditional notions of rank and deference, rather than class in the more modern sense. Some evidence indicates that the poor and the working classes, threatened by industrialization, supported democratic localism in times of technological transition. However, a middle-class attempt to secure advantage for their children as technological change heightened the importance of formal education ensured the success and acceptance of universal, elaborate, graded school systems. The same result emerged from the fear of a growing, unschooled proletariat. Education substituted for deference as a source of social cement and social order in a society stratified by class rather than by rank.

In each instance, the organization was in the middle. It was the medium through which groups or classes organized their response to social imperatives. In short, to repeat my hypothesis, organization mediated between social change and social structure. Hence, men brought to the design of their organizations their values, their ambivalences, their fears, and, above all, their aspirations for the shape of American society.

V

Two general points about the significance of the organizational debate remain to be made. First of all, it refocuses the issue in the decreasingly profitable debate between proponents of consensus and controversy as keys to the American past. If my underlying contention is valid, men did argue over fundamental value differences, which they articulated in reference to the practical problem of organization building. Their interchange, the competition among organizational forms and the visions they expressed, did provide a dynamic of controversy to nineteenth-century history. But it is a dynamic that implies no lack of faith in Lockean liberalism, no desire to subvert the existing social order, and no lack of commitment to America. The politics of organization building *were* politics of value clash, but the nature of that clash is not described by conventional categories of economic or class division. Determination of just what those categories are—how to go beyond the empirical facts of organizational form to organized systems of values and their relationship to social structure—should be, I would argue, the major goal of American social historians.

The other point of significance regards alternatives. Men did see alternatives in the American past. Those whose vision embraced a path other than bureaucracy lost. But, if the present was inevitable, it did not seem so to men at the time. Perhaps, if they had been that much wiser—who can say? Their failure and their vision provide, respectively and at once, enduring notes of pessimism and hope, to which we cannot afford not to listen today.

Adolescence and Youth in Nineteenth-Century America

Joseph F. Kett

The modern concept of adolescence was created by Hall and his colleagues at Clark University in the 1890's and given full expression in Hall's two-volume *Adolescence*. Hall described adolescence as a second birth, marked by a sudden rise of moral idealism, chivalry, and religious enthusiasm. In the context of Hall's celebrated theory of recapitulation—the idea that the child passes in succession through the various historical epochs already traversed by man—the adolescent became a kind of noble savage. His activities were inevitable reflections of psychic echoes out of a distant past. Weird and pseudo-scientific in retrospect, Hall's concept had a profound impact in his day. A parade of books on the teen years, the "awkward age," the high school, and the juvenile delinquent followed, while a virtual profession of advisers on the tribulations of youth emerged.

One can also argue that adolescence has become a unique topic of interest in the twentieth century because of social conditions peculiar to our own time—specifically, the emergence of a yawning time gap between the onset of sexual maturity and the full incorporation of young people into the economic life of the adult world. Before we can rest content with this explanation, however, we have to confront the historical fact of numerous references to adolescence or youth long before Hall's time.

In the Middle Ages, speculations about the "ages of man" had usually included a stage of youth or adolescence and, at times, two separate stages. Such speculation had often centered more on the exact number of the ages than on their moral or psychological content, however. Indeed, the fascination with dividing the life cycle by whole or magical numbers survived into the early 1800's. Humanists and philosophers—Elyot and Ascham in the sixteenth century, Comenius in the seventeenth century, and Rousseau in the eighteenth century—had also located moral as well as physical changes at adolescence. Of these, Rousseau was assuredly the most emphatic, and the direction of both European and American medical literature in the late eighteenth and early nineteenth centuries paralleled his insistence on a profound change at puberty. One indication was the rise of a scientific literature on masturbatory insanity, touched off by the publication of the Swiss physician Samuel A. Tissot's *Onania, or a Treatise upon the Disorders*

Reprinted from *The Journal of Interdisciplinary History*, II (Autumn, 1971), pp. 283–98, by permission of *The Journal of Interdisciplinary History* and The M.I.T. Press, Cambridge, Massachusetts. Copyright © 1971 by *The Journal of Interdisciplinary History*.

Produced by Masturbation (Lausanne, 1758). A popularization of this species of literature took place in early-nineteenth-century America in the form of innumerable "candid talks with youth" books and pamphlets.

Writers on physiology displayed another side of the growing interest in adolescence. Dunglison, in his influential physiology text, found at puberty a freshening of the external senses, a rise of idealism, a qualitative leap in intellectual capacity, and the dawn of a tender modesty. Like Hall, Dunglison insisted that adolescence was a moral and psychological stage of life that began with puberty and terminated with the end of physical growth in the early twenties. There was, indeed, a connection between the two sides of the emerging concept of adolescence, for the more writers celebrated the idealism of adolescence, the more befoulment they saw in masturbation.

Simply to note scientific and medical references to adolescence before the work of Hall tells us little, however, about the origin of popular ideas about adolescence. To revert specifically to the American context, we may well ask whether a writer such as Dunglison was simply giving scientific expression to long-standing popular assumptions, or whether he stood at the end of a relatively short line of development. This is, for many reasons, a more difficult question to answer. An abundant and systematic literature on adolescent guidance did not exist in America before 1900. The word "adolescence" appeared only rarely outside of scientific literature prior to the twentieth century. But the absence of an elaborate literature on adolescent guidance before 1900 does not mean that ideas about adolescence did not exist, or that they were of only marginal concern. It indicates merely that adolescence was not the public, official concern prior to 1900 that it has since become.

The evolution of popular, as opposed to strictly scientific, ideas about adolescence can be understood by studying the changing usage of "youth," the word usually employed before 1900 to denote the intermediate stage of development. Numerous references to "youth" can be found as early as the seventeenth century. New England Puritans, Cotton Mather in particular, published numerous sermons on the rising generation. Yet, one is left with a feeling that Puritans used "youth" more as a noun than as a concept. Their sermons routinely mixed up children, youth, young people, and young men. This slippery use of designations, in turn, reflected various aspects of the mentality and social experience of seventeenth-century New England Puritans. As John Demos has suggested, adolescence scarcely existed as a private issue in seventeenth-century New England. In a stable, agrarian society, the range of occupational and religious choices open to young people was so narrow as to preclude a period of doubt and indecision. One generation passed quietly into the next. But, even if adolescence had existed as a social experience in seventeenth-century New England, Puritans would have had difficulty in coming to terms with it. They hardly believed that individuals moved through stages of life. To take their favorite analogy, life was a highway. There were various signposts along the way, and older individuals had a greater physical and mental capacity than younger ones. But the sum of forces at one point on the highway did not necessarily determine direction at the next. Childhood was the beginning of the continuum of life, but the course of childhood did not necessarily determine later development.

Verbal distinctions between childhood and youth, practically nonexistent in the seventeenth century and still rare in the eighteenth, became much more common after 1800. A growing conceptual segregation of childhood and youth paralleled the sharpening of terminology. If the favorite analogy in the 1600's was the comparison of life to a highway, the darling metaphor of the 1800's was the comparison of human life to the cycle of the seasons. One illustration of the new understanding of human development was the changing nature of biography and autobiography. Biographers and auto-biographers in the seventeenth and eighteenth centuries either ignored the childhood of their subjects or treated the events of childhood simply as indications of later development. The focus was more on remarkable in-stances—close scrapes with death, providential good fortune, and the like —than on organic growth. After 1800, in contrast, chapters on childhood increasingly replaced the family tree as the introduction to the subject's life, and the tendency now was to concentrate on a recounting of the unex-ceptional events of childhood. Finally, after roughly 1830, more and more biographies and autobiographies emphasized that the early years provided a positive thrust for, rather than merely an indication of, later development.

The heightened awareness of childhood in early-nineteenth-century America involved not only a recognition of the organic character of human growth, but also a tendency toward preserving juvenile innocence rather than stimulating children to imitate adults. The celebration of juvenile in-nocence, in turn, produced the fear of precocity so pervasive in nineteenth-century thought. Since Puritans had viewed childhood as a condition to be worked off with all due speed, they tended to applaud children who acted like adults. The different direction of nineteenth-century thought can be traced in the emphasis placed in biographies after 1800 on the ability of subjects to get along with their peers in childhood. It was illustrated, also, in the immense importance that common-school reformers attached to the location of schoolhouses away from the busy scenes of secular life and to the gradual conversion of the school into "an asylum for the preservation and culture of childhood." Inevitably, the fear of precocity in children was carried over to a concern with the premature development of adolescents, an anxiety that pervaded the popular literature of the nineteenth century on masturbatory insanity. In the popular image, the precocious lad and the compulsive masturbator had so much in common—a stooping gait, a shift-ing eye, a sunken chest—that one is entitled to view many references to precocity as euphemisms for masturbation. Here, again, the break with tradition was profound. Samuel Danforth's sermon of 1674, *The Cry of Sodom Enquired into . . . Together with Solemn Exhortations to Tremble at God's Judgements and to Abandon Youthful Lusts,* condemned "self-pollution" along with other sexual indulgences, but never suggested that masturbation threatened psychological or even physical stability. The more sentimentalized became the image of early childhood in the nineteenth century, the more threatening became the onset of youth. The preoccupation of nineteenth-century writers with masturbatory insanity thus reflected a keen, if often quackish, sensitivity to the psychological dangers of adolescence.

The disposition to view the life cycle as divided into a series of disparate stages, the tendency to sentimentalize childhood, and the rising fear of precocity, all had the effect of throwing youth, the intermediate stage of development, into sharper relief. For the first time, a class of books aimed specifically at youth appeared. Addressed to those who had recently left the security of Protestant homesteads for life in urban countinghouses, the "advice to youth" books celebrated the idealism of youth but warned incessantly of the dangers of fast living and rash judgment.

To unravel the intricate web of social and attitudinal changes that lay behind this conceptual segregation of childhood and youth is not easy. Broadly speaking, the changes can be correlated with the rise of romanticism. But romanticism is a vague term; reference to it illuminates but does not explain historical change. Yet, to be more specific is risky. A heightened awareness of childhood and youth emerged at different places in the Western world after the middle of the eighteenth century, amidst widely differing social conditions. Population concentration in America after 1800 probably gave children a new degree of conspicuousness. As the Demoses have noted, the decline of the family as a working unit in an urban setting gave rise to "an important 'discontinuity of age groups.' Children and adults are much more obviously separated from each other than is ever the case in a rural environment." But it is also true that many were led to an appreciation of the innocence of smaller children by personal experiences of a religious rather than a social nature. We can see this connection in the life and thought of Catherine E. Beecher. Like any daughter of Lyman Beecher, she was expected to experience a religious conversion, was told that it was her own fault if she did not, and yet was told that there was nothing that she could do to bring about her own salvation. She initially despaired and ultimately rebelled, turning toward liberal religion and a belief that the instincts of the small child were a truer guide to morality than the solemn syllogisms of New England orthodoxy.

While the sentimentalization of childhood in early-nineteenth-century America owed something to urban liberalism, a fresh focus on both children and youth grew contemporaneously out of the very opposite source, rural and village Calvinism and the revivals of the Second Great Awakening—that massive outpouring of religious enthusiasm that swept first one and then another section of the nation from the 1790's onward. Teenagers became truly conspicuous for the first time in American history, and evangelicals involved in the Awakening noted time and again the singularly important role of children and youth, especially the latter, in the revivals. This role had been foreshadowed in the Great Awakening of the 1740's,

but, as the Great Awakening waned, there was a general return to the pattern of aged church membership. During the Second Awakening, in
The frequency of teenage conversions in the Second Awakening is signifi-
contrast, teenage conversion became the norm.
cant for a number of reasons. First of all, it was a reflection of increasing pressures on young people for choice and commitment. The spread of commercialization, pressure on the land in older sections of the nation, and internal migrations—all fundamental aspects of American social life after 1800—altered both the opportunities and [the] life patterns of young people. The rise of new religious denominations, such as Methodism, Universalism, and Unitarianism, was no less important and more directly relevant to the religious experience of young people. Religious diversity had always characterized American life, but, in the colonial period, dissenters could always be sealed off in watertight compartments like Rhode Island. By 1820, the various denominations were competing for converts in the same towns and villages. Religious alternatives were at the parental door.

The argument is often advanced that the choices available to young people are greater today than in former times, and, hence, that in our day generations more quickly become strangers to each other than in the past. But social change is as much a subjective as an objective phenomenon. It exists not only in reality but also in the eye of the beholder. Boys subjected to the traditional modes of child-rearing, in which an absolute value was placed on submission to adult norms, found the appearance of even a small degree of social change profoundly unsettling. For many, religious conversion in the teen years proved to be at least a temporary therapy for doubt and uncertainty.

While the pattern of teenage conversion reflected social change, the phenomenon of teenage conversion became a subject of inquiry and speculation on the part of the evangelical ministry, the group with the most consistent institutional and intellectual concern with young people throughout the nineteenth century. The principal by-product of this interest was the emergence of a conviction among evangelicals that adolescence was the ideal time to induce a religious conversion. By 1820, there was a disposition among evangelicals to argue that something in the nature of youth, a combination of idealism, plasticity, and emotional enthusiasm, rendered it especially suited to conversion. By all accounts, the youth involved in the Second Awakening ranged in age from five to twenty or twenty-five, but the majority of references were to young people between twelve and twenty. Prior to the 1830's, few viewed conversions under twelve with any enthusiasm; at the same time, few were eager to put off conversion until after a youth had left home to make his way in the world. Partly by this negative process of addition and subtraction, and partly by the positive affirmation of the idealism of youth, evangelicals came to embrace the ideal of teenage conversion.

Although the practice of calling up teenagers to give testimonials of a conversion experience survived into the late nineteenth century, it had lost much of its significance by the Gilded Age. Hall himself, born in 1844, belonged to one of the last generations of New England boys expected to go through an elaborate ritual of conversion during adolescence. When he and his co-workers at Clark University, in the 1890's, were developing the modern concept of adolescence, they resurrected the old adolescent-conversion nexus by establishing a practically automatic connection between puberty and a kind of ultimate concern that manifested itself specifically in religious conversion. The connection had never been so neatly fixed in practice, but Hall and his colleagues paid homage to a nineteenth-century initiation rite that had affected millions of boys. Only if we grasp the profound roots of adolescent conversion in nineteenth-century America can we comprehend why so many of the writers on adolescence between 1890 and 1905 came into the field not by way of social reform and the juvenile courts, as the later history of the concept might suggest, but from religious psychology.

The pattern of teenage conversion that, as a matter of both expectation and reality, grew out of the Second Awakening, had the effect of forcing people to clarify the traditionally nebulous distinction between childhood and youth and of riveting attention on the psychological reactions as well as on the physical growth of youth. If religion were to be a matter of the heart as well as of the head, and if youth were the time for religious conversion, then youth had to be characterized by a rise of emotional sensibility. Indeed, the evangelical clergymen who wrote the "advice to youth" books were often led to a concern with the problems of youth after personal experience with young people during revivals. So, too, if some conversions were authentic, others, everyone conceded, were spurious—the products of mere "sympathetic enthusiasm." The inevitable implication was that the emotional reactions of young people were at times unreliable, and, specifically, that some adolescents, especially girls, were prone to insanity. The propensity of youths toward mental instability—melancholy for males and hysteria for females—was set down by medical writers from the 1830's onward under the rubric "pubertal insanity." In a sense, youthfulness had acquired a psychological as well as a chronological content.

The new concern for distinguishing childhood and youth had a variety of institutional effects. In the war against the rum demon and the grog shop, for example, both the Cold Water Army, designed for younger children, and the Cadets of Temperance, designed for teenagers, grew rapidly in the 1840's. In Sunday Schools, the holding of special classes for those in their middle teens indicated the importance attached to those years by evangelicals. It is, indeed, worth noting that evangelical Sunday Schools were often more carefully age-graded than were most secular schools.

By the 1830's, however, demands for separating boys and youths affected secular education, as well. In the late eighteenth and early nineteenth centuries, schools at any level were rarely graded by numerical age. One could meet pupils from four to twenty-three in district schools, from eight to twenty-five in academies, and from thirteen to thirty in colleges.

By the 1830's, school promoters were showing visible concern over these jagged fluctuations. Their agitation hardly resulted in the quick establishment of a graded school system. The entire process of gradation had a jerky quality that left many areas unaffected until the late nineteenth century. Prior to 1850, moreover, few educational writers showed much interest in setting age ceilings; in 1860, one could still find twenty-five-year-old academy students and thirty-year-old college students. But age floors were under construction in the 1820's and 1830's, especially in the colleges. Conditions in colonial colleges had never been altogether orderly, but, after a series of unusually violent college riots in the early 1800's, the situation grew desperate at many institutions. The disposition of students to view their horizontal ties to their peers more seriously than their vertical ties to adults not only indicated an emerging solidarity among students but also focused public attention on the need to reform college discipline. Two ideas were common to most of the proposals for reform. First, an increasing number of writers on education recognized that the older method of detecting offences by tutorial espionage had no future, and that faculty "weasels" who peeked over transoms and through keyholes were only exacerbating the problem. The sole recourse was to make a direct appeal to the honor and good sense of youth. Second, such appeals would be fruitless, many felt, as long as colleges continued to accept "mere boys" of thirteen or fourteen. Ideally, then, the colleges were to become institutions for young men rather than for children.

It is easier to note the existence of a concept of youth in early nineteenth-century America than to delineate its scope. There is a temptation to argue that references to youth in the 1830's meant the same thing as Hall implied by adolescence. Certainly, the differences between medical definitions of adolescence in the 1830's and Hall's later formulation of it were slight. But significant differences do exist between popular references to youth in the early nineteenth century and the connotation of adolescence in our century. For adolescence is now applied mainly to teenagers, while the early nineteenth-century concept of youth extended over a broader span of years from the middle teens to the middle twenties. Hall himself insisted that adolescence embraced the long period from puberty to the end of physical growth in the twenties, but he was running against the tide even in his own day. From the 1870's, there was a growing disposition to define youth narrowly as the years from fourteen to nineteen, and virtually all of the writers on adolescence who followed in Hall's wake equated adolescence with the teen years. Paradoxically, while we think of prolonged adolescence as a twentieth-century phenomenon, the definition of youth in the early 1800's was broader than the generally accepted meaning of adolescence in the twentieth century.

The concept of youth was not only more extensive in the early nineteenth century, but the focus was primarily on those in their late teens and early twenties. The famous Currier and Ives sequence dating from the 1860's—"The Four Seasons of Life"—is indicative. Childhood is symbolized by a group of tiny tots at play in a field; youth, by a sober twenty-year-old walking down a country lane arm in arm with his inamorata. So, too, the youth of the "advice to youth" books were closer to manhood than to childhood: They comprised those who had recently left Protestant homes for life in the city. In a word, the youth of the 1830's and 1840's was more of a burgeoning independent than a frustrated dependent.

There were frustrated dependents in the 1830's, and the concept of youth did extend downward to include boys at puberty. But, for a variety of reasons, few either chose to focus on the crisis around puberty or thought it more significant than later crises.

First of all, in the early 1800's, it was difficult to formulate horizontal concepts about juveniles, especially about those in their middle teens, because teenage experiences in preindustrial American society were not graded in any precise way by numerical age. There was no set age for leaving school or for starting work. Fourteen was the usual age for apprenticeship, but there were so many exceptions in practice, especially in the case of farm boys, that no one could draw an automatic connection between arrival at the age of fourteen and the commencement of work. Even those boys who entered apprenticeships at fourteen had frequently started to do chores or farm tasks years earlier. The relationship between school and work, moreover, was far less definite than it has since become. Today, we assume that entry into the labor market follows education, but, in the 1830's, education and labor were interwoven. Most boys worked for part of the year and then attended school. The structure of educational institutions complemented this process. Academy students, for example, usually attended only one or two terms a year, after harvest and before planting. District schools were divided into summer sessions, taught by women and intended for girls and very young boys, and winter sessions, taught by men and attended by farm boys of all ages. Seasonal education thus complemented seasonal labor. The nature of education and labor combined made it difficult to say whether a fifteen-year-old boy was dependent or semidependent, a child or a youth, for at different times of the year he was likely to be each.

The onset of male puberty failed to coincide with any fundamentally new life experience. Boys at puberty simply were not conspicuous in the way they later became. In contrast, by Hall's day, school gradation had reached the point where, at fourteen, the great majority of boys left elementary school and had to choose between high school and the job market. It is not surprising that Hall's theory of adolescence, and virtually all of the popular literature on adolescence between 1900 and 1915, assigned overriding importance to puberty. The twentieth century has argued that, no matter where the boy is, what he is doing, or what he has been through, with the onset of puberty he becomes an adolescent. In the 1830's, in contrast, popular definitions of youth took their cue more from social status than from physiology. If a sixteen-year-old boy [was] in district school, he was called a child and, for the most part, treated like one. If in college, he was usually described as a youth. Strictly speaking, the same boy could be a child for part of the year and a youth for the remainder. Or, again, one could meet seventeen-year-old children and fifteen-year-old youths.

A second reason for the relative emphasis on later adolescence was simply that the kind[s] of perils that confronted youths in their late teens were of more absorbing interest than those of the early teens. One such peril, that of leaving home, has already been noted. As the image of home became more sentimentalized in the nineteenth century, one's entry into the world of affairs appeared more threatening. Or, we can argue, the more menacing the world became, the greater the disposition to drench home and family in sentiment. Whatever the priority, by the 1840's more and more individuals were inclined to view the first few years after the break with home as critical ones. But other events of the late teens and early twenties gave rise to equally pertinent anxieties. Individuals so diverse as Orestes Brownson, John Humphrey Noyes, and Horace Bushnell, for example, all experienced a pattern of religious drifting in their twenties after premature, teenage conversions, and a clear tone of anxiety in the "advice to youth" literature suggests that such vacillations were widespread. Alongside these crises, those of the early and middle teens seemed less significant.

There was one notable exception to the lack of interest in the middle teens; paradoxically, the years around puberty were thought to be extremely critical for girls. The description of the tribulations of adolescent girls was a standard feature of sentimental novels from Susanna Rowson's *Charlotte Temple* (published as *Charlotte, A Tale of Truth* [Philadelphia, 1794]) through James Fenimore Cooper's *Tales for Fifteen* (New York, 1823), just as the tendency of racy tales of love and seduction to induce hysteria in teenage girls was a principal argument against the novel as a literary genre. The paradox arose from the fact that girls were not really viewed as having, like boys, a period of youth. A society that failed to provide a significant social role for women outside of marriage had difficulty envisioning girls passing through a protracted period of adjustment to responsibility, but no trouble recognizing the threat to female virtue posed by the sudden onset of sexual maturity. Stated another way, girls were seen as experiencing a wrenching adolescence between fourteen and sixteen, but not as having a stage of youth; boys went through a relatively painless physical adolescence, but followed it with a critical period of youth. This helps to explain why one scarcely meets any male versions of Charlotte Temple in antebellum literature, that is, with fourteen- or fifteen-year-old boys. In contrast, a considerable number of youths of eighteen to twenty, from Brown's Arthur Mervyn to Simms' Ralph Colleton (in *Guy Rivers*) to Melville's Pierre Glendenning, appeared in the same literature as central figures.

In all of this, was there any sense in antebellum America that youth should be prolonged—that pressures for achievement or choice should be removed or relaxed in youth? We usually assume that the prolongation of adolescence is a relatively recent idea. It was certainly the central message of Hall's work, and, in one form or another, it has pervaded most twentieth-century literature on youth. But was the idea present even before Hall wrote?

In some respects, the desirability of prolonged adolescence was a nineteenth-century discovery. In the 1840's, Fowler had pleaded for a reduction of academic pressures during adolescence and had lauded the value of a late ripening of the faculties. So, too, school reformers in the 1830's and 1840's often spoke of the need to preserve adolescents from premature knowledge of the world. Yet, such declarations were not equivalent to Hall's defense of a moratorium on career and intellectual commitment during adolescence. It was one thing to complain about excess study or premature sophistication and another to say that young people should be indulged in their doubt and allowed time to reflect on life's possibilities and choices.

The idea of prolonging adolescence by encouraging a postponement of choice was not prominent before 1860, at least partly because of the kind[s] of institutions that middle-class boys encountered, which permitted a certain amount of stumbling about before one was settled in a calling. The loose and informal character of the academies, and the ease with which those over twenty-five could start their college education, allowed a number of false starts. The feebleness of licensing requirements made it possible to switch from occupations to professions, or from occupation to occupation. Occupations simply did not have the rigid quality that they later acquired, and, in practice, many people had more than one occupation. Characteristically, antebellum books of advice aimed at mechanics usually assumed that the reader had already settled in a line of work and needed only to improve his competence.

Although the problem of career choice did not arise before 1860 with its later intensity, young people could still be confronted by agonizing decisions, especially in religion. Yet, despite the many declarations in the 1830's and 1840's about the desirability of reducing academic pressures on young people, there was a widespread reluctance to allow young people a period of doubt and indecision even on religious matters. There was a sense that, if young people were given time to choose, they would make the wrong choices. As the nineteenth century wore on, the need to fix religious character early in life became nearly an obsession among Protestants. By the 1850's, many Protestants were committed to the ideal that religious growth should be so gradual and steady that the Christian would be unable to say exactly when the change of heart had come.

Voiced early in the century by Unitarians, fully articulated by Horace Bushnell in *Views of Christian Nurture* (1847), and adopted increasingly by most Protestants after mid-century, the ideal of linear human development challenged long-standing Calvinist assumptions about the need for a radical regeneration of the soul. Even evangelical Calvinists, who could never accept Bushnell's liberalism, were, by mid-century, placing more emphasis on inducing early religious decisions, on bringing down the age of conversion from eighteen or nineteen to fourteen or fifteen. By the 1850's, religious conversion had ceased to be a resolution of religious doubts in late adolescence and had become, instead, a kind of Victorian initiation rite, a capstone of childhood and a prelude to youth.

Whether liberal or Calvinist, American Protestant thought about juveniles was increasingly marked not by declarations of the need for a regimen of prolonged doubt followed by conversion, but by a veritable culture of early conversions, teenage temperance pledges, and institutionalized revivals for young people, all aimed at fixing character so firmly that no amount of jarring in later youth could drive the individual off course. Thus, the ultimate paradox of nineteenth-century thought about youth was that it viewed the postponement of choice and fixed purpose as inconsistent with the protection of young people from worldliness, while, in the twentieth century, we have come to view the prolongation of adolescence as a corollary of protectiveness.

Family Patterns and Social Values in America, 1825–75
William E. Bridges

The history of the American family is presently in quite as disorganized a state as the family itself is often said to be. The conceptual sophistication of both sociology and social history since 1920 has left the only existing survey of this crucial social institution quite obsolete, for that survey was published during World War I. In no major area of American social history will the investigator find so little work available and so much misconception passing for established fact. The situation is like that which would prevail if study had stopped forty-five years ago in the fields of religious or educational history. In a sense, the situation is actually worse than that; for, in disregarding the family, historians are disregarding what Margaret Mead has called "the basic institution of society."

Before much sense can be made out of the family patterns in nineteenth-century America, the basic social function of the family must be clear. As the context into which a child is born and within which he spends his most impressionable years, the family plays a double social role: First, it transforms an asocial biological entity into a human being, and, by instill-

Reprinted from *The American Quarterly,* Volume 17, Number 1 (Spring, 1965), pp. 3–11, by permission of The University of Pennsylvania, publisher, and the Author. Copyright, 1965, Trustees of The University of Pennsylvania.

ing in him the values endorsed by his culture, it prepares him to meet the demands that his society will make upon him; second, it serves thereby to convey the culture's values across a critical gap in the social continuum —that separating one generation from its successor—and thus perpetuates the culture itself. This basic double function is performed in ways that are most appropriate to the values of the culture in question. The way in which a child is acculturated is the product of the very values to which he is being acculturated. If, for example, his society is organized hierarchically, the child will be instructed in social subordination by domestic subordination; if his society expects sons to follow fathers in type of work and social station, the family patterns will aim at reproducing the father in the son; if his society emphasizes the importance of getting along with, and fitting into, "the group," the child will be encouraged to act in such a way that he will be popular with his juvenile peers. From a society's methods of acculturation, therefore, it is possible to predict the general outlines of its value patterns; conversely, a knowledge of cultural values will help one to make an educated guess as to the domestic methods by which they could be conveyed from generation to generation.

If all this is familiar to the student of American civilization, it can only be said that the widely held conception of what nineteenth-century American family life was like suggests otherwise. For, before the historian can make much headway in the task of describing that family life and its relationship to the society of which it was a part, he must deal with a surprisingly tenacious stereotype. *Snow-bound*, "The Old Folks at Home," Currier and Ives prints, "The Children's Hour," Rogers Groups, "Home, Sweet Home"—from hundreds of such sources comes the image of a closely knit, stable, patriarchal, self-sustaining, well-disciplined family group. As Carl Degler has recently suggested, . . . , this kind of family forms the basis for Riesman's study of "inner directedness" in *The Lonely Crowd*. The socialization of the child in such a family would presumably involve training in such qualities as self-control and self-denial; naturally, the methods appropriate to such an end would call for considerable parental control and rigid discipline.

The person who brings such assumptions to the study of the nineteenth-century American family will find himself in a state of confusion very quickly. Surely, the date of the following passage cannot be 1861; but for the diction, it sounds more like 1961.

> In the genuine New England home of today, still that good old-fashioned thing called *obedience* lingers. In too many homes, judging by what we see and hear, it is deemed intrusive and turned out. . . . One may gather from his own observation and experience the most atrocious instances of disrespect and misrule, such as would disgrace an age of barbarism.

Nor was a mid-century writer being affected in calling obedience "old fashioned," for Americans and Europeans had been noting its absence for more than a half century. In the 1850's, the Pulskys wrote that American children "have their own way" and described them as "tumbling and dragging about books and cushions and chairs and climbing up and down just as they please." In the same decade, Adam Gurowski complained of "the prodigality, the assumption, self-assertion, and conceit" of the American child. When James Fenimore Cooper listed the "defects in American deportment" twenty years earlier, he began with "insubordination in children, and a general want of respect for age." The children encountered in 1817 by De Montlezun "are absolute masters of their fates. The authority of the parents is no restraint at all." And so it goes—the endless record of those who had been jostled, bellowed at, and spilled upon by the pre–Civil War American child.

It may be objected, of course, that these were mostly observers who were generally disapproving in their views of American society, so let us turn to one less suspect on this score. Tocqueville devoted a chapter of his second volume to the American family, and it is well worth reading. Obviously, he saw the very things of which the other observers complained, but he did not confuse a lack of subordination and new patterns of training with insubordination and a lack of training. Instead, he argued that the same forces that undermined the principle and practice of civil subordination also removed the need for most of the domestic subordination that was familiar to the European. He reasoned that the same principles on which the Americans had rejected the past politically and socially led them also to care less for the arbiters of, and spokesmen for, that past and, thus, to "the general want of respect for age" of which Cooper had complained. In keeping with his own domestic experience, he analyzed the situation in terms of the role of the father rather than that of the parents, but nonetheless many of his observations are astute. What he described was not a family in an advanced state of disintegration (as contemporary Europeans tended to) but rather a family that was being reconstructed so that it might more successfully acculturate the American child and prepare him thereby for life in his society. The kind of correlation he found between the values of American society and the patterns of its domestic life is evident [as] he writes:

> When the condition of society becomes democratic and men adopt as their general principle that it is good and lawful to judge of all things for oneself, using former points of belief not as a rule of faith, but simply as a means of information, the power which the opinions of a father exercise over those of his sons diminishes as well as his legal power.

In this statement, one can see the way in which Tocqueville's analysis differs from that of Riesman. Whereas Riesman associates individualism with a process of close parental supervision, under which the child "internalizes" parental restraints, Tocqueville associates individualism more logically with minimal parental supervision and early instruction in the importance of learning things for oneself. The complaints of most contemporary observers could be summed up in the words of an Englishwoman who wrote, in 1848, that the American child "is too early his own master." Her opposition to the system was almost as much one of principle as of results. If one could forget the principle and attend to the results, he might see the sort of thing observed by another Englishwoman, who reported in amazement:

> Little creatures feed themselves very neatly, and are trusted with cups of glass and china, which they grasp firmly, carry about the room carefully, and deposit unbroken, at an age when, in our country, mamma or nurse would be rushing after them to save the vessels from destruction.

The only thing to add to such an account is that it seems very likely that the same child that carried the cup with such care also infuriated other visitors who tried to be helpful by taking it away from him. One suspects that much of the "willfulness" noted in the American child was triggered by the behavior toward him of the visitor who observed it.

It is significant, of course, that many of the criticisms of the American child's independence were voiced by those who found American men presumptuous, materialistic, and restless. For the children were being fitted for life in a society whose main outlines were dangerous by European standards. It is interesting to compare the kind of child that we have been describing with the conclusions that several historians have reached about the demands made on the individual by society in this period and the kind of man who was best suited to meet them. In his study of the effects of economic abundance on the American character, David Potter wrote:

> Historically, as new lands, new forms of wealth, new opportunities, came into play, clamoring to be seized upon, America developed something of a compulsion to make use of them. The man best qualified for this role was the completely mobile man, moving freely from one locality to the next, from one economic position to another, or from one social level to levels above. . . . In a country where the entire environment was to be transformed with the least possible delay . . . mobility became not merely an optional privilege but almost a mandatory obligation, and the man who failed to meet this obligation had, to a certain extent, defaulted in his duty to society.

Potter's conclusion is supported by that of another historian whose approach and purposes are very different; in his study of Jacksonian democracy, Marvin Meyers wrote:

> The central economic figure is . . . the speculative enterpriser who scents distant opportunities and borrows or invents the means for grasping them. A preference for high-risk, high-gain transactions is found at all economic levels. . . . Thus the American, in his urgent quest for gain and advancement, becomes to many witnesses the very opposite of the sturdy, stable citizen-producer; becomes an adventurer steered only by a bold imagination.

To Potter's "completely mobile man" and Meyers's "adventurer," we may add the Adamic figure of self-containment described by R. W. B. Lewis as "an individual emancipated from history, happily bereft of ancestry, untroubled and undefiled by the usual inheritances of family and race."

The composite image that can be formed from these three figures is very close, I would submit, to the image of man that the nineteenth-century acculturation practices were designed to produce. This impression is supported, moreover, by the findings of Daniel Miller and Guy Swanson, who summed up their survey of nineteenth-century child-guidance literature by identifying the following as one of the central and unifying themes in it:

> . . . the notion that a youngster must be able independently to go out into the urban world, to capitalize on such opportunities as it may present, to carve out a life for himself which, in a rapidly changing society, may well require different tasks to be performed than were required of his parents. His is to be the active, manipulative approach to people and things.

This statement may remind the reader of Riesman's figure, the inner-directed man; and, assuredly, the self-reliance and self-direction that Riesman emphasizes are present. What is also present, and what has not been hitherto sufficiently remarked, is a cluster of values that can be described as impersonality and emotional nondependence. The enemy of mobility is not only a static social structure but also the personal attachments that the individual develops in such a structure. Individualism, in these terms, is not so much an intellectual freedom as it is an emotional disengagement from others. This disengagement was an important element in Emersonian individualism. What appeared to many observers to be domestic disintegration and lack of strong emotional ties within the family is better understood as training in detachment.

The relationship between domestic practices and their social context in this matter of emotional independence was reciprocal. That is, the patterns of acculturation can be studied as both results and causes of an increasingly atomistic, impersonal, competitive socio-economic order. One area in which this two-way relationship is evident is that of paternal participation in family life. Contemporary reports make it clear that fathers were playing less and less of a part in domestic activities as their work took them out of the home for the major part of the day. In this matter as in so many like it, modern historians have underestimated the similarities between past and present—similarities that are clear in such a passage as this, written in 1860:

> The pressure upon a multitude of business and professional men is really frightful; combined with the necessity in many cases of going long distances to their places of duty, it produces little short of an absolute separation from their families.

Not only is this the product of socialization along patterns of emotional independence; it also encourages such patterns in the next generation by fragmenting the family and by placing the father's central social concerns outside the domestic context.

It would be a mistake to assume, however, that this training in detachment was wholly successful, for one of the striking features of nineteenth-century family life resulted from its partial failure. There is plentiful evidence that striving to be the "completely mobile man" was a lonely and frustrating task. What Miller and Swanson called "the active, manipulative approach to people and things" dehumanizes not only others but oneself as well. The economic roles filled by these men were often narrow and not conducive to broad self-fulfillment. The problem and its bearing on family life have been described thus by Margaret Mead:

> In much of his ordinary adult activity, the individual expresses his personality in a segmented fashion. One aspect finds expression in his work or profession; another may be elicited from his social and recreational interests; still another may be called forth in his religious life. In the intimacies of family association, on the other hand, the entire personality is capable of integrated expression and receives response in terms of the whole rather than its parts.

Here is another area in which the differences between the last century and this have been emphasizing at the expense of the similarities. For, although the social scientist's vocabulary would have been foreign to the nineteenth-century American, the notion behind the words would not. In the best-selling *Reveries of a Bachelor* (1850), the narrator decides that, among the many attractions of home life to a man, the greatest is "the ecstasy of the conviction, that *there* at least you are beloved; that there you are understood; that there your errors will meet ever with the gentlest forgiveness . . . ; and that there you may be entirely and joyfully—yourself."

According to this view, the home became a retreat from the world, a shelter from the impersonality and competitiveness of the society that surrounded it. This is, of course, the domestic image that fills the poetry and visual art of the period and is, thus, the source of the stereotype of nineteenth-century home life. In practice, however, the notion of "home as retreat" could only confuse domestic life, for it burdened the institution that was preparing children to face their society's demands with the task of rehabilitating adults that found those demands too great.

This confusion was compounded by another that stemmed from the father's absorption in extradomestic activity. In his absence, the task of child-raising, the acculturation process, fell largely to the mother. This shift of responsibility might have had less impact on our culture if, at the same time, the vigorous reform movements active in the society had not turned to the American mother, and the acculturation process over which she presided, as their best avenue of advancement. Mothers were barraged with a many-sided campaign to save the world by means of the family. While the specific goals of the campaign were as various as the groups engaged in it, one of them deserves our notice. Its central figure was the editor of *Godey's Lady's Book*, the influential Sarah Josepha Hale, and its purpose is evident in the following passage from one of Mrs. Hale's editorials:

> In this country, there being no established rank and privileged class, wealth has been found to be the surest letter of introduction into the highest and most polished circles. . . . There is a cramping and debasing influence exerted by this systematic, absorbing pursuit after wealth. . . . And here it is that our country needs the power of female talent to be exerted, the efficiency of moral training to be tested. Let this besetting sin of our times be studiously watched by the Christian mother. Let us guard against this insidious influence of Mammon.

Mothers were being urged, in short, to undermine the very pattern of values that the emerging economic order demanded.

The resulting tension between the values of the success ethic and those of Mrs. Hale's crusade did little to further domestic solidarity. But, in the period between 1825 and 1875, it did achieve a precarious balance that was important. The home and the market place became the foci of opposite sets of values, one stultifyingly static and the other recklessly dynamic. Each was the more extreme for the presence of the other, while each acted as a brake on the other. The result was a tense amalgam of advance-with-safety, progress-with-restraint, exploit-with-control. It is the pattern of checks and balances that one finds in Howells's *The Rise of Silas Lapham*, in which the male principle of material advancement is restrained by the female principle of moral advancement.

The hold of this polarity between home and market place upon the American imagination is considerable, even today. But just as the last quarter of the nineteenth century brought public criticism of the market as a threat to the individual, so the same period saw a disenchantment with the home on the same score. Huck Finn's flight from social control at both the beginning and the end of the novel is an escape from the domestic context. "Aunt Sally she's going to adopt me and sivilize me, and I can't stand it"—this is the complaint lodged against an institution and a set of values that it seeks to convey.

Yet, even these attitudes are not new. The same narrator of *Reveries of a Bachelor* who depicted the home as a happy retreat decided, finally, to remain a bachelor, because of the freedom he enjoyed in that state. Describing his house, he writes:

> I take a vast deal of comfort in treating it just as I choose. I manage to break some article of furniture, almost everytime I pay it a visit; and if I cannot open the window readily of a morning . . . I knock out a pane or two of glass with my boot.

He concludes that his behavior would "make a prim housewife fret herself into a raging fever." His attitudes, though much more self-conscious, are like those of Huck, who announced, "There warn't no home like a raft, after all. Other places do seem so cramped up and smothery, but a raft don't."

In comparing Huck's sentiments with those of the mid-century "bachelor," I am again suggesting that attitudes that we often consider modern do, in fact, run back well into the nineteenth century. Throughout the period, the American family was equipping new generations to fit the social patterns described by Potter, Meyers, and Lewis—an activity on which we have far too little information. At the same time, the family, under maternal guidance, was serving as a counterweight to the effects of those values and as a retreat from the confusion they often produced. Most of our misconceptions about the nineteenth-century family come from assuming that its second, compensatory role was its only role. But the family's primary role, as we began by noting, is the acculturation of children. And, until we know far more than we do now about the way in which the nineteenth-century American family functioned, vitally important pages will be missing from the historical record.

The "New Departure" in Quincy, 1873–81: The Nature of Nineteenth-Century Educational Reform

Michael B. Katz

Charles Francis Adams, Jr., and John Dudley Philbrick should have been friends and colleagues. Philbrick, with the exception of one year, was superintendent of schools in Boston from 1856 to 1878. He was an intelligent and successful educational administrator and spokesman on the city, state, and national levels. "Mr. Philbrick," proclaimed the editor of the *New-England Journal of Education* in 1878, "is a representative American educator. . . . Whatever of credit is attached" to the Boston school system "belongs, in a large measure, to Mr. Philbrick's study, care and administration." At one time or another, Philbrick was president of virtually every important state and national educational association. If the schoolmen of the United States had an official spokesman, it was John Dudley Philbrick. Adams, brother of Henry and Brooks, was a lay educational reformer. As a member of the Quincy school committee, he helped to precipitate and sustain a revolution in the town's schools between 1875 and 1880. Adams broadcast the successes of the colorful and charismatic new superintendent, Francis W. Parker, and visitors by the thousand trooped in to view the "new departure" in the Quincy schools. Parker's methods, moreover, were

Reprinted by permission from *The New England Quarterly,* Volume 40, Number 1 (March, 1967), pp. 3–20.

those that Massachusetts educational reformers had been trying to introduce for a long time. They were methods urged by Philbrick's mentors, like Horace Mann; they were the epitome of enlightened pedagogy. Philbrick, one would expect, should have been delighted with the schools of Quincy. Moreover, Adams and Philbrick both were ardent advocates of enlightened supervision of the schools, champions of the importance of that still rather new institution, the professional superintendency.

Surely, Adams and Philbrick *should* have been fellow reformers, a potent lay and professional team leading Massachusetts education to new glories. But, in 1881, Philbrick published a scathing *ad hominem* attack on a paper Adams had delivered to the National Education Association. Philbrick's attack suggests that there was more to the Quincy system, as it was often called, than the protoprogressivism usually noted by educational historians; his bitterness prods us to look closely to discover the sources of tension that made antagonists out of two men who agreed upon so many issues. A location of these sources will enable us to understand much better the dynamic of late nineteenth-century educational reform.

I

The granite quarries helped to change Quincy from the rural nursery of Presidents to a bustling, economically diversified town. After 1830, mining operations in the town began to acquire the features of large-scale industry, and, especially after the mid-1840's, an influx of Irish immigrants to labor in the mines swelled the population and altered irrevocably the town's ethnic homogeneity. From a town of a little over two thousand people in 1830, Quincy grew to an urbanized center with a population [of] over nine thousand in 1870. The mid-1840's brought more than the immigrants; for, in 1845, the Old Colony Railroad began operations between Quincy and nearby Boston. In the twenty-five years between 1845 and 1870, Quincy became, in the words of Charles Francis Adams, Jr., a "sleeping compartment" for Boston business executives.

Economic and ethnic changes ruptured the traditional social fabric of the town. New animosities and cleavages arose as politics became increasingly partisan; drunkenness became a problem; in short, Quincy experienced the growing pains associated with rapid and unplanned urbanization. The process of urban growth put new burdens on the schools. One very real problem was finding space for the children of the new inhabitants, and as the school population grew, so did the school budget. Reflecting on its problems, the school committee accurately analyzed the cycle of change in Massachusetts schools. From, very roughly, the 1840's to the 1850's a wave of reform had hit the schools; but, during the 1860's and early 1870's, reform had slowed or stopped. To the committee, the reform spirit had waned because the limits of reform under the popular style of educational practice had been reached. "This immobility," they wrote, "seems to show that a point has been reached which is near the natural term of such force as our present system of schooling is calculated to exert." For a decade, from 1863 to 1873, wrote Adams, "there had been no perceptible improvement" in the schools, but "during those years the annual cost to the town of educating each child in the public schools had increased from six to fifteen dollars." Here, then, was the basic problem for the Quincy school committee. How, amid an expanding population and increasing social complexity, could the operation of the schools be both economized and improved?

Precisely what was wrong with the "present system of schooling?" The committee decided to see for themselves. Usually, the annual examinations of Massachusetts schools consisted of a teacher putting some well-rehearsed questions to the class as the school committee watched benignly. But, in 1873, the Quincy school committee itself took charge of the examinations, each member choosing a different subject. The results were shocking. In his diary, Charles Francis Adams, Jr., commented that he had spent the day "slaughtering" classes in grammar, and, in the committee's reports, he observed, "[A]s now taught in our schools, English grammar is a singularly unprofitable branch of instruction." In retrospect, he was even more blunt. When he looked back at the condition of the schools at the start of his tenure on the committee in 1872, Adams asserted: "The examinations assumed a wholly new character. . . . The result was deplorable. The schools went to pieces. . . . In other words, it appeared, as the result of eight years' school-teaching, that the children, as a whole, could neither write with facility nor read fluently." Criticism of the schools appeared, too, in the press. One anonymous letterwriter noted the prevalence of private schools in Quincy and wondered why the people of the town supported them. His answer was the deficiency of the public schools and their teachers. "There is much fault found privately, and now some publicly, but the same teachers, who have taught eight and ten or more years, are still employed. Every class sent out of their schools . . . are found deficient in the fundamental principles."

Besides increased expense and poor results, the problem of attendance troubled the school committee. The high school had too few pupils; too many children were truant. Indeed, in many of the schools, reported the committee, "the attendance is irregular, and often intermittent, and ceases before a fair result can be expected." Such complaints were neither new nor limited to Quincy. For decades, they had permeated almost every report of a Massachusetts school committee. The Quincy committee, however, thought they saw two ways of keeping children in school. "The first of these is the employment of a thoroughly competent and energetic superintendent of schools, at a salary which will permit us to insist that his whole time and thought shall be devoted to no other end than their improvement; the second is the establishment of a truant school."

The "intermittent and relaxed attention of gentlemen engaged in other engrossing pursuits," argued the committee, "can never secure the exact and smooth perfection in every quarter which a really able man who is singly devoted to that duty can ensure." Convinced of the necessity of a full-time superintendent, the committee took its case before the town meeting, where it was opposed by those who argued that this innovation would add another chunk to the already burdensome school taxes. Committee members countered by asserting that the salary of the superintendent would be more than offset by savings that would result from efficient management. The committee won its case in 1875, when the town voted to appoint a superintendent for a trial period of one year.

Actually, the changes in school administration recommended by the committee were one phase of an attempt, spearheaded by Charles Francis Adams, Jr., and his brother John Quincy Adams, to alter the conduct of town business. Two aspects of town affairs alarmed them. For one thing, the Irish were wresting control of town business from the Yankees; patronage, ethnic divisions, and partisan motives were replacing the influence of learning and the Adams family name in the affairs of Quincy. Second, inefficient management was increasing taxes and plunging the town deeper and deeper into debt. To counter this situation, the Adams brothers managed to get themselves elected to a number of town offices. Then, they pushed through the town meeting a method changing that meeting's business. Previously, the articles in the town warrant were read, debated, and voted on, all at the same meeting. When Quincy had been small and homogeneous, this system had worked well. But now the town meeting had swelled in size and, so Charles Francis Adams, Jr., thought, declined in intelligence. Sometimes, articles were not given sufficient attention; amid the noise of the meeting, debate was impossible; it was difficult to pass a coordinated and thoughtful program for the town. In 1874, the Adamses won on a motion to divide the town meeting into two parts. At the first, officers were elected and the articles on the warrant assigned to committees. These committees reported their recommendations to the town at a second meeting, when the vote was taken. The Adams brothers and their associates made certain of their appointment to the most important committees and either wrote or directed the most important reports. The new system represented a way of removing, by one step, town decisions from the immediate province of the people as a whole. Through the committee system a coordinated policy could be formulated and, usually, pushed through the town meeting with minimum difficulty. Hiring a superintendent was an extension of this policy, for it represented removing educational administration from popularly elected officials and giving increased control to an appointed expert. The school committee's desire for a superintendent was one aspect of an attempt to reestablish intelligent control of town affairs by counteracting the weaknesses of urban democracy.

John Quincy Adams and James H. Slade, another member of the school committee and a prominent lawyer and insurance agent, were appointed to hunt for the superintendent of schools that the town had voted to hire. Slade, who took on the burden of the search with no idea how to proceed, advertised the position (a highly unorthodox procedure) in three Boston newspapers. Candidates, the advertisement said, were to apply at his

Boston office. Slade, a yachtsman, customarily sailed from Quincy to Boston; however, on the appointed morning a lack of wind delayed his trip, and, "Upon his arrival all available space was filled with applicants. . . . It was the greatest medley of men out of a job that one could care to see." "The distinguishing characteristic" of most of the applicants was "their peculiar unfitness for the position. Ministers without pulpits, lawyers without briefs, schoolmasters gone to seed, and pretty much every species of educated men out of employment, seemed to think themselves specially ordained to assume the management of the Quincy Schools."

Slade quickly eliminated all but one of the candidates, who was told to return in a few days. On the morning of that day, however, "a man strolled in, wearing the worst hat he had ever seen, and as he was ushered in he remarked that he would like to be considered a candidate for the superintendency in Quincy." Slade was about to tell him that the position had been filled, "but catching the earnest eye of the stranger he hesitated and asked why he thought himself eligible." For two hours, the young man of thirty-eight enlightened Slade "upon the great essentials in the spirit of educational reform." At the end, Slade was a "disciple." Next, Slade took the man to John Quincy Adams, "and at once" he "began educational evangelistic work upon him. Pedagogical zeal was at white heat, and Slade and Adams sat under the spell for a long time—three hours, more or less." Adams's conversion was soon followed by that of the rest of the committee. Thus did Colonel Francis W. Parker come to Quincy.

Both before and after the Civil War, Parker had had experience in education in his native New Hampshire and in Ohio. After receiving a $5,000 legacy in the late 1860's, he had traveled to Germany to study the latest advances in pedagogy. When he wandered into Slade's office, Parker had not long returned and was looking for a chance to put into action the ideas he had acquired abroad. Indeed, Parker was almost as fortunate to find Quincy as the town was to obtain his services. As Adams aptly pointed out, Parker "found a committee strong in the confidence of the town and holding office with a degree of permanence most unusual, the members of which were in a singularly disgusted and dissatisfied frame of mind." Second, the committee members "were not, as under similar circumstances is too frequently the case, jealous of their little authority." They listened to Parker's plans, and, "once those plans were approved, he had a free field in which to carry them out, with the understanding that by the results, and the results alone, would he be judged." With this remarkable degree of freedom, Parker commenced his duties as superintendent of schools in Quincy on April 20, 1875, and energetically began the pursuit of the twin goals that the school committee had set for educational reform.

II

One goal was improvement in the quality of teaching. The other was to check the increase in expenses. In 1874, the school committee noted: "However cheerfully borne, the burden of taxation for school purposes is not light. There is a necessity for economy in the expenditure of our teaching force." The "burden of taxation" was a theme repeated time and again during the depression of the 1870's. In fact, it was during the decade's first year of national financial crisis, 1873, that the cry for educational reform was raised in Quincy. Financial and economic fluctuation spurred the committee to seek economies; the first goal was to obtain 100 cents worth of value for every dollar spent on education.

However, economy and improvement were not considered antagonistic. A fact of critical importance in nineteenth-century educational reform was the assumption that economy and improvement went hand in hand. "Efficiency," explained a writer in *Education*, meant "the wise selection of an agency with reference to the best possible results attainable under the most favorable circumstances." In the management of city school systems, declared the writer, "*Efficiency* and *economy* must both be kept in constant view, each by itself and each in relation to the other." The assumption that efficiency or improvement and economy should occur simultaneously underlay two important innovations of the reform movement earlier in the century: the feminization of the teaching force and the grading of schools. The second wave of reformers, represented here by the Quincy school committee in 1873–80, championed the extension of these innovations and argued that economy and improvement should complement each other. Charles Francis Adams, Jr., insisted [that] the "object of . . . changes and experiments" was "to secure . . . a thoroughly good common-school education at a not unreasonable cost. The two points of excellence and economy were kept in view, and neither was to be subordinated to the other."

The committee's arguments for the consolidation and more efficient grading of schools revealed its aim of simultaneous economy and improvement. It contended that, "to have first-rate common schools, you must collect your pupils in a few centers, and then classify them as thoroughly as possible." The committee found "that success follows in a direct ratio any improvement in grading." As schools become larger, moreover, "the best results will be obtained at the least expense," because one man could be placed in charge of an entire graded school of five hundred students. Under his direction could be placed a number of female assistants. Females "are not only adapted, but carefully trained, to fill such positions, as well [as] or better than men, excepting the master's place, which sometimes requires a man's force; and the competition is so great, that their services command less than one-half the wages of male teachers." Thus, through consolidating schools, the population explosion in the town could be met without hiring additional, expensive male teachers. The beauty of the plan was that the quality would improve while the cost went down.

The same assumption underlay the arguments for a superintendent. The committee had hired a superintendent because "It was thought that this measure would impart an increased efficiency and economy to the management. . . . The intellectual culture, not less than the financial interest of the people, in short, demanded this reform." Thus, although it would be incorrect to say that educational reform in Quincy sprang solely from a desire for improved schools, it would also be inaccurate to say that it arose strictly from parsimony. The problem of mounting expense was very real, and financial caution was justified. More than that, reformers believed quite firmly that expenses could be checked and the schools improved. The inefficiency that raised expenses also produced poor education. Reformers believed they could have their cake and eat it.

This account of educational reform in Quincy would be incomplete without some notice of the ways in which the committee tried to cut costs. For some time the town had had a graded system of schools, which included primary and grammar schools and a high school. The committee tightened up this system of grading: Where possible, they consolidated schools, finding it cheaper to transport a few pupils who lived at a distance than to maintain a separate school; they put grammar school masters in charge of supervising all the primary schools in their vicinity and made sure that only the high school and six grammar schools had male teachers; the superintendent watched carefully over the outflow of money for purchases and repairs to avoid duplication and waste. For the first time, the schools were subjected to the same tight accounting procedure as a large business. All these steps, introduced in the first few years, failed to provide enough economy when rough financial conditions returned in 1877 and 1878. Then, the committee took its most drastic (and, as we shall see later, perhaps fatal) step. Taxpayers had been urging the committee to cut the salaries of teachers, an expedient followed in many other towns. This, in itself, the committee refused to do, fearing most teachers would leave. However, the committee did vote a sizable reduction in the salaries of new teachers. Since the turnover of teachers in any circumstances was fairly rapid, the committee pointed out, this action would yield a gradual reduction in the instructional budget. Likewise, in spite of its satisfaction with Parker's work, the committee refused to raise his salary.

The committee justified its economy moves with pleas of poverty. Quincy, it lamented, could not afford to pay salaries and have a per pupil expenditure rivaling those in nearby, wealthy towns, such as Milton, Brookline, and Newton. Actually, the committee was not crying wolf; the per capita valuation of Quincy was considerably lower than that of the towns that the committee singled out as more fortunate. It was even lower than the average both for Norfolk County (in which Quincy was located) and for the state as a whole. The need for economy, even without financial crisis, was very real, and the drive to lower expenses was, in fact, successful. Not only did the committee manage to decrease per pupil spending, it also kept the total expense for schools very stable, in spite of continued population growth, and at the same time it presided over an educational revolution.

III

As the school committee trimmed the budget, Francis Parker introduced pedagogical innovations that transformed the educational process within the Quincy schools. Parker observed that his methods contained little that was new or original. "The principles of instruction that I am trying to make the foundation of all the teaching in Quincy were long since discovered and established," he wrote. "There has been no famous teacher for the last two hundred years who does not owe his fame to the application of them." He asserted that his methods were not experiments: "They have been tested for thirty years in Germany, and for several years in parts of our own country."

What, then, was Parker's system? He summed it up in a sentence: "The essence . . . is the *teaching of things*, and not *words* alone." No well-read Massachusetts schoolman would have raised his eyebrows at this statement. Horace Mann and other educators had said the same thing. The stress on "things," object teaching, was an idea that had been around the state for a long time. So had Parker's more specific innovations. One of the most notable was the teaching of reading through the whole-word method instead of a strictly phonic approach. But Horace Mann had vigorously argued for this practice thirty years earlier. Parker repeatedly stressed that educational methods should proceed from the interests of the child; he urged teachers to make the child's natural curiosity and eagerness the foundation of their practice. Because of his emphasis, Parker has usually been considered a forerunner of "progressive education." But, again, thirty years earlier, Massachusetts schoolmen had urged exactly the same point. Here, too, then, Parker was right. He was proposing nothing new. Yet, read Parker and you realize that a new generation of educational reform has begun. Still, the era of Dewey had not yet arrived, for Parker offered no sophisticated theoretical rationale for his work, and his psychology is that of the earlier nineteenth century. What, then, is the difference between Parker and earlier reformers? What is Parker's place in educational thought and practice?

First of all, Parker was far more explicitly utilitarian than earlier reformers. Already, in the 1840's and 1850's, some schoolmen were arguing that education should bear a direct, practical relation to life, but their timid arguments retained prevailing goals. Education, almost all agreed, had to develop mental discipline. Moreover, schooling had to help the formation of character. The central process in character building was a kind of sublimation, the substitution of "higher" for "lower" pleasures. As one commentator observed:

> Those whose minds and whose hearts have been properly trained and disciplined by education, have control over their passions. Having cultivated a taste for simple and innocent pleasures, rather than a love for vicious excitement, their desires are awakened by objects higher than any gratification merely animal.

No subject could be justified in terms of practicality alone. All had to meet, finally, the criteria of mental discipline and character formation. One writer, for instance, argued for the inclusion of drawing in the curriculum and described its financial value "to almost every class in the community." But he could not leave the argument at that point, without adding:

> . . . independently of its utility as contributing to success in business, its refining and elevating effect is by no means unimportant. He who has learned to depict the beauties of nature and art, more highly appreciates and more keenly relishes those beauties; and hence has within himself an additional source of innocent enjoyment, and a new motive to moral excellence.

Unlike earlier reformers, Parker was willing to express educational aims in purely utilitarian terms, without obeisance to other ideals. He wrote, "We have steadfastly endeavored to teach the children that which will do them the most good—to dispense with the useless and put in its place the most useful." By "useful" Parker meant that which would assist an ordinary person to carry out well his everyday duties and tasks. Thus, under Parker, the teaching of the English language stressed letter writing and clear, oral expression instead of isolated, carefully memorized rules of grammar. In arithmetic, children considered problems similar to those they would encounter outside the classroom; in geography, they worked with models and learned about the terrain around them instead of memorizing definitions and routes of navigation.

Parker differed from earlier reformers in a second important way. One of the key words in contemporary social thought was "restraint." Behind reformers' stress on the substitution of "higher" for "lower" pleasures was a fear of the passionate and sensual. They insisted repeatedly that schools should teach restraint. Restraint it was that separated children from adults and formed the basis of civilized life. Over and over again, reformers denounced any passion not intellectual. The emphasis on restraint and the denial of passion are totally absent from Parker's writing. To him, the most valuable qualities of childhood were its spontaneity, its buoyancy, its eager curiosity. Indeed, one suspects that Parker was the first prominent American educational reformer who really liked children. Certainly, in mid-nineteenth-century educational thought there is no love for children, except as they promise to become refined, passionless men. More than anything else, Parker wanted "sunshine in the schoolroom." He urged the importance of play in the primary school, and he introduced features of the kindergarten into the first years of school life in Quincy. Describing his method, Parker wrote, "The little folks play, sing, read, count objects, write, draw and are happy." Thirty years earlier, happiness was neither a consideration nor a goal in education.

What Parker wanted to remove from the schoolroom was "repression." Remove "repression," make school a happy, enjoyable place, and the need for punishment, he claimed, will disappear. The trouble with most education was that "The usual treatment of young children in school is unnatural and almost barbarous. Instead of turning the full, freely flowing current of their active, buoyant lives upon the new work and into the new world found in the schoolroom, all this is repressed, and an unnatural, artificial routine begun." Previous reformers had been caught in a bind. They had argued that education should proceed from the interests of the child, but they had also contended that the child's lack of restraint had to be corrected. Reformers' fear of the spontaneous and physical had cast a pall over their efforts to humanize the schoolroom. Because of their fear of the passionate, they were afraid to cut loose and create schooling in harmony with the nature of childhood. Parker was one of the first to emancipate the older theory. Under his direction, the schools of Quincy underwent a revolution, because he seriously followed the older theory. Without the fear of the passionate lurking in every corner, the schools of Quincy became places where a child could be happy. Leila Partridge, an experienced teacher who came to observe the Quincy schools, recorded her impression that "The old order seemed literally to have passed away, and a new atmosphere of enthusiastic but normal activity filled these schools; a new attraction held these happy pupils."

Without doubt, Parker's personality contributed much to his success. Again and again, individuals testified that the zeal that had captivated James Slade and John Quincy Adams affected most people with whom Parker talked. The school committee wrote of his "pervasive magnetism as a man." The town newspaper described his success in captivating an audience as an after-dinner speaker; *The New-England Journal of Education* cited praise of his boyish qualities: "Col. Parker is one of those happy men to whom God has given the grace of inclosing a splendid, big boy and a wise, good man in one skin. . . . There is no end to the good a man so natural, catholic, and truly child-like in spirit can do in our country." A. D. Mayo, an associate editor of the *Journal*, exuberantly noted the same qualities. He lyrically described Parker as "[a] born genius in elementary schoolkeeping, an eternal boy in temperament and sympathy with childhood, combining the rare qualities of reverence, humility, and wonderful openness of soul, in the presence of children." In front of a classroom, continued Mayo, Parker was constantly " 'stirring in' a score of things of which he is only half-conscious; balancing, modifying, watching the flitting moods of children; following the lead of happy inspirations and flooding the schoolroom with irresistible enthusiasm, joy, and love." He was, in short, "the poet of the new elementary education." According to another writer in the same journal, Parker "set all his teachers on fire with his 'crazy-brain notions.' " Parker's inspirational ability was admired, too, by George Walton, agent of the Massachusetts Board of Education: "A remarkable power was possessed by the superintendent for aiding the ambitious, for encouraging the worthy timid, for stimulating and rousing the sluggish." Another agent of the Board of Education commented that Parker's zeal and enthusiasm were the most important factors in the transformation of the Quincy schools. The picture that emerges of Parker is that of a large, ebullient, and charismatic man, a natural leader capable of diffusing through a school system his own love of life and zeal for reform.

Parker, however, did not rely on chance for spreading his infectious desire for educational change. From the very beginning, he met weekly with his teachers and visited their schoolrooms, often taking the class himself. In his reports, he was always careful to praise the teachers under his supervision. He attributed faults in the Quincy schools to an outmoded system of education, not to the failings of the instructors. Quite obviously, he was working hard to bolster the teachers' morale. Perhaps his most important single innovation was his training class. Parker wanted instructors who loved children and were "cultivated, refined, trained artists in teaching." To get these, he immediately started a class for female graduates of Quincy High School who wanted to become teachers. Here, Parker combined observation, practice teaching, and instruction with his own charm; and, as vacancies occurred, he filled them, as often as possible, with the teachers he had trained himself.

Both the school committee and Parker were dissatisfied with the high school. The attendance was low; the curriculum was badly cluttered; and the Latin and Greek requirement seemed irrelevant to most of the students who did not intend to go to college. For those preparing for college, an academy was opened in 1872, with money left by the late President John Adams. The head of the academy, hired on the recommendation of Harvard's President Charles Eliot, was extremely able, and the school offered an excellent, classical college preparatory education. Out of the first graduating class, fourteen entered Harvard and one another college. Moreover, the academy was not beyond the means of poor Quincy boys. At first, there was no tuition for Quincy residents; later, the tuition of local poor boys was entirely paid out of the interest on the endowment. Thus, it seemed pointless for the high school to offer a classical education. Instead, Parker's aim was to make the school similar to the "Real Schools" he had admired in Germany; to do this, the curriculum was radically changed and the number of subjects reduced; students now had a choice between Latin and French; and emphasis was placed on bookkeeping and surveying. In the first year, the course even included instruction in "structure and drainage." However, not everyone in Quincy accepted Parker and his innovations as enthusiastically as the School Committee.

IV

Parker had his critics within the town. One school committee member complained that he was a "libertine," but Parker apparently convinced the Adams brothers of his innocence. A satirical attack on Parker and his methods noted, "It would do your . . . heart good to see what fatherly care and affectionate regard he has for the female teachers." To prove such allegations is impossible, but it is hardly surprising that a dashing young widower should excite gossip. More serious was an anonymous accusation charging Parker with corrupt financial practices in awarding contracts. However, after John Quincy Adams's virtually unanswerable refutation, similar charges did not appear again. Once educational reform proved to be economical, local criticism was, in fact, sporadic. Most citizens probably took pride in the fame that had come to their town.

Charles Francis Adams, Jr., and James H. Slade actively promoted the reputation of educational reform in Quincy. Slade lectured on the Quincy schools as far afield as California. Adams also lectured, and, in 1878, he published a pamphlet entitled *The New Departure in the Common Schools of Quincy*. Widely circulated, the pamphlet helped to attract visitors to see for themselves, and their reports spread the fame of the "new departure." In one year, Parker reported that 6,396 observers had visited the schools of Quincy! The secret of the attraction undoubtedly extended beyond its reputation for enlightened pedagogy. Throughout the 1870's, per pupil spending was actually falling across the entire country as communities tightened their belts amid financial hardships. When harried school committees studied the "new departure," they could learn how a town had not only retrenched on spending but had, at the same time, improved its schools. They could go to Quincy to see the realization of the nineteenth-century assumption that economy and improvement went hand in hand.

Besides the stream of enthusiastic visitors, the school committee and Parker discovered other reasons for proclaiming the success of the "new departure." "The most evident result of the new work was a decided change in the spirit of the schools, in the pupils, and in the teachers," reported one observer. The pupils "immediately manifested an increased interest in their school-work; they were impelled by motives within themselves; they worked from the gratification felt in the attainments they were making." As for the teacher, he "ceased to be a task-master, and became a co-worker with the children; he was at once transformed from a mechanic or machine to an artist, and his work, before drudgery, became a fine art." The change in atmosphere was a prerequisite to one of the main goals of reform. Parker had argued that the repressive nature of the schools caused most attendance problems. Improve the schools, make the children happy, he urged, and such problems will disappear. In the early 1870's, the percentage of enrolled children who daily attended the Quincy schools was not impressively high, and irregular attendance and truancy worried the school committee. Two years after Parker began his reform, the attendance had increased markedly. In 1877–78, for instance, an average of 97 per cent of enrolled children daily attended the Quincy schools. Early in the 1870's, the town had passed bylaws to cope with truancy and had appointed truant officers. Sometime after Parker's reforms began, the truant officers were no longer necessary.

In Quincy, as in neighboring towns, only a fraction of eligible children enrolled in high school. During the year following the alteration of the curriculum, however, the enrollment of Quincy High School doubled; and, in succeeding years, it retained its new, higher level while the high school enrollment in neighboring towns failed to increase. With much justification, Parker felt that the improvements in attendance and high school enrollment had vindicated his thesis, and, in 1878, he reported to the town that the struggle for good attendance had ended. When one considers that for roughly forty years almost every school report in the state lamented the low irregular level of attendance, it becomes clear that Parker's assertion heralded an educational revolution. Here, most graphically, reform had been a success.

The regular attendance was one measure of success, but what had happened to the quality of education? Three years after Parker had been at work in Quincy schools, George Walton, an agent of the Massachusetts Board of Education, surveyed the educational achievement in all the schools of Norfolk County. In each town, Walton tried to study random samples of children who had received four and eight years of schooling. They were tested in reading, arithmetic, and composition (including spelling and punctuation). By any reasonable modern standards, the survey was very crude, and its results must be looked at with skepticism. However, even allowing for a generous amount of error, one result is undeniable. "An examination of the schools of Quincy in connection with the other schools of Norfolk county, . . . after the improvements had been some time inaugurated," wrote Walton, "showed results superior to those obtained in any of the other towns of that county." On every measure except arithmetic, the children of Quincy far outstripped the children of all other neighboring towns. More than that, the children who had been in school roughly four years, that is, those who had been in schools under Parker's supervision for three-fourths of their school life, outdistanced children in rival communities by considerably more than did the children who had been in school for eight years, ones who had been affected by reform for less than half of their educational careers. Quincy children's lack of superiority in arithmetic is explained by the fact that this was the last subject whose teaching Parker reformed. Indeed, he did not begin his reform of arithmetic teaching until the year the survey began. "That the tests favored the Quincy work is no doubt true," commented Walton; "that was not the discredit of the examinations, however, but to the credit of the methods employed in Quincy . . . they may be considered as indicating that the new lines of work adopted in that town were and are producing superior results." Thus, on the dimension of achievement as well as attendance, the "new departure" deserved its fame.

Improvement by itself, however, was not the critical test. Adams asked, "At what money cost was it bought? If it involved a heavy addition to taxes, no matter how great the improvement, it was none the less a failure." But, as we have noted, since school expenditure in Quincy was checked, and per pupil spending actually fell during the period of educational improvement, Adams felt that the "most important" of the committee's propositions had been demonstrated. "That a good common-school education could be had at some cost, no one ever doubted; they [the committee members] claim that they have shown it could be had at a reasonable and average cost." The "average" was important; for the school committee had kept its expenses at a level just below the average for the state as a whole. They were confident that they had shown how economy and improvement could be attained together.

For a few golden years, it seemed as though the committee had really proved its point. But soon its two goals split apart. Quincy continually paid lower salaries to teachers than did a number of nearby communities, and the school committee justified this with continual cries of poverty. Early the low salaries began to have a consequence that boded ill. Teachers trained under Parker were being lured from Quincy by higher salaries. This became especially noticeable after the committee voted to lower the salaries of new teachers, putting the town at an even greater disadvantage. A year after the cut was introduced, Parker criticized the action in his annual report. For reform really to take hold, he admonished his readers, stability was a necessity; too much economy could vitiate all his efforts. Parker, in fact, must have been aggrieved himself, because with one hand the committee praised his work, with the other it refused to raise his salary.

Very likely Parker felt that the parsimony of the town was beginning to frustrate his efforts, and less than twelve months after he had registered his complaint at the inability of the town to retain its teachers, he resigned to become a Supervisor of schools in Boston, at a salary nearly double the one he was receiving in Quincy. Parker did not leave alone. With him went thirteen teachers, including three of the town's six grammar school masters. In 1880, the town of Quincy lost its superintendent and one-quarter of its teaching force. Parker's immediate successor lasted but a short time and failed miserably, and the next superintendent reported severe difficulties because of the number of new teachers needed in the schools. The report of trouble in the schools was echoed by the committee itself. According to the town newspaper, Parker was taking revenge on the town: From his new post in Boston, armed with higher salaries, he was stealing Quincy's best teachers. The school committee had failed to see just how insecure the "new departure" was, how great was its reliance upon one exceptional man. In retrospect, it was probably the charisma of Parker that had exerted the centrifugal pressure on the teaching force; it was probably his enthusiasm and zeal, as much as his methods, that had raised the teachers' morale, transformed the atmosphere of the schools, and counterbalanced the economy measures. In the long run, the school committee proved that the twin goal of simultaneous economy and improvement provided reform with a foundation that was bound to crumble.

As the leading spokesman for organized educators, John Dudley Philbrick had cause for reservations about the "new departure" in the schools of Quincy. Philbrick was in a singularly angry and sensitive mood. A little over two years earlier, a reforming Boston school board had voted him out of office, and, at the next school board election, Charles Francis Adams's brother Brooks had been elected. Brooks took command of the reformist forces, tried to introduce changes modeled on Quincy, and destroyed a number of the innovations of which Philbrick was most proud. Philbrick, moreover, must have looked with less than enthusiasm on a school committee that boasted of lowering per pupil expenditure and that reduced teachers' salaries. He must also have been embarrassed that the most notable educational reform in Massachusetts for three decades had been given its original impetus not by professionals but by a lay committee. When the Quincy committee flaunted the inferiority of Massachusetts schools, it was implicitly attacking the career educators who for decades had been striving to improve their standing within the community, and it was doing this at a time when an angry howl of lay criticism was being heard throughout the country. It did the reputation of the group Philbrick represented no good when Charles Francis Adams, Jr., published his accusation that Massachusetts was wasting two of the four million dollars it annually spent on its schools.

Adams, however, provoked Philbrick even more directly. Philbrick had been a city superintendent for more than twenty years; he had been the first president of the national association of superintendents. What Adams said about the occupants of that position was hardly ingratiating:

> Accordingly, very much as Bentham defined a judge as "an advocate run to seed," the ordinary superintendent is apt to be a grammar school teacher in a similar condition. Where he is not this, he is usually some retired clergyman or local politician out of a job, who has no more idea of the processes of mental development or the science of training than the average schoolmaster has of the object of teaching English grammar. The blind are thus made to lead the blind, and naturally both plunge deeper into the mire.

In the speech to the NEA that immediately prompted Philbrick's wrath, Adams had charged:

> Most of you, indeed, cannot but have been part and parcel of one of those huge, mechanical, educational machines, or mills, as they might more properly be called. They are, I believe, peculiar to our own time and country, and are so organized as to combine as nearly as possible the principal characteristics of the cotton-mill and the railroad with those of the model state prison. The school committee is the board of directors, while the superintendent—the chief executive officer—sits in his central office with the time-table, which he calls a programme, before him, by which one hour twice a week is allotted to this study, and half an hour three times a week to that, and twenty hours a term to a third; and at such a time one class will be at this point and the other class at that, the whole moving with military precision to a given destination at a specified date. . . . From one point of view children are regarded as automatons; from another, as India-rubber bags; from a third, as so much raw material.

Philbrick was stung badly, and his reply was vague, poorly argued, and largely *ad hominem*. He tried to discredit Adams as unqualified to comment on schools; he attacked Adams's wealthy background, implying that the Quincy system was an aristocratic attempt to keep the masses down by teaching them only the three R's. Philbrick quoted Parker's assertion that there was little new in his pedagogical innovations and said that the same sort of education had long been customary in many other places; finally, he attacked the Walton survey as proving nothing. It was actually Philbrick's attack that proved nothing—nothing, that is, except that a new stage had been reached in educational development, in the relation between the community and the educator, between the lay reformer and the professional.

With motivation similar to Philbrick's, the strongest local teachers' organization, the association of Boston grammar school masters, had, in the 1840's, attacked Horace Mann. The masters had argued that the slurs Mann cast on the current state of Massachusetts education reflected unfairly on their own efforts. They had attacked his knowledge of schools and criticized his innovations. But Mann and his associates had marshalled political forces to silence the masters. In fact, Mann and his associates created a situation in which it would be professional suicide for a teacher to criticize the reformist line, and public attacks, at any rate, stopped. From the late 1840's onward, the organized teachers identified themselves with the cause of reform and echoed the ideology of the lay reformers, and, for a little over a decade, a wave of reform, built partly on cooperation between pedagogue and lay community leader, swept the state. As the charismatic phase of reform waned, its results were left partly in a more organized teaching force and in fledgling educational bureaucracies. Urbanization, population growth, and the consequently increasing size of city school systems combined with dwindling lay interest in education to nourish the growth of these fledgling bureaucracies into the rigid and powerful machines described by Adams.

Educators characteristically justified their increasing command of community resources by pointing to their own importance, their critical role in the salvation of mankind. Because they were eager to convince the community of their own worth, educators often stressed their own accomplishments and ignored their own faults; they became almost intolerant of basic criticism, incapable of generating reform. Adams, for one, deplored "the self-sufficiency of Eastern educationists, as a class—their satisfaction and thorough contentment, both with themselves and with the situation." Thus, if the crust of sterility was to be cracked, if reform was to start anew, the impulse had to come from outside the professional establishment. This is precisely what happened in Quincy. A lay committee took the lead and even found a superintendent who, through peculiarity of background, was not yet a member of the educational establishment, who had no vested interest in the *status quo*.

To convince people of the need for educational reform, men like Adams and other school committee members had to expose the deficiencies of current educational practice. As soon as Charles Francis Adams, Jr., decided to become an educational reformer, it was inevitable that he would antagonize John Dudley Philbrick, that he would create, as had Horace Mann, a gulf between the lay reformer and the professional educator. Although professional educational organization was still rudimentary in 1880, the proliferation of associations and journals made it far stronger than it had been in the mid-1840's. Thus, unlike Horace Mann and his associates, the new generation of reformers could not silence their professional critics. The same voice of hostility raised by Philbrick to Adams would be heard again and again—sometimes stridently, as in the 1890's, when educational journals attacked the muckraking articles of Joseph Mayer Rice; sometimes sneeringly, as in the 1960's, when professional journals dismissed Admiral Rickover. The hostility of Philbrick to Adams and the "new departure" revealed that a lasting tension between professional schoolman and lay reformer had permeated American public education.

3. From College to University

The traditional story of American higher education is one of decline and rebirth. It goes something like this:

Higher education began in a promising way as settlers made enormous exertions to erect nurseries of piety and learning in the wilderness. Although the colleges educated a relatively small proportion of the population, their educational standards were surprisingly high, and they trained a remarkably high percentage of the men who led early America into independence. As a consequence largely of evangelical religion, newly formed, competing denominations dotted the country with hundreds of rival institutions in the first half of the nineteenth century. Founded on the narrowest of sectarian bases, inadequately supported, dividing the meager resources available, these new institutions represented, in the words of the late Richard Hofstadter, a "great retrogression." Their narrow curriculum was taught by young men using the recitation method, a stultifying form of rote learning. Believing their duty to be to act *in loco parentis,* college tutors and presidents paid more attention to the morals of their students than to their minds. Whatever vital intellectual life there was in America went on outside of the colleges.

After the Civil War, all this began to change suddenly. New wealth, the influence of Germany, secularism, and the increasing prestige of science, together, produced something new in the history of the world: the American university, combining undergraduate colleges with centers of higher training in academic and professional pursuits. The lecture system, the seminar, and the Ph.D. invaded American education;

the university as we have come to know it took shape in the years between, roughly, 1870 and World War I.

This traditional interpretation is valid in some respects. The number of small colleges did expand astronomically between the Revolution and the Civil War, and the university did acquire what have come to be its typical structural features in the late nineteenth and early twentieth centuries. Nonetheless, serious problems of interpretation remain. The social function of the colonial college, for one thing, is not at all clear. Historians are not certain just who went, for how long, and why, or what effect attendance at college had upon the subsequent careers of students. Nor is it at all certain that conditions in the early nineteenth century were entirely unsatisfactory. It may be the reflex of ingrained academic snobbery to dismiss the small antebellum colleges simply on account of their size and lack of distinction. To the contrary, we must ask seriously what role they played within the hundreds of small towns and cities that harbored them. Should they be considered nurseries of sectarianism or aspects of local popular culture? What difference did it make to the life of a town to have a college within the town's boundaries? There is mounting evidence that the answers to these questions will put these colleges in a much more sympathetic light. Similarly, some recent research points to the presence of a small but active and serious scientific community composed of professors at nineteenth-century colleges.

These modifications in the traditional view tend to soften the distinction between the college and the university. Although the transition was undoubtedly less abrupt than we often think, nonetheless it was real, and its existence poses questions that still remain unanswered. Why did American higher education change in precisely the way, and at precisely the time, that it did? Changes in higher education were controversial. As in the case of public education earlier in the century, there were competing models for the future of higher learning, and we lack a fully satisfactory explanation for the success of the one with which we live today.

Part of the answer must rest with the university's clientele, for its aspirations and demands must have influenced strongly the shape that higher education assumed. Yet, we know far too little about student life and culture. In fact, we know little about their identity. Studies of the social composition of the student body and life histories of individual students are critical, however, if we are to interpret the social role of the university correctly or assess the impact of higher education on the life chances of students and on American society. That assessment must be made accurately, for it affects the interpretation given to the contemporary disenchantment with the university.

At least three extreme positions are possible with respect to current problems in higher education, and each one implies a different view of history. It may be argued that the problems of universities stem simply from unregulated growth and dispersion within a fundamentally sound and socially useful structure. Consequently, careful and systematic reform within the present structure can resolve whatever problems exist. Or it may be argued that the fault lies with students and the expectations they have acquired as a result of permissive methods of nurture; they are pampered and spoiled children venting their unresolved difficulties with authority onto the university. Still another perspective is that the problems are embedded in the structure of the university itself. They are, thus, not ephemeral but basic; it is not reform but a recasting of internal relations and social role that is required for any fundamental improvement in higher education.

The five selections in this section cover the sweep of American higher education from the colonial period to the present. The first selection, by the late Richard Hofstadter, outlines the features of colonial colleges that became fundamental characteristics of American higher education. In the next selection, David B. Potts takes on the theme of the "great retrogression" and argues effectively that early and mid-nineteenth-century colleges were more local than denominational in their sources of support and their impact; in fact, he argues that it was after the Civil War that they became increasingly sectarian. Laurence Veysey concentrates primarily on the period when the university began to dominate the college, pointing to both continuity and change in American education, competing conceptions of the university's future, and to a number of sources of change in the late nineteenth century. In the next selection, John P. Rousmanière considers one of the groups most affected by new forms of higher education: women. His essay is a brilliant exploration of the relations between changes in the nature of higher education for women, female role conflict, and the origins of a new institution, the social settlement. Finally, Samuel Bowles considers the relationship of the recent history of the university to its current problems, arguing that university crises represent the eruption of internal structural contradictions that no longer can be contained or ignored.

The Colonial Colleges
Richard Hofstadter

By the middle of the eighteenth century, there had emerged an American system of collegiate education different not only from the English models

From Richard Hofstadter, *Academic Freedom in the Age of the College*, New York: Columbia University Press, 1955, pp. 115–26, 144–51; by permission of the Publisher.

with which Americans were most familiar but from all others as well. In three features, the early American system was unique. First, while American collegiate education, like that of Europe, was·the ward of religion, its pattern of essentially private denominational sponsorship, with a modest admixture of state supervision, was new. Second, unlike the European universities, American colleges had no connection with professional and advanced faculties—that is to say, they were colleges but not, strictly speaking, universities. American colleges did not, like those of Oxford and Cambridge, multiply and cluster at great centers of learning; they were small and scattered, and, after the Revolutionary era, they were to become numerous as well, so that the educational effort of the American people was increasingly diffused. In the nineteenth century . . . this tendency got completely out of hand. The third unique characteristic was that the early American colleges developed a system of lay government—that is, a system in which the major decisions were made by boards of nonresident governors who were not teachers—that remains characteristic of American higher education to this day.

*　*　*

THE AMERICAN PATTERN: DENOMINATIONAL SPONSORSHIP

The first three colleges, Harvard (1636), William and Mary (1693), and Yale (1701), were founded by the established churches of their respective colonies. Then, after the settled churches had become too austere, too doctrinal, and too remote from the religious needs of the people, the religious scene was revitalized by the Great Awakening, inspired by the preaching of such men as Theodore J. Frelinghuysen, William Tennent and his sons, [and] Jonathan Edwards and by the five rousing evangelistic trips of the great English revivalist George Whitefield. This series of revivals led to splits in the Congregational, Presbyterian, and Baptist groups that had important consequences for education. Princeton (1746) was founded by New-Side Presbyterians, who hoped to show that they, too, for all their revivalist fervor, could continue the New England tradition of an educated ministry. Both Brown (1764) and Queen's College (1766; later Rutgers) were founded by revivalistic groups, the first among the Baptists of Rhode Island, the second among Frelinghuysen's followers in the Dutch Reformed Church. Dartmouth (1769), the last of the colonial establishments, grew out of an Indian missionary school organized with Whitefield's help by Eleazar Wheelock, a Congregational pastor who had caught the current "enthusiasm." The two most secular of the colonial schools, King's College (1754; later Columbia) and the College of Philadelphia (1755; later the University of Pennsylvania), were still not untouched by religious rivalries, since both were shared and fought over by Anglicans and Presbyterians.

While the early colleges developed under religious sponsorship and a large measure of religious control, it does not follow that their religious purposes wholly account for their character. The common statement that they were, in effect, theological seminaries is altogether untrue. . . . Harvard was never a mere religious seminary with the sole purpose of training ministers. The stated purposes of other early institutions, as expressed in their charters, also included references to liberal education and the service of the public. What is true is that the desire to educate a suitable, orthodox body of native clergymen could be plausibly asserted to be the most urgent and immediate reason for founding the majority of the colonial colleges, perhaps seven out of nine. But it is equally true and equally important that their curricula were not those of divinity schools but of liberal arts schools, and that, among those denominations that tried to maintain high standards for their clergy, additional postgraduate study in divinity was expected. It must also be remembered that, early in the eighteenth century, the clergymen graduates became a minority among all graduates. The proportion declined sharply throughout the eighteenth century, at the close of which about four-fifths of all graduates were going into other vocations. Not one of the colonial colleges required students to subscribe to a particular religious creed as a condition of admission. The founders of Brown, the most liberal college among them, not only ruled out sectarian differences as an object of classroom instruction but barred religious tests for members of the faculty.

The sectarian allegiance of a college was usually expressed by the religious adherence of its president. The charters of King's College, Brown, and Queen's College specified that their presidents must be, respectively, an Anglican, a Baptist, and a member of the Dutch Reformed Church. And, although their charters did not demand it, Yale and Harvard could hardly think of anyone but a Congregationalist; Princeton, [of] anyone but a Presbyterian.

The most noteworthy departure from the practice of the first three colleges to be made by those institutions that were founded around the middle of the century and afterward is the introduction of interdenominational representation on boards of control. While the last six colonial colleges were all identified, in varying degrees, with a single, dominant church, five had interdenominational representation. With the exception of Dartmouth, they did not enjoy, as had the earlier colleges, the privilege of being founded by an established church. The founders of the later colleges, in order to establish their institutions, had been forced to allay the hostility of other denominations by allotting them some place on governing boards, while their subsequent need to broaden the base of their financial support and enlarge their student bodies also contributed to softening their sectarian features. King's College, despite its Anglican affiliation, had among its charter members the pastors of four churches of other denominations in New York City. The College of Philadelphia, which grew out of a nonsectarian academy chartered in 1749, was reorganized and broadened in 1779 as the University of Pennsylvania (although it had already been infiltrated by the Presbyterians), an arrangement under which six of the twenty-four trustees were to be the senior members of each of the principal religious denominations of the city, including the Roman Catholic. The pretensions of the two most prominent denominations were recognized by making the first provost an Anglican divine and the first vice-provost a Presbyterian. At Brown, where the Baptists had a clear preponderance in both units of the dual governing board, the Congregationalists, Anglicans, and Quakers together held fourteen out of thirty-six seats among the trustees, while among the fellows only eight of twelve could be Baptists. The spirit of interdenominational concession was least in evidence at Queen's College, yet even Queen's included four state officials among its forty-one trustees, and still others of the twenty-eight laymen named to its original board were not members of the Dutch Reformed Church. Only a little less sectarian was Dartmouth, where three members of the first board were Anglican laymen and New Hampshire officials.

The tendency toward interdenominational representation, though a sign of growing tolerance, did not mean that the denominations had composed their differences and forgotten their hostilities. On the contrary, interdenominational representation came about precisely because sectarian bickering was so acute that hostile factions had to be quieted in some diplomatic way if the new institutions were to have a chance of success. The founding of King's College seemed for a time to be seriously jeopardized by animosities between Anglicans and Presbyterians, while differences between the same groups affected the early development of the College of Philadelphia. Brown was founded only after an angry tussle between Baptists and Congregationalists. Sectarian pride kept the governing board of Queen's College from accepting union with Princeton at a time when Queen's was staggering toward total collapse. As for Dartmouth, the mere suspicion that the Bishop of London might be made an ex-officio trustee caused Eleazar Wheelock to consider removing his projected college from New Hampshire to another province. As late as 1779, the suspicion inspired in the dissenting sects of Virginia by the Anglican background of William and Mary destroyed Jefferson's plans to revamp the institution, even though these plans involved a diminution of its denominational character.

In sum, the desire to dominate and the fear of being dominated had by no means died out in sectarian breasts, but the capacity to do mischief to each other had been greatly diminished, and the necessity of reckoning with outsiders brought about a greater flexibility in educational planning.

The later eighteenth-century colleges were opened at a time of expanding religious liberty. To be sure, this expansion was, for the most part, neither planned nor welcomed. The articulate Protestant leaders of colonial settlement had been—with few notable exceptions, like Roger Williams and William Penn—firmly opposed to toleration. But, while they rejected it as a principle, they yielded increasingly to it out of necessity or expediency. A large number of sects poured into, or emerged within, the colonies during the eighteenth century, and none was strong enough to attain dominance.

In the absence of a majority strong enough to exercise coercion, some mutual forbearance became a simple necessity. Indeed, the situation of the various sects provided an example for free political organization that was not lost upon American observers. "In a free government," wrote Madison in Number 51 of *The Federalist*,

> the security for civil rights must be the same as that for religious rights. It consists in the one case in the multiplicity of interests, and in the other of the multiplicity of sects. The degree of security in both cases will depend on the number of interests and sects.

Also working for tolerance were the example of English opinion and English law under Cromwell and after the Act of Toleration of 1689, as well as the influence of English governors who reflected the preference of the mother country (and of some of the Catholic and Quaker proprietors) for economic prosperity rather than sectarian bickering. The developments of the eighteenth century accentuated the trend toward tolerance, as the sects moved somewhat closer together in the face of common problems—the threat of an Anglican episcopate and the rise of rationalism and Deism. Even the development of revivalistic factions among the Presbyterians, Baptists, and, later, the Methodists contributed surprisingly to the atmosphere of religious latitude. The New-Side apostles, despite their intolerant impulses, realized that their type of emotional religion would only benefit by the destruction of the formal institutions and establishments that had been created by their predecessors and opponents; such destruction would clear the way for movements that exalted the force of spirit over external discipline and traditional arrangements. Finally, the growth of rationalism itself created a liberal-minded elite, the flower of which were such men as Franklin, Adams, Jefferson, and Madison, and which was fundamentally indifferent to doctrinal issues and impartially tolerant of all the sects.

THE AMERICAN PATTERN: LAY GOVERNMENT

Of great significance for later struggles over intellectual freedom was the American system of academic government, which had taken on its essential features by the middle of the eighteenth century. Nowhere outside the United States and Canada are modern universities governed by boards of laymen. The system of lay government has created special problems for free teaching and scholarship in America. The essence of lay government is that the trustees, not the faculties, *are,* in law, the college or university, and that, legally, they can hire and fire faculty members and make almost all the decisions governing the institution. This has hampered the development of organization, initiative, and self-confidence among American college professors, and it has contributed, along with many other forces in American life, to lowering their status in the community. Other professional groups have far greater power to determine the standards and conduct of their own professions.

To contrast, without qualification, the European system of academic self-government with the American system of lay government would, however, be misleading. While European universities, particularly those of the Continent, are formally self-governing, they are still not entirely free from the influence of church and state. American universities and colleges, particularly the best private institutions, have developed a system under which the balance of governmental power is actually distributed among trustees, administration, and faculty. Formally empowered with almost all the prerogatives of government, trustees in such institutions have, in fact, delegated most of them to the administrations or the faculties, retaining chiefly the prerogative of budgetary decisions and the right of intervention in broad policy. Faculties have a very large voice, often, in effect, the controlling voice, in matters of appointment, promotion, and curriculum. Legally still powerless, they are nonetheless potent agencies of academic government in the most reputable colleges and universities. How this measure of informal self-government has grown up within the framework of the plenary legal powers of the trustees is an important part of our story.

When all necessary qualifications have been made, however, the fact remains that lay government has been one of the most decisive factors in the problem of academic freedom in America, and its origin and development are central to our concern. The American system of lay government was not planned by the founders of the colonial colleges, who were themselves familiar chiefly with the altogether different system of the English universities. Rather, it grew out of the conditions of religious and social life in the New World.

In at least three important respects, the American situation was unique. The first was that, while the European universities had been nurtured for centuries on the medieval guild traditions of faculty self-government, the American colleges were not only Protestant institutions but had been founded in a totally Protestant milieu, sharply cut off from many medieval traditions. The medieval universities were ecclesiastical agencies, founded at a time when the church was still effactually guarding its institutions from the incursions of lay power. Both the church principle of ecclesiastical independence and the guild principle of corporate self-government provided the universities and society at large with dominant models of autonomy. This autonomy the Protestant Reformation had sharply circumscribed. . . . [T]he proud self-sufficiency, and, with it, much of the intellectual freedom, that had been characteristic of the medieval universities at their zenith went into decline. Moreover, the principle of the freedom of the church hierarchy from intervention by laymen was sharply challenged—not least by the Puritans, of whom it has been remarked that they gave the layman a larger part in the control of the local church than he had enjoyed since the Roman emperors became Christian. Now, it was not a very drastic step from admitting men who were not clerics into the government of churches to admitting those who were not teachers into the government of colleges. Just as guild self-government and church autonomy were models for the organization of the medieval universities, so nonconformist Protestant church government provided new and different models for the American colleges. In England itself, while the method of founding colleges at Oxford and Cambridge was not changed by the Reformation, educational foundations of lower than university grade had begun to be placed under the control of incorporated bodies of lay trustees in the sixteenth century.

American Protestants did not consider that they were destroying intellectual freedom by extending the policy of lay government from churches to colleges. Indeed, they considered it one of their contributions to civilization that they had broken up the priestly autonomy of advanced education and had brought it under the control of the community. Of course, the early founders of American colleges did not depart very far from the traditional assumption that institutions of higher learning should be run largely by clerics; but, if clerics were expected to share the government of churches, they might also be expected to share the government of colleges. Such early efforts as were made to increase the corporate autonomy of teaching bodies were not identified with any movements toward greater liberality in thought but, rather, with narrow clerical interests, conservatism, and orthodoxy. . . . Mather at Harvard in the seventeenth century and tutors Sever and Welsteed in the early eighteenth century sought to augment corporate autonomy for reasons that had little to do with freedom, while the clerics at William and Mary seem to have been interested only in their own salaries and privileges. Likewise, Thomas Clap at Yale, defending the independence of that institution against the intervention of the Connecticut legislature, was fighting for conservative theology and sectarian purity. Paradoxical as it may seem to those who read the situation with twentieth-century values in mind, the growing religious and intellectual liberalism of eighteenth-century America was identified in the colleges not with corporate autonomy but with lay government. Not until the nineteenth century, when lay government had been long established, was this situation reversed.

The second reason for lay government was that, while the European universities evolved out of long-established communities of scholarship and teaching, the first American colleges were created, in a sense, as artifacts by communities that had to strain very limited resources to support them. This meant that infant institutions in the American colonies had to be carefully nursed for many years before they developed into stable colleges capable of standing on their own feet. During this period of infancy, the lay boards of control exercised sweeping powers that they were later reluctant to give up, being, like other parents, unwilling to accept the fact of their own obsolescence. Moreover, the prominent role of private benefactions guaranteed that this obsolescence would never be complete; institutions dependent upon renewed surges of good will in the lay community were more sensitive to lay opinion than were those that relied upon stable clerical livings or regular parliamentary appropriations.

Finally, while in Europe a body of men belonging to what could be called a teaching profession existed before the emergence of the universities, the colleges in America were created first, and only afterward did a considerable body of professional teachers emerge. The idea of the self-governing university had been based upon the assumption that teachers were mature professionals; the first American teachers were preponderantly youthful amateurs. In a raw community like early colonial America, the opportunities for a man of learning outside the realm of teaching were too great to leave many first-rate men available for the ill-compensated, low-status positions that were the lot of those whose whole lives would be given to the instruction of boys. . . . [T]he first teaching staffs at Harvard were composed of future ministers, for whom teaching was only a temporary occupation, a preamble to a clerical career. In the later colleges, this was also the case, with the exception . . . of William and Mary. So long as the bulk of college teaching was in the hands of groups of youngsters for whom teaching was only a by-path to more desired careers, faculty self-government was bound to seem less acceptable, indeed less meaningful, than it did in European universities numbering among their masters many great and influential men of learning. For over a century and a half, American collegiate education relied chiefly on young tutors, having in all its faculties only a handful of professors of some maturity and length of tenure. Harvard had been established for more than eighty-five years, Yale for more than fifty, and Princeton for more than twenty before each had its first professor, and it was to be many years more before regular professors outnumbered transient tutors. The only secure and sustained professional office in American collegiate education was that of the college president himself. He alone among the working teachers of the early colleges had, in the community and before the governing boards, the full stature of an independent man of learning. To this situation can be traced the singular role and importance of the American college or university president.

Lay government created more problems than it solved, and to these problems the college president provided an answer—at least, the best answer that could be found. Lay boards of trustees were absentee proprietors, and, in the bustling America of colonial days, they usually had very little leisure to devote to their colleges. Small as they were, these colleges had promotional problems, staff problems, disciplinary problems, servant problems, curricular problems—and to none of these could the busy trustees consistently give enough attention. Thus, between the trustees, who had the legal capacity but not the time or energy to govern, and the teachers, who were considered too young and too transient to govern, there was created a power vacuum. This vacuum the presidents quickly began to fill.

The early college president played a multiple role. As a cleric and learned man, he taught. As a member of the governing board, he participated in major decisions. As a leading citizen of his community, he promoted his institution. As a faculty member, he led the teaching staff. As a preacher, he prayed and sermonized for the students. Since he was subject, in most cases, to dismissal by governing boards, he was the subordinate of the trustees, and yet, as the man most familiar with college affairs, he was also the leader of the governing board. In relation to his tiny teaching staff, he was a leader or a boss, depending upon his situation and temperament. Unlike the European rector, he was not elected by the teachers nor, in any formal way, accountable to them. Teachers came and went as a matter of course. The president remained until he died or resigned or, in rare cases, was ousted by his board. The tutors, being temporary servants, had little reason to resist or hamper his authority. The trustees, although they appointed and could replace him, could not displace him. In legal theory, they were the college, but, in the eyes of the community, and often in his own eyes, the president was the college. Upon his reputation and his promotional energies its place in the community chiefly depended. He became at once its dynamic center of authority, its symbol, and its spokesman. He occupied and, in a sense, created an office that has no equivalent in academic systems outside the United States. The prestige and pride that elsewhere were vested in the faculties came to center in him—and there, with some modification, they have remained to this day.

For a long time, in most colleges, the president was the only teacher who possessed enough status, power, and confidence to wage a battle with the trustees or repressive forces in the community on behalf of religious or intellectual freedom. Thus, from the time of Henry Dunster down to the Civil War period, the outstanding college controversies of this sort involved presidents more often than professors, and tutors hardly at all. In some of these cases it is hard to determine to what extent the controversy was a purely administrative affair and to what extent it involved intellectual issues. But the fact remains that in the transition of both freedom and power from lay trustees to faculty members, insofar as that transition has taken place, the president played an important and constructive part. In the early days of the colleges it was quite difficult for trustees to find a man endowed with all the qualities needed for vigorous college leadership. Those institutions that could not find a strong president or would not give him sufficient powers frequently languished. The man who had the necessary qualifications thus found himself in a good bargaining position, and if he was astute, he often saw to it that he came into his office with a strong hand. Strong presidents, to be sure, could make great difficulties, as the opponents of Mather and Clap could testify; but strong presidents, like Ezra Stiles and John Witherspoon, made strong colleges, and ultimately—though this was much later indeed—they made strong faculties. In the transit of powers of decision to the faculties, as in the struggle for freedom of thought, many of the outstanding college presidents contributed their full share.

SUPPORT AND CONTROL

The earliest colleges had been founded at a time when private resources were much too feeble to maintain them, and support by the state was a necessity. The close of the colonial period saw the ideal of the private college well established. The intimate relations between the first colonial colleges and the states have caused one student of the subject to declare that the first three colleges were, in effect, under state control, and to imply a vague analogy with the state universities of a later age. But, since all three institutions were founded under the aegis of established churches, this statement can easily be misleading. It is hardly more valid than the assertion that the colleges were controlled by the churches. It is perhaps less startling but more correct to say that the colleges were governed by the church-state complex. In Massachusetts, the magistrates usually consulted and often deferred to the ministers. Anne Hutchinson, for instance, was condemned and excommunicated by a church synod, but she was tried and banished by civil authorities. Similarly, the clergy took the initiative in the prosecution of the Quakers, but the legislation controlling them was enacted by the General Court and enforced by the magistrates. In similar fashion, the General Court often interfered in the affairs of Harvard—and not merely through the Overseers, on which board it was represented, but also directly through legislative action. It was the General Court, not the Overseers, that took action against President Dunster and received his resignation and that called upon Increase Mather either to reside in Cambridge or vacate the presidency. In Connecticut, the Assembly, though not represented on the governing board of Yale, showed its interest by ordering the trustees to finish a building at New Haven, intervening in the choice of a rector and the permanent location of the school, examining finances on many occasions, and looking into the religious condition of the college. Dependent as they were upon state aid, the two New England colleges were in no position to resist such interference even if they so chose. William and Mary, in a stronger position because of its larger fixed income, was subjected to less detailed intervention; but the personnel of the board of visitors there was closely interlocked with the membership of the Governor's Council and the House of Burgesses. The college's situation at Williamsburg, the capital of the province, was a token of its intimate relation with the state, as well as a great academic advantage.

In the last thirty years before the outbreak of the Revolution, both state aid and state interference diminished as the burden of support shifted from government to private individuals. The first three colleges had relied chiefly upon governmental support in the form of annual grants or assigned revenues from a particular source. But the later schools, largely because of sectarian hostilities and inhibitions, could not safely call upon the state governments and thus benefited from state aid only in a marginal and incidental way. King's College got some public help, the College of Philadelphia less, and Dartmouth only two very small grants, while Princeton, Brown, and Queen's College received nothing.

The founding and continuation of the later colleges were made possible by the development of a widespread interest in higher education among the well-to-do, an interest intense enough to bring contributions from thousands of individuals in the colonies, the British Isles, and even other parts of the Empire. Important bequests were still quite rare; most of the funds were raised through subscriptions, some through the riskier and less popular means of private lotteries. The pressing need for private funds gave prestige to trustees like Gilbert Tennent of New Jersey and Morgan Edwards of Brown and administrators like William Smith of the College of Philadelphia and John Witherspoon of New Jersey, all of whom were outstandingly successful as fund raisers. It also underlined, however, the importance of the churches, through which a great deal of the solicitation was carried on, especially in the British Isles. British contributors were often impatient of American sectarian disputes, and the necessity of raising funds from them added some leverage to the movement toward tolerance in the colleges. Colonial assemblies seem not to have been disposed to intervene officiously in the management of educational institutions that they were not supporting, and the later colonial colleges manifest a decided shift toward private control along with private support. Harvard and Yale, with their traditional involvements with the states, became disentangled more slowly, receiving their last grants in 1823 and 1831, respectively. They were legally relieved of their liability to substantial state intervention after 1819 by the implications of the Dartmouth College case.

Direct legislation was not, of course, the only measure of state interest in the colleges. With the exception of Yale, Brown, and the College of Philadelphia, the colonial colleges had ex-officio representatives of the state officialdom, including the governors, on their boards of control, a relationship which arose out of the necessity of securing either a state charter or a royal or proprietary charter with some governor's benevolent intervention. Where political matters, factional feuds, church differences, or the interests of the state or Crown were involved, trustees representing the political order were thus on hand to express themselves. On the Harvard Overseers and the governing board of Dartmouth, the state officials comprised about half the membership. At Philadelphia after 1779 and Yale after 1792, state officials were added, leaving only Brown, an inheritor of Rhode Island's church-state separatism, without such a relationship.

The respective places of laymen and clerics on boards of control also deserve notice. By the terms of the charters (and these arrangements tended to perpetuate themselves for long periods), four of the colonial colleges—Harvard, Princeton, Brown, and Dartmouth—had governing boards on which clerical and lay trustees were quite evenly balanced. Three—William and Mary, King's College, and Queen's College—were mixed but clearly dominated by the laymen, while one, the College of Philadelphia, consisted entirely of laymen. Yale's board, until its reconstitution in 1792, was the only one composed entirely of clergymen.

A mere enumeration of the number of clerical and nonclerical trustees, however, perhaps underestimates the religious character of the colleges. Ministers tended to be more assiduous in their attendance at meetings. The presidents who, as we have seen, provided so much of the dynamic leadership were clergymen. And laymen themselves were very commonly chosen with their denominational affiliations clearly in mind and often with reference to their position as pillars of their church communities. Perhaps most important of all, the college itself seems to have been thought of very largely in the light of its religious relationships, and the role of a college trustee had more of the pastoral character than it came to have in later times. Trustees, while governing the business affairs of the colleges, thought of themselves also as the moral and spiritual guardians of the students and, indeed, often of the faculties; and pious laymen, leaving their businesses to attend board meetings, seem to have shorn themselves, to a degree, of their usual roles to assume the moral and intellectual garb of pastors-for-the-moment, inquiring closely into the regularity and character of religious services at the college and examining the spiritual nature and moral discipline of the under-graduates.

Thus, even though the colleges were committed to the governance of lay-men, these laymen found in the role and demeanor of the clerics a subtly influential archetype for their own behavior; the religious inheritance of the colleges created a kind of priesthood of the trustees. This was a process that could also work in the opposite direction, for the responsibilities of fund raising and administration tended to make men of affairs and business managers out of the clerics who became college presidents. The manage-ment of colleges was indeed one of the many areas of life in which the un-specialized society of the eighteenth-century colonies created its versatile men.

One may find difficulties in disentangling the roles of church and state in college sponsorship, but one thing seems clear: Aristocratic control and aristocratic values were universal. Colonial America may have been a more democratic society and may have offered more opportunities for class mo-bility than the contemporary societies of Europe. But, as compared with the open and fluid society of the first half of the nineteenth century, or with the image of "frontier democracy" that is all too often freely pictured in gen-eral books on American history, the society of the American colonies was one dominated by an aristocracy of land and commerce, an aristocracy dif-ficult of access to rising members of the middle class and all but closed to those who started very poor. To be sure, opportunities to earn an independ-ent livelihood, to be free from poverty and gross insecurity, were exception-ally good for those who started in life with little but a willingness to work; but this was a far cry from opportunity to enter the ranks of the rich and powerful. A privileged class, strengthened by ties of intermarriage, existed in each province and, at length, spread across colonial boundaries; it seems to have grown stronger and become more sharply defined in the eighteenth century than in the seventeenth. "There was, in fact," writes a distinguished student of the colonial period, "in almost every colony a definite ruling class [that] dominated the local political machinery, filled all or nearly all the important local offices, . . . spoke on public matters in behalf of all . . . [and] used its power very largely for the benefit of its own members. . . ." Attached to this ruling class were the outstanding professional men of the colonies, and on its periphery were the most acceptable leaders of a class of solid citizens of the sort represented by Benjamin Franklin. It was to serve the traditional and aristocratic needs of this upper crust that the colonial colleges, with their conservative adherence to the classical curriculum, were designed; while the middle classes beneath them, whose base was small shopkeeping and special crafts, were generally satisfied to send their children to good private academies with curricula based less upon the classics and more upon a program of practical studies.

It was the aristocracy that was primarily concerned with the colonial colleges, the well-to-do class that gave the bulk of private support, and the ruling group that provided the trustees. When a governing board sat down to consider the affairs of the colonial college, there was usually assembled, at the same table, a group of men who were accustomed to seeing each other frequently at the counting houses, in each others' homes, and in the vestries of the churches, and whose family relationships could be represented only by a complicated network of crisscrossing lines. Even in Connecticut, which a man like Samuel Johnson considered hardly better than a mobocracy, and which was, in fact, less clearly aristocratic than many other colonies, the bonds of kinship were conspicuous, and the clerical founders of Yale were quite elaborately interrelated.

In sum, each of the early colleges was under the governance of men representing a fairly homogeneous social class and sharing a common conception of education. Although colonial politics was often the field of sharp partisan dispute, the social homogeneity of the immediate sponsors of the colleges, together with the absence from the curricula of topical economic or political subjects, kept the colleges relatively free from urgent controversy of this sort. The chief problems to appear within them—and they were by no means negligible—were those arising out of religious and intellectual differences within the governing group. On the whole, the colonial elite need not have been ashamed of its educational achievement, for the colonial colleges, with all their weaknesses, made remarkable gains during the eighteenth century, not only in the direction of higher standards but of greater liberality. The sponsorship of an enlightened aristocracy has often been identified with such gains in American higher education.

American Colleges in the Nineteenth Century: From Localism to Denominationalism

David B. Potts

The general contours of nineteenth-century collegiate development, as found in the histories of American higher education, probably need substantial re-examination and extensive reshaping. Traditionally, colleges associated with various denominations are characterized largely in terms of sectlike religious zeal and are assigned the early nineteenth century as their period of importance. The few monographic studies of late-nineteenth-century colleges and the more numerous works on the emergence of universities are correspondingly cast in a framework of increasing secularism in higher education. It seems more likely, however, that the current historical conception of the denominational college more closely coincides with realities of institutional development *after* rather than before 1850. In terms of support, control, and functions, there is evidence of a strong and increasing denominationalism in a large majority of late-nineteenth-century colleges. For most of the institutions with founding dates prior to 1850, this degree of denominationalism is a departure from the primary role played by localism in founding and nurturing these educational enterprises during their earliest years. Although additional research will be necessary to confirm this contrast, there is good reason to anticipate that the traditional generalization concerning a basic trend from sectarianism toward secularism, when applied to American collegiate history during the nineteenth century, will have to be inverted.

I

A re-examination of nineteenth-century colleges might appropriately begin by asking to what extent the connections between pre–Civil War colleges and various denominations were important to the founding, financing, and functioning of these institutions. Existing answers to this inquiry are almost unanimous in their stress on the religious roots and roles of antebellum colleges. From the early nineteenth century to the present, these institutions have been portrayed, with few exceptions, as struggling sectarian enterprises.

Major pieces of evidence used to support this predominant interpreta-

Reprinted from *The History of Education Quarterly,* Volume 11, Number 4 (Winter, 1971), pp. 363–80, by permission of the Publisher.

tion, and even the tone and thrust of the analysis, are largely derived from the writings of nineteenth-century educational reformers. Francis Wayland, president of Brown University and one of the early reform leaders, provided, in his book of 1842 and pamphlet of 1850, the scenario of collegiate retrogression that has been so frequently repeated. He pictured colleges during the late colonial period as "eminently successful." Following the Revolution, however, "the character of education deteriorated, and after some years had passed it had sunk lamentably low. It has since improved, but I doubt whether in many points it has yet surpassed its ante-revolutionary standing." Whereas Wayland only mentioned in passing that "almost every college in this country is either originally, or by sliding from its primitive foundations, under the control of some religious sect," his contemporaries in the small but outspoken group advocating reform of higher education usually emphasized a causal connection between deterioration and sectarianism.

Philip Lindsley, president of the University of Nashville in the late 1820's, viewed the multiplication of sectarian colleges as "a grievous and growing evil" that limited the usefulness and retarded the prosperity of higher education in the states of Tennessee, Ohio, and Kentucky. Julian Sturtevant, president of Illinois College, found the same trend in his area to be "disastrous to the interests of liberal education." By blurring all distinctions between denominationalism of early-nineteenth-century America and an older and generally unlovely religious phenomenon, sectarianism, these critics attributed the low state of antebellum colleges to a ubiquitous villain: narrow-minded sectarian zeal. The contours, critiques, and tone found in Wayland, Lindsley, and Sturtevant were perpetuated and augmented in documents authored by late-nineteenth-century university promoters. Charles Kendall Adams, F. A. P. Barnard, and others argued that denominational colleges were so narrow and shallow in their curriculum, largely due to their excessive multiplication under the impetus of sectarianism, that they failed to meet public needs. And, for this reason, their never more than minuscule public patronage had been declining (relative to population growth) since as early as the 1830's.

It is more than a little ironic that these key pieces of evidence employed by subsequent historians to establish the parochialism of pre–Civil War colleges are themselves extremely limited in their angle of vision. Wayland, looking outward from an urban environment highly atypical for colleges of his day, draws only on the New England states for the data supporting his observations. Research on sixteen early-nineteenth-century colleges affiliated with Baptist interests indicates that, although Wayland was probably the most prominent Baptist of his times, his writings exhibit little understanding of the nature and functions of colleges, other than Brown, affiliated with his own denomination.

Lindsley, a Princeton graduate and subsequently a professor there during an early portion of his career, expressed distaste for many practices of frontier America, ranging from tobacco-chewing to revivalism. Acceptng the presidency of a new nondenominational college in Nashville, Tennessee, Lindsley arrived in 1824 with the long-range goal of establishing, in this town of about five thousand inhabitants, a university equivalent to any of the major European centers of learning. In his attitudes, intellectual outlook, and ambitions, he appears far removed from the realities of grassroots educational activity and thus not very well equipped to report on its particular characteristics with accuracy or insight.

Sturtevant, in his autobiography and especially in several articles on colleges he wrote for the *New Englander,* displays a high level of what might be termed Congregational ethnocentrism. He consistently assumes that collegiate education occurring outside the circle of enlightened Congregational sponsorship must be sectarian, even if one bows to semantic convention and calls it denominational.

In the late nineteenth century, the obvious need of university reformers for a foil to dramatize their promotions of new directions for higher education renders their observations of equally limited utility. Even when they offer, as Columbia's President Barnard did, extensive enrollment statistics to buttress their case, the conclusions drawn from such data are highly questionable. We have, then, the history of early-nineteenth-century colleges written from an urban Northeast, European-inspired, Congregational, or university-reformer point of view that seems severely limited—one might even say parochial—when compared with the fact that the overwhelming majority of antebellum colleges bore little relationship to any of these elements.

Building on this limited angle of vision, subsequent historical approaches to pre–Civil War colleges have, aside from the picturesque and amusing aspects, heavily stressed curricular characteristics. With the exception of Wilson Smith's study of moral philosophers, however, curricular analyses have been so quality-oriented that they do little more than set a conservative, bleak backdrop against which one can view the progressive rise of science, technological education, and the research-oriented university in the late nineteenth century. The major implication of such a picture can hardly be avoided: Classical, sectarian, superficial, and, therefore, separated from the needs and desires of an industrializing and urbanizing nation, colleges have little significance beyond their curricular backwardness. The vastly more important story for American higher education, it is then assumed, lies in the exciting new intellectual and institutional developments that come in the late nineteenth century.

Easily dismissed in this fashion, nineteenth-century colleges have received scant attention from professional historians. And, yet, there is still much to be learned from a broadly conceived, institutional history point of view. This would not be the internal, buildings-and-personalities institutional history that has for too long been predominant in the literature of higher education. New investigations might focus on points of intersection between institution and society. Among the many possible dimensions deserving examination in depth are the relationships between institution and sponsoring denomination and [the] relationships between institution and surrounding communities in terms ranging from cultural to economic. These explorations are likely not only to provide new data concerning an important aspect of American cultural history but also to challenge current generalizations, such as the one about sectarianism helping to isolate colleges from the true needs and desires of antebellum Americans.

A look at the colleges of one denomination from this noncurricular, local history point of view yields the conclusion that they were neither predominantly sectarian nor separated from society. Baptist colleges, prior to the Civil War, were essentially local enterprises. Denominational ties were of secondary importance. This holds for both the founding and functioning of these institutions at least up to 1850. Baptist ministers who played important roles in the founding of almost all pre-1850 colleges affiliated with their denomination were rarely driven by narrow denominational motives. Vital assistance in the creation of these institutions came from Baptist laymen, but their objectives were probably even less characterized by evangelical enthusiasm. And, since only a small minority of college towns could be classified as Baptist strongholds, support from non-Baptists was essential. Whereas communities provided substantial contributions and large numbers of students, the official organizations of the denomination provided little more than their sanction and verbal encouragement. The fundamental element in college-founding was the alliance forged between college promoters and a particular town or county. Initially, this alliance was usually expressed in terms of the promoters agreeing to locate the college in a particular community in return for a sum of money raised within that community.

Once the agreement concerning location was made and an institution established, the process of sinking roots into community life and binding the cultural and economic fortunes of the town and immediate vicinity with those of the college proceeded rapidly. Preparatory departments and special nonclassical courses served many educational needs of the community. Graduates of normal courses and students working their way through college helped to staff local schools with unusually well-qualified teachers. Companion institutions for female education were frequently founded. The college president or some other distinguished member of the denomination from the faculty often filled the local Baptist pulpit. Public lectures by faculty members, literary society exhibitions, and numerous other influences emanating from the college also served to augment local cultural resources. Some economic benefits to the community, such as the boarding of students with townspeople, might reflect carefully calculated policy. Others, such as the money put into the local economy by students and the increases in land values near the college, were inevitable.

Communities responded to all these tangible benefits of an educational institution by supporting their college in several ways. The college town and nearby settlements supplied a large percentage of each institution's students. Citizens contributed liberally to meet operating expenses, erect buildings, and create endowment funds. College events, such as the annual commencements, were attended in great numbers by a broad spectrum of local residents. Throughout the antebellum period, the immediate vicinity of the college was a crucial and generally dependable source of support for Baptist-affiliated colleges.

The essential point about these institutions is not curricular conservatism buttressed by religious zeal but, rather, their role in widely dispersing the nation's cultural resources and their efforts to increase public demand for higher education. On the latter point, the curricular outlook of the Yale Report, in terms of its emphasis on mental discipline fostering success, served a broad, cultural-institutional function. Agents were employed by individual institutions to travel extensively and cultivate grassroots support for the particular collegiate enterprises they represented. A key element of their message to parents and potential students was the claim that a classical liberal arts education was the all-important first step toward power, wealth, and influence. Mental discipline was pictured as the best means for meeting the challenges and opportunities of a fluid society. Reports on campus piety and data on subsequent careers indicate that enrollments resulting from [the] efforts of these educational salesmen were characterized more by secular ambition than by denominational affiliation or religious zeal.

If the Baptist-affiliated colleges are representative (as I will suggest below), then it is time to abandon the practice of describing and dismissing early-nineteenth-century colleges as sectarian or even as merely denominational. The adjective "sectarian" is particularly inappropriate; its use by educational historians ignores the precise definition employed in the sociology of religion and derived from Ernst Troeltsch's *Social Teachings of the Christian Churches* (1912). And, even if the term "denominational" were consistently used in the very broadly evangelical and nonsectarian sense that scholars in American religious history tell us is appropriate to most of the Jacksonian era, it would still obscure the essence of antebellum colleges. They were, above all else, *local* colleges. This adjective does not exclude religious zeal as one element of localism, but it does give secular forces their rightfully predominant role. In this era of institutional multiplication and dispersal, colleges were closely tied with the local, cultural, and economic ambitions of citizens, parents, and students; special religious interests became of major significance only in the unusual cases where these ties were weak or absent.

II

In the existing historical writings on higher education in the late nineteenth century, the vast majority of American colleges tend to do a vanishing act. Consistent with the limited points of view on early colleges, our scholarly writings on late-nineteenth-century higher education focus on universities as products of reform movements and on Congregational colleges, especially those of New England. Given this selective situation, it is hardly surprising that trends from piety to intellect and [from] evangelicalism to progressivism march steadily across the available pages. Searchers of the secondary literature in this period will find little, if any, reason to question Richard Hofstadter's observation that, of the several major themes commanding the attention of the historian of American higher education, "the oldest and longest sustained is the drift toward secularism."

But, if the early-nineteenth-century colleges should turn out to be predominantly secular, is the next half century or so merely a period during which they become even more secular? Probably not. Given the phenomenon of localism as a reference point in the antebellum years, there is considerable evidence within the collegiate mainstream of a subsequent drift toward denominationalism rather than secularism. This inversion of the commonly employed historical trend seems to hold not only for the Baptist-affiliated colleges but for those of most other major denominations as well.

By 1850, there were, among Baptist-affiliated local colleges, signs of increasing denominationalism. With college towns becoming less able or willing to sustain the role of primary supporter, appeals for funds shifted emphasis from college as contributor to the public good to college as instrument of denominational interest. There were efforts to make faculties thoroughly Baptist. An increasing proportion of students was being drawn from outside a sixty-mile radius of the college but within the confines of the state. It seems highly probable that students coming from this considerable distance were more likely to be of Baptist backgrounds than those from the immediate vicinity of the college. Questions of denominational control were raised, and boards of trustees were reorganized to reduce the large number of local members and increase statewide denominational representation. Proposals to move colleges to sites more centrally located in terms of the Baptist constituency appeared in many states during the 1850's.

After the Civil War, institutional ties with the Baptist denomination on a statewide level generally continued to grow in strength and number. Lingering secular orientations prompted two colleges—Colby in Maine and Richmond in Virginia—to make unsuccessful efforts toward being designated as land-grant institutions under the Morrill Act. But they and several others soon found their primary source of funds among a few wealthy Baptists residing in urban centers. These patrons regarded colleges from a strongly denominational point of view. Colleges lacking such support concentrated their fund-raising efforts on the denominational grassroots level, employing as president a Baptist leader with widespread reputation and appeal.

The growing denominational grip on colleges is reflected in several college removals effected by Baptist state conventions and in an increased incidence of charter revisions and trustee reorganizations to make institutions more clearly the servants of statewide Baptist constituencies. And, unlike the large majority of original charters issued prior to 1850, which

Theodore Lownik Library
Illinois Benedictine College
Lisle, Illinois 60532

were now being revised, charters for Baptist-affiliated colleges founded in the late nineteenth century rarely failed to stipulate Baptist control of the board of trustees.

Further impetus to a denominational orientation came with the founding of national Baptist educational agencies, beginning in 1870. At first operating in the area of encouraging increased Baptist student enrollment in the denomination's colleges, these national influences acquired substantial monetary dimensions with the founding of the American Baptist Education Society in 1888. Financed by John D. Rockefeller, the Society made its largest single matching grant to the new University of Chicago. But, in the years from 1889 to 1914, it also gave a total of more than $500,000 to twenty-three other Baptist colleges, which themselves raised almost $2 million in matching funds. Additional support for Baptist academies strengthened their role as "feeders" for the denomination's colleges. Shortly after World War I, both the Northern and Southern Baptist conventions conducted campaigns that brought additional millions to their colleges.

Widely scattered data on the religious composition of faculties and student bodies, general comments on the tenor of campus life, and the institution of courses and departments in Biblical literature also indicate that Baptist colleges were reaching a high point of denominationalism in the 1880's and 1890's. With few exceptions, this intensity of religious identity was sustained well into the 1920's. Southern Baptist college faculty and presidents suspected of doctrinal impurity were being closely and effectively monitored by the denomination's state conventions well into the 1930's. When a group of fundamentalists within the Northern Baptist Convention set out, in 1920, to determine "the loyalty of our Baptist schools" to Christ and denomination, their thorough investigation found almost all colleges firmly under denominational control and uncovered very few signs of any drift from orthodoxy.

III

With the available evidence regarding Baptist-affiliated colleges suggesting an inversion of the traditional generalization about increasing secularism in nineteenth-century colleges, it is necessary to confront the central question: How representative is this group when compared with institutions affiliated with other denominations? Are Baptist colleges more likely to be local because of a very decentralized denominational polity or more sectarian due to peculiar and staunchly defended beliefs concerning baptism? In exploring these questions, one finds that, beyond histories of individual colleges, the only detailed secondary sources available for comparative analysis are monographs on higher education among Methodists and Presbyterians (published, respectively, in 1928 and 1940), an unpublished dissertation on Episcopal education completed in 1958, and portions of a multidenominational study done in 1929.

Looking at Methodist-affiliated colleges in the years prior to 1869 largely through official denominational sources, Sylvanus Duvall makes the following observation: "As the Methodist Episcopal Church has always been a highly organized and bureaucratic body, its lack of control over these educational institutions stands out in striking contrast to the strict control exercised over its churches and other activities." Duvall finds these colleges to be "local endeavors" involving "no attempt to direct activities with reference to what others were doing, or to the needs of a denomination as a whole." He further suggests, but does not explore, the idea that even service to local denominational needs was not the primary objective. Calls for greater denominational control over this "unregulated" accumulation of nominally Methodist colleges appear as early as 1840, but they do not become significant in volume or influence until the 1860's. Duvall's monograph concludes with the Methodist General Conference establishing a national Board of Education in 1868 and the incorporation of that board in the following year.

Data from C. Harve Geiger's work on Presbyterian colleges suggest a similar contrast between local initiative in the early nineteenth century and growing denominational supervision in subsequent years. Almost two-thirds of the colleges dating from 1802 up to the Civil War were founded "privately" rather than by Presbytery or Synod. For those institutions established between 1866 and 1895, the origins are just the reverse: two-thirds denominational and one-third private. Not until 1848 does the Presbyterian General Assembly take strong steps to increase denominational control over the early pattern of decentralization. By 1887, the national denominational agency distributing financial aid was stipulating that not only must the receiving institution have firm legal ties with the Presbyterian Church but also, in the event such organic connection was severed, all property received would revert to the denomination. In 1919, a requirement was added to the effect that colleges receiving aid must give sufficient evidence of sustaining "vital relations of cooperation with the [General] Board [of Education] and its Presbyterian constituency." This cooperative relationship was specified four years later in terms of evangelical requirements for faculty membership, campus worship services, and curricular objectives.

Episcopal and Congregational patterns in higher education are, respectively, smaller-scale and diluted versions of the Baptist, Methodist, and Presbyterian experience. The handful of Episcopal colleges reached a comparatively earlier peak of denominationalism in the mid-nineteenth century. A resurgence of educational effort within this denomination in the late nineteenth century was restricted to the level of secondary education. Although the Congregational-based Society for the Promotion of Collegiate and Theological Education at the West (1843) was probably the first denominational organization to give direct aid to institutions, connections between college and church were slow to develop and never became very extensive. By the mid-1890's, the Congregational Education Society was stipulating that, in order to qualify for grants, a college must be approved by state and local denominational bodies and make annual reports to the state conference. And, should a college have a self-perpetuating board of trustees, a majority must be "members in good and regular standing in Congregational churches." Despite the persistence of such stipulations into the late 1920's, the Educational Survey Commission reported to the National Council in 1921 that previously strong, informal college-denomination relationships had greatly diminished and were now very tenuous.

Yet, compared with the approximately fifty colleges more or less loosely affiliated with Congregational and Episcopal churches by the 1920's, there were more than four hundred institutions whose connections with denominations such as the Baptist, Methodist, and Presbyterian had probably increased in strength during the years between the Civil War and World War I. Not until the early 1920's did denominational appropriations to colleges reach their peak. And as late as 1899 colleges identified with a denomination in the annual report of the U.S. Commissioner enrolled 46.2 per cent of the undergraduate population in American higher education. In sum, it appears that the institutional mainstream of American higher education, for at least the second half of the nineteenth century, was composed of colleges, like those of the Baptists, moving in the direction of denominationalism rather than secularism.

IV

Reconstruction of the contours of late-nineteenth-century higher education from data concerning the majority of colleges and students might shed new light on a number of developments. One that can be cited by way of illustration and also used to support the preceding argument concerns the Carnegie Foundation for the Advancement of Teaching. The foundation, incorporated in 1906 with firm prohibitions against admitting denominationally controlled colleges to its faculty pension plan, is commonly cited as an important force that accelerated the secularization of American colleges. Several of the well-known institutions that severed denominational ties in order to qualify their faculties for Carnegie pension benefits are usually cited to illustrate the foundation's impact on higher education.

Re-examination of the Carnegie Foundation's role within a context of collegiate denominationalism that was waxing rather than waning would yield a considerably altered emphasis. Close inspection of the foundation's annual reports reveals that, of the 615 institutions surveyed by the foundation in 1905, 509 had denominational entanglements to a degree that barred them from joining the pension plan. What is perhaps more important, only fifteen colleges during the first fifteen years severed denominational ties to join the initial group of fifty on the accepted list. It would be difficult to conclude from these data that the Carnegie Foundation made anything more than a small dent in the prevailing denominationalism.

One major reason for such minor impact can be found in the activities of John D. Rockefeller's General Education Board, established in 1902. Unlike the Carnegie Foundation, the board's policy included provision for "systematic and helpful cooperation with religious denominations." Prior to World War I, the General Education Board distributed matching grants to 103 colleges and universities. Some 35 of these were also members of the Carnegie pension group, but almost 50 were clearly denominational colleges. Whereas the Carnegie Foundation assumed pension obligations that, by the close of 1934, resulted in expenditures of approximately $27 million, the General Education Board, by 1925, had already appropriated nearly $60 million to the endowment funds of 291 colleges and universities. Matching requirements added another $140 million to endowments of these institutions.

The impact of the board on just the portion of those institutions closely linked to denominations similarly overshadows any potential influence of the Carnegie Foundation. All but a few of the approximately fifty denominational colleges receiving Rockefeller money during the years from 1902 to 1915 belonged to the Baptists, Methodists, and Presbyterians. To these colleges, grants were made totaling approximately $4 million. With matching funds added, the total raised for endowments approached $16 million. Since very few of these colleges probably operated with an annual income of more than $100,000 in 1915, the returns from enlarged endowment funds presumably represented at least a 10–20 per cent increase in annual income.

With the General Education Board pursuing a policy of substantial support for the most promising denominational colleges in terms of location and academic standards, the various national denominational boards of education founded after the Civil War could continue their policy of allocating large portions of their resources to the smaller and weaker colleges within each denomination. Rather than succumbing to financial pressures from the Carnegie Foundation, denominational colleges were in a financial position to anticipate a brighter future unimpaired and probably enhanced by close church affiliations. Of the handful who altered charters to benefit from Carnegie pensions, some even returned to the more promising denominational fold. Randolph-Macon went back to the Methodists after only a few years; Franklin completed a return to the Indiana Baptists in 1919 by restoring its previous charter; Centre, in Kentucky, resumed close Presbyterian ties in 1922.

The primary sources and the secondary works employed to suggest an important trend from primarily secular localism to denominationalism at the grassroots level of nineteenth-century higher education in America hardly scratch the surface of this phenomenon. To establish the widespread existence of such a trend, to chart its interior dynamics, and to determine its impact on American cultural development will require a great deal of broadly conceived yet meticulous research at the local and individual institution level. The detailed analysis of student origins, motives, and subsequent careers so necessary to such an enterprise can, for example, only proceed in depth when limited to one or a small group of colleges. By venturing outside New England to probe the institutional depths of the nation's collegiate development, and by looking at this remarkable phenomenon through eyes other than those of reformers, historians can greatly increase our understanding of American higher education.

The Rise of Academic Reform

Laurence Veysey

To the men who experienced it, the time around 1870 seemed to mark "almost the Anno Domini of educational history" in the United States. Watching the rapid flow of events with a skeptic's eye, President Noah Porter of Yale commented upon American higher education in 1871:

> Never, perhaps, did this subject occupy the thoughts of so many persons and occupy them so earnestly. It certainly never excited more active controversy, or provoked more various or confident criticism, or was subjected to a greater variety of experiments than with us in these passing years. The remark is not infrequently made that college and university education are not merely agitated by reforms; they are rather convulsed by a revolution—so unsettled are the minds of many who control public opinion, so sharp is the criticism of real or imagined defects in the old methods and studies, and so determined is the demand for sweeping and fundamental changes.

Not everyone has agreed with Porter in invoking the term "revolution" to describe the movement that produced the American university in the decades after the Civil War. Again and again, academic reformers were to insist that they believed in gradual change, that they sought to balance the "progressive" against the "conservative." Then, too, while enrollments in universities appeared to soar by the turn of the century, producing an unprecedented impression of expansion, the percentage of Americans of college age attending college rose only from 4.01 to 4.84 in the decade from 1900 to 1910. These figures would not have made an exciting graph of business sales during a comparable span.

Yet, the fact remains that the American university of 1900 was all but unrecognizable in comparison with the college of 1860. Judged by almost any index, the very nature of the higher learning in the United States had been transformed. Intellectually, purposes were being nurtured of which the mid-nineteenth-century academic custodian had had only an alarming

From *The Emergence of the American University* (Chicago, University of Chicago Press, 1965), pp. 1–18; by permission of the Publisher.

premonition. The complexity of the university made the former college seem a boys' school in contrast. And a profession, pridefully jealous of its status, had come into being in the interim, replacing what had been a gentlemanly amateurism of spirit. The decades after 1865 thus saw a definite process of metamorphosis, operating on many levels, occur within what was an already venerable corner of American life. Despite significant elements of continuity in the change, the college scene before 1865 seems archaic indeed when set against the new and rapidly working forces of academic reform.

These new conditions were several. Given labels, the most important of them might be termed Europhilic discontent, available national wealth, and immediate alarm over declining college influence. The university is, first of all, the distinctive creation of Western Europe. Universities have eventually appeared in other parts of the world, in the United States as in India or Japan, as a result of the outward spread of European patterns of cultural activity. This fact underlies the transformation of American higher education in the late nineteenth century. An intellectual leadership had come into being in the United States that yearned for . . . equality with that of Europe even while it cherished a certain posture of independence from foreign standards. This leadership fervently sought national progress, but it was likely to cast its glance eastward across the Atlantic whenever improvement needed specific definition. Increasingly, as the nineteenth century advanced, the moral, religious, and political scruples that had operated as powerful deterrents to the adoption of recent European intellectual forms grew weaker among an educated minority of Americans. This leadership, separating itself from orthodox evangelical piety and continuing to reject Jacksonian vulgarity, became receptive to European scientific and educational developments that might offer a counterweight to the cruder tendencies manifested in the surrounding society. At the same time, the lack of a suitable focus for their talents, the absence of a vehicle to command, left men of this educated stamp restless and discontented. Looking at Europe, they saw what they needed. The university, hallowed yet newly thriving on the Continent, could uniquely satisfy the social idealism, the personal ambition, and the prideful American urge to equal the best of European achievements that these men possessed.

From this perspective, it is by no means startling that the university took root in the United States during the several decades after 1865. But such aspirations might have come to nothing had they not received assistance of more tangible sorts. To begin with, there is the blunt fact of the surplus capital that was newly available. Earlier efforts at innovation in the field of American college education had proved abortive, in large part, simply because there had not been money to sustain them. American colleges and universities have always been basically dependent upon philanthropy, whether public or private. In the post–Civil War years, the university could not have developed without the Cornells, Hopkinses, and Rockefellers, without the taxpayers of Michigan and Wisconsin.

Wealth, again, was a necessary precondition but not a sufficient cause for the academic change that took place. The same money may buy castles as easily as classrooms. For some of it to be·directed toward academic reform, further incentives were required. Education had to be warmly regarded by at least a few men of surplus means. It is easy to exaggerate the passion for education, especially in its higher reaches, that was held by Americans during the mid-nineteenth century. Practical men of that period often showed contempt for "useless" books. One can too easily forget that both of the prominent academic donors of the period before 1890, Ezra Cornell and Johns Hopkins, were Quakers motivated by an uncommon humanitarianism; only after that year would benefactions toward higher learning become widely fashionable. Yet, the college did still manage to function as an important symbol of respectability. And the university, as an outgrowth of the college, promised to move higher education much closer to the ways of thinking shared by the practical and the wealthy. Academic reform thus held out the hope of salvaging a somewhat quaint ministerial survival and transforming it into an agency that would cater to newer, secular desires. Slowly at first, but then with increasing speed, education began to be identified with material success, bringing it into the notice of those whose financial backing was necessary for its widespread growth. University development in the United States before 1890 fed on a mere trickle from the nation's wealth, but that trickle was sufficient to register dramatic gains.

Neither wealth nor the temptation to match European achievements could have produced reform in American higher education had not the existing colleges been in troubled circumstances. In fact, the American college, with more than two centuries of history already behind it, now found itself in deepening difficulty. Ever since the Jacksonian period, college enrollments had remained static amid a growing national population. In the years after 1865, these discouraging figures drew more and more notice within academic circles. During the 1870's, attendance at twenty of the "oldest leading colleges" rose only 3.5 per cent, while the nation's population soared 23 per cent. In 1885, less than a quarter of all American congressmen were college graduates, as compared with 38 per cent ten years earlier. "In all parts of the country," Charles Kendall Adams of Michigan declared, "the sad fact stares us in the face that the training which has long been considered essential to finished scholarship has been losing ground from year to year in the favor of the people."

In one respect, it could be said that the unfavorable statistics represented a false alarm. European immigration accounted for a substantial share of the national population growth. The immigrants were usually in no position to attend college, even when they were of the proper age. For the same reason, throughout the 1880's the ratio of those attending school to the total school-age population of the United States also fell. But, of course, this factor does not account for the total picture. Immigrants came in greater numbers after 1890, but college attendance began its steady climb upward around that date. To an important degree the static quality of American higher education reflected the changing tastes of the established population.

The college, with its classical course of training, had hitherto been a means of confirming one's respectable place in society. Now many young men—for example, the younger brothers of college graduates—for a time became convinced that sufficiently attractive rewards were available to them by direct effort in business or in the professions. (The number of lawyers and doctors who had college degrees declined in the late nineteenth century.) The large city also brought with it altered expectations. The highest conceivable prominence was no longer that of the small-town physician, lawyer, or minister. The prospect of a business career in the city lured many who otherwise would have been content as village clergymen. This kind of prospective student the college lost. As T. H. Safford, a professor at Williams, remarked in 1888: "The varied attractions of city life restrain intellectual tendencies in the minds of many boys, and the variety of careers which they see opening before their older schoolmates leads to a strong tendency to follow business rather than classical courses." The trustees of the University of Vermont pointed in the same direction in 1871 when they said [that] the most important cause of a thirty-year drop in attendance was a growth in the mercantile spirit, consequent upon "our close connection by railroad and telegraph with our great cities." Unless they changed, the colleges seemed destined to play an increasingly minor role in an urban, "materialistic" society.

The mid-nineteenth-century decline in college influence showed itself in nonstatistical ways that are perhaps the most significant. Testimony throughout the 1950's and 1960's unanimously echoes the fact that the intangible prestige of the American college graduate was sinking. When G. Stanley Hall, a Massachusetts farm boy, was admitted to Williams College in 1863, he attempted to conceal the fact from his rural companions, "but it was found out and I was unmercifully jibed," he recalled. This kind of incident reflected the uncertain social position of the educated man in a restless society. Colleges were identified with the elements that had dominated the population, particularly in New England, before the day of Jackson. American Bachelors of Art comprised "something of an educational aristocracy." Those who stood within the charmed circle might talk easily of the "inherent respectability" of classical training. But they formed a minority that was becoming less honored within the nation at large. As for the college professor, he shared in the esteem common to members of the Eastern aristocracy, but within those ranks his place was near the bottom. He lacked the comfort of a well-marked professional position akin to the lawyer's or the minister's. He might have to wait for years until a chair became vacant, and then he was likely to be appointed as a result of casual social contacts (or religious loyalty) rather than in recognition of academic competence. As late as 1870, William Graham Sumner complained: "There is no such thing yet at Yale as an academical *career*. There is no course marked out for a man who feels called to this work, and desires to pursue it." Once given an appointment, a professor almost required independent means to supplement his nominal salary. His duties were monotonous: the hearing and grading of memorized recitations, usually in the ancient languages or mathematics. Harvard's President Eliot remarked at his inaugural in 1869: "It is very hard to find competent professors for the University. Very few Americans of eminent ability are attracted to this profession. The pay has been too low, and there has been no gradual rise out of drudgery, such as may reasonably be expected in other learned callings." Families of social prominence usually looked down upon the professor. Paid little, burdened by an unexciting routine, the professor of this period clung to the coat tails of the slowly sinking New England tradition.

Many of the most prominent college presidents who held power in 1865 were old men, and in perhaps as many as nine cases out of ten such presidents were still recruited from the clergy. At Williams, Mark Hopkins, who had become president in 1836, held the reins until 1872. Theodore Dwight Woolsey, who had first instructed Yale students in 1823, was not to retire until 1871. William A. Stearns, who headed Amherst until 1876, had been an unusually pious youth at Harvard back in the 1820's. Such men as these reacted with caution to the challenge of the late 1860's. Mark Hopkins spoke out plainly against academic expansion. "There is a false impression," he declared in 1872, "in regard to the benefit to undergraduates of the accumulation of materials and books, and of a large number of teachers." One of Hopkins' eulogists remarked: "He was not . . . in haste to substitute a new text-book for an old one." Stearns of Amherst was described by those who knew him as a moderate conservative in matters educational, political, and theological. Philosophically, Stearns rejected "the thick German fogs" in favor of Scottish common sense. Too much literary or intellectual content in the curriculum might, he feared, turn Amherst into "a nursery of pantheism." "Reverence for the aged, veneration for parents, for sacred institutions, for wisdom and goodness in character," were among the qualities he would inculcate in his students. As a teacher, Stearns held aloof from his classes and was said to lack both enthusiasm and inspiration.

Yale and Harvard then stood pre-eminent among colleges, and both their presidents were somewhat more alert than most. Yet, it would be easy to exaggerate their relish for change. Woolsey of Yale had studied classical philology in Germany. But, when he returned home, he stressed the teaching of metaphysics, and, for this purpose, he used exclusively the English and Scottish philosophers, not Kant or Hegel. During the long Woolsey administration, emphasis upon science, history, and economics had declined at New Haven. And Woolsey's classroom manner could also be characterized as "chilly and forbidding." President Thomas Hill of Harvard was a self-made man. This fact set him apart socially (he was once taken to task for removing his shoe in public to extract a pebble);

perhaps it contributed to a certain open-mindedness on his part about educational innovations. Hill enjoyed drawing up grand, abstract schemes that would encompass the whole of human knowledge. Nonetheless, he made it plain that intellectual training "should be most carefully watched and guarded," so that Harvard youth might "keep the heart open for simple and refining pleasures." Colleges, he urged, must more carefully segregate liberal education from the taint of vocationalism. Hill's yearning for reform, which was unsupported by any vigor of personality, remained tepid. He was to resign on account of ill health in 1868.

These were the men who led some of the major American colleges in 1865. Either they opposed change or they spoke of reform in vague, half-hearted terms. It is not surprising that the college has often been overlooked in an assessment of American conditions on the eve of Reconstruction. Most of its managers had been reared in the world of Fisher Ames and John Quincy Adams. For these men, the Civil War may have resolved a set of troublesome, important political issues, but it offered no invitation to alter fixed beliefs about the fundamentals of society, religion, or learning. These presidents and their faculties comprised a very small group within a dynamic, unintellectual nation. They did not wish vulgarly to attract the public's attention. They minimized the declining support for their institutions by blaming transient particulars, local in nature: the disruption of the war, rivalries with their neighbors, financial troubles, the failings of secondary schools, factional discords, and higher entrance standards. The only course of action that these men could urge was to hold on, perhaps making minor concessions, and hope that their institutions would be able to survive. These were tired men, and one suspects that they were less militant than the younger conservatives who replaced them at such campuses as Yale and Princeton a few years later.

The old college order was far more complex and somewhat more defensible than these few remarks can indicate. It attracted able partisans down through the 1880's, men whose reaction to the academic transformation around them will be worth an extended look. Under the banner of "mental discipline," a phrase that referred to the sharpening of young men's faculties through enforced contact with Greek and Latin grammar and mathematics, the old-time college sought to provide a four-year regime conductive to piety and strength of character. Unitarian Harvard, enduring doldrums that live in the pages of Henry Adams, was not characteristic of the old order, whose best moments required less sophistication for their appreciation. For ambitious village boys, the old-time college had offered genuine satisfactions, even if few of these came directly from the curriculum. Before the Civil War, hardly anyone had scoffed at the pleasures of a religious revival. Yet, when this is said, it remains true that the old regime had entered a decadence made self-conscious ever since the Yale Report of 1828, when, for the first time, attacks upon academic orthodoxy had required an articulate answer. The American college had been a thriving institution in the eighteenth century; in the early nineteenth, it tended to become a bit artificial, despite the deceptive ease with which its managers had thus far maintained themselves in power.

In 1865, beneath the calm façade afforded by their aging presidents, several colleges harbored would-be leaders of a different and far more vital potential. These younger figures, as yet on the margins of academic life, were the heirs, direct or indirect, of a number of prewar efforts toward college reform that had already left behind them what their historian calls "a tradition of aspiration and experimentation." Occasional Americans had been studying in Germany since 1816, and, by the 1850's, considerable interest had developed concerning Continental universities, the German then being without doubt pre-eminent in the world. Henry P. Tappan, on assuming the presidency of the University of Michigan in 1852, had prematurely declared that the German institutions could serve as "literal" models for American higher education. (He moved too fast and was replaced by a docile clergyman.) Other prewar stirrings, such as those initiated by Francis Wayland at Brown in the 1840's, had emulated foreign ideas less directly but also tended toward a flexible, more departmentalized curriculum. Several colleges had briefly tried to offer graduate work. Carefully segregated "scientific schools" had been founded at Harvard and Yale, and these, unlike the other experiments, were taking root and incidentally nurturing several of the leading academic reformers of the generation to come.

The 1850's and 1860's marked the budding season for a new and discontented group of future American academic leaders. Jolts provided by newly released wealth and an awareness of static or declining college enrollment were to bring some of these reformers to power far more suddenly than they could have foreseen in 1865. The clergymen who still held control in that year were exiled from a number of prominent seats of learning during the following decade. That the reformers gained leverage so rapidly indicated several facts about the change that was taking place. First, it showed that, even at its nadir, academic life was still sufficiently prominent in America to attract a remarkable group of potential chieftains with ideas about its improvement. Further, it demonstrated that the trustees of the existing institutions, more than a third of them clerical, sometimes preferred to risk experimentation rather than to continue in the unpromising ways of the past. Since those older ways were firmly identified in everyone's mind with religious piety and innovation with unsettling intellectual influences, the reform-minded trustees whose votes were essential in selecting new presidents had obviously shifted to a primary concern over educational rather than religious problems. Finally, once any one respectable institution moved in a new direction, others found themselves under a powerful compulsion to follow suit. The changes, if they meant anything, were bound to attract more students. Colleges that lagged behind for any reason, including religiously motivated traditionalism, had to face the threat of eventual starvation.

Fear, thus, might often spur change. But, in many quarters, a more positive sense of intellectual urgency could be discerned. The 1860's will longer be remembered as the decade of Darwin's reception than as the time of growing panic in the colleges. Knowledge, particularly in the sciences, was beginning rapidly to expand. No longer could the old curriculum even pretend to account for all major areas of fact, nor could it adequately explore the "laws" that men of that time believed could almost effortlessly be derived from fact. Europe offered exciting challenges to accepted ways of thought. Intellectual respectability demanded new academic forms.

Down into the 1860's, proposals for major reform in America had been regarded rather vaguely by their proponents and opponents alike. The word "university" was already much in use in discussion, and, indeed, a number of small colleges, especially those with public endowments, bore this name in their title. But the phrase lacked clear definition. According to one observer in 1860, the term meant nothing more specific than "an educational institution of great size, and which affords instruction of an advanced grade in all learning." The then president of Harvard, Charles C. Felton, appears to have conceived of a university as an expanded country college with a somewhat larger library.

From this primordial, scarcely thought-out vision of "the university" there appeared, in the period from 1865 to 1890, three much more specific conceptions. These centered, respectively, in the aim of practical public service, in the goal of abstract research on what was believed to be the pure German model, and, finally, in the attempt to diffuse standards of cultivated taste. (A fourth group of academic leaders . . . continued, in effect, to say no to the university altogether.) . . . [A]t the outset, it is important to realize the underlying power of the undifferentiated dream of "the university," which, in a sense, was to swallow up the followers of the more particular educational philosophies once again after the turn of the twentieth century. Like so many moving forces in American history, the simple urge toward "the university" in this unqualified sense did not lose power because it lacked concreteness. Before 1865, the dream of an American university standing on a par with those of Europe had been a vague but increasingly insistent urge. Again in the twentieth century, rhetoric about the university (with some notable exceptions) was to lean toward hazy generalities. Only for one generation, while the university was actually coming into existence, did clearer, more articulate lines of debate find widespread expression. Only for the approximate years of this study, and then only for some of its protagonists, did the American university generate what could be called a coherent intellectual history. Before that, the *college* had had such a history, closely bound to the history of American religion. Afterward, the university tended to lose itself among individual disciplines, and thinking about the institution as a whole retreated to the level of slogan.

None of the three particular conceptions of academic reform that appeared after 1865—those of service, research, or culture—was original in mid-nineteenth-century America. The goal of practical service, linked with congeniality toward applied science, was less European than the other two and has sometimes been acclaimed as the genuinely American contribution to educational theory (though utilitarian enthusiasm could be traced back at least to Francis Bacon). The idea that higher education should be attuned to the teaching of vocational skills could claim American ancestry in Benjamin Franklin and Thomas Jefferson, but these had been cosmopolitan figures very much in touch with the European Enlightenment. The other two reforming ideals of the post–Civil War period were even more clearly borrowed from abroad. Enthusiasm for research came from Germany, though with complications that will merit exploration. Finally, culture was perhaps the most Europhilic conception of all, deriving basically from British attitudes, with additional sustenance from Romantic Germany, the Renaissance, and classical civilization.

There is no reason to claim a native originality for the several late-nineteenth-century conceptions of the American university when, in fact, such independence can easily be exaggerated. Educated Americans of this period could not afford to be without European influence. One of the most obvious, yet unsung, functions of the American university, especially in its formative years, was to feed ideas from the center of Western civilization into an area that still stood in great need of them. The danger was that European ideas, including those about the university, would too soon lose their force when they began to be applied throughout the vast American Continent. Here, it may be noted that American academic imitativeness would nearly always prove selective; scarcely any major university leader who came to power in the 1860's or 1870's wanted to import the whole of the German university without change. Indeed, such leaders often boasted reassuringly of how American their conceptions were—a fact that should not obscure their continued concern for the latest European developments.

Meanwhile, at home, the new American academic reformers would have to face a restless and, for the most part, ill-educated population. The American public had little enthusiasm for the foreign, the abstract, or the esoteric. Yet, some of this public must be tapped if enrollments were to expand. To win popular sentiment for a venture that, by its nature, had to be somewhat alien must have seemed a dishearteningly difficult task, especially in the period between the Civil War and about 1890. This was the time when industrial leaders liked to issue acid statements about the uselessness of higher education. In 1889, a banker attracted attention by his declaration that he would hire no college graduates anywhere in his office. Most publicized of all were Andrew Carnegie's ringing words of the same year:

> While the college student has been learning a little about the barbarous and petty squabbles of a far-distant past, or trying to master languages which are dead, such knowledge as seems adapted for life upon another planet than this as far as business affairs are concerned, the future captain of industry is hotly engaged in the school of experience,

obtaining the very knowledge required for his future triumphs. . . . College education as it exists is fatal to success in that domain.

Mistrust of the bookishness and cultivation that academic life symbolized was also to be found at all the less prosperous levels of the society: in textbooks for primary schools, among farmers and their spokesmen, and in the infrequent pronouncements of labor organizations on the subject. A life of virility and action seemed irreconcilable with . . . higher learning. As William P. Atkinson observed: "The popular idea of a young scholar is that he should be a pale and bespectacled young man, very thin, and with a slight and interesting tendency to sentimentality and consumption. Parents send their weakly children to college; and it is supposed to be an ordinance of nature that a large proportion of what are called promising young persons should die young.

The newer purposes of the university long failed to register in the public mind; when they did become clear, the gap between scholar and ordinary citizen might thereby grow wider instead of disappearing. The student always continued to be judged by his friends and relatives in terms of a material scale of prestige. In many communities, a young man's decision to attend college was regarded as a "questionable experiment." All that his parents and neighbors usually asked—in these early years, with skepticism —was: "Will he make more money, will he secure a better position in life, will he become more distinguished than if he had remained at home, and married young?" In rural areas, positive fear of the college long existed. A California newspaper reported, in 1892, a belief, "to a surprising and alarming extent" throughout the interior of the state, that it was "worth a young man's soul to send him to the State University at Berkeley," where he would be surrounded "by an atmosphere entirely Godless, not to say vicious." In the South, "Pitchfork Ben" Tillman promised to abolish the University of South Carolina during his gubernatorial campaign of 1891. It was in such an unfriendly climate as this that the American unviersity initially had to make its way.

Signs existed, however, that educational promoters might lead the public from its fitful hostility by judicious pleading and maneuvering. These tactics, abetted by favorable political circumstances, had already been responsible for the passage of the Morrill Act of 1862. Under the terms of this act, the federal government offered aid to states that would support colleges whose curriculums included agricultural and mechanical instruction. Only potentially would these colleges be more than pretentious trade schools, but academic reformers with loftier intentions often secured control of them in their infancy and made them entering wedges for their own plans. The delicate process of gaining support was then repeated at the state legislatures, where sustenance had to be obtained for the publicly endowed institutions that were coming into being. Only very gradually and unevenly, and with frequent setbacks, was state support for higher education gained. In the early years, victories were due less often to widespread public sympathy than to other, more particular motives. The Morrill Act provided a basic incentive; what the states could obtain for nothing, they were likely to take. Then the alumni of the state universities gradually grew to be powerful minorities within a number of legislatures; acting more from their own loyalty than from their constituents' wishes, these delegates frequently tipped the balance when appropriations were being considered. Finally, state pride was invoked once a neighboring state had acted vigorously. Despite these favorable tendencies, legislatures were always ready to interfere with or curtail the operations of state institutions (as, for example, at Michigan in 1877, when faculty salaries were reduced), and, by 1900, only a handful of states had provided outstanding public universities, fit to be compared with the leading private establishments.

The would-be academic reformer also had to cope with a suspicious public in the form of well-defined pressure groups. Prominent among these were the proponents of the various organized religions, political factions of all persuasions, and, away from the Eastern seaboard, agricultural societies such as the Grange. Religious leaders often resented the trend toward secularization augured by the university. They might even seek, by legislative means, to hamper a foundation that harbored alien styles of thought, and which, at the same time, drained students from the local colleges operated by the denomination. Meanwhile, politicians found a device for votes in anti-intellectual oratory. Grangers, for their part, demanded the teaching of agriculture rather than literature and succeeded in tampering with several state universities when their movement achieved power. Everywhere and at all times, newspapers gleefully emphasized academic misdoings, real or imagined. The absence of a prayer on a public platform, as at the Johns Hopkins in 1876, might damage one's public relations for months or years ahead. So frightened of sectarian hostility to the new Cornell University was the governor of New York in 1868 that he backed out of a promised attendance at the opening exercises.

During the early years of the American university movement, until about 1890, academic efforts burgeoned largely in spite of the public, not as the result of popular acclaim. It was observed, for instance, that John Hopkins "came into existence unasked for and uncared for; and so must first create a demand and then supply it." Josiah Royce, writing from Berkeley in 1880, declared: "The public says very little about us, and knows, I fear, even less." Academic and popular aspirations seemed rarely to meet. Even the advocates of a higher education dedicated to practical social service often revealed that they were not attuned to what the public, or the groups that offered to speak for it, [was] really thinking. Far less did "the people" ask for a higher education that was centered in abstract research. Nor did they care for culture in the deep and demanding sense that was desired by its academic partisans. The distance between popular modes of thinking and the nascent universities was one that increasing talk about "democracy" on both sides of the dividing line tended more often to obscure than to eradicate.

For the internal development of the new universities, these difficulties over public relations heralded two widely divergent consequences. First, such problems tended to produce academic leaders whose careers were molded by their insistent efforts to woo a recalcitrant clientele. Reasoning that popular support was essential for the success, numerical and financial, of the new institutions, these men leaned as far in the direction of non-academic prejudices as they dared. They stumped the surrounding country with ingratiating speeches; they made friends with the influential; they campaigned like politicians in seasons of crisis. With one hand, they built the university, borrowing from Europe and improvising as they went; with the other, they popularized it. This group of academic executives emerged with a battle-scarred sensivitity to the subject of public opinion. Knowing its power, fearing its force, these men could develop an almost obsequious habit of submissiveness to it. But, secondly, the very aloofness of many academic concerns from public sympathy tended also to attract men to the university who sought to separate themselves from the other elements of the society. This second kind of academic man, more often a professor than a president, relished the distinctiveness of . . . higher learning. He wished to build the university in an almost deliberately unpopular style. While, naturally, he hoped to win the loyalties of a certain number of students, he assumed that these students would have to meet the standards he imposed, not that he should have to go forward to bargain with them. The academic life, for this kind of believer in the university, must set its own terms.

For a while, as universities began to develop, the contrast between these two kinds of person[s] who were attracted to it revealed itself only rarely, and then in the exalted realm of debate over academic purpose. The question of how far the university should bend to meet the public remained rather abstract so long as public acceptance continued to be an uncertain novelty. No one at Cornell or Johns Hopkins was likely to turn away the first flock of students as they appeared. Yet, the very difficulty of gaining support, the very sharpness of the distinction between academic life and "real" life in the mid-nineteenth century, had set in motion opposed expectations that were to reflect themselves in major internal tensions after 1890. On the one hand, an almost insatiable need for the feeling of public approval developed; on the other, a hope that the university could serve as a refuge.

From the point of view of those who sought a distinctive role for the university, it was the best possible circumstance that higher education remained relatively unpopular for more than two decades after 1865. In this period, the young university enjoyed a temporary (if partial) liberty of action. Not overwhelmed by vast numbers of students, it could afford to experiment with fewer restraints. Since its leaders lacked the "feel" of what the public might be willing to accept, new ideas from Europe could penetrate with fewer [impediments]. Indeed, it was the luxury of widespread public indifference which permitted such a variety of abstract conceptions of the university to blossom immediately after 1865. In this fluid time, before the pressure of numbers had irrevocably descended, entire universities might even be founded or reorganized in the name of such particular conceptions. Presidents and professors could engage in debate among themselves over the guiding aim of the university with the feeling that their words really mattered. It could be hoped that deeply held convictions would realize themselves in institutional structures. Thus, one's academic partisanship became shaped by the definition one gave to the process of learning. For the professor—and for those presidents who had not yet fully learned that their art centered in public relations—it was a season of unparalleled idealistic anticipation.

Cultural Hybrid in the Slums: The College Woman and the Settlement House, 1889–94

John P. Rousmanière

Students of American culture have, since Tocqueville, celebrated this country's voluntary associations. We have long praised the large numbers, active programs, and enthusiasm of political parties and pressure groups, philanthropies and professional organizations, athletic and alumni clubs. But the student concerned with social history rather than historical sociology, with change and process rather than statics, must admit that his fellows rarely consider the key question of origins with the same care they use in their descriptions of the activities of mature associations. Certainly, this student exclaims, the latter is important, but is it not at least equally valuable for an understanding of changing norms and values to understand why an organization was founded at a precise moment in American cultural development?

This study of the origins of the first women's (and first successful) settlement organization in the United States was stimulated by just that question, rephrased in this manner: Why did a *particular* group of women found a strikingly *unique* philanthropic organization *in 1889?* The answer has important implications, specifically about the impact of changes in women's higher education in the Gilded Age and, more generally, about the link between social marginality and organizational structure.

Reprinted from *The American Quarterly,* Volume 22, Number 1 (Spring, 1970), pp. 45–66, by permission of The University of Pennsylvania, Publisher, and the Author. Copyright, 1970, Trustees of The University of Pennsylvania.

Emily Greene Balch, reformer, teacher, and peace agitator, once wrote, apparently in criticism of neo-Freudian attacks on spinsterhood: "If the educated unmarried woman of the period between the Civil War and the [First] World War represent an unique phase, it is one that has important implications which have not yet been adequately recognized by those who insist upon the imperious claims of sex." A popular and influential activity of educated women in the later years of this period was residency in settlement houses. Three-fifths of all settlement residents between 1889 and 1914 were women and, of these, almost nine-tenths had been to college.

Several writers have claimed idealism as the main stimulus to settlement residency for both men and women. To Allen F. Davis, the settlement movement was engined by "a broadly religious humanitarian urge to help solve the problems of urban industrial America." A historian of higher education has viewed the settlement as an outgrowth of the introduction of courses in "social harmony" into the college curriculum. Settlement activity, this historian has argued, provided "an exciting release to the feelings of purposelessness" for students whose learned idealism had no extracurricular outlet. On the other hand, Staughton Lynd has claimed that middle-class young people joined the settlements on a "radical impulse" to ease the guilt occasioned by the period's discovery of poverty.

Other writers have traced more unconscious factors. Richard Hofstadter argued, in *The Age of Reform,* that the settlement was an outlet of tensions created by the breakdown of religious institutions through which middle-class Protestants had traditionally articulated their strong sense of responsibility for social order. Jane Addams saw societal hypocrisy as a major cause of the settlement movement. The young woman returns home from college, Addams wrote in 1892, and "begins to recognize her social claim to the 'submerged tenth.'" But society, which has heretofore pressed "altruistic instincts" upon her, now asserts the "family claim" and tells the young woman that she is ill-advised in her desire to share the "race life" with the poor. Thus, the settlement was the product both of the altruistic desire to fulfill the social claim and of the alienation that came in reaction to society's hypocritical assertion of the family claim. Cristopher Lasch has generalized from Addams's argument to argue that this clash between the social and the family claims took on the proportions of a cultural crisis, generating a revolution of the young. The educated young of the 1880's and 1890's suddenly found themselves unable "to pursue the goals their parents held up before them and also unable to explain why they felt themselves [in Addams's words] 'simply smothered and sickened with advantages.'" They moved into the slums to actualize their renunciation of middle-class values.

An analysis more subtle than any of the above has traced a complex social dynamic spawning the women's settlement. College women of the 1880's and 1890's, Jill Conway has written, shared a sense of mission as pioneers on an educational frontier. And, as educated individuals, they were strongly in need of a challenging activity, so they took as their model the active man. But these women were trapped by accepted norms in their role of inactive woman. By defining a new role for themselves in the settlement house, college women were able to satisfy the demands of their sense of mission and of their need for activity.

There are many problems with each of these explanations, but I shall start and end my discussion of them with a question that none satisfactorily answers: Why did college women express their ideals, guilt, or frustration through the novel *structure* of the settlement house? Unlike all preceding charitable institutions, the settlement was a "colony": It was a home as well as a philanthropy. Why, we must ask, was it necessary to merge these two characteristics? This close study of the first five years of the College Settlement Association is addressed to this and the other questions I have posed.

The College Settlement Association's (CSA) residents were not all college women. Three-fifths of the 92 residents who spent any time in the houses between 1889 and 1894 had been to some college. College women, however, were more committed to settlement work, judging by their tendency to stay longer than noncollege women. The college-educated residents represented twelve schools, three of which—Vassar, Smith, and Wellesley—provided all of the sixteen first-year residents, almost half of the 1889–94 residents, and a majority of the long-term residents.

Close analysis of CSA annual reports reveals an interesting recruitment pattern (see Tables I and II). One-half of the Vassar women and the great majority of the Smith and Wellesley women joined the settlement in a total of eight groups composed of two or more actual or near peers. Over three-fourths of these and the Bryn Mawr women (in sum, more than three-fifths of all college-educated CSA residents) had the opportunity of knowing well, at school, at least one other woman who was also to become a resident. And over two-thirds of all college-educated residents who remained longer than the requested three months were members of actual or near peer groups.

These figures reveal only a statistical correlation between residency and college peer groupings; they do not tell us who knew whom, although evidence in college records, memoirs, and autobiographies reveals close friendships among many founders. The correlation strongly indicates, however, that the settlements were not the outlets for the spontaneously expressed ideals or frustrations of Gilded Age college women that several historians would like us to see. Instead, these figures stimulate two interesting questions: Why were three colleges so heavily represented? And why was there so much variation in patterns of representation? We should start our inquiry by coming to an understanding of the state of women's higher education in the late nineteenth century.

The founder of Wells College nicely summarized the educational philosophy of pre-1875 women's colleges and seminaries when he pictured the ideal college as

TABLE I

CSA Peer Group Recruitment by College Class
and Year of Entry, by Percentage

College/ Peer Group	Vassar	Smith	Welles- ley	Bryn Mawr	Total	Others	Total
Primary[a]	20%	83%	50%	67%	58%	0%	46%
Secondary[b]	30	0	42	0	19	0	15
Primary and secondary	50	83	92	67	77	0	61
Nonpeers[c]	50	17	8	33	23	100	39
Total	100%	100%	100%	100%	100%	100%	100%
N	(10)	(18)	(12)	(3)	(43)	(11)	(54)

[a] Women from the same or successive college classes entering the settlement in the same year.

[b] Women from the same or successive college classes entering the settlement in successive years.

[c] Women not qualified for primary or secondary peer groups.

TABLE II

Summary: Number of Primary and Secondary
Peer Groups, by College

Groups/ College	Primary and Secondary Groups
Vassar	2
Smith	4
Wellesley	2
Bryn Mawr	1
Total	9

a "Home" in which, surrounded with appliances and advantages beyond the reach of separate families, however wealthy, young ladies may assemble to receive that education which shall qualify them to fulfil their duties as women, daughters, wives, and mothers, to practice that pleasant demeanor, to cultivate those womanly graces, to exercise that winning courtesy, which so befit those whom our mother tongue characterizes as "the gentler sex."

Wells, Mount Holyoke, Elmira, and Vassar were the more established of the early seminaries and "female colleges" in New England and upstate New York. These schools accommodated girls in their midteens to early twenties whose parents demanded little more than a couple of years of training in the feminine "accomplishments"—sewing, music, art, and "moral philosophy" or elementary religion. The degree was worth so little at Wells

that, in 1883, for example, there were twenty freshmen, fourteen sopho-
mores, nine juniors, and only two seniors. The authoritarian "lady principal" controlled social life, and the students were crammed into large, stuffy
dormitories or rooming houses. Prevailing medical opinion held outdoors
activity to be unhealthy for young women, so the students' extracurricular
life was limited to chapel, sewing, and discussions of religion. All involved,
from the trustees and the distant president down to the lowly student, were
single-minded in their devotion to what a Mount Holyoke teacher called
"that highest conception of the nineteenth century—a complete and consecrated womanhood." Following Barbara Welter, I shall call this all-important ideal "true womanhood." It was a cult on whose altar were displayed
the icons of purity, innocence, virtue, affection, service, and devotion to
duty.

Vassar was the most famous of the early women's colleges. Matthew
Vassar, a Poughkeepsie brewer, founded the school in 1860, firmly believing in the intellectual equality of men and women. Although the emphasis at
the school rapidly changed from the intellect to true womanhood, Vassar
differed from other women's colleges and seminaries in picturing its alumnae serving in places other than the home. College women, President John
H. Raymond said in 1871, would be lifted above "the average level" by
their education to become "wiser, truer, purer, nobler women," whose mission would be to commend high culture to the less fortunate by exemplify-
ing its beneficial effects.

By the mid-1870's, a competing philosophy of education for women
emerged. In two new colleges, Smith and Wellesley, intellectual discipline
received more emphasis than the accomplishments. The founding trustees
of Smith College first preached the gospel of discipline in their announce-
ment in 1872. The school's main purpose, they wrote, was to produce disciplined women who would be influences "in forming manners and morals,
moulding society, and shaping public sentiment" as teachers, missionaries,
and writers. Smith opened in 1875 to fourteen students carefully chosen by
the first president, the Rev. Lawrence Clarke Seelye.

Seelye, who was to remain at the college's head until 1910, was no less
devoted to the ideal of true womanhood than were his peers at older
schools, but he was careful to mix disciplined intelligence with purity in
his pedagogical brew. He felt that college aided women in two ways: It increased their efficiency, making them more valuable to society. But, more
importantly, as he once told his students, education forced women "to enlarge [their] capacities, that [they might] receive more of God's fullness
and to quicken [their] apprehension of those eternal verities out of which
right affection springs." Smith's original motto well summarized Seelye's
educational philosophy: "Add to your virtue, knowledge."

Wellesley College was founded in 1875 by Henry Fowle Durant, a colorful, pietistic, Boston philanthropist who tried to inspire moral purity, religious commitment, and feminine militancy in his students. "Moral

strength" best summarizes his educational philosophy, passed on after his death in 1880 through Wellesley's presidents and trustees. Everything he did—from making rowing mandatory to checking, like a nineteenth-century Cotton Mather, on the state of his students' souls—testified to his sense of mission. Durant firmly believed that God was calling woman "to come up higher, to prepare herself for great conflicts, for vast reforms in social life, for noble usefulness." Higher education was "but putting on God's armor for the contest," he wrote. . . . Durant's choice of a motto reveals, in a sentence, his commitment: from Dante he selected *"Incipit vita nuova"*— the new life begins. Although he differed with the heads of the other two colleges on the precise role of the educated woman, Durant shared with them a strong faith in her high status. The college-educated woman was now privy to an exclusive, extrafamilial calling.

As the emphasis in female higher education changed to the uniqueness of college women, such relatively unimportant details as curriculum and social arrangements came to be considered vital to proper schooling. The reforms of Charles W. Eliot at Harvard in the elective system and of Herbert Baxter Adams at Johns Hopkins in the teaching of the social sciences first began making their impact at the three colleges in the early 1880's. In Vassar's early years, the "discipline of the faculties" and the "furnishing of the mind" were not, as we have seen, of the highest priority. Eventually, faculty and alumnae pressure brought improvement in admissions and academic standards. By the mid-1880's, all three of the new colleges required laboratory science courses of their students. Smith and Wellesley offered multicourse programs in political science and political economy by the late 1880's. These were taught by such reformers as the Christian Socialist John Bates Clark, who was writing the essays that were to make up *The Philosophy of Wealth,* and Katherine Coman, an activist who was to help found the College Settlement Association.

Clark, who taught at Smith, fully agreed with President Seelye's conception of the active woman. He felt that the importance of his courses lay in "the direction that is given to the life studies that are to follow." At Wellesley, Katherine Coman gave courses that included discussion of the competitive system, of poverty and relief, of "the uses and abuses of public charity," and of anarchism and Christian Socialism. Wellesley, she once wrote, aimed to prepare women for active lives in a variety of fields. In a sentence highly revealing of her moderation as well as of her commitment, she voiced the hope that her courses would enable her students "to be tolerant and just in their action on the temperance question or on the textbook question, or the servant question."

A college does not manifest an educational philosophy through its curriculum alone; it also works through such social arrangements as regulations, social activities, and housing—what Cotton Mather long ago called "The Collegiate Way." A Smith alumna recognized the value of the Way in 1886:

I got something at Smith, in the way of class-feeling and college pride, which I value as much as anything I learned out of books there. There is a kind of discipline in the community of interests which a number of persons living together necessarily have.

In the same vein, the editors of the 1891 Wellesley yearbook wrote of the typical student club that, "by its work, its influence, its results, may be measured with considerable accuracy the conditions and value of the college education."

At Vassar, the students slept, ate, studied, and prayed together in the huge main hall. Their few clubs were class-centered, to the extent that a girl with friends in classes other than her own was thought unusual. These large organizations gathered periodically to discuss religion, to sing, or to put on plays. If anyone cut across class lines it was the suffragette Quaker astronomy teacher, Maria Mitchell. An annual party in the college observatory for "her" girls saw her lauding the students as persons who,

> lifting their hearts to the heavenly blue,
> Will do women's work for the good and the true
> And as sisters and daughters, or mothers or wives,
> Will take the star-sight into their lives!

Though a suffragette, Mitchell had a limited vision of the capabilities of college women.

The circumscribed group life of women's college[s] came under attack in the mid-1870's. As *Scribner's Monthly* suggestively put it, the women's college was a breeder of "diseases of body, diseases of imagination, vices of body and imagination—everything we would save our children from." These unnamed evils surely included neurasthenia and nervous breakdowns and might have included homosexual behavior. *Scribner's* felt that their origin lay in the strains of crowded living, and the magazine urged that students be housed in small cottages, so that *"there shall be a real family in every house,* and it shall not be hard for every woman to feel that, for the time, she is a member of it."

From their founding years, Smith and Wellesley honored this ideal. Privacy was as respected in social life as independence was eventually to be in intellectual activity. Most students occupied not large dormitories but single rooms in 25-resident cottages, each watched over by a housemother who, an alumna once wrote, was more "a counsellor and friend than a supervisor." Academic life was bounded by the class, but, unlike [at] Vassar, in social activities groups were small and independent. Each cottage had its own club, common room, and dining facilities. The two newer schools had one or two college-wide organizations to which all students belonged, but the focus of attention was on the small cottage clubs, some of which even sponsored newspapers and literary journals.

The faculty were influential at each of the three colleges and, in those pre-AAUP days, echoed their presidents' and founders' educational philosophies. Maria Mitchell's moderate feminism reflected Vassar's conception of the young lady, and she touched many of her students, judging from alumnae comments. At Smith, John Bates Clark's ideal of the active, constantly learning young woman matched that of President Seelye. But it is at Wellesley where we best see how the founder manifested his educational goals. The militant Durant established a policy of hiring only female instructors. He felt that strong, active women set the best example for their students. By the late 1880's, the Wellesley faculty included Katherine Coman, Vida Scudder, and Katherine Lee Bates, all founders of the College Settlement Association, and Ellen Hayes, who later, as Emily Greene Balch put it, dragged the Communist Manifesto into her astronomy lectures. Durant succeeded; the editors of the 1890 yearbook urged the freshmen to take the "noble faculty" for their model.

To summarize this discussion about life at the three schools, I should emphasize five elements differentiating it from that at older and more traditional colleges and seminaries. First, more emphasis was placed on student freedom and initiative, in social life as well as studies. Second, the schools encouraged the students to be well-rounded, to balance their studies with participation in extracurricular activities. Third, many of the students came into contact with what was, for the period, moderately advanced social thought, stressing women's activities outside the home. Fourth, the value of small, independent peer groups came to be emphasized, especially, at Smith and Wellesley, in the cottage system. And fifth and most important, the newer schools constantly impressed on the students their uniqueness and superiority to other young women. In a while, we will trace how the students bloomed in the hothouses of a new conception of womanhood. But, first, we should see how two later colleges, founded in the 1880's, differed from the three just described.

The Harvard Annex, soon to become Radcliffe College, was little more than an extension school, where most students took but one or three courses taught by Harvard instructors. Students lived in boarding houses or in their own homes and met for classes and tea in a small Cambridge house. Consequently, there was nothing approaching the intense community life institutionalized at Vassar, Smith, and Wellesley. There was not even a degree to identify the school—something a visiting Smith student found inconceivable.

The other new school was Bryn Mawr, certainly the most radical woman's college before the founding of Bennington in 1932. The educational philosophy of Bryn Mawr and of its determined dean, M. Cary Thomas, assumed a revolutionary conception of the role of the educated woman in America. Like the three colleges on which I have focused, the new college promised an education equal to that offered men. But Cary Thomas carried this promise to its logical conclusion. The older schools worked for a modified true womanhood; their alumnae would be educated, certainly, but they would be educated *women,* superior to their less disciplined sisters because they were hybrids of intellect and virtue. Thomas argued that the world of the intellect existed above considerations of sex. Only marriage and sexual needs—which the truly disciplined woman could control—stood between the educated female and high achievement. The Bryn Mawr woman's uniqueness was defined by her isolation from considerations of true womanhood. Her model of behavior was the male; the model of the Vassar, Smith, and Wellesley woman was the disciplined yet noble female.

Judging from undergraduate literature, the students at the three colleges shared their institutions' faith in their uniqueness. Vassar's class of 1878 floridly articulated this belief in its senior ode:

> The pioneers have bravely cleared the way,
> And claimed for us a better, broader life,
> A richer future, and they cannot pour
> The ripe fruits in our laps: 't is for us
> Which they so boldly claim for womanhood.

At first, they expressed this sense of mission in competitiveness with men. The motto of Smith's first student society (self-consciously called the Alpha) was *"Cur Non"*—why not, if such societies existed at men's colleges. President Seelye thought this fighting spirit unfeminine, but, by 1884, he was able to note happily that "the young ladies have ceased to fear that the intellectual character of the college will suffer by developing the utmost womanly traits."

The hybridization of discipline and womanliness was a constant theme in undergraduate essays, though the authors were more concerned with domesticity than with social activism. "Has the educated woman a duty towards the kitchen?" a Vassar student asked. Her answer was that the kitchen is exactly where the college woman belongs: The orderly, disciplined, independent graduate is the woman best prepared to manage the home, in which lies the salvation of the world. A Smith alumna argued that "the breadth of college culture" reveals to the young woman, "the necessities and duties of a practical and useful life," among them housekeeping. "We are making experiments here on a small scale in our miniature households, clubs, and societies," a Smith student confidently noted. "We are gaining in experience, self-confidence and readiness of resource. . . . We are acquiring the prudential virtues of social life." And a Vassar undergraduate challenged her classmates to "do our part royally, then, as becomes daughters of our Alma Mater, thinking no work too humble for our hands, no ideal too lofty for our lives."

Thus it was that the college woman's values, expectations, norms, and self-perceived status were defined by her college experience. Her referent was not solely that of the sexless college graduate, as symbolized by the intellect alone, or purely that of the true woman, as symbolized by the accomplishments alone. Rather, it was that of a new hybrid of these two cultures—an individual with a responsibility to the union of disciplined intellect and home. Secure in her status, this young woman left the college and "returned" to late-nineteenth-century society. She had her hopes of what to expect of middle-class America, but what was middle-class America to expect of her?

Like her less-well-educated sister, the female college graduate of the 1880's was meant to serve society in one of three socially approved activities: marriage, charity work, or teaching. The highest calling was marriage and child-rearing. "The true profession of every woman is that of Queen," went a typical comment. "For this she was created, to rule wisely and well over 'A Woman's Kingdom,' a well-ordered home." It is well worth noting that this quotation comes from an educational journal that closely followed the continuing development of women's higher education. The single woman did volunteer charity work, if she had an independent income. But, if she lacked for money, she was left with but one approved occupation: "How much," a wail went up in 1885—"How much is the time to be desired when so many avenues of useful and honorable work shall be open to women that teaching will no longer be regarded as the one available resource of the cultivated but impecunious lady."

The iron hand of the service norm policed Vassar, Smith, and Wellesley graduates as strictly as it did other young middle-class women in the Gilded Age. The popular image of the college woman—both then and now—is that of a liberated spirit. But close study of the postgraduate lives of some five hundred Smith and Vassar alumnae leads one to agree with a contemporary observer who described college women as "conservative, retiring, and more apt to disappoint expectation by differing too little than too much from other respectable, conventional folk—exactly as college men do." Only four of these women, from ten classes between 1868 and 1891, never married or taught school. The majority of the 37 women who went to graduate school became college teachers or doctors, and most of the doctors married.

The standard voluntary way to satisfy the service norm was activity in organized charity, imported from England in the 1870's to replace the old relief societies. With their faith in the economic benefits of moral purity, their emphasis on record-keeping and "friendly visiting," and their terror of the consequences of class antagonism, the Charity Organization Society activists set two goals for themselves. They were to get the jobless off the relief rolls, and they were to bring to the workers something a mere job could not provide—culture, which, Josephine Shaw Lowell believed, would "make their lives not only easier, but richer and nobler, and more what a human life should be."

The founders of the first social settlements shared in organized charity's faith in the moral causes of poverty. The first one, Toynbee Hall, was formed in East London in 1884 by a group of Oxford students inspired by Matthew Arnold's faith in the redeeming influence of culture. They wanted the poor to come into contact with "the best thoughts and aspirations of the age" through knowing university men. The residents would themselves gain from their experience, which would "react most practically upon the thought of the educated classes upon whom, in a democratic country, falls so deep a responsibility for local and central good government."

In the fall of 1887, when Stanton Coit formed America's first settlement, the short-lived Neighborhood Guild, and two years before Jane Addams was to decide to move into the slums of Chicago, a group of Smith alumnae visiting their alma mater got to talking about charitable institutions. One of these young women was Vida Dutton Scudder, of the class of 1884, an Episcopalian disciple of that Gilded Age religious phenomenon, Phillips Brooks, and a Christian Socialist like her teacher John Bates Clark. She had spent half a year at Oxford and told her companions of her work with the Salvation Army in London and of Toynbee Hall, which she knew only by reputation. The settlement idea immediately appealed to the young women, but their attempts to raise funds for such a project met with parental fears about their safety. Unlike the wealthy orphan Jane Addams, they had parents who asserted control through the pocketbook.

An article Scudder wrote at the time for an Episcopalian weekly indicates how openly college women received the settlement idea. She most admired Toynbee Hall for its realism; for, unlike organized charity, the settlement did not waste its energies on the jobless—the most helpless of the poor. Rather, it wisely focused its attention on "the most-valuable and self-respecting of the working class," whose greatest needs were for beauty, brightness, and culture. Why, Scudder asked, should not women take part in this kind of work, in which "the most effective instruments are usually supposed to be womanly tact, sympathy, and devotion"? Volunteers, "united and sympathetic in tastes, ideals, desires," would live together in a boardinghouse, where they would teach their neighbors "a few of the practical things which the better classes of the poor in our great cities so desperately need to know," especially housekeeping. In addition to teaching these skills, the settlement residents would work to instill in their neighbors "the spiritual and hidden wealth of a sensitive nature attuned to beauty, a mind rejoicing in its own fair powers, a soul rejoicing in the unseen." And the residents would also benefit, Scudder continued. Their confrontation with the basic facts of life would be educational, and the resulting "hearty, mutual comprehension and friendship between classes" would help society to "avert our social dangers."

Vida Scudder joined the Wellesley faculty as an English instructor in the fall of 1888. Her enthusiasm for the settlement was contagious, and soon two colleagues, Katherine Coman and Katherine Lee Bates, and a young trustee, Cornelia Warren, were helping her to raise funds from a variety of college women, philanthropists, and clergymen. They bought a house—"one of the wonderful old survivals of a formerly aristocratic quarter"—on Rivington Street on New York's Lower East Side and appointed as paid head resident Jean Fine, a member of the group that first discussed settlements at Smith two years earlier. Five other Smith and Wellesley women, paying six dollars a week for room and board, moved in with her in September, 1889.

What were their intentions? We can summarize the founders' conception of the needs of their neighbors in four words: virtue, entertainment, work, and home. The first would be satisfied by constant contact with the noble residents—women, a visitor reported, honest, truthful, gentle, kind, unselfish, and helpful. But, Jean Fine told the visitor, only the younger children could possibly benefit from the residents' example; it was too late for their elders to unlearn their bad habits.

Children's clubs would satisfy the second need with constructive entertainment. The girls could join the Good Seed Club to learn about flowers; the boys had the Hero Club, which revealed the "elements of success," and the Knights of the Round Table, where they learned how to be "chivalrous and true." Dues were charged to inculcate self-respect, to encourage self-government, and, probably, to exclude the offspring of the "helpless" and "useless."

The founders shared a Puritan's faith in the redeeming nature of work, especially for children. "It is not the lack of money which is the poverty we most deplore," wrote the head resident of the Philadelphia settlement, "but the lack of self-hood, that self-hood that comes from work and makes it a blessing even though it is a bitter struggle for existence." The settlement, she continued, should urge work on the young jobless, "happy in an idleness that means soul-stagnation."

For us, the most interesting of the needs of the poor as seen by the founding settlement residents was that for a proper home life. As William E. Bridges has documented, Americans at this time saw the home, the family, and true womanhood united in defense of traditional morality against the encroachments of materialism. The popular preacher and writer Edward Everett Hale could define "home" not in social or economic terms but as a collection of feminine virtues: "With this word always comes the idea of family, of feminine presence, of woman's patient sympathy and tender care." The settlement was to exemplify to neighborhood women the virtues of "pure, true, simple living," with the residents recreating the genteel atmosphere of their own upbringing. Settlement life, wrote a founder years later, "was all very satisfying and natural."

Her pleasant memory gives us a clue to the expressive value of the settlement house for its residents: Perhaps the life was so satisfying *because it was so familiar*. We might now take a look at the self-conceptions of the early settlement residents to see what they reveal about the attractiveness of the settlement as home, as "colony." The self-image of the founders breaks up into three general attitudes, each reflecting a self-consciousness about being well-educated women living together among the poor. One was a strong sense of adventure, "an abandonment," a founder wrote, "of ourselves to the life and to whatever might come along that charmed us all." They were inspired by the British Christian Socialists and Tolstoy to embrace "Lady Poverty" and lead a simple life. Abandonment also took form in claims of brotherhood with the poor, which the "Return to the People" movement of the young Russian aristocrats and Walter Besant's novels about peasant hospitality served to inspire. To the founders, brotherhood precluded charity; this was not a relationship between donor and receiver but one between equals, and the founders were sensitive about being labeled philanthropists.

But beneath these claims of equality lay a second attitude, a sense of *noblesse oblige*. Tolstoy did, after all, have his work shirts tailored in silk. For example, residents contrasted the simple beauty of the settlement house—its paintings showing "refinement, taste, travel, culture"—with the dirty children playing within. One founder emphasized this vivid contrast in picturesquely describing an encounter between a resident and a neighborhood boy:

> She met him in the hall [of the settlement house], as she came home from church, and with the street door wide open, she stooped and kissed him, as she would have her own small brother, making quite unconsciously a beautiful picture for the stunned inhabitants of Rivington Street.

Clearly, then, for all the claims of equality and brotherhood, there was a gulf between the residents and their neighbors.

The founding residents also saw a gulf between themselves and other women. They thought of themselves as unique, not because they were the first settlement residents, but because they were members of the first generation of college women. Ascribing to themselves a new and special status—"a new factor in the social order," Vida Scudder said of them in the late 1880's—the settlement founders saw college women acting as mediators between the idle rich and the working poor. These new women had the best of two virtues, true womanhood and discipline. They were, Scudder boasted, "women of the new order," no longer willing "to be put in niches and worshipped as saints . . . nor to be put in the chimney-corner and relegated to stockings." Instead, through such institutions as the settlement, they were able to join in doing the world's work.

These feelings of uniqueness and mission were formalized in the founding of the College Settlement Association in 1890. The CSA would "unite all college women, and all who would count themselves our friends, in the trend of a great modern movement; would touch them with a common sympathy and inspire them with a common ideal." The CSA, then, was *a voluntary association of college women rather than an association of settlement residents*. On this basis, the founders emphasized the benefits of the settlement and the settlement movement for themselves, as college women. "Many of us feel that the new conceptions of life we have gained are of far more worth than anything we have been able to give our neighbors," a resident wrote. "We feel that we know life for the first time." They used academic terminology: The settlement was "a graduate school in life" for women "whose university is the outer world." And they used academic institutions: A resident drew up a syllabus of suggested readings;

fellowships were awarded [to] one or two recent college graduates to pay residency expenses.

The family and home aspects of settlement life received even more attention than the academic. A critic once accused the house of being little more than a women's club. Vida Scudder angrily responded that only men instinctively form clubs: women form homes. The self-contained, independent settlement "family" consisted of a paid head resident, who was more advisor than supervisor; her assistant; a resident doctor; one or two fellowship residents; a half dozen or so paying residents who were expected to stay at least three months and a few visitors who could stay for several weeks at a time. Each resident had her own room on an upper floor. Claims about the moral benefits of work notwithstanding, the residents hired a cook and a maid for heavy housework.

The head resident and the nonresident Association secretary jointly selected residents from among the many applicants. Judging from the backgrounds of 36 of the 188 CSA residents in the first ten years, the typical worker was small-town-born and college-educated. She was likely to have taught in a private secondary school immediately after graduation, although several taught in public schools and colleges, became librarians, and went to graduate school, in declining order of preference. Graduate students studied medicine and nursing in the United States and academic subjects in Europe. The typical settlement resident was active and had traveled, if only to get to her college. She seems to have been uninterested in organized charitable work.

Having come to an understanding of the goals of the settlement founders, of the self-conceptions and recruitment patterns of the early residents, and of their backgrounds in the women's colleges of the Gilded Age, we can begin to develop answers to the questions stimulated by the statistics at the opening of this essay, which can be summarized: Why was the settlement house so attractive to college women and especially to groups of women from three colleges? This summary analysis will take the form of a discussion of the four ascriptive characteristics of the CSA settlements: as charity, as social movement, as "colony," and as voluntary association.

Although its founders were repelled by the word, most Americans would regard the settlement as a charity. As such, residency satisfied what I have called the service norm and thus made the settlement a socially approved institution, a functional alternative to marriage, teaching, and organized charity. However, this characterization only tells us why the settlement was a charity; it does not indicate why it took the form it did.

The CSA shared another characteristic with organized charity, since they were both social movements. But, where the National Conference of Charities and Correction unified supporters of a value—the merits of organized, "scientific" charity—the CSA brought together women of a common status, "all college women, and all who would count themselves our friends." Social movements centering, like the CSA, around a group norm and expectation are generally fostered by strains creating "demands for readjustment in the social situation." These strains result when a sub-system of society changes more rapidly than other subsystems and its members experience an alteration of expectations. As we have seen, with the development of the disciplined, true woman hybrid at Smith, Wellesley, and, to a lesser extent, Vassar, a rather sizable number of college women assumed a new self-image and, simultaneously, a group norm centering around their uniqueness and felt superiority. As Katherine Coman put it, these women were "particularly sensitive to the principles of *noblesse oblige*. So much has been given them of intellectual and spiritual treasure that they feel under heavy obligation to the world."

Yet, when these women, overflowing with confidence and optimism, left the closed group of their college years, they entered a culture not only unused to well-educated females but, more importantly, also utterly unfamiliar with women so self-conscious about their uniqueness vis-à-vis other women. They felt scorned, rejected. Emily Greene Balch was annoyed that going to college in the 1880's "was to feel oneself a marked character in the neighborhood, when returning as a college graduate meant to be constantly met with the would-be amusing protest that people were afraid to talk with me, I was so learned." College *men* encouraged no such cynical honor. A *Nation* parody of how an older woman of the period felt about college women was probably not too much of an exaggeration. The educated female, this lady would think,

> is undomestic in her habits and unfeminine in her tastes . . . [,] takes the initiative in conversation, is perpetually agitating for some "cause," or "reform," is ill-dressed and untidy, in fact regards dress as an unimportant matter, and the desire to attract the attention and interest of men as "frivolous."

The point here is not that this description was true. In some cases it must have been, in most cases it probably was not. Rather, this quotation is valuable because it reveals, even as a parody, a widely believed myth articulated in type-casting.

Facing such antagonism, some young college graduates, like Marion Talbott of Boston University's class of 1880, were forced to doubt the value of their education because it provided neither friends nor a niche in their communities. In 1882, Talbott helped found the Association of Collegiate Alumnae, which was "to unite alumnae of different institutions for practical educational work"—mainly, it appears, by encouraging girls to go to college and helping to resocialize them into middle-class America when they graduated.

Other college women, however, were more convinced of the worth of their education, however unsure they were of America's ability to agree. The problem was not simply one of fitting in; rather, as one CSA founder put it. "Some of us were not yet sure that the world needed us—in any case it was not evident where, or for what." They required, Jean Fine wrote, "a place in the world where we may *help* and be helped." So convinced were they of their own uniqueness and talents, and so set were they in their mission, that they could not simply retire into the inward-looking Associate of Collegiate Alumnae and lick their wounds. "We were looking," Vida Scudder proudly wrote, "to widen horizons beyond our own borders."

So, these young women needed an institution and an activity that would, first, satisfy the service norm as well as their sense of mission and that, second, would support their vulnerable status so that they might regain the equilibrium they had been secure in at college. The seminary woman had no such need, for her education had but socialized her into the traditional female role. Likewise, the Bryn Mawr graduate had few of these problems, since her expectations had not been raised by a faith in the ultimate compatibility of true womanhood and sexless intellect. The problem was unique for the cultural hybrid—the Vassar, Smith, and Wellesley woman.

To solve the problem, she innovated by constructing a new institution and a new role out of bits and pieces of the most familiar institutions and roles. Thus it was that the third of the settlement's ascriptive characteristics, its "colony" structure, was a reproduction. The founders appropriated the most indelible institutions of their alma maters, which had literally fostered and mothered the self-conceptions whose clash with dominant standards made these women so ill at ease. We have already seen how they borrowed academic jargon. Even more interestingly, they imitated the Smith and Wellesley cottage. Both the settlement and the cottage were "homes" for "families" of women "with congenial tastes, common interests, and independent convictions." Both were self-sufficient and self-contained institutions, serving as moral and social centers for the occupants and the immediate community. In each "home," the emphasis was on individual privacy alongside group activity overseen by older and more experienced women, more friendly advisors than supervisors.

In addition, the settlement's recruitment patterns clearly reflect the cottage system's emphasis on small peer groups. The high proportion of Smith and Wellesley women who entered the College Settlements at the same time as classmates and near-classmates indicates that peer group influence was an important factor behind their decision to become settlement residents. Vassar, where there was relatively less emphasis on small student groups, was represented in the CSA settlements by fewer and smaller peer groups. The prevalence and patterning of peer and near-peer groups among residents was not accidental, and neither was the structural similarity between the settlement and the cottage. Both represented the need of certain college women for a familiar and stable "home" in a hostile world. Through its social arrangements and "family" and academic rhetoric alone, the settlement as colony was functional.

Its geographical location was also functional. These young women felt a uniqueness that society did not recognize as constructive. In their attempt to define and institutionalize a unique, but socially approved, role, the founders constructed a social class that was above, yet part of, all other classes—a kind of superclass characterized by living a genteel, middle-class home life in the midst of poverty. The doctrine of the settlement as home, not charity, supported this uniqueness. Since the poor were not clients but guests invited to share the benefits of "respectable" home life, the hostesses could restrict the right of entry to those most appreciative of the values within. Not only could a resident kiss a poverty-stricken boy in the doorway of a middle-class home, but she could also choose which boy to kiss.

But the self-image of these women was not limited to uniqueness, for the hybrids saw themselves as superior women of rare ability and dedication. To defend this high status against the ravages of an unbelieving society, they isolated themselves through the mechanisms of an exclusive voluntary association. By tightly restricting membership, such organizations served a vital function for members of felt and actual high-status groups by re-affirming hierarchy. In the CSA settlements, noncollege women desiring admission as residents had to swear fealty to values asserting the special mission of college women. The former thus made the latter group their referent, even though they were not natural members. In this way, the settlement's founders asserted their felt superiority as college women by asserting an aristocracy of merit that was identical with a defense of a vulnerable status.

The settlement, then, was functional for our college women in four inter-connected ways. As a philanthropy, it was a socially approved alternative to a very few service activities. As a "colony," the institution was dually functional: It was a reconstruction of a familiar ideological and social "home" for young college women confused by a hostile world; and it was a middle-class outpost that concretized an otherwise abstract sense of uniqueness. Finally, as an exclusive voluntary association, it articulated—as no other institution could—the college woman's sense of superiority over other young women.

My analysis of the settlement as the product of a cultural rather than of a purely moral or ideological conflict is not an attempt to denigrate it as an institution that was eventually to play an instrumental role in social and political reform. Neither am I arguing that all Vassar, Smith, and Wellesley women were even to be attracted to settlement residency. As a student of English Puritanism has written in a somewhat similar analysis, "None of these group experiences make individual conversion predictable, each of them makes it comprehensible." To view the settlement as I have is to see it as a child—a rather gangling child—of a period of painful cultural transition and not simply as an impulsive, institutionalized Topsy.

The Integration of Higher Education into the Wage-Labor System*

Samuel Bowles

INTRODUCTION: FROM IVORY TOWER TO SERVICE STATION

> At least there is tolerably general agreement about what a university is not. It is not a place of professional education. Universities are not intended to teach the knowledge required to fit men for some special mode of gaining their livelihood.—J. S. MILL

> More knowledge has resulted from and led to service [by the university] for government and industry and agriculture. . . . All of this is natural. None of it can be reversed. . . . The campus has evolved consistently with society. . . . The university and segments of industry are becoming more and more alike. . . . The two worlds are merging.—CLARK KERR

The appearance of a radical student movement and the organization of radical professional and other white-collar workers in the late 1960's and early 1970's raise important questions: Will this radicalism among the highly educated play an important role in bringing about revolutionary changes in U.S. society? Or will unemployment and job insecurity among college graduates, along with the financial crisis of higher education, discipline young people to accept—if begrudgingly—the contours of U.S. society more or less as they are? Is the recent relative quiet of the campuses a sign that the movement has been assimilated, bought off, isolated, or destroyed? Or will it reappear, grow, and coalesce with radical movements among women, blacks, and workers in other sectors of the society?

Answers to these questions will be sought in an analysis of the economic and social forces underlying the movement. I will argue that the student movement and radicalism among young white-collar workers and professionals are manifestations of structural weaknesses endemic to the corporate capitalist system and that the continuing evolution of the capitalist

* This paper grew out of discussions with Herbert Gintis and owes much to his "The New Working Class and Revolutionary Youth," *Review of Radical Political Economics*, II, no. 2 (Summer, 1970). I have benefited from the comments of many friends: from John Judis, Eli Zaretsky, Margaret Levi, Keith Aufhauser, and Bill Lazonick, and particularly from the members of the Union of Radical Political Economics seminar at Harvard. An unabridged version appears in the *Review of Radical Political Economics*.

Copyright © 1973 by Samuel Bowles.

system will exacerbate these weaknesses and thus help to create the opportunity for radical change in the United States.

Central to my argument is the new political and economic importance of colleges and universities. Two hundred years ago, the college was an elite cultural community existing on the periphery of the social and economic mainstream.

At Harvard, Yale, William and Mary, and a few others, some—but by no means all—of those who would enter the learned profession were trained and certified. The tradition of classical scholarship was maintained. Even among the economic elite of the day, college attendance was the exception rather than the rule, a cultural luxury more than an economic or social necessity. In fact, no part of the formal educational system, not even elementary education, was particularly central to the process by which the economic order was reproduced and extended.

Higher education in the United States has come a long way in two centuries. Half of the relevant age group now attend post-secondary educational institutions. Colleges and universities have come to play a crucial part in the production of labor, in the reproduction of the class structure, and in the perpetuation and emendation of the dominant values and ideologies of the social order.

Higher education has taken its place alongside other types of schooling and the family as part of the process by which the corporate capitalist labor force is reproduced: Higher education has been integrated into the wage-labor system. This fact is of the utmost importance, for it bids us broaden our theoretical perspective on the sources and processes of social change and the nature of contradiction in the capitalist system.

In this essay, I will formulate both a description and a theoretical interpretation of the ways in which the contradictory developments of the forces of production and the relations of production are manifested in the evolution of higher education in the United States. I hope that this analysis will provide a useful framework for the development of strategies for radical social change.

In the second section of the paper (condensed from a longer version), I trace the historical role of schooling in ameliorating and depoliticizing the class conflicts associated with the accumulation of capital and the extension of the wage-labor system. In addition I discuss the ways in which the present structure of higher education operates to reproduce the class structure of the United States. In the third section, I survey the recent evolution of the social relations of production in the U.S. economy and the accommodation to these changes in the transformation of the structure and content of higher education. In the fourth section, I explore the ways in which these changes impinge on student life and argue that the strains associated with the transformation of higher education are manifestations of fundamental contradictions that have their origin in the structure of the corporate capitalist economy. The student response—at once radical and backward-looking—is analyzed and the possibilities for radical change are assessed in the concluding section.

THE SOCIAL FUNCTIONS OF HIGHER EDUCATION

I have never considered mere knowledge . . . as the only advantage derived from a good . . . education. . . . [Workers with more education] are more orderly and respectful in their deportment, and more ready to comply with the wholesome and necessary regulations of an establishment. . . . In times of agitation I have always looked to the most intelligent, best educated, and the most moral for support. The ignorant and uneducated I have generally found the most turbulent and troublesome, acting under the impulse of excited passion and jealousy.—A Lowell, Mass., textile manufacturer writing to Horace Mann, Secretary of the Massachusetts Board of Education, 1841

Capital accumulation has been a driving force behind the transformation and growth of the U.S. economy. Living labor is combined in production with increasing amounts of past labor—in the form of schooling and training as well as machinery and other equipment. Two important aspects of the process of capital accumulation may be identified. The first is an expansion of the forces of production—the productive capacities of the economy—with a consequent rapid and sustained increase in the output of goods and services per worker. The second is an equally dramatic transformation of the social relations of production, manifested in the reduction of ever increasing segments of the U.S. population to the status of wage labor. By the social relations of production, I mean the rules of authority among those engaged in production, the system of control over the work process, and the relations of property that govern the ownership of the product. The continued proletarianization of the U.S. labor force—which may be considered the other side of the ever rising gross-national-product coin—has not been a placid process of gradual accommodation to economic progress. Workers, at least since the 1840's, have fought to retain control over their labor and its products.

The structure of U.S. education evolved in response to political and economic struggles associated with this process of capital accumulation and the extension of a structure of production—the wage-labor system—in which the vast majority of workers surrender control over their labor in return for wages or salaries. The main periods of educational expansion and reform are coincident with the integration of major groups of workers into the wage-labor system and were a response by the capitalist class to the political and economic conflicts arising from this continued expansion of capitalist production relations. Thus, the two decades prior to the Civil War—which saw the rapid extension of public primary education and the consolidation of schools —were also a period of labor militancy associated with the rise of the factory system and the "degradation of the worker." The progressive education movement, spanning the period from the 1890's to the 1920's, can be seen as a response to conflicts associated with the integration of peasant labor, both immigrant and native, into the burgeoning corporate capitalist relations of production.

The modern U.S. educational system had its origins in the need of the capitalist clans to ameliorate class conflict and obscure class interests so as to facilitate the uninterrupted accumulation of capital and extension of the wage-labor system. The recent political conflict and impetus for reform in U.S. colleges and universities are hardly unprecedented; indeed, they are merely the manifestation at a higher level of forces that earlier propelled the history of U.S. education at the elementary and secondary levels. A crucial force behind the current ferment, I will argue, is the continuing proletarianization of white-collar and previously self-employed labor, which has brought both student expectations and the structure of U.S. higher education into conflict with the social relations of production of the corporate capitalist economy.

The particular intensity of recent conflict and reform efforts in U.S. education is a response to the integration of two major groups into the wage-labor system: uprooted Southern blacks and the once-respectable "solid" members of the precorporate capitalist community: the small-business people, the independent professionals, and other white-collar workers. Both groups have made an impact on education, the first mainly in elementary and secondary education, the latter chiefly in higher education. The expansion of the wage-labor system has also made an impact on the position of women and on the family. An important impetus for the current women's movement can be found in the integration of women into the wage-labor system and the penetration of commodity relations to the core of family life, as more and more "household services" are bought and sold on the market. The historical coincidence of the integration into the wage-labor system of these three groups—women, blacks, and previously independent nonmanual workers—and the associated confluence of political movements associated with the process are a reflection of the law of uneven development. The fact that all these groups are undergoing a similar process, but from very different starting points, presents at once a great opportunity and challenge to radicals: How can the disparate consciousness of these three groups be brought together with other potentially revolutionary groups? A theory and description adequate to our political needs would, of course, require a unified treatment of women, blacks, students, white-collar workers, younger or blue-collar workers, and others. The objective of this paper is more modest. I will dwell primarily on the political opportunities associated with the proletarianization of the previously independent white-collar group.

Assessing the political implications of the contradictions of the corporate capitalist economy and educational system requires an understanding of the two major social functions of higher education, namely, the reproduction of the social relations of production and the expansion of the forces of production.

The social relations of production are reproduced by equipping workers, technicians, and bosses alike with a set of skills, attitudes, and values that strengthen both the legitimacy of the hierarchical division of labor as a structure and each person's sense of deserving treatment within that structure. The social relations of production are reproduced in yet another sense: An individual's position in the hierarchical division of labor is to an important extent dependent upon the class position of his or her parents.

For the past century, at least, schooling has contributed to the reproduction of the social relations of production largely through the correspondence between school structure and class structure. Specifically, the social relations of education—the relations between students and teachers, students and students, and students and their work—replicate the social relations of production. The conditions of office or factory are reflected in the student's lack of control over his or her education, in the irrelevance of school work to the student's own interests, in the motivation of work by a system of grades and other external rewards rather than by the student's interest in either the process of production (learning) or the product (knowledge), in the persistent and ostensibly objective ranking and evaluation of students, in the emphasis on discipline and acceptance of authority, and in the supremacy of strict and unvaried routine. By attuning young people to a set of social relations similar to those of the work place, schooling teaches future workers not so much how to work as how to behave.

Moreover, the amount and kind of education received by each child are closely correlated with the position of his or her parents in the hierarchy of work relations. Those whose parents occupy subordinate positions in the production hierarchy are ordinarily enrolled in schools that lay heavy stress on the types of behavior required in those work roles: obedience and the ability to follow instructions. The sons and daughters of people holding positions of authority in the work hierarchy are usually educated in more "progressive" institutions—suburban high schools and liberal arts colleges, for example—which lay greater stress upon developing the student's ability to use information and to make independent decisions. Thus, the educational system plays an important part in the intergenerational reproduction of the social relations of production.

The fact that colleges and universities have often been centers of radical discontent should not lead one to believe that higher education is an exception to these general principles. Like the rest of the school system, higher education has aided in the expansion of the productive capacities of the nation, the reproduction of the social class system, and the legitimation of the resulting inequalities.

Higher education in the United States has made a major contribution to economic growth. Recent economic development has depended heavily upon organizational and technical change—in short, upon the ability to devise new things to be produced and new ways to produce old things. Rapid technical and organizational change and the associated increase in output per capita have led to major shifts in the occupational structure. Particularly notable has been the rapid increase in the number of technicians and other white-collar workers—highly skilled and well educated but excluded from the central decision-making powers. Higher education has had a hand in the development of new technologies, both through the research sponsored at major universities and through the training of research personnel to work for private firms or for the government. Equally important, higher education has been a major producer of labor—labor with the skills and attitudes appropriate to the new methods of production and the changed occupational structure. Higher education is the last stage of the long process of socialization and training for those who will move into positions of authority or expertise in the occupational hierarchy of our society. It has been called the most complex initiation rite ever devised, but it is not simply a labeling ceremony. A college education contributes to a person's future income, in part through the knowledge gained in college. Of equal or greater importance are the patterns of behavior and the attitudes toward work, toward one's fellow workers, and toward authority that are inculcated in college. It is these attitudes and behavior patterns, more than the cognitive skills acquired in college, that facilitate the entrance of college graduates into the upper levels of the hierarchy of work relations.

The fact that, until recently, students in higher education were destined for relatively similar positions at the top of the occupational hierarchy allowed colleges and universities to perform this socializing function through the imposition of a set of rules or procedures that effectively prepared students for positions of power in business, the professions, and government. The social relations of the colleges reflected the social relations of production into which the students would enter in their adult life. There were few rules, and most of them could be gotten around; a wide choice of courses and majors was offered; the student was trained to exercise a considerable amount of independent discretion, as well as authority over much of his or her own affairs.

Thus, the social relations of college education have helped to produce graduates capable of the effective exercise of authority in large organizations. At the same time, the content of the curriculum has been geared to the production of graduates with the specialized knowledge and skills needed in the performance of the high-level bureaucratic and technical roles into which college graduates move.

But it is not merely through its contribution to the forces of production that higher education has served to maintain existing social institutions. It has also played a direct role in the reproduction of the social relations of production.

Whatever determined the occupational success of the older generation of the corporate elite—inherited wealth, nepotism, ability, theft, political power, or ambition—it is clear that, in order to reproduce this success, the next generation is virtually required to obtain a college degree. This reproduction of class standing has been facilitated, to a remarkable extent, through unequal access to higher education. Although the class position of parents is only weakly approximated by their income level or other measures of social "status," such as educational level or occupation, some notion of the extent of differential class access to higher education can be gained from the following data. According to U.S. Census data for the late 1960's, even among those who had graduated from high school, children of families earning less than $3,000 per year were over six times as likely *not* to attend college as were the children of families earning over $15,000. Children from poorer families were also much less likely to graduate from high school; and, for those who did attend college, much more likely to enroll at the inexpensive, less prestigious colleges, particularly two-year rather than four-year institutions..

Access to higher education by a limited number of children of working-class families has served a number of important functions. It has lent credence to the myth of equal opportunity. At the same time, it has allowed the recruitment of new talent for the positions of power or expertise in the occupational hierarchy. Last, by allowing some aggressive and able working-class children to make it, it has provided a safety valve for the class system and, thus, served to drain off potential leadership from the working class.

Higher education in the United States has served not only to reproduce the class structure but to justify it. The fact that inequalities in educational credentials "fairly" gained have been added on to inequalities of class background has served to hide the importance of class itself in getting ahead. And, because higher education has ostensibly been open to all, and promotion within the educational system has appeared to depend solely on one's own achievements, those who are successful tend to be seen as deserving. Partly for this reason, the bitterness arising from one's job or one's income or status is often directed against oneself rather than against the social system or those whose "success" was facilitated—if not predetermined —by that system. Radical thrusts against the dominant groups in society are blunted by the sentiment that "It's only fair; they have the education to do the job." By this same line of reasoning, poverty is often "blamed" on the poor: They are referred to as the "economically weak," not as the exploited.

Successful completion of higher education has thus come to confer a modern form of "right to rule" at least as persuasive and politically invulnerable as any of its divine, aristocratic, or plutocratic predecessors.

The growth of higher education itself has offered apparent verification of the myth in people's daily experiences. Because of the rapid growth of education at all levels, children are almost certain to attend school for a significantly longer period than their mothers and fathers did and so are likely to achieve a level of schooling that, in their parents' day, would have ensured high status and a good job. Thus, the educational system appears to be open and to sponsor a significant amount of mobility.

Quite apart from its role in verifying the myth of equal opportunity, college expansion, like the growth of per capita income, has helped to legitimize the capitalist system by demonstrating its capacity continually to produce more of everything. For many parents who themselves did not make it, the rapid growth of higher education has offered the satisfaction of having been able to provide well for their children.

THE PROLETARIANIZATION OF WHITE-COLLAR LABOR AND THE VOCATIONALIZATION OF HIGHER EDUCATION

> If we can no longer keep the floodgates closed at the admissions office, it at least seems wise to channel the general flow away from four year colleges and toward two year extensions of high school in the junior and community colleges.—AMITAI ETZIONI, *Wall Street Journal,* March 17, 1970

Continued capital accumulation and economic growth have provided the basis for a rapidly expanding system of higher education; they have also drastically altered the relationship of the educational system to the economy. The rapidly changing social relations of production under corporate capitalism has had two facets: The self-employed have become increasingly peripheral to the economy, and, at the same time, entire new cadres—technical and lower supervisory workers—have come to occupy a central role in the production system. Recent changes in U.S. higher education are an accommodation to these trends.

The expansion of capital, largely through accumulation by large corporations, has continued the integration of workers into the wage-labor system. Over the past century, the proportion of self-employed professionals and entrepreneurs to all economically active individuals has fallen from about two-fifths to less than a tenth; the relative numbers of salaried managers and professionals have multiplied by a factor of seven. And the relative number of wage earners has continued its steady rise. But these gross occupational categories obscure as much as they reveal: The nature of the labor process within occupations has been changing, too. Work tasks have become more fragmented, the mental processes associated with them more specialized, and the social relations defined by work roles more limiting. Even in many well-paid, high-status jobs, the worker's discretion is increasingly limited.

The case of teaching provides a good example. It is easy to imagine teaching as relatively integrated, unalienated labor. The teacher is in direct contact with his or her material and has at least a modicum of control over his or her work; given a sufficiently vivid imagination, he or she may even entertain illusions of social usefulness. However, the teacher's job has undergone subtle change. The educational efficiency binge of the 1920's led to the application of business-management methods to the high schools. The concentration of decision-making power in the hands of administrators and the quest for "economic rationalization" had the same disastrous consequences for teachers that bureaucracy and "rationalization" of production had on most other workers. In the interests of "scientific management," control of curriculum, evaluation, counseling, selection of texts, and methods of teaching were placed in the hands of "experts." A host of specialists arose to deal with minute fragments of the teaching job. The tasks of thinking, making decisions, and understanding the goals of education were placed in the hands of educational experts and bureaucrats.

Ostensibly to facilitate administration and reap economies of large-scale production, schools became larger and more impersonal. The possibility of intimate or complicated classroom relationships gave way to the social relations of the production line.

The fragmentation of tasks and the demise of intimate personal contact has not been limited to teaching but, rather, has pervaded all the "service" professions. The medical sector, for example, has seen the rise of large, impersonal medical bureaucracies, the ascendancy of specialists, and the demise of the general practitioner, who once ministered to the health of the whole body and the whole family.

Along with the virtual demise of the self-employed worker and the integration of white-collar labor into fragmented and hierarchically stratified work roles, the expansion of corporate capital has brought the rapid growth of new kinds of work. These new cadres include technicians, lower-level supervisory personnel, secretaries, nonretail sales workers, dental assistants, draftsmen, and paraprofessional personnel in medicine and education, to name just a few of the rapidly growing occupational titles.

The rapid growth in college enrollments has been in part a response to the needs generated by this changing occupational structure. The expansion of enrollments has, in turn, brought about two important changes in the social position of higher education. First is the increasing scientific, cultural, and social role of the college community. Second is the frank recognition that colleges have become the training ground for much more than the economic elite; community colleges and many four-year institutions have taken up the task of training the middle-level bureaucrats and technicians of the future. While the adaptation to both of these consequences of growth has, for the most part, preserved the fundamental functions of higher education, the adjustments are far from perfect and have revealed some of the underlying weaknesses of the corporate capitalist system. In the remainder of this section, I will argue, first, that the culture of the college community is anachronistic and dysfunctional, given its now greatly enlarged clientele, and, second, that the community-college movement may be seen as only a partly successful attempt to deal with some of the unsettling consequences of the increasing diversity of socialization functions that have been imposed on higher education by the increasing enrollments.

Over a century ago, Marx (in *Capital*, vol. I) foresaw that the continued expansion of the forces of production under capitalism might necessitate the development of a labor force whose skills and outlook would bring it into conflict with the social relations of production:

Modern industry compels society . . . to replace the detail worker of today, crippled by life-long repetition of one and the same trivial operation, and thus reduced to the mere fragment of a man, by the fully developed individual, fit for a variety of labors ready to face any change in production and to whom the different social functions he performs are but so many modes of giving free scope to his own natural and acquired powers.

But will such a labor force acquiesce in the social relations of corporate capitalist production? André Gorz expresses the problem succinctly:

> The problem for big management is to harmonize two contradictory necessities: the necessity of developing human capabilities, imposed by modern processes of production, and the political necessity of ensuring that this kind of development of capabilities does not bring in its wake any augmentation of the independence of the individual, provoking him to challenge the present division of social labor and distribution of power.

As long as the vast proportion of college students were destined for positions of leadership, the tradition of scholarship and unfettered inquiry was probably an appropriate context for college training. Yet, with over half of each age cohort continuing schooling after high school, it is clear that both leaders and followers are being trained. The educational processes best suited to training an elite may be less successful in fostering quiescence among followers. Incompatibility of functions seems certain to arise as higher education is forced to combine the teaching of intellectual skills with an increased role in the perpetuation of a conservative social mythology and the socialization of docility among middle-level workers. Moreover, the contradictions of the larger society increasingly impinge on the classroom. The struggles of blacks, women, Third World peoples, welfare recipients, and others have starkly revealed the seamy side of American reality and are rapidly serving to explode the legitimating ideologies taught in our colleges and high schools.

The political ramifications of a failure to adapt the culture and objectives of the university community to its new diversity of social functions are fairly obvious. The economic consequences are no less important. Skilled and professional labor power, like all labor power, is embodied in people. The process of embodiment—training and education—is time-consuming and is, for good economic reasons, undertaken at a young age, in large measure in specialized institutions: schools, colleges, and other training institutions. But skills are not learned in a vacuum. Because of the cultural environment of the traditional college community and the nature of many of the skills themselves, the educational process seems increasingly to provide the means but not the motivation to be a useful cog in the corporate capitalist system. Moreover, the fact that high-paid skills and competence are embodied in workers—and, unlike capital, cannot be severed from them—provides an insurance against dire poverty and economic hardship and thus relieves some of the economic pressures that force less well-educated labor into the labor market at the mercy of employers.

As a result, there have been strong barriers to the development of a market in skills and ideas in which services flow readily to the highest bidder. Teachers, researchers, and other college graduates may increasingly impose qualitative as well as monetary conditions upon the rental of their services to business and the government.

Recent tendencies in high-level teaching and research may be seen as only a partially successful attempt to deal with this problem. With the specialization of jobs in the economy has come a fragmentation of studies and research. Increasingly, no student, no researcher, is encouraged to deal with a whole problem, any more than a worker is allowed to produce a whole product. The artificial compartmentalization of intellectual pursuits allows the development of advanced technique within each area and simultaneously militates against the application of comprehensive moral standards or the consideration of the larger social consequences of one's work. The narrowing effect of academic specialization is furthered by the modern conception of professionalism, in which the intellectual is seen as a technician whose success may be adequately judged by his skill in devising technical solutions to technical problems.

In addition, the research functions of the intellectual community are increasingly severed from their university base, to be carried out in large private or government laboratories and institutes where the cultural climate is more favorable.

But these strategies are met with resistance from all sides. Researchers ordinarily prefer to be associated with a university, partly for reasons of status emanating from the peculiar culture of intellectuals and partly to maintain easy access to graduate students and the broader scientific community. Far more important, students at both the graduate and undergraduate levels increasingly reject specialization and "professionalism," demanding, instead, multidisciplinary approaches to whole problems.

The increasingly "vocational" orientation of intellectual pursuits fostered by today's colleges is but one outgrowth of the conflict between the traditional elite-training function of the university and the greatly expanded numbers of students enrolled. The growth of two-year colleges and postsecondary technical institutes is another manifestation of the same underlying problem—namely, the impossibility of accommodating half of each age cohort in "elite" institutions. The booming community-college movement has created a class stratification within higher education parallel to the hierarchical relations of production in the modern corporation. An expansion of the number of students in higher education has thus been made possible without undermining the elite status and function of the established institutions.

With a small fraction of each age group attending college, most could be accommodated at four-year institutions, graduation from which virtually ensured future economic and social success. Of course, there were always institutions that could not automatically confer status, but these were confined largely to a few fields (such as education and divinity) and to the South (particularly black colleges).

The idea that those who had made it into college had made it to the top did not survive the tremendous increase in enrollments. But it is not merely the expectation of success that has to change; the entire structure of higher education has become inadequate. A relatively uniform system of higher education enrolling so large a fraction of each age group would fail in a number of ways. The right to rule and the expectation of privilege would be extended to social groups that, in their jobs and their political activities, had previously exercised very little influence over their own lives or those of others. Unrealistic occupational and status expectations would be encouraged in working-class children; disappointment would undoubtedly result in discontent. Equally important, the social relations of the educational process itself—based on the notion that the colleges and universities were socializing an elite—would prove inappropriate when these institutions began training middle-level workers. Thus, a uniform system of higher education would foster discontent and competition for power, for it would legitimize the aspirations for power and wealth among much more than the old elite and would fail to inspire the expectations and submissiveness appropriate to the future work roles of most of the newcomers to postsecondary schooling.

Structural change in educational processes has thus been necessitated by two parallel movements: the growth in enrollments and the continuing change in the social relations of production, manifested in the fragmentation and routinization, in short, in the prolitarianization, of white-collar labor. The 1960's and 1970's thus present many parallels to the period around the turn of the present century, which saw the expansion of secondary education as a means of integrating peasant and working-class children into the wage-labor system.

The repetition in our colleges and universities of the high school expansion and stratification process has been under way for some time and for similar reasons. Concerns about poverty and racial discrimination and the desire to placate previously excluded middle- and lower-income families have given increased impetus to the movement.

Enrollments in community colleges are over three times what they were ten years ago and include by far the most rapidly growing body of college students. Higher education has developed a multitiered system, dominated at the top by the Ivy League institutions and the great state universities, followed by the state colleges, and ending with the community colleges. This system reflects both the social-status structure of the families of the students and the hierarchy of work relations into which the various types of students will move after graduation.

The results of a recent study of one of the more equalitarian systems—California's—illustrate this stratified system. Over 18 per cent of the students at the University of California in the mid-1960's came from families earning $20,000 or more, while fewer than 7 per cent of the students in community colleges (and fewer than 4 per cent of the youth who were *not* receiving higher education) came from such families. Similarly, while only 12.5 per cent of the students attending the University of California came from families earning less than $6,000, 24 per cent of those attending community colleges and 32 per cent of the youth not enrolled in higher education came from such families.

The segregation of students not destined for the top has allowed the development of procedures and curricula more appropriate to their future "needs" as defined by their actual occupational opportunities. The vast majority of students in community colleges are programed for failure, and great efforts are made—through testing and counseling—to convince students that their lack of success is objectively attributable to their own inadequacies. The process of bringing student hopes into line with the realities of the job market is facilitated by a tracking system within the community college much like the channeling system of high schools, with "four-year-college transfer programs" for the "promising" and vocational programs for the "dead-enders." The magnitude of the task of lowering student expectations can hardly be exaggerated, for at least three times as many entering community-college students want to complete four or more years of college as actually succeed in doing so. Fewer than half of community-college entrants receive even the two-year Associate of Arts degree. For those who stay, studies at community colleges are, much more often than in four-year colleges, explicitly vocational, emphasizing such middle-level goals as training in nursing, computer work, and office skills. The connection between the needs of business and the curricula of community colleges is fostered by business representation on advisory boards. The continuing vocationalization of the community-college curriculum is now actively being pushed by the business community, the federal government, and major private foundations, particularly the Carnegie Corporation.

The needs of the corporate elite are also reflected in the social relations of education at the community colleges. The student is allowed little discretion in selecting courses. Systems of discipline and student management resemble those of secondary education more than those of the elite universities; these colleges have been called "high schools with ashtrays." The teaching staff is recruited heavily from the corps of high school teachers. State legislatures exert pressure to increase teaching loads and class sizes and, in some cases, even to standardize curriculum and teaching methods. The social relations of the community-college classroom increasingly resemble the formal, hierarchical impersonality of the office or the uniform processing of the production line.

All this, of course, must be seen not as a failure of the community-college movement but, rather, as a successful adaptation to the tasks they were set up to perform: processing large numbers of students to attain that peculiar combination of technical competence and social acquiescence required in the skilled but powerless upper-middle positions in the occupational hierarchy of the corporate capitalist economy.

The vocational orientation of the community colleges is becoming more typical of U.S. higher education as a whole. This process is in large part a result of the rapid increase in the proportion of all college students who are enrolled in community colleges. Nor is this proportion likely to level off: Current projections are for the community-college enrollment to continue its rapid rise while total enrollment in all colleges slowly moves toward a plateau in the late 1970's or early 1980's. Four-year institutions thus stand to *lose* enrollments over the next decade. Moreover, the four-year institutions are likely to come under pressure for a "rationalization" of curriculum and educational method as the financial crisis of the colleges and universities intensifies. State legislatures and other funding bodies are already pushing for more job-relevant curricula, heavier teaching loads, and more teacher accountability at the four-year institutions.

THE EXPANSION OF CORPORATE CAPITAL AND THE CONTRADICTIONS OF STUDENT LIFE

We refuse to buy the right not to die of hunger by running the risk of dying of boredom!—Student slogan, Paris, May, 1968

Student life has been radically changed by the transformation of higher education. The rapid increase in enrollments over the past half-century, the central role of university research and personnel in the domestic and international expansion of corporate capital, the social stratification of higher education, the vocationalization of the curriculum, the rationalization of methods in order to process more students more cheaply—all these changes have impinged on students' daily experience. The process of change, though carefully engineered by university administrators and adroitly sold by apologists for the new order, has not been a placid one. Since the Berkeley uprising of the early 1960's, students in revolt against mechanized, mass-produced education have announced that they will not be folded, spindled, or mutilated. Attempts to relate the college community more directly to service to the state and the business community are met with ever more direct resistance. Attacks on ROTC and other campus war-related establishments have been widespread. The protest has extended to graduate students and young professionals. Dozens of radical professional organizations have sprung up, in medicine, sociology, the physical sciences, economics, psychiatry, engineering, law, city planning, and Asian, African, and Latin American studies, to mention just a few. These groups give tangible political expression to a growing commitment among students, young teachers, and other professionals that their function is not to administer society but to change it drastically. Dr. Edward Teller's recent assessment of the strength of the movement was clearly extravagant but heartening nonetheless. He told a Presidential commission that events in universities in 1969 and 1970 had "practically cut the connection between universities and defense related industries. . . . In twenty years," he warned, "the U.S. will be disarmed."

At least during full-employment periods, campus recruiters for big business and the government find a cooler reception than in the past. Direct political action, which was originally focused against companies in the war business, is now aimed at a much broader range of targets—General Motors, General Electric, Polaroid, and the Peace Corps, for example. Student attacks on campus recruitment by the U.S. Information Service, Department of State, and companies with substantial international operations are indications of the repugnance felt by many students at being trained to administer the U.S. world empire.

Assaults against the multitiered educational stratification system, pressures for open enrollment, and (among students already enrolled) demands for access to prestigious institutions have mounted. In New York City, Black and Puerto Rican students took the lead in "opening up" the previously highly selective city colleges. In Seattle and elsewhere, minority students have resisted being shunted into the newly formed vocational tracks at the bottom of the educational pyramid. Lagging attendance in specifically vocational programs has reflected a hostility, or at least massive indifference, to these curriculums. Across the country, women and blacks are demanding not middle-level vocational skills but an education that can help to fight sexism and racism.

Other responses have been less political. Some decide not to go to college at all. Some drop out. Many go and stay but turn on to drugs and turn off from intellectual and political pursuits.

Thus, the integration of U.S. higher education into the wage-labor system has produced political strain and a deep-seated malaise. This strain, this malaise, persists even during periods when an uneasy calm characterizes most campuses. For what we are witnessing is not the growing pains of a healthy organism but, rather, the manifestations of fundamental contradictions in the larger society.

The nature of the contradiction may be briefly summarized: The expansion of enrollments, like the expansion of capital, continues to be essential in legitimizing the class structure and allowing its reproduction from generation to generation. Yet, the material well-being and transformed social relations of production induced by the expansion of capital have produced an incongruence between the aspirations of college students, on the one hand, and the manpower requirements of the economy, on the other. In short, colleges can no longer make good their promises: Most students are simply not getting enough of what they want out of higher education. To the extent that students see college as an investment in a better job, three broad types of objectives may be identified: money, status, and rewarding work. Of the three, the expectation of a monetary payoff is most likely to be fulfilled, at least for the minority who manage to receive a four-year degree. That a college degree continues to be a well-paying investment no doubt helps to explain the hold colleges continue to exercise on the public imagination. But, increasingly, students—particularly the more affluent ones —see their education as a means of access to rewarding work. Desirable jobs are coming to be regarded as those that make a contribution to social betterment or are an aid to the continuous development of one's creative, aesthetic, emotional, intellectual, and other capacities. Like the dispossessed artisans and farmers of the nineteenth century, students increasingly reject the fragmentation of tasks and the hierarchy of production in the modern corporation; they want to be their own boss. Less well-off students often see further education as the route to respectability through access to a high-status job.

With the rapid expansion of higher education, with over half the age group continuing education beyond high school, there are simply not enough either rewarding or high-status jobs to go around. The increasing discrepancy between jobs and expectations is no passing phenomenon. Both the change in student consciousness and the declining opportunities for rewarding and high-status work are firmly rooted in three aspects of the process of capitalist expansion: namely, in the level of material affluence, in the stratified and alienating social relations of production, and in the pervasiveness of waste and irrational production necessary to absorb the surplus productive capacity of the economy.

The ever increasing level of material well-being—both of the students' families and that which they reasonably expect to enjoy after they leave college—has reduced the urgency of immediate consumption needs. Thus, the success of the economic growth process has itself undermined much of the monetary rationale for getting a college degree, for it has changed the way in which many students value the economic payoff to their studies. For many, the calculation of monetary gain has become secondary to other aspects of education; the other job-related objectives—rewarding work and status—have become primary. With the lure of the external monetary reward on the wane, students—particularly the more affluent—demand that education be intrinsically rewarding: College study must be interesting and enjoyable and must contribute to the individual's personal development.

The social relations of production under corporate capitalism represent a major obstacle to meeting student aspirations for either rewarding work or status. Alienated labor now characterizes most of the occupational slots open to college graduates. Most now move into jobs in which they exercise little control over the disposition of their own labor power and neither own nor identify personally with the product of their labor. Thus, work tasks tend to be repetitive, fragmented, and meaningless. The time spent on the job is not only physically and emotionally draining, it is worse; for it stunts the creative and personal development of an individual, channeling energies into the development of those skills and capacities that are valued only insofar as they bring a little more job security or a slightly larger paycheck.

The social relations of production thwart the status aspirations of students as much as they obliterate the possibility of rewarding work. The continued expansion of corporate capital has altered the system of status differentiation. Many of the high-status occupations—the independent businessman, the self-employed professional—are losing numbers. The job vacancies open to people who have been to college are now found in the well-paying but lackluster middle rungs of the corporate hierarchy. Even without changes in the availability of high-status jobs, there would not be enough status to go around. The nature of the status objective itself—based, as it is, on invidious distinctions—makes it unattainable to most of the vast numbers of students now enrolled in two- and four-year institutions. The promise of high status seemingly offered by admission to community colleges is a particularly cruel hoax. The occupational opportunities and likely incomes of workers with fewer than four years of college fall far short of the opportunities open to four-year college graduates. Four-year-college graduates are over twice as likely to end up in the high-status professional or technical jobs as those who have been to college fewer than four years. Those without four-year degrees are over twice as likely to end up in clerical jobs. As of 1968, the difference in expected lifetime income between high school graduates and four-year college graduates (as calculated by the U.S. Census Bureau) is $47,000; for those who have been to college, but for fewer than four years, the advantage over high school graduates is a paltry $7,000.

The waste and irrationality that characterize production under corporate capitalism also limit the opportunities for rewarding work. The alienated white-collar worker lacks a personal identification with the product of his or her labor, not simply because the product is owned by the capitalist, but because, in many cases, the product does not meet any real human need. The product of work may be as alienating as the process. The ecology and consumer-protection movements, the pervasive demands for more adequate social services, and the Third World liberation movements have all helped to reveal the massive waste and irrationality of what is produced in the United States. Having a hand in producing it has little appeal to more and more young people. The growing number of such people, who feel that too many commodities for private consumption are produced already, balk at most work prospects available in a capitalist economy. Others, sensitive to concerns such as environmental issues, can feel nothing better than ambivalence about their work. And, while employment in military and war-related work was not long ago seen as a social contribution, it is now more often taken on with only a sense of humiliation, embarrassment, or even contempt. The new armies of workers involved in packaging, product design and redesign, advertising, and other aspects of the sales effort are face to face with the fact that the object of their labor is capitalists' profits, not the satisfaction of consumer needs. Even work in the production of education itself has lost much of its appeal. The smug ideology that once celebrated the enlightening and equalizing mission of the teaching profession has given way under the pressure of radical political movements and radical critiques to a more persuasive, though less inspiring, view of education, stressing its inegalitarian and repressive functions.

The uninviting job prospects for college students are thus a manifestation of contradictions in the evolving structure of the corporate capitalist economy. On the one hand, the expansion of corporate capital has provided much of the impetus for the increase in enrollment. On the other, the changing social relations of production and the growing waste and irrationality associated with corporate capitalist expansion have altered the structure of work so as to thwart student aspirations. Much of the student protest of the past decade has been reflective of this basic contradiction.

Student protest has its roots in other contradictions of the larger society as well. Attacks on campus racism arise less from the peculiarities of college life than from the nationwide movement for racial self-determination. The fight against ROTC and campus military recruiters is just a small part of the worldwide anti-imperialist struggle. Likewise, the radicalism of many young teachers, technicians, social workers, and other professionals is a response to the continuing failure to place the nation's productive capacities and fiscal resources in the service of the people.

Similarly, the fact that the political manifestations of the movement are confined largely to the campuses and the professional organizations should not obscure their broader social importance. The weakening of the reproductive role of higher education represents an opportunity for radical change, not only on the campuses, where the contradictions are now most acutely felt, but also in other sections of the society, where the crisis in higher education will help destroy the mythology of opportunity and progress and thus reveal the shortcomings of the social institutions regulating our lives.

THE CONSEQUENCES OF CONTRADICTORY DEVELOPMENT: PETTY BOURGEOIS CONSCIOUSNESS AND THE REVOLUTIONARY POTENTIAL

> The tradition of all the dead generations weighs like a nightmare on the brain of the living. And just when they seem engaged in revolutionizing themselves and things, in creating something that has never yet existed, precisely in such periods of revolutionary crisis they anxiously conjure up the spirits of the past to their service and borrow from them names, battle cries and costumes, in order to present the new scene of world history in this time-honored disguise and this borrowed language.
> —KARL MARX, *The Eighteenth Brumaire of Louis Bonaparte*

Like the nineteenth-century labor movement, the student movement today is, in large measure, a product of the proletarianization of labor that accompanies the accumulation of capital. Like the early labor movement, too, it has combined militant action and a sometimes radical rhetoric with a backward-looking consciousness.

The skilled factory hands who sought to regain the freedom they lost with the demise of craft production, the agricultural workers and farm tenants who bemoaned the bygone respectability and independence of the family farmer, find their twentieth-century echo in the college student who despises the thought of salaried work in the corporate bureaucracy and longs for the free-wheeling personal independence of the self-employed professional or owner-entrepreneur. The same backward-looking consciousness finds expression in the teachers or engineers who agonize at the loss of status and independence as they are absorbed into large bureaucracies.

The precapitalist Jeffersonian ideal—the small community of property owners—that captured the imagination of dispossessed farmers and craftsmen a century or more ago was gradually extinguished, for it had been by-passed by the growth of the competitive capitalist system. Today, the competitive capitalist ideal—the individuality and respectability of the individual entrepreneur or professional—is expressed in slightly altered form in students' definitions of a good job and in their desire to "do their own thing." Like the precapitalist Jeffersonian ideal, this competitive capitalist vision conflicts sharply with the reality of the corporate capitalist economy. The underlying aspirations that unify the student movement, contemporary youth culture, and the malaise of many young white-collar workers are thus a hip emendation of petty-bourgeois consciousness.

Unlike the nineteenth-century workers and farmers, whose precapitalist consciousness was often rooted in their own experience as independent producers, today's discontented students draw their backward-looking consciousness largely from their parents. The student values of independence, initiative, individuality, and social service reflect the often unrealized aspirations of a parental generation of independent craftsmen or professionals and small business people. These values were passed on to the younger generation through patterns of "progressive" child-rearing, as well as by more formal "indoctrination." Well before the 1960's, the accumulation of corporate capital had undermined the economic basis of the parents' entrepreneurial values. The social relations of production of corporate capitalism had been radically transformed, leaving the parents of the college generation more often than not in wage or salary employment and drastically altering the occupational structure open to their children. The result was a massive discrepancy between the backward-looking consciousness of the college generation and the contemporary and future structure of jobs and work for which students were preparing.

For all the discontent that has been generated, the contradiction between the structure and growth of higher education, on the one hand, and the expansion of corporate capital, on the other, has thus not produced a revolutionary or socialist consciousness among students. Yet, the contradictions underlying student protest are likely to intensify, for they are deeply rooted in the process of capitalist expansion. As the continued proletarianization of white-collar work continues to propel the vocationalization and stratification of U.S. higher education, the political expression of the contradictions in higher education may begin to take a more radical form. Two tendencies, though of seemingly minor importance at the present, are likely to manifest themselves in strength over the next decade.

First, by escalating serious class and racial inequalities from secondary to higher education, the expansion of enrollments has done much more than increase the awareness of the degree of inequality in our school system. It has created, in the mass of nonelite college students, a group of people who have had at least a taste of inequality and hardship, who are old enough to be politically active and yet young enough to have dreams and take chances, and who are brought together on a day-to-day basis through common experiences and, in some cases, common residence. No such potential political force could be found when the main work of social class selection was being done at the high school level. For until recently, at least, the high school students themselves were barely aware of what was being done to them, and were perhaps too dependent on their elders to act. The parents, in turn, were both too busy providing for themselves and their children and too diffuse and unknown to each other to be a potent political force. Not surprisingly, only rarely did working-class and minority-group parents of high school students develop cohesive political movements with the staying power to engage in more than episodic struggles over the schooling of their children.

Campus political discontent outside the elite colleges may signal the beginning of a broad struggle for greater equality in higher education. Certainly, events such as the strike at San Francisco State College in 1968 and the struggle for open enrollment have revealed the shortsighted and narrow limits within which the corporate elite and other privileged groups are willing to make concessions to Third World and less affluent students. These conflicts have thus helped to clarify the fundamental role of the community colleges and some state colleges in the class hierarchy of higher education, thereby undermining one of the central legitimizing beliefs of the capitalist order.

A second source of potential radicalization arises from parallel contradictions in U.S. higher education and in the evolution of the class structure. Until recently, professional workers and white-collar labor have smugly accepted the comforting view that they constituted a privileged group—a modern aristocracy of labor. They had greater job security, greater control over their work, and, of course, more money. They had little reason to be critical of the hierarchical social division of labor. Along with the substantially overlapping group of property owners, they were the main beneficiaries of the capitalist system and constituted the foundation of its political defense.

While the earnings of professional and other white-collar workers have continued to exceed those of blue-collar workers by a good margin, the resulting consumption privileges accruing to this labor elite have become increasingly unimportant for many. At the same time, highly valued privileges in production have rapidly been withdrawn. The working conditions of office and "brain" labor have increasingly been coming to resemble those of the production line. The widespread unemployment and job insecurity of engineers, teachers, and technicians are symptomatic of these changes.

Although the labor force remains highly segmented by occupational level as well as by race and sex, the process of capital accumulation itself has greatly reduced the number of workers with a direct personal interest in the perpetuation of the social relations of corporate capitalist production. The concentration of capital and the demise of the small property-owning producer have narrowed the base of support for private ownership of the means of production. The concomitant decline in the number of workers exercising independence and control in their work has created a great mass of working people—now the overwhelming majority—who experience production as a social rather than an individual process, and who have little to lose and much to gain by the overthrow of the hierarchical division of labor in favor of collective control of production. The continued expansion of corporate capital may belatedly create a common condition of work among all segments of the labor force and, thus, provide the objective economic basis for a comprehensive working-class consciousness.

But consciousness does not change automatically in response to a changing economic reality. Much will depend on the objectives pursued by students, by organizations of young white-collar and professional workers, and by the groups with which they ally themselves. If they act out the retrospective consciousness of many students and other young people, if they seek to restore their lost privileges in the hierarchy of production—as independent decision-makers and directors of the labor of others—they will isolate themselves from other workers. Attempts by teachers' unions to limit student or community power in the educational process provide a glaring example of strategies that reinforce rather than undermine the corporate capitalist order. Similarly, if white-collar workers seek compensation for their lost autonomy and faded status in higher earnings, allies will be hard to come by. But, if these goals derived from looking backward are rejected in favor of demands for a wider, collective participation in control over production, the movement will find roots in a broad segment of the population. For it is possible that, over the next decades, workers in all occupational categories, as well as students, will increasingly trace their frustrations to a common set of obstacles barring their pursuit of rewarding work and a better life. The corporate capitalist economy—with its bias in favor of hierarchy, waste, and alienation in production and its mandate for a school system attuned to the reproduction and legitimation of the associated hierarchical division of labor—may then be seen as a source of the problem.

As individual salvation through access to higher education is shown to be an empty promise, the appeal of political solutions will increase. With much of the legitimizing ideology of the capitalist system destroyed by everyday experience, the ground would be laid for a broad-based movement demanding participatory control of our productive and educational institutions and the development of a liberating education and its complement: a humane and efficient social technology of production.

The contradictions of corporate capitalism will not, by themselves, create a revolutionary movement, but they do give birth to a revolutionary potential. The contradictions now manifest in higher education provide us with the opportunity to organize, to continue the uphill struggle to bring that revolutionary potential to fruition.

REFERENCES

1. Bowles, S., "Understanding Unequal Economic Opportunity, the Role of Schooling, I.Q., and Social-Class Background," *American Economic Review*, May, 1973.

2. Bowles, S., "Unequal Education and the Reproduction of the Social Division of Labor," *Review of Radical Political Economy,* III, no. 3 (Fall, 1971).

3. Bowles, S., and H. Gintis, "I.Q. in the U.S. Class Structure," *Social Policy,* January–February, 1973.

4. Edwards, R., M. Reich, and T. Weisskopf, *The Capitalist System* (Englewood Cliffs, N.J.: Prentice-Hall, 1972).

5. Karabel, J., "Community Colleges and Social Stratification," *Harvard Educational Review,* November, 1972.

4. Cities, Immigrants, and Educational Reform

There was more to progressivism in education than John Dewey, the child-centered school, and the project method. Between the late nineteenth century and World War I, educational reform had, in fact, four major components. The first was the attempt to alter the political control of education; this meant substituting a small, centralized, elite-controlled board of education for the larger, ward-based, and allegedly boss-ridden and corrupt boards in most cities. As such, progressivism in education was part of a larger movement designed to create honest, efficient, and less expensive urban government, removed as far as possible from the influence of immigrants and their political representatives. The movement's leadership came from business and the professions, often from the same people who led the campaign to restrict immigration into America.

The second component, which perhaps has received an undue share of attention from historians, was the reformulation of educational thought. Generally speaking, progressive educational thought stressed the incorporation of the experience of the child into the curriculum, the softening of pedagogy, the breaking down of barriers between subjects, and the active participation of the learner. At times, as in the writings of Dewey, these themes intertwined with a strong emphasis on the contribution of education to social reform. There are, however, less appealing motifs in progressive educational thought, as we shall note in Part VI. What is important to consider here is the relation of educational thought to educational practice. What influence did progressive education theory have upon the schools? Did changes within schools represent a response to theory or to concrete problems and pressures, such as the vast expansion in high school enrollment? These are extremely important historical issues, but issues to which the answers are not at all clear.

Educational change forms the third component of the reform movement of the period. During these years, schools adopted a number of major innovations, such as industrial education, the kindergarten, guidance, ability grouping, and testing. In part, these can be related to themes in progressive thought, although they grew from different impulses, such as the need to reconstruct secondary education in the face of its invasion by immigrant and working-class children.

The fourth component was the perfection of educational bureaucracy. By the late nineteenth century, large urban school systems had acquired all the characteristics that sociologists associate with bureaucracies. However, adocates of administrative change did not attack the hierarchical, specialized, rule-governed, secretive operation of school systems. In effect, they argued, to the contrary, that problems within school systems arose from the failure to implement the bureaucratic model fully; inefficiencies and imperfections could be corrected through the adoption of a more highly specialized, even more expertly administered structure. They argued, that is, for a more perfect bureaucracy.

Serious interpretative problems arise if we accept these four components as characteristics of educational activity in the late nineteenth and early twentieth centuries. What was the relationship of educational to other social and political activities? Can progressivism be considered a broadly humanitarian, enlightened movement to improve the schools or the nation? Or was it, in Robert Weibe's phrase, part of a "search for order," an attempt to control what many people saw as the increasingly chaotic and disorderly quality of American life?

It would be easier to answer these questions if we knew more about changes in social and family structures in this period. However, our hard knowledge is sketchy at best. We do have evidence of some things, including the development of what Weibe has called the "new middle class" (professionals and experts dedicated to introducing order into social and political affairs through the application of science and expertise); the emergence of a greatly expanded class of very rich families, searching for ways of affirming their wealth through symbols of status and exclusiveness; and the assumption of much more active social roles by women, who spearheaded not only the settlement-house movement but also many municipal reform campaigns. At the same time, the demographic character of the population altered as immigrants from southern and eastern Europe entered America in large numbers, making poverty a pressing and undeniable national problem.

The perception of immigrants and their families by reformers and educators is, in fact, one of the most important topics for historians to consider. Usually, they are pictured as disorganized, poor, and confused, unaware of the value of education and anxious to send their children to work in the factory. The school and the settlement, in this view, had to compensate for the deficiencies of the home. Yet, there is evidence that appreciation of education was widespread among the new immigrants and that their family and communal ties were strong and stable. If this should prove to be generally the case, the job of the historian will shift: He will have to account for the distorted perception of immigrants that has marked social and educational writing for at least the past century.

The selections that follow touch on all these themes. David Tyack's essay shows that bureaucracy had spread across the country by the late nineteenth century. It points as well to the relationship of bureaucracy with educational reform, of both progressive and preprogressive varieties. William Issel explores the relationship between municipal and educational reform, showing how they reflected both class interest and divergent images of the city's future. In the next selection, James McLachlan relates the remarkable growth of private boarding schools for the wealthy to the simultaneous spread of the public high school, the development of university reform, and some of the family problems of the rich. Marvin Lazerson writes about an institution—the kindergarten—that also began as an aid for wealthy families but, unlike the boarding school, quickly became associated with urban social reform directed at the uplift of poor immigrant families. He demonstrates how the conflict between the desire for reform and the commitmnt to order, coupled with the quest for "efficiency," changed the kindergarten's role. Finally, Timothy L. Smith revises commonly held ideas about the educational attitudes of immigrants, suggesting that their economic, cultural, and nationalistic aspirations combined to produce remarkably high commitment to the education of their children.

Bureaucracy and the Common School: The Example of Portland, Oregon, 1851–1913

David Tyack

The most fundamental principle observed in the present conduct of the Portland school system is the maintenance unchanged of a rigidly prescribed, mechanical system, poorly adapted to the needs either of the children or of the community." So concluded a team of educational experts led by Ellwood P. Cubberley of Stanford in a 1913 study of the Portland Public Schools. "Because of lack of opportunity to exercise initiative," they observed, teachers and administrators were "carrying out a system in whose creation they had little or no part. The result is a uniformity that is almost appalling." Administrators were mere inspectors, certifying or compelling compliance with rules. The curriculum was "vivisected with mechanical accuracy into fifty-four dead pieces." Children trotted on one stage of the treadmill until they could advance to the next by passing an examination. "School board and superintendent, as well as principals, teachers, and pupils, are victims of the system for which no one is primarily responsible." The origin of the bureaucracy was a mystery; pride, ritual, and fear maintained it.

Cubberley and his colleagues were describing—with some caricature—a social pathology that had afflicted urban schools for decades. In 1880, Charles Francis Adams, Jr., blasted school superintendents as "drill sergeants" and described their schools as "a combination of the cotton mill and the railroad with the model State-prison." In a series of articles in the *Forum* in 1892, Dr. Joseph M. Rice attacked regimentation in city schools of the East and Midwest. That same year President Charles W. Eliot of Harvard denounced mass education, which "almost inevitably adopts military or mechanical methods . . . [which] tend to produce a lock-step and a uniform speed." Inflexible routine degraded the "teacher's function. . . . There are many persons who say that teachers in the graded schools ought not to serve more than ten years at the outside, for the reason that they become dull, formal, and uninteresting; but, if this be true, it is certainly the fault of the system rather than of the teachers."

During the mid-nineteenth century, most American urban school systems became bureaucracies, though schoolmen did not use that term. They de-

Reprinted from *The American Quarterly*, Volume 19, Number 3 (Fall, 1967), pp. 475–98, by permission of The University of Pennsylvania, publisher, and the Author. Copyright, 1967, Trustees of The University of Pennsylvania.

veloped elaborate rules to govern the behavior of members of the organization, and a great premium was placed on conformity to the rules; they created hierarchies of appointive offices, each with careful allocations of power and specified duties; and objective qualifications governed admission to the various roles (whether "superintendent" or "third grader"). The schools, like other organizations, were trying to cope rationally with large numbers of heterogeneous pupils. Indeed, schoolmen commonly thought bureaucratization essential to progress. In 1890, the Committee on City School Systems of the National Education Association quoted Herbert Spencer on the value of "a differentiation of structure and a specialization of function," and concluded that urban schools needed not only "combination and unification for general purposes" but also specialized administrative structures "with well-defined functions and powers." In the actual organization of the schools, however, schoolmen of the nineteenth century tended to favor simple military or industrial bureaucratic models in which uniformity of output and regularity of operation took precedence over functional differentiation. Thus, in practice, they often created a curriculum that was identical for all children, preferred teaching methods that promised standardized results, and based the hierarchy more on a distribution of power than on specialized expertise.

The educational statesmen of Horace Mann's generation had tried to create system where they saw chaos. Urban school bureaucracies institutionalized this quest for standardization. Reformers believed that, in order to unify the people, they must first unify the common schools. They were dismayed by the heterogeneity of typical public schools: teachers untrained, mostly young and inexperienced, lacking a sense of professionalism; curriculum haphazard, textbooks miscellaneous; classes composed of students of wildly varying age and ability, irregular in attendance and unruly in behavior; buildings rough and messy, serving as general community centers for church services, lantern slide lectures, social occasions, and political assemblies. The rural school was especially subject to the caprice of the community, the tyranny of the tribe that Edward Eggleston describes so clearly in *The Hoosier Schoolmaster*. In the small district school, authority inhered in the person, not the office, of the schoolmaster; the roles of teachers were overlapping, familiar, personal, rather than esoteric, strictly defined, and official (the same teacher in a rural school might be brother, suitor, hunting companion, fellow farm worker, boarder, and cousin to the different boys and girls in the class). Normally, the only supervisors were laymen, school board members, or ministers who dropped in from time to time on the local school. The school played a relatively small and often unpredictable part in the total socialization of the young.

Reform, then, meant standardization. Schoolmen sought to grade classes, to prescribe a uniform curriculum and textbooks, to train teachers in approved methods, to give them a sense of vocational identity and spirit, and to appoint officials to supervise the schools. Such bureaucratization was easiest in cities (where the population was concentrated and the tax base adequate). Urban residents were familiar with bureaucracies arising in manufacturing, commerce, transport, the military, and government. Posing the rhetorical question "Why the expense and machinery of a superintendent?" one school administrator replied:

> In industrial establishments, as well as in enterprises requiring unskilled manual labor, employers insist upon abundant supervision. A great railroad company places one man to boss three or four. Every factory, large or small, has its foremen and its bosses. Experience has taught that such an arrangement pays financially. The conclusions are quite as reasonable in the conduct of schools; where even a small aggregation of schools is, there an able superintendent can be profitably engaged.

Increasing ease of transportation and communication, together with the migration of teachers and administrators, spread the new patterns of organization. Richard Wade has observed that the new cities arising by the banks of the Ohio and the Mississippi—St. Louis, Cincinnati, and the rest—emulated the educational systems of "the great cities across the mountains," even though they were "freed from . . . old restraints and traditions." Louisville sent a new principal to study Eastern schools to eliminate the need for "expensive errors and fruitless experiments." Similarly, Portland, Oregon—a fir forest in 1840—had organized, by the 1870's, a school system based on Eastern models. By copying the most recent organizational reforms, such cities could skip earlier, piecemeal stages of bureaucratization.

In 1874, leading American city and state school superintendents and college presidents signed *A Statement of the Theory of Education in the United States*, written to explain American educational practices to Europeans. In this outline, they justified bureaucratization in matter-of-fact rather than crusading language. "The commercial tone prevalent in the city," they said, "tends to develop, in its schools, quick, alert habits and readiness to combine with others in their tasks. Military precision is required in the maneuvering of classes. Great stress is laid upon (1) punctuality, (2) regularity, (3) attention, and (4) silence, as habits necessary through life for successful combination with one's fellow-men in an industrial and commercial civilization." They seemed to accept employers' specifications as to the ideal character of workers. They saw the school as "a phase of education lying between the earliest period of family-nurture . . . and the necessary initiation into the specialties of a vocation." Because "the peculiarities of civil society and the political organization draw the child out of the influence of family-nurture earlier than is common in other countries," the American school had "to lay more stress upon discipline and to make far more prominent the moral phase of education. It is obliged to train the pupil into prompt obedience to his teachers and the practice of self-control in its various forms, in order that he may be prepared for a life wherein there is little police-restraint on the part of the constituted authorities." Therefore, urban schools must socialize children to take part in an increasingly bureaucratic society: The new size and complexity of "corporate combinations . . . make such a demand upon the community for directive intelligence that it may be said that the modern industrial community cannot exist without free popular education carried out in a system of schools ascending from the primary grade to the university."

Across the nation, urban school bureaucracies won acclaim. The best teachers and administrators flocked to these systems in search of higher pay and prestige. But the reformers' very success became an affliction, as is often the case when reforms become institutionalized. Orderly grooves became ruts. In 1903, Charles B. Gilbert, the superintendent of schools in Rochester, New York, warned that large institutions tend "to subordinate the individual. . . . This is particularly true in great school systems. . . . The demands of the organization itself are so great, it requires so much executive power to keep the machine running, that the machine itself attracts undue attention and we are in danger of forgetting that the business of the school is to teach children." He knew, he said, superb teachers who were "driven from the school system because they did not readily untie red tape." Worst of all was a "shifting of conscience" from teaching to pleasing pettifogging superiors. "I know of cities in which supervisors go about from schoolroom to schoolroom, notebook and pencil in hand, sitting for a while in each room like malignant sphinxes, eying the terrified teacher, who in her terror does everything wrong, and then marking her in that little doomsday book." A school is not a factory, he said, "with a boss, sub-bosses, and hands." Like Charles W. Eliot, Gilbert looked back with nostalgia on "the small unpainted schoolhouse in the remote country district" as a place where the individual child, the individual teacher, counted, where flexibility flourished. When the urban school bureaucracy turns children into robots and "grinds out the power of initiative from the teacher," said Gilbert, "then it is time to smash the machine; and there are countless machines all over this land that need to be smashed."

Just such a machine was the Portland school system when Cubberley and his colleagues arrived in 1913. There, they found all the dysfunctions that Robert Merton describes in his essay on "Bureaucratic Structure and Personality." What had originally been a thoughtful response to problems of disorganization in mass education became archaic ritual. "Passive, routine, clerical"—these adjectives described "the attitude of principals and grammar school teachers toward their work," said the investigators. "And the attitude of the pupils is inevitably the same." With the exception of one lesson, they "heard not a single question asked by a pupil, not a single remark or comment made, to indicate that the pupil had any really vital interest in the subject matter of the exercise." Like experienced enlisted men, teachers "feared to advocate anything out of the routine, for that would mean more work, and more work—with its intended accomplishment—in one part of the system, would threaten other parts of the system with a like affliction!" The system was bound by rules that had so long outlived their usefulness that no one could recall their origin or state their rationale.

"There is no study," Charles Bidwell has observed, "of the prevalence or incidence either of bureaucratic structures or processes in school systems." This oversight is not coincidental. As Marviñ Bressler has pointed out in his essay on "The Conventional Wisdom of Education and Sociology," scholars in education have tended to stress individual volition, broad social needs, and a "credo of unlimited hope." Reformist and optimistic in temper, many educationists have written from an individualistic, psychological perspective. They have often represented teaching styles and philosophies of education as if they were options independent of organizational patterns. The behavioral effects of institutional structure have more often been taken for granted than examined, while tacitly it was assumed that a teacher could choose to be "progressive" or "traditional." But the experience of Portland up to the time of the Cubberley survey suggests that the rigid bureaucratic system had an internal momentum and influence that largely shaped the conduct of teachers, administrators, and students. The persistence of this system in the face of major social and intellectual changes cannot be explained simply by conventional categories of individual intent, rational adaptation, or psychological or social needs. Although the founders of the bureaucracy knew the reasons for their actions, before long the structure of the organization began to produce in its members what Veblen called "trained incapacity" and what Dewey deplored as "occupational psychosis." People acted the roles that the institution demanded with little thought about the purpose of education.

So it was with the Portland bureaucracy. While this essay deals, perforce, with the individuals who built the system, the bureaucracy itself is the central subject rather than the actors. The essay will also explore the relevance of bureaucracy to "progressive education," in the conviction that this reform movement was a "revolt against formalism" quite as much in educational organization as in educational thought.

When the Rev. Thomas L. Eliot, a public-spirited, Unitarian minister in Portland, became superintendent of schools in Multnomah County in 1872, he was convinced that Portland needed the kind of educational system his father had helped to build in St. Louis. "Economy of power and efficiency in our schools," he wrote in his annual report in 1873, "depends in great degree upon a proper division of responsibilities. As in the army, so here; and I have suggested to the Directors [of the Portland schools] some steps looking towards a more thorough supervision by the Principals of their subordinates." The next year, he welcomed the appointment of a city superintendent (Eliot worked only part-time as county superintendent and his territory was far too large to supervise adequately):

> This measure was . . . dictated by that common sense which sees the need of a head to every organization consisting of diverse and complex parts. Our 25 schools, like so many separate units, or 'feudal baronies,' were governed by as many systems and precedents as there were teachers. The grades were, indeed, supposed to be defined, but

were in a decidedly nebulous state. It was not, nor could it be, expected of the Directors to spend their whole time in the details of school methods, discipline and examinations. It remained . . . to follow . . . the example of other cities throughout the country where Superintendents or visiting principals are appointed.

The early days of public education in Portland had a certain rustic charm: The first teacher, bearing the unfortunate name of John Outhouse, unloaded ships and built roads when he was not teaching school; a successor "graded" her ninety pupils by ranking them on steps in the old loft that served as her classroom; one dapper teacher went for his certificate to the home of a minister who was serving as county superintendent, found him at the washtub, and smartly answered his questions while the minister was drying himself and rolling down his sleeves; a canny class of children persuaded their teacher not to use the rod by threatening her with a roomful of mice.

But for Eliot and his predecessor as county superintendent, the Rev. George Atkinson, such haphazard schooling had grave flaws: How could such teaching render the next generation "homogeneous in habits of thinking, feeling, and acting"? Atkinson was a pioneer Yankee Congregationalist minister who taught for a while in the Oregon City schools. He patterned the system of grading and examinations in Oregon City on the Boston plan, and, when he moved to Portland, he sought to standardize its schools as well. Eliot agreed; graded classes and strict examinations brought healthy uniformity, hard work, and moral indoctrination. "As a field of clover, well rooted, admits no weeds," he wrote, "so the mind of a child, thoroughly employed and interested, has little room for the culture of low imagination and vice . . . an ill-regulated school system will bear fruit in the lack of self-control, punctuality, order, perseverance, justice, truth and industry, in its citizens." Eliot believed that well-run schools could counter "the pitiful fallacies which plunge nations into years of social misery and political disorder. . . . The barest knowledge of political economy, widely diffused, would prevent the notion of sumptuary laws, communism, and interference with trade and circulating media, which even now delude the minds of large portions of the people." Immigration, immorality, class conflict, corruption —these threats demanded efficient schools.

These two ministers, architects of the Portland school system, borrowed freely from Eastern educational ideology and structure. The product of the schools was to be the homogeneous good citizen—sober, moral, industrious, one who would preserve rather than question the social and economic system; the means of production was to be a prescribed curriculum and a semimilitary bureaucracy. Atkinson and Eliot were educational strategists: They saw the schools as only part of a total process of socialization and civilization, and they worked as well to establish libraries, churches, colleges, and a host of other stabilizing institutions and associations. But many of the schoolmen who followed them were not strategists but drillmasters who mistook bureaucratic means for social ends.

When Samuel King, first city school superintendent, took office in 1874, Portland had about ten thousand residents, 1,168 of whom were enrolled in the public schools. A consummate bureaucrat, King believed that children's behavior must be precisely controlled, reliable, predictable. Regular attendance and punctuality—surely necessary prologues to schooling—became an obsession with King. His war on irregular attendance, also waged vigorously by his successor, Thomas Crawford, made Portland students, in a few years, the most punctual in comparable cities across the nation (by 1881, only .04 per cent were reported tardy). Superintendents continued well into the twentieth century to report attendance and tardiness statistics down to the second and third decimal point. In 1876, the school board adopted a policy of suspending any student absent (except for sickness) or tardy four times in four consecutive weeks. King and his successors also publicly reported the tardiness of teachers, and fined principals for not opening schools at 8:30 A.M. sharp. "A school with an enrollment of fifty, daily attendance fifty and none tardy," King wrote lyrically in 1876, "is a grand sight to behold in the morning and afternoon." So great was the stigma of tardiness, and so keen the competition among schools for a good record, that children sometimes hid all day to avoid coming into class late and teachers sometimes sent children home to avoid marking them tardy. Sometimes, Crawford complained of teachers who had "overdrawn the evils of tardiness"; but he set the style by patrolling the streets to spot absent or late children. And Crawford proudly listed in a roll of honor the names of children who had perfect attendance from one to six years.

Getting the children and teachers to school on time was only the beginning. King and his principals worked out a "system of instruction and a division of school labor" that included a uniform curriculum, primary, intermediate, and grammar departments divided into six grades (further subdivided into A and B sections), and a plan of written examinations to ensure that the children had been "thoroughly drilled in the work assigned." As a Yankee who believed that "a perfect system of school management is indispensable to the welfare of our Public Schools," King paid examinations the supreme compliment: "System, order, dispatch and promptness have characterized the examinations and exerted a healthful influence over the pupils by stimulating them to be thoroughly prepared to meet their appointments and engagements. Next to a New England climate, these examinations necessitate industry, foster promptness, and encourage pupils to do the right thing *at the right time.*"

The results of the first round of examinations might have dismayed a heart less stout than King's. In seven classrooms out of a total of twenty-one, none of the children passed. Only in six classrooms were more than half of the children promoted. But King maintained that the operation was a great success, though most of the patients died. Not surprisingly, in the next examinations teachers and pupils improved somewhat: This time, between 13 and 75 per cent of the children were promoted (in some of the classes, though, fewer than three-fourths of the students got up nerve to take the test). King published the results of the examinations in the newspaper, with the child's score and school next to his name. Parents could draw their own conclusions about the diligence of the child and the competence of the teacher, and they did. Incensed and anxious, the teachers joined irate parents to force King's resignation in 1877.

The new superintendent, Crawford, promptly abolished the practice of publicizing the test results. He wrote, in his report in 1878, that "incalculable injury has been done, both to the teachers and to the pupils of our free schools, resulting from a spirit of rivalry on the part of the teachers." Some teachers had gone to great lengths to protect their reputations, urging children to withdraw from school shortly before the examination and even advising the superintendent to suspend slow students for trivial offenses, so that they wouldn't drag down the percentage of promotions. The system of publicity had led, he said, to cramming, "bitter animosities," and "unpleasant wranglings, over arbitrary standards in marking papers." Yet, Crawford was no Paul Goodman; he was a good bureaucrat who wanted harmony in the ranks. He retained the examination system, elaborating it in Mandarin detail while softening its rigors, but he kept the examination results the property of the bureaucracy.

Despite occasional rhetoric about independence of mind, King and Crawford made it clear in their reports that the school system was to inculcate certified thoughts and proper deportment. "Habits of obedience, attention, promptness in recitation, neatness of copy-books, and a carefully prepared program of the daily work, are some of the characteristics and attractions of most of the schools," said King in 1875. He believed that "children should be taught to obey the commands of their teachers at once, and a slight tap of the pencil [should] be intelligible to any class." As children passed from class to class, they displayed "a military air and discipline that is truly commendable and pleasant." Even compositions should display martial virtues as pupils "draw up their words in orderly array and march through many sentences preserving order in the ranks and an unbroken line." Eliot believed that, in their handwriting, students "should strictly conform to given positions and rules, however awkward and constrained they may seem at first; for in penmanship, as in everything else of man's development, true liberty is obedience to law." And the law, there was no doubt, was the curriculum prescribed by the bureaucracy.

The uniform curriculum of the common school—an unbroken "chain," King called it—included the three R's, grammar, and a smattering of natural and social science. From test questions, it is possible to discover what children learned to remember long enough to repeat on the examinations. The curriculum was neatly parceled into semester segments, the teachers were closely supervised and had to drill students on the material covered in the tests, and a premium was placed on uniformity of output. King's report for 1877 listed the questions asked at the end of the eighth grade and the examinations in the various high school subjects. With few exceptions, the questions required definitions, facts, memorization of textbook explanations. These are some examples (the last three are aimed at eighth graders, the others at high school students):

A man pays 6 dollars yearly for tobacco, from the age of 16 till he is 60, when he dies, leaving to his heirs $500; what might he have left them if he had dispensed with this useless habit and loaned the money at the end of the year at 6 per cent compound interest?

Define Imaginary Quantity, Surd and Pure Quadratic Equation.

What system did Kepler adopt? Give his three laws. Tell how he discovered each.

Define Diction. What is necessary to give one a command of words? What kind of New Words should be avoided? If any, specify the objections to the use of each of the following words: Exit, talkist, alibi, conversationalist, boyist, skedaddle, donate.

How do the two kind[s] of engines differ? How is the power of steam engines estimated?

What was the Kansas-Nebraska Bill?

What causes earthquakes? Describe the Desert of Sahara. Give the area of the Atlantic ocean.

Write and punctuate the Lord's Prayer.

Give the principal parts of the verbs *lay, lie, go, cut, shoe.* Give the second person singular of *elect* in all its moods and tenses.

Give the five provisions of the Compromise of 1850.

Spell: Burlesque, Ichneumon, Heliotrope, Analytically, Diaphragm, Panegyric.

The fact that about 93 per cent of the high school students answered questions like these correctly that year testifies to the marvelous capacity of the human race to suffer trivia patiently. Year after year, until the bombshell of the Cubberley report in 1913, the curriculum changed but little; it was mostly taken for granted.

An essential phase of the bureaucratization of the schools was the establishment of definite qualifications, salaries, and duties for teachers. In 1881, Crawford complained about untrained and inexperienced teachers and decried the pressure on the school board to hire incompetent teachers with influential friends. He urged that professional competence be the only criterion for employment. He also suggested a normal "training class" for high school students intending to teach. In 1881, the school board adopted a uniform pay schedule for teachers based on years of experience and level of instruction. Two years later, the board set standards of eligibility and performance for each position and published twenty-two rules regulating teachers' examinations and certificates. Although, technically, there was no segregation into positions by sex, in effect a class system soon developed in which men became predominantly the supervisors and women the supervised; only in the high school was it respectable for men to teach. This feminization of elementary school teaching had gone so far by 1905 that all teachers of the grades were women. Twenty-three out of twenty-seven elementary school principals that year were men—almost, but not quite, a caste system, for some upward mobility was possible for women. This sex differential, coupled with the low pay, low prestige, and inadequate education of the elementary school teachers, helped to reinforce the autocratic structure of the bureaucracy.

Although certification is regarded today as a form of professional licensure, in its early stages in cities like Portland certification was a branch of civil service reform: a means of ensuring that public servants possessed at least minimal competence for their tasks and a way of preventing an educational spoils system. These objective standards of competence and rewards were common characteristics of bureaucracies in all fields, though in public agencies during the Gilded Age corruption and special favors were notorious problems. In Portland, however, civil service reform came early, and, with the exception of alleged improper influence of the "book trust" of the American Book Company, in the 1890's, Portland was relatively free from scandal.

In 1883, the school board issued a booklet of *Rules and Regulations* that codified the practices standardized during the previous decade. There was bureaucracy, in black and white: the classification of schools, the uniform curriculum, the hierarchy of offices and delineation of duties, the time schedules, the elaborate plan of examinations and promotions. As chief policeman, the superintendent was required to "see that the grade work is strictly followed, that the rules and regulations are observed and enforced, and [to] report any and all delinquencies to the Board." Principals were the intermediate inspectors and disciplinarians, instructed by the board, among other duties, "to prohibit the playing of marbles on or about the school premises." Nothing was left to chance in the duties of the teachers. They were told to open the windows at recess; to suspend a thermometer from the ceilings and to keep their rooms between 67 and 71 degrees; to assemble, for at least two hours, at their monthly institute (they were fined two dollars for failing to attend and one dollar for being tardy); "to subscribe for, take and read, at least one periodical devoted to educational work"; and to "*cheerfully* cooperate with the City Superintendent in executing the prescribed work of the grades." Uneven in education and skill, teachers were to be governed by rules, not professional norms. Once a month, the teachers read to the students the "Duties of Pupils" commanding obedience, punctuality, industry, and respect for school property. Thirty-seven rules dealt with absense, tardiness, excuses, and suspensions; eight outlined examinations and promotions. Obscurity was not one of the faults of the Portland Public Schools; complacency was.

The bureaucratization of the schools had not gone unchallenged in Portland or elsewhere. In 1880, the crusty and conservative editor of the *Oregonian*, Harvey Scott, launched an attack on the "cumbrous, complex and costly system" of the public schools. "In nearly every city there has been growing up during the last ten years an elaborate public school machinery," he wrote, "largely managed and directed by those whom it supports. Nominally it is controlled by the taxpayers of the districts, but in reality by associations of persons who live as professionals upon the public school system." What was needed, he said, was a return to "the simple yet effective system of the old common schools." Scott was sure that citizens were "decidedly in favor of reducing the 'establishment,'— as the system has been called since it grew to its present proportions." Methods of instruction have grown "to a complexity which puzzles the learner and which works the teacher harder out of school hours in making up trivial reports, calculated on percentages of proficiency, behavior, etc., than in the . . . schoolroom." (Perhaps teachers not inclined "cheerfully [to] cooperate with the City Superintendent" had been talking out of turn.)

Scott sent reporters out to gather the opinions of the businessmen of Portland about the "new-fangled, finical stuff" going on in the schools; the complex machinery, the new subjects introduced into the grades and the high school (which Scott thought quite unnecessary for the common child). Most of the businessmen interviewed thought common schools necessary, but many questioned the need for expensive "flummery." "A child who has a good English education, if he has any snap about him," said one, "will succeed better than the average graduate of the high school who knows a little of every thing." Another said flatly: "The prominent and useful men of this city are not men of high education." Some glorified the simple, cheap, old-time district school: just the three R's, under the eye and thumb of the community. And one believed that the Portland schools were "being controlled by a school ring and not by taxpayers or directors." Just inculcate the right values cheaply, said the self-made men.

Even George Atkinson had misgivings about the dominant role the school was beginning to play in the life of the child. During pioneer days, children had learned the discipline of manual labor at home, he wrote in 1879; but, as the school took over more and more of the student's life, there was a danger that it might "graduate whole regiments of sickly sentimentalists: young gentlemen unused and unfit to work, and young ladies decked in the latest fashion." Parents should be forced to certify that their children were doing some manual labor for at least six months of the year, thereby correcting "a good part of the evils which are likely to grow out of improved public instruction."

Atkinson's comment that "evils . . . are likely to grow out of improved public instruction" suggests the complexity of the issues raised in the revolt of 1880 against the school bureaucracy. Many motives impelled Scott and his fellow critics. Scott thought the schools were producing "shyster lawyers, quack doctors, razor-strop and patent-soap peddlers, book canvassers, and bookkeepers"—not willing workers. Many opposed higher taxes, especially for secondary education. Some believed that education beyond the common school should be the province of private schools (and they were encouraged in this belief by many private schoolmen who luxuriated in laissez-faire rhetoric). Some wanted the simple days of the old district school, when parents saw the school as a community center in which families were more citizens than subjects. Others resented the fact that the schools were taking over functions previously performed by family, church, and economic units. And, above all, the schools seemed to be out of touch, insulated, irresponsible and irresponsive to the public, remote, and haughty.

Scott had said that no one could expect self-criticism from the professional establishment; the letters to the press of administrators like Crawford and the state superintendent of public instruction displayed a shocked and self-righteous attitude. The depth of feeling against the bureaucrats was illustrated in a letter from "C" that appeared in the *Oregonian* on February 26, 1880: "We, the defenders of the common school system, are between the upper and nether millstones, the impracticables and the destructives. . . . It can only be perpetuated by relieving it of the complex character it has assumed by reason of the inflated, pedantic and self-aggrandizing character of the faculty, who from one entrenched foothold of aggression against popular rights have advanced to another, until we see the result in the superficial, overloaded and overtaxing system now prevailing."

Such attacks hurt and bewildered Crawford. He had earnestly gone about his business of liquidating tardiness and ignorance, organizing the schools according to the best Eastern models, cultivating his own bureaucratic garden. The impersonal rules, the uniform curriculum, the school hierarchy—did these not serve as a buffer between the teacher and the community, affording protection against the tyranny of parents, the spoils system of urban politicians, the insecurity of ambiguity? Crawford did admit that school patrons "have an undoubted right to sit in judgment on the general and even particular conduct of teachers who are public servants. What a teacher does out of the school room as well as in it comes within the purview of the public." Then, as now, the superintendency was an anxious profession, and the school a vulnerable institution. Bureaucracy became the schoolman's moat and castle, and bureaucrats tended to regard an attack on their particular system as an attack on the principle of public education. That label which would be heard again and again in the years to come—"enemies of the public school"—they tried to pin on their opponents.

In 1880, the main task of defending the schools fell to the Rev. George Atkinson, then general missionary for the American Home Mission Society. Atkinson knew how to smother brush fires by committee. Thus, at a heated meeting of taxpayers on March 1, 1880, Atkinson, as private citizen, diplomatically proposed an impartial investigation of the charges that had been leveled against the system and a report on the condition of the schools. He summarized the complaints: that the machinery of the schools was too costly and cumbersome; that the studies were too difficult and numerous; and that the high school was not properly a part of the common-school system (certain college preparatory subjects had been singled out for attack). Atkinson was chosen chairman of the investigating committee. This was rather like asking the Pope to study irregularities in the Vatican, for Atkinson was the most eloquent advocate of the bureaucracy (though not, technically, a member of the "school ring").

As author of the report, Atkinson said that the "machinery" of education, far from being too cumbersome and costly, "seems hardly to keep pace with the growth of the city." He maintained that "large classes permit the best division of labor," and that the systems of grading and examinations "encourage every class in habits of promptness, order and diligence." Over a third of the grammar school graduates of the past five years were continuing their education, over one-half were working at home or in trades, and only 1 per cent were "of questionable character." But Atkinson reiterated that parents should "train their children in manual labor," and teachers should give "lessons about the real work of life." The best proof of the quality of the schools was "that few idlers or hoodlums have ever been connected with the public schools of Portland." The high school he saw as an "extension of the grades and classes," well justified as a means of spreading "the purest morals and the best possible culture among great masses of people, who make and execute their own laws."

In this report, Atkinson reminded the people of Portland of the rationale for uniform and efficient public education: "The self-government of the people is still on trial, and every hour great currents sweep from other lands against its foundations and test the pillars of its strength. How shall the incoming tens and hundreds of thousands be moulded into our body politic and made homogeneous with ourselves except by the public school—training every child in our own tongue and habits of thought, and principles of government and aims of life?" The perils of diversity dictated uniformity in the schools. Thomas Eliot concurred:

> The justification of our public school system really lies where people seldom look for it, viz.: In the necessity of a republic's preserving a homogeneous people; the necessity of having one institution which effectively mingles and assimilates *all* classes and castes. It is the 'imperium in imperio,' the democracy *within* the democracy of our national existence. The nation can afford to trust education of every kind to the parental instinct; but, it cannot afford to trust to chance the unifying processes; the sentiment which welds the people; and the common school as bringing all classes together at an impressionable age is the forge it sets up and maintains as its most powerful instrumentality against aristocracy and mobocracy (communism) and every other 'ocracy.'

Still grumbling about the establishment, Portland accepted Atkinson's report and its rationale. Not until Cubberley and his team of experts descended in 1913 would there be another full-scale investigation of the bureaucracy.

When Crawford resigned from the superintendency in 1888, the basic character of the school system was well established. For the next three years, a talented woman, Ella Sabin, was superintendent. During her brief tenure, she attempted to recast the curriculum and teaching methods in accord with "the enlivening influence of the 'new education'" (the movement that later became "progressive education"), but the patterns of behavior already established in the bureaucracy persisted and were reinforced by the regimentation required by her successors; she left her mark chiefly by a residue of progressive rhetoric, here and there, in the teachers' guide. Irving Pratt, who took her place in 1891, became best remembered for declaring that "19 of his teachers [were] excellent. . . . All the rest were a poor lot."

Frank Rigler spent his seventeen years as superintendent (1896–1913) largely in perfecting the machine he had inherited. In his first report, he assured the taxpayers that *he* was no devotee of the "new education": "The friends of our schools who are apprehensive that the schools have become too modern are needlessly alarmed. I am not aware that our schools have any (approved) features that were not to be found a generation ago." Like a good general, he supported his troops: "[E]very teacher now in our schools is making an effort, each according to her ability, to do the kind and extent of work that has been done by the best teachers for many years." The *Oregon Journal* reported the claim of one of Cubberley's colleagues that there had been no changes for the better during Rigler's long regime, an accusation that infuriated the superintendent. In Rigler's final report, written just before his resignation, he listed the improvements made during his tenure—manual-training schools, a program for deaf and defective children, medical examinations of pupils, and so on—but his sense of priorities was evident in the first three items on his list of achievements:

1st. The construction of the buildings has changed from wood to steel and concrete.

2nd. A system of ventilation and heating has been introduced which expresses the latest views of competent ventilating engineers.

3rd. The toilet facilities of the schools have been made equal to those of the best dwellings and hotels.

Indeed, a committee of leading educators admitted, in 1890, that community pressures on imaginative administrators were such that "It is not surprising that so many really capable superintendents settle down to the running of the school machine as it is . . . the strongest and wisest of educators may be pardoned if he degenerates into a not ignoble specimen of arrested development."

Rigler, however, never was tempted to be anything but a guardian of tradition. His maxim "was to play the game straight according to the prescribed rules." Criticized he was, for conservatism and autocracy—never for being too liberal. Stern, efficient, logical, a master of detail, he ran the bureaucracy like an army. At teachers' meetings, he went through the textbooks page by page, telling his staff what questions to ask and what answers to accept. It was common knowledge in Portland that Rigler "could sit in his office and know on what page in each book work was being done at the time in every school in the city." He revived Crawford's plan of internships in teaching for high school graduates and personally indoctrinated the young girls in his rigid course of study. (The bureaucracy in Bel Kaufman's *Up The Down Stair Case* seems permissive by comparison.) The basic curriculum remained what it had been in the 1870's: the three R's, grammar, history, civics, geography, drawing, and various subjects in natural science. But Rigler took great pride in splitting the former thirty-six divisions of the curriculum into fifty-four "cycles" (each spelled out by pages in the textbooks) and, in turn, subdivided them into fast and slow sections.

In Rigler's monotonous reports, one looks in vain for reflections on the philosophical or sociological rationale of his administration. A fellow superintendent, Aaron Gove of Denver, was not so reticent; in an NEA address, he bluntly expressed the premises that underlay the Portland bureaucracy as well as his own. Gove opposed " 'soft pedagogy' and 'mellow education' " and believed that the grammar school years were "the time for drill, memory training, severe application to tasks with an accounting for their accomplishment." Similarly, he had no taste for democratic school administration. The limits of the superintendent's authority should be clearly stated, he said, "in the formal rules and regulations of the board of education." Within these bounds, the superintendent's authority was unlimited, though he would be well advised to exercise it politely: "The autocracy of the office of the superintendent of a public-school system is necessary for the accomplishment of his purposes, but that despotism can be wielded with a gloved hand." Teachers can no more constitute a democracy than can policemen. Teachers may, from time to time, give *advice*, but "dictation must come from the other end." The teacher has only "independence like that of a man in a shoe factory who is told tomorrow morning to make a pair of No. 6 boots"—that is, he "can work rapidly or slowly," but he must make the boots. Gove saw in the "War Department of the nation" the best analogy for proper school organization. The general —the superintendent—must control all his troops, but must leave first-hand inspection up to his inspector-general's department. "The executive department of a school system of thirty thousand pupils would be ideal with one superintendent and four school inspectors who shall spend their entire time, as does the inspecting officer of the army, in reviewing and examining in detail every part of the enterprise and reporting promptly and often, in a very careful way, what he finds."

So far had bureaucracy gone down the down staircase that the nature of education had been subordinated to the demands of the organization. To the survey team in 1913, schooling seemed a vast percolation of words for the student; teachers, robots; administrators themselves, captives of the rules and the system. This was the trained incapacity, the blindness to alternatives, that bureaucracy often (though not necessarily) produced. Cubberley and his colleagues were determined to jar Portland out of its rut.

To Cubberley's group, Portland symbolized much that was wrong with "traditional education." They deplored the abstract, uniform curriculum and gagged on grammar tests that asked students to define attribute complements and independent elements. They attacked the military model of teaching by routine and drill. They satirized the autocratic and rule-constipated structure of the schools. They believed that the new science of education, new conceptions of learning, new tasks for the school, and new views of the teacher's role had rendered obsolete most of the bureaucratic system that Portland had labored for fifty years to build.

Cubberley was convinced that education should be functionally differentiated according to the needs of students and society. Furthermore, he was committed to professional expertise for both teachers and administrators. These are elements of what has come to be called educational progressivism. The old-fashioned military model of bureaucracy, in which hierarchy depended more on power than on function, made sense only so long as the goals of education were stated in very generalized terms, such as producing homogeneous good citizens. By 1913, many school administrators believed that educational progress depended on Spencer's "differentiation of structure and . . . specialization of function," and their model of such functional specialization was contemporary industrial organization. In Cubberley's view,

> Our schools are, in a sense, factories in which the raw materials [children] are to be shaped and fashioned into products to meet the various demands of life. The specifications for manufacturing come from the demands of the twentieth century civilization, and it is the business of the school to build its pupils to the specifications laid down. This demands good tools, specialized machinery, continuous measurement of production to see if it is according to specifications, the elimination of waste in manufacture, and a large variety in output.

Cubberley believed in "large variety in output," for one of the key faults of traditional education was its lack of specialization. Portland's schools were "much in the condition of a manufacturing establishment which is running on a low grade of efficiency," said Cubberley, for it was based on an antiquated bureaucratic model. "The waste of material is great and the output is costly—in part because the workmen in the establishment are not supplied with enough of the right kind of tools; in part because the supervision of the establishment is inadequate and emphasizes wrong points in manufacture; but largely because the establishment is not equipped with enough large pieces of specialized machinery, located in special shops or units of the manufacturing plant, to enable it to meet modern manufacturing conditions." Cubberley believed that urban schools should "give up the exceedingly democratic idea that all are equal, and that our society is devoid of classes," and should adapt to existing social classes. Portlanders "should apply to the management of their educational business principles of efficiency similar to those which control in other forms of manufacturing." He believed that the school system should train students for specialized roles in the economy while still striving to produce *morally* homogeneous citizens.

The school should have a highly trained staff headed by a captain of education similar in stature to a captain of industry. A bureaucracy it should be, but a specialized one controlled by professionals, not drill sergeants. The caliber of a school, said Cubberley, "depends much more on the quality of the leadership at the top and the freedom given the leader or leaders to work things out in their own way, than upon any scheme of organization which can be devised." The Portland School Board was still trying to oversee minute administrative details and relied on rules rather than men, not realizing that "What a school system is, it is largely because of the insight, personality, and force of the Superintendent of Schools." Likewise, this leader should be given responsibility to select administrators and teachers who could exercise professional discretion within their specialized spheres. Cubberley believed that a staff that had grown from 294 in 1900 to 928 in 1913 needed effective supervision; but he also was convinced that no one man could decide what was best for the 43,000 children in the district. To professionally trained teachers fell "the responsibility, under wise guidance and leadership, of adapting the educational process, both in content and method, to individual needs." In short, the bureaucracy was to be looser structurally, the superintendent and his administrative staff adapting the schools as a whole to the needs of society, and the teachers adapting lessons to the needs of the child. A new tension was thus introduced that had hardly existed in Rigler's despotic system: the uneasy and sometimes conflicting demands of consistent and orderly administration, on the one hand, and professional autonomy and freedom to experiment, on the other.

Cubberley had really stated a dilemma rather than solved a problem, a dilemma faced by urban schoolmen everywhere. As Cubberley knew, bureaucracy in some form was here to stay in large American school systems, however it might be modified by new conceptions of education, and inherent in bureaucracy was the impulse toward regularity. In a small, rural school, or in a Freud-inspired private school, an individual teacher might single-handedly put the tenets of progressive education into practice. Progressives might protest against the regimentation common in urban school systems at the turn of the century, but the effects of rigid bureaucratization could not easily be erased by reading *Democracy and Education*, by introducing new subjects into the curriculum, by workshops on new methods, by developing new ways to classify pupils, by new theories of administration, by new patterns of professional training. It was difficult indeed to capture the spirit of progressive education in a crowded slum school, to transform a class of forty polyglot children into the sort of family at cooperative work that Dewey described as the ideal school. As a result, many "progressives" like Cubberley sought essentially to substitute a new version of bureaucracy for the old. But, at the turn of the century, perceptive schoolmen recognized that the quest for standardized schooling—that once had been a reform—had become a kind of depotism. It would require all their ingenuity to control their creation and to subordinate the schools to education.

Modernization in Philadelphia School Reform, 1882–1905
William Issel

Edwin A. Van Valkenburg, muckraking editor of the *North American*, hailed the Philadelphia Public School Reorganization Act of 1905 for bringing "the modernization of Philadelphia's school system." The product of a twenty-year campaign by school reform organizations, the laws in the Reorganization Act defied the definition of law as congealed custom. The school reformers had deliberately designed a precedent-breaking measure that would radically transform the old ways; for, as the new conditions became urban, industrial, and (in the argot of the reformers) "foreign," the old ways had become repulsive and outmoded. The Reorganization Act brought an end to the uncoordinated localism and informality characteristic of the public schools of an agrarian culture, and symbolized the establishment of the centralized, standardized, and bureaucratic educational system characteristic of urban America today. In short, the Act brought educational modernization to the nation's third largest city. Investigation of the social basis for, and the political process behind, this modernization throws considerable light on both the history of urban education and the nature of Progressive Reform.

An integral part of reform to modernize Philadelphia municipal administration in general, the campaign to reorganize the public schools began in the flurry of insurgency of the 1880's and ended in the heat of what Clinton Rogers Woodruff called "Philadelphia's Revolution" of 1905. Upper-class Philadelphians staffed the municipal and the school reform organizations and advocated a similar set of political goals for both City Hall and Board

From *The Pennsylvania Magazine of History and Biographies*, Volume 94, Number 3 (July, 1970), pp. 358–83. Reprinted by permission of The Historical Society of Pennsylvania.

Officers of the Civic Club (1904)

Total number	9
Number in Blue Book	9
Number in Social Register	5
Per cent in either	100%

Delegation to Harrisburg Supporting the 1891 Reorganization Bill

Total number	25
Number in Blue Book	22
Number in Social Register	14
Per cent in either	88%

Board of Public Education After the 1905 Reorganization Act (1906)

Total number	21
Number in Blue Book	16
Number in Social Register	4
Per cent in either	76%

Officers of the Public Education Association (1882–1912)

Total number	24
Number in Blue Book	18
Number in Social Register	11
Per cent in either	75%

Board of Public Education Before the 1905 Reorganization Act (1904)

Total number	42
Number in Blue Book	20
Number in Social Register	5
Per cent in either	47%

Delegation to Harrisburg Opposing the 1891 Reorganization Bill

Total number	18
Number in Blue Book	5
Number in Social Register	0
Per cent in either	27%

Ward Boards of Education Abolished by the 1905 Reorganization Act (1904)

Total number	540
Number in Blue Book	63
Number in Social Register	8
Per cent in either	12%

SOURCES: Philadelphia *Social Register* (New York, 1893, 1895, 1903, 1910); Boyd's *Philadelphia Blue Book* (Philadelphia, 1887, 1893, 1905, 1908); Philadelphia Board of Public Education, *Annual Report,* 1904, 276–296, and *Annual Report, 1906;* Public Education Association of Philadelphia, *A Generation of Progress in Our Public Schools* (Philadelphia, 1914), 63; Civic Club of Philadelphia, *Annual Report, 1904,* 3; *Public Ledger* (Philadelphia), May 12 and May 22, 1891.

of Public Education: separation of municipal administration from state and local politics; centralization of power in the hands of a few, nonpartisan experts; extension of civil service and scientific business administration methods.

The first attempt by upper-class reformers to modernize the Philadelphia municipal government began in November, 1880. Led by disgruntled Republicans, including Anthony J. Drexel, Edward Longstreth, Justus C. Strawbridge, John Wanamaker, and Rudolph Blankenburg, and operating under the name of the Committee of One Hundred, the reformers nominated a reform slate for the February, 1881, municipal elections. Their goals suggested the later course of municipal reform in the city: a nonpartisan police force; limiting the salary of the receiver of taxes; prosecution and punishment of those guilty of election fraud, maladministration of office, and misappropriation of public funds. After failing to gain the support of the incumbent mayor, the Committee succeeded in securing the election of Samuel G. King on a nonpartisan ticket. The Committee approved of King's administration, but, by 1884, the regular party organization won back the mayoralty. The Committee chose to answer local resistance with state legislation, and, led by John C. Bullitt, drew up a reform charter. The Bullitt Bill, as the charter was called, passed the legislature in 1885, centralizing power and responsibility in the hands of the mayor and consolidating the twenty-five municipal bureaus into nine departments.

The Committee of One Hundred had demanded election of the school board without regard to party affiliation and the appointment of teachers on merit. Shortly after the 1881 municipal election, members of the Society for Organizing Charity organized the Public Education Association (PEA) in order to fight exclusively for these and other public school measures. The PEA immediately distributed a circular of information in which it linked its goals directly to those of the Committee of One Hundred: "It is the object of this Association to promote the efficiency and to perfect the system of public education in Philadelphia, by which term is meant all education emanating from, or in any way controlled by, the State." The PEA decided to adopt frankly political methods, for "These objects the Association hope[s] to attain through appeals to the local authorities and to the Legislature, and by any other means as may be deemed expedient."

The Committee of One Hundred had aimed to increase the power of the central city administration, but, for Philadelphia's public schools in 1882, there was no central administration to strengthen. Supervising principals administered the ward schools; committees of principals managed teacher examination and other necessary duties; committees of the Board of Public Education carried out the overseeing of the high school. Such decentralization of authority seemed incredible to the members of the PEA. Looking, unlike the members of the ward school boards and most of the members of the Board of Public Education, to other large cities for comparison, they pointed out that Philadelphia's arrangement was an anachronism, for Boston, Cincinnati, and St. Louis, with smaller school populations, all had city superintendents. "The Board of Education," argued the PEA, "hold the same relation to the Public Schools as a Board of Directors hold to a bank or railroad. It would be as reasonable to argue that the Board of Directors of the Pennsylvania should run the road, and dispense with a President, as to argue that the Board of Education should assume the duties of superintendents."

Early in 1882, the PEA set up a subcommittee to meet with the Board of Public Education on behalf of gaining an appropriation from the City Councils for a superintendent. At the same time, they organized several public meetings to stir up sympathy for reform, and utilized the newspapers to publicize the campaign. In April, the Board of Public Education adopted a new bylaw to allow for an office of superintendent, as well as for assistants, and the City Councils shortly thereafter authorized funds for salaries.

Encouraged by their success in lobbying for a City Superintendent, the PEA decided to carry their interest in centralization further, and met with the legislative subcommittee of the Committee of One Hundred to suggest that the Bullitt Bill, then in the process of formation, include a section providing for the reorganization of the public schools. The ward school boards, they argued, should be abolished; in their place the PEA proposed managers and superintendents appointed by the Board of Public Education. The architects of the Bullitt Bill, though interested in the principle of centralizing school administration, refused to back a proposal that would deny to residents of the wards the power to elect their school directors. Such a clause would almost certainly reduce the chances that the reform charter could gain enough support to pass the legislature.

Aware of the odds against them, now that their plan to abolish the ward school boards had been rejected by the Committee of One Hundred as too radical, the PEA worked even harder to gain support. The schools, they argued, were in a situation of crisis proportions brought about by the lack of "consistent and homogeneous methods of administration," and "the unification of the governing body and undivided authority over, as well as the responsibility for, the administration of schools must be secured." The PEA quietly increased its membership, gradually gained the support of newspaper editors, and tirelessly followed the deliberations of the Board of Public Education in an effort to gain influence. By 1885, the PEA codified its legislative program into two resolutions that would guide, with no substantive changes, its political activity for the following twenty years.

> *Resolved,* That it is the deliberate judgment of this Association that the advance of public education in Philadelphia is grievously retarded by the imperfect system of control of the public schools now existing; that the interests of this community demand a radical change in this system, which shall include the appointment of numerous assistant superintendents to co-operate with and act under the direction of the Superintendent of the Public Schools, and the abolition of the local school boards, and the vesting of the powers of disbursing money and appointing and removing teachers and otherwise controlling the public

schools of this city in the Board of Public Education; that all merely local and artificial divisions should be abolished both in the management of the schools and in the appointment of the members of the Board of Public Education, so that the interests of the whole community may always be kept in view and the system of education treated as a unit, sub-divided as convenience may require, and not as a mass of separate divisions, each independent of the other and subject to no common control such as exist at the present time.

Resolved further, That this Association and its individual members will not rest satisfied until these measures are accomplished and will use their utmost endeavors to carry them through.

By 1891, the PEA had enlisted the support of several members of the Board of Public Education; most important, they had convinced Edward T. Steel, its president, of the necessity for reorganization of the school administration along the lines they advocated. And, by 1891, the modernizing reformers who had supported the Committee of One Hundred had decided that the Bullitt Charter, while necessary if the municipal government was to be transformed, was not sufficient of itself to accomplish the task. Using the Committee of One Hundred as a model, a small group of reformers organized the Municipal League; the League demanded the familiar goals of civil service, separation of municipal administration from state and national party politics, and business principles of management. In February, 1891, Edward T. Steel asked the Secretary of the PEA, lawyer William W. Wiltbank, to draw up a bill to be presented to the legislature for reorganization of the Philadelphia schools. The Porter bill, so-called after the Philadelphia Senator who managed the measure, followed the lines of the 1885 PEA resolution, and provided for the abolition of the ward school boards, increased financial autonomy by the Board of Public Education from the City Councils, prohibition of federal, state, or municipal officials from membership on the Board, and extension of power for the Superintendent of Schools. By the time the bill had passed second reading in the Senate, the PEA began to get a taste of the opposition, and it organized two meetings to gain support among the city population. Of the newspapers, most of which had already been enlisted as supporters of the bill, the most enthusiastic was the *North American,* owned by Thomas Wanamaker, son of the famous merchant, and edited by Edwin Van Valkenburg. Van Valkenburg used his paper in support of the Municipal League and to hold up the school reformers, as he did the League members, as men "with no incentive but a conscientious feeling of the duty which as citizens they owe to the community."

The opponents of the Porter bill saw it and its advocates in a different light. When the Senate Education Committee held its hearings on the measure on May 11, almost half of the ward school boards sent representatives to Harrisburg to help defeat reorganization. They pictured the bill as a scheme in the interest of centralized power and decried it as a vicious attempt by Edward T. Steel to increase his personal influence. At the meeting of the Philadelphia Board of Public Education the following day, they introduced a resolution asking the Board officially to condemn the bill. The Board squashed this resolution as beneath its dignity, but the bill's supporters were taken aback by the vehemence of the opposition represented by such a move.

The Senate was less moved by the vehemence of the opposition than by the arguments of the reformers that "The schools of Philadelphia are suffering for want of a system. They are now hampered by the local committees, made up for the most part of the worst element of ward politics." With the help of Boies Penrose and the endorsement of the Republic Party organization, for the state and city organizations were working to break the independent strength of the ward organizations, the bill passed the Senate easily.

The situation was different in the House. The only Philadelphia member on the Education Committee opposed the bill, and the Philadelphia delegation, experiencing heavy pressure from their ward constituents and their ward party committees to oppose the bill, and reluctant to jeopardize their seats, prepared to defeat the measure with whatever help they could get from the rural members. The supporters of the bill who attended the hearings before the Education Committee on May 21 argued with the legislators until 3:00 A.M., at which time the Committee agreed to report the bill favorably. But, when the time came for reporting out bills, the Chairman of the Committee could not be found. Later, when the supporters attempted to report the bill out of place, the Philadelphia delegation refused to grant the necessary unanimous consent and thus killed the reorganization bill of 1891.

By May 23, editor Van Valkenburg knew that the bill would be defeated, but he urged the reformers to take heart, for their victory was inevitable. "The man," he wrote, "who doubts the doom of the sectional boards in the near future must be willfully blind." While it was true that the ward school boards were "doomed," Van Valkenburg's timetable was faulty, for the opposition was to prove stronger than he or the reformers imagined in 1891. Their attempt to introduce a reorganization bill into the 1893 legislature was completely frustrated; for, while Senator Porter read the bill on the first day of the session, it was never reported out of Committee.

In January, 1894, several women college graduates from Philadelphia's upper social levels, determined to promote "by education and active cooperation, a higher public spirit and a better social order," organized the Civic Club. Led by Mrs. Cornelius Stevenson, educated in Paris, holder of a graduate degree, and an amateur archaeologist, the Club members were profoundly disturbed by what they saw as the failure of women of their class and status to assume a public role in keeping with their intelligence and education. "The deep shadows which now darken our present moral condition," said Mrs. Stevenson in her first address to the Club, "have been brought about mainly by love of ease, of self-indulgence, and of luxury, and we women are not without blame with regard to this. The poor use which many of our privileged sisters have made of their fine feathers, not so much to attract as to dazzle others into something akin to covetousness, has led many a man, like the jay of the fable, to devote his entire energies to decking himself and his brood with peacock's feathers." The members of the Civic Club were as anxious to be realistic as they were to assume a political role, and they decided to avoid the stigma of idealistic, utopian, petticoat politicians. "The days of useless martyrdom are over," said Mrs. Stevenson, "and heroic sacrifice, even in the shape of unnecessarily facing ridicule, is not required of us." "For those who wish to point the way, it is not enough to be good, they should be clever." To be clever was to be politically realistic, and to be politically realistic was to know the strength of organization. In the twentieth century, since the "growing necessity for organization and concerted action in every direction is now so keenly felt," the voluntary and unofficial union of reform activity represented by the Club would become official. In the meantime, she felt that the Civic Club could "not only do serious good, but that it can win for itself the respect of the community by preparing the way for such unification of effort."

The modernization of the Philadelphia public schools stood high on the list of problems to which the Civic Club intended to devote its energy; scarcely two months after the Club organized, it arranged with the PEA for a joint meeting to consider the question. Encouraged by the large attendance at the meeting on March 3, and pleased with the citywide publicity granted by the newspapers, the Club asked the PEA Executive Committee to appoint a subcommittee to formulate a joint proposal that would lead to the drafting of a new school reorganization bill. The joint committee of the two organizations, with the new President of the Board of Public Education (also a member of the PEA Executive Board) and Mrs. Stevenson among their number, met throughout the spring and fall of 1894 to consider the content of the bill. Senator Porter agreed once again to sponsor the measure, which he introduced on January 16, 1895.

This bill, had it passed, would have radically transformed the character, duties, and powers of the Board of Public Education. Power to choose members would have been shared by the mayor and the judges of the common pleas courts, instead of [being] held solely by the judges. The Board would have been reduced in size from more than thirty members to ten; the ward school boards would have been abolished; the Board of Public Education, not the City Councils, would have received all state school funds, and the Board would have had authority to levy a special city school tax. All teachers would have been appointed by the central board rather than the ward school boards, and only after an examination administered by the Superintendent of Schools.

Because this first 1895 reorganization measure was sponsored by Senator Porter, it was never to be considered. For, during the week that followed the introduction of the bill, Porter supported the attempt by David

Martin to seize control of Pennsylvania's Republican Party organization from Matthew Quay and Israel Durham. Martin, at the last minute, refused to support the Quay-Durham mayoralty choice, Boies Penrose, and shifted his delegates to Charles F. Warwick, City Solicitor. Taking his opponents by surprise, Martin won the convention, thereby allowing Warwick to win the election in February. Porter's support of Martin won him a place in the "Hog Combine," as the Martin faction was called, and lost him the support of Penrose in the Senate. Consequently, his bills were killed, for most members of the Senate were sympathetic with Quay's desire to punish the rebellious Philadelphians.

Because Penrose opposed Senator Porter rather than the bill to reorganize the public schools, the second 1895 bill received a more sympathetic hearing in the Senate. The Civic Club and the PEA, furthermore, noting the newspaper opposition to placing any appointive power over school board members in the mayor's hands and criticizing the complete abolition of the ward school boards, revised the initial measure considerably. The new bill provided for a twenty-one rather than a ten-member board, replaced the ward school boards with ward boards of school visitors (a provision that would hopefully take the sting out of the stripping of power from the boards), abolished the ward lines as the basis of school districts in favor of lines drawn according to administrative "convenience," and required the City Councils to appropriate school funds to the Board of Public Education in a lump sum, to be distributed by the Board according to its own decisions. The Board, furthermore, would be authorized to levy a special school tax on the city residents to be used strictly for school purposes. As stated in the PEA resolution of 1885, the central Board of Public Education would take over from the ward boards all duties, such as teacher hiring, building-site selection and maintenance, and examination and certification of teachers, as well as determining and supervising curriculum. Prohibition of school board membership to municipal, state, or federal officeholders, a clause that had antagonized potential supporters in 1891, was omitted.

By the time Mayor Warwick took office in the beginning of April, the bill was in the legislature, and Warwick, acknowledging the support he had received from the members of the Municipal League and the Independent Republicans, made it clear in his inaugural address that he favored the activities of their allies in the PEA and the Civic Club. "I am," he noted, "strongly of the opinion that the bill recently introduced into the Legislature, and urged by the Civic Club of this city . . . if passed will do away with the present cumbersome and involved system, and result in securing greater efficiency in school work." By April 8, opposition had developed in the legislature to the autonomy granted the Board of Public Education relative to the City Councils by the financial arrangements of the bill. Granting the strength of the opposition, the bill's supporters amended the measure so as to retain in the hands of the Councils the power to raise all school funds (except the state appropriation) and to delegate to the Board whatever funds it would receive. In this amended form, the bill passed the Senate unanimously.

The successful reorganization bill left the Senate with the support of both the Martin and the Quay-Durham-Penrose factions of the Republican Party organization and with the backing of Mayor Warwick and District Attorney Graham as well as the Civic Club and the PEA. Their support explained the fact that the members of the House from the other areas of the Commonwealth began "being besieged with letters from the best citizens of Philadelphia to support it." The Philadelphia delegation, however, was beginning to receive pressure from citizens of presumably a different sort, as the members of the ward school boards began putting pressure on their representatives to defeat the bill. When the bill came to the House to be placed in Committee, the Speaker (who later denied that he had deliberately tried to kill the measure) ordered the Committee on Municipal Corporations (popularly known as the "Corpse" Committee) rather than the Education Committee to take the bill. Whereas only four Philadelphia men were on the Education Committee, twelve were on the Committee on Municipal Corporations, and, as a member of the Philadelphia delegation told Senator Porter, to support the bill would be political suicide.

The battle to decide the fate of the reorganization bill during the six weeks that followed separated the modernizing reformers from the traditional enemies of reform. The reformers worked to destroy what they saw as an outmoded, inefficient, wasteful, and corrupt, systemless way of carrying out public education. The enemies of reform worked to maintain what they saw as a reasonably successful means of schooling that, most important, was controlled by people of their own class, status, and neighborhood, and to which they had immediate and personal access. On the one side were the PEA and the Civic Club, joined by both factions of the state and city Republican Party organization. On the other side were at least half of the ward school boards, particularly those in the lower- and middle-income wards of the city, and the ward political party organizations, the very ward organizations that Israel Durham and the Vare brothers had been working for a decade to mold into a centrally directed, citywide Republican organization.

The criticism by the large circulation newspapers of the city that the ward school boards passed resolutions against the bill for "personal selfish fear of losing their petty political positions," and that "the election of School Directors by the people is a theory, not an actual condition" because the nominations were made by "the organization," contained a measure of truth. But it was deceptively simple as an explanation for the strength with which the ward school boards could fight, given the fact that "the organization" supported the reform bill. Newspaper editors supporting the bill never took it upon themselves to wonder how, since "the organization" had enlisted on the side of "the people at large," "the organization" could also be charged with responsibility for, in some shadowy way, opposing the passage of the measure. Newspaper editors opposing the bill, on the other hand, were as anxious to argue that the bill did not represent a popular and widespread demand as supporters of the bill were eager to argue that parents and guardians "are almost a unit in their support of the bill."

But Mrs. Stevenson of the Civic Club, speaking before the House Committee on behalf of the bill on May 7, did not refer to the sentiment of the people at large as the justification for the bill's merits. Instead, she pointed out that, given the modernizing perspective, the bill was simply necessary in order to do away with the traditional practices now that they were outmoded. That they were outmoded was not determined by canvassing the citizens of Philadelphia. The reorganization bill looked beyond the city, and it was drawn up "after extensive correspondence between prominent members of both associations [the Civic Club and the PEA] and the leading educators of the country, and after a careful study of the latest reforms brought into the educational systems of the various states."

Mrs. Stevenson had no opposition counterpart in the Committee hearings except the delegations from the sectional school boards and the editors of the opposition newspapers. William Taggart, editor of *Taggart's Times*, emerged as the most vociferous critic of the reformers, and used his paper, as well as the Harrisburg hearings, to condemn the reformers as elitists anxious to impose their values upon the city population as a whole. "The agitation over this subject," he wrote, "does not represent a general demand or sentiment in this city. The great majority of the people are abundantly satisfied with the schools, and know that they are better today than they ever were as regards instruction, comfort, good teaching, and the general welfare of their children." Taggart's frame of reference, and the frame of reference he presented to his readers, was not, like that of Mrs. Stevenson, one that compared Philadelphia public schools with those of other large cities according to criteria derived from writers on educational administration. Instead, Taggart looked at the Philadelphia public schools in the context of the earlier years of the nineteenth century, and he was correct, according to even Mrs. Stevenson's criteria, that the schools were better in 1895 than they had been in 1845.

"Where," wrote Taggart, "does this bawling and whining about the 'degradation' and 'inefficiency' of our schools come from? Chiefly from the old maids in the Civic Club, from a handful of educational cranks, from the University clique which is anxious to boss the whole school system, and from the newspapers which are anxious to please powerful advertisers." Mrs. Stevenson and the reformers were indeed anxious to place control of the public schools in the hands of educational experts under the direction of a small group of college and university-educated businessmen and professionals. And the reformers did not deny that they were largely "women who have never experienced the joys of maternity and have no practical ideas whatever about the training of children" rather than argue that Taggart's criteria were irrelevant to the teaching of children in school. According to Taggart, "the real object [of the Porter bill] is an effort of the so-called social status people, who have no faith in the wisdom of boilermakers, carpenters, painters—in short the bone and sinew as well as the good common sense element to be found among our mechanics as well as business men in all our wards—to take a hand in the management of our public schools." The reformers again pointed out that such an argument missed the point; simply stated, "Education is a science. Every chance citizen cannot administer it."

Advocates of the bill, argued the editor of the Philadelphia *Telephone*, "are in a majority of cases persons who have not been educated in the public schools of the city, and several of the most ardent opponents of the present system are not even residents of the city." The cosmopolitan, modernizing perspective of the reformers made that argument irrelevant like the others. And explicit in the reform bill was the destruction of criteria for selecting teachers held up by the *Downtown Record* as admirable; most teachers, the editor pointed out, were natives of Philadelphia, but the bill would threaten the custom of hiring the teachers from the city Normal School on the basis of their family's residence in a ward.

Finally, the reformers were opposed to continuation of the traditional system of school control because it fostered a mentality they defined as destructive to educational excellence, because it fostered a point of view essentially parochial and neighborhood oriented rather than scientifically oriented. The editor of the Manayunk *Advance* told his readers that "the underlying principal of the measure is wrong, and it should be defeated." Referring to the transfer to an appointive from an elective central Board of Public Education earlier in the century, he argued against strengthening an appointive system by abolishing the ward school boards altogether. "Our ward," he argued, "has not been more advantageously represented in the Board of Education since the controllers were appointed than it was when they were elected." It was just such efforts by the delegates from ward school boards to the Board of Public Education to act as members of a log-rolling political caucus on behalf of their constituents, according to the school reformers, that were inimical to the creation of a modern school system administered according to the latest principles of business management and devoted to the dissemination of curriculums organized on the basis of scientific educational theory.

To the members of the Civic Club, the arguments raised by the opposition consisted merely of "well-sounding nonsense, such as has been used at all times by the crafty, by the ignorant, or by the thoughtless." From their point of view, "school revision . . . must, of course, appeal to all those . . . who have had intellectual training, and who take an interest in the good standing of our city." But to the members of the House Committee on Municipal Corporations, sympathetic to the pressure from the ward school boards and to the arguments raised by the opposition press, the bill had only enough appeal to induce them to "study" the measure. Needless to say, when the legislative session ended, they were still hard at work "studying."

The traditionalist opposition to reform kept the 1895 reorganization bill

from consideration by the entire House, despite the efforts of the reform coalition of Civic Club, Public Education Association, most of the city's newspapers, and the leaders of the state and city Republican organizations. But
the fight for the reorganization bill had not been the Civic Club's only fight
in the first months of 1895; at the same time, the Club had worked to elect
women school directors to the ward school board of the Seventh Ward.
This campaign sheds further light on the nature of the school reform politics that eventually destroyed decentralized school control in Philadelphia.
The model for the Civic Club campaign came from the old Committee of
One Hundred, which had nominated two women school directors for the
Twenty-ninth Ward in 1882 who had subsequently served on that school
board for fourteen years. Since that time, eleven women had been chosen
for ward school boards out of a total of about 440 ward board members.
Determined to work on a strictly nonpartisan basis, the Club sent to the
Democratic and Republican leaders of ten wards, as well as to the newspapers and the Municipal League, the names of women who would run for
the offices if nominated. The Municipal League nominated the Club's
choices in three wards, and, when the Democrats endorsed the League
nominees in the Seventh Ward, the Club decided to put all its efforts toward the campaign in that section. A downtown ward, it ran from the
Schuylkill River to Seventh Street, and from Spruce to South Street—a
long and narrow strip bordering businesses and shops on the north and a
lower-income and ethnically diverse area of single-family homes, with a few
tenements, on the south and east. Its population was one-third Negro, and,
of the other two-thirds, half were either foreign born or second generation
(with a substantial group of Russians, Poles, and Italians), while the remainder were native-born whites.

The Civic Club pointed out that the ward political party leadership of
this predominantly Negro and recently arrived immigrant section was representative of its population, and tracked down the occupations of the Democratic and Republican Executive Committees in an attempt "to make perfectly clear the forces with which a canvass like ours has to contend." The
Civic Club candidates did not expect to win the election with ease, but they
were surprised by their difficulty in even obtaining a hearing. They nevertheless persisted, refusing to participate in the petty bribery that was part of
the political culture of the ward, and lost by a smaller margin than they had
expected. They lost with the help of the ward school board, the ward Republican organization, and the ward public school teachers. The school
board made it known that they would not suffer a woman on their board,
and the teachers followed the lead of their employers: Fifty-four of the
sixty-three teachers in the ward issued a manifesto to the voters opposing
the Civic Club hopefuls and praising the incumbents running for re-election.

Looking back at the election campaign after a space of several months,
the architect of the fight attempted to explain to the members of the American Academy of Political and Social Science that the campaign results were
not surprising. "The wealthier part of the ward," she admitted, "has only a

platonic interest in the public schools. Its members do not send their children to these schools, as under their present political management no parents will send their children to them if they can send them to better schools. The most moral and conscientious Catholics," she claimed, "send their children to their own parochial schools. The only class of which," in her opinion, "the religious and moral portion interest themselves in the public schools, are the colored population, because they send their children to them, and are obliged to do so, or keep them at home, none of the private schools admitting them." As the Civic Club campaigners were people from the "wealthier part of the ward," the fact that their interest was platonic was not lost on those from the less wealthy parts. And, besides the organized opposition to their candidacy, the Club admitted that the confidence of the voters in "the men who had taken the trouble to make their acquaintance before they asked for their vote" partly explained the women's defeat. Furthermore, they had failed to convince electors that women could "really manage the schools better than men."

Despite the rebuff in the Seventh Ward, the Civic Club continued, working with the PEA, to campaign for women school directors during the years that followed. And, while they failed to elect more than a handful of women, their political acumen increased considerably. The major efforts of both organizations, however, went to the slow but quiet task of building enough support among the members of the legislature and among the state and city Republican organizations to ensure the eventual success of a reorganization bill. In 1897, another bill was prepared, but it failed, like the 1895 measure, and, in 1899, the PEA appointed a committee to make a systematic investigation of the organization and financing of schools in the larger cities of the country. The committee made the report public in 1900, and used it as their rationale for a resolution to investigate the schools of the entire state, which they introduced unsuccessfully in the 1901 session of the legislature. In 1902, the Civic Club and the PEA continued to build their case against the Philadelphia schools by gathering still more empirical evidence with which to compare their administration with that of other large cities. Together, the groups memorialized the City Councils to support reorganization, sending along, as the fruits of their research, a list of contradictory and confusing laws in force that had been passed since the middle of the nineteenth century. Such empirical data impressed the Councils less than they did the reformers, and, when a sympathetic Councilman introduced an ordinance to set up a commission of nationally recognized educational experts to investigate the Philadelphia schools, the Councils defeated it. Most Councilmen opposed the importation of outsiders to evaluate their Philadelphia public schools.

Frustrated once again by their failure to gain reorganization, the reformers sought to take advantage of the opportunity afforded by the sensationalist press coverage accorded to the conviction of three school directors from the Twenty-eighth Ward for conspiracy, bribery, and extortion in connection with hiring and promoting teachers in early 1903. At the same time, Miss Dora Keen, Secretary of the PEA and a member of the school board of the Ninth Ward, experienced a highly emotional personal confrontation with John K. Myers, Republican leader of the ward, over teacher hiring. According to Clinton Rogers Woodruff, sympathetic to Miss Keen and sharing her point of view that teachers should be chosen according to criteria other than strict seniority (the view of Myers), the ward leader "made a personal and profane attack upon Miss Keen of so virulent at [sic] nature that she was compelled in self-respect to leave the room." The "Twenty-eighth Ward Scandal" and the confrontation between Miss Keen and Mr. Myers provided the reformers with potentially powerful issues with which to support their case against the existing organization of the Philadelphia schools. The three articles that appeared in national magazines in the months immediately following added momentum to the reform campaign. Lincoln Steffens labeled Philadelphia "Corrupt and Contented" in July; Clinton Rogers Woodruff attacked "A Corrupt School System" in December; Adele Marie Shaw castigated "The Public Schools of a Boss-Ridden City" in February, 1904.

The muckrakers offered little in the way of concrete suggestions for change in the public schools, but Charles W. Eliot, President of Harvard, recommended a detailed reorganization program in his address to the PEA on January 16, 1904. Eliot reiterated, in considerable detail, a program for modernization sketched out in the PEA resolution of 1885. Legislation for the schools should be strictly in the hands of a small board representing the city as a whole; executive functions should be confined to educational experts; all school finances should be controlled by the Board of Public Education, whose income should be predictable in advance and determined by law irrespective of the City Councils. In April, the PEA began distributing copies of Eliot's address throughout the city, urging readers to "throw your influence in favor of some similar reorganization of *our* system at the *next session of the Legislature*. Reorganization is needed in order to abolish sectionalism, but can not take place until public opinion is agreed what to substitute."

In the fall of 1904, the reformers changed their tactics and emphasized dishonesty and corruption in the management of the schools as they never had before. Whether they deliberately decided to make such a change in order to dramatize their case, or merely shifted their emphasis as a result of the muckraking exposures and the convictions of the previous year, the school reformers stressed honesty versus corruption rather than the modernizing rationale behind the reorganization plan. The same was true of the arguments of the municipal reformers, who, reorganizing the nearly dormant Municipal League into a Committee of Seventy, launched a campaign on November 14, 1904, "to rescue Philadelphia from political degradation." And, two days before the organization of the new Committee, the Philadelphia Teachers' Association, itself recently organized and already a potential political force, having enrolled a majority of the city's teachers, declared its sympathy [with] reorganization. The editor of the *North Amer-*

ican, having dedicated his resources to the service of "honesty," then began a systematic campaign of exposure against the ward school boards. Stressing the obsolescence of the constituent orientation of the ward school boards as a group, Van Valkenburg made clear that "We propose to remedy the deficiency by adapting to conditions here the methods which created a political revolution in Chicago. That city was cleansed, not altogether by exposing graft and corruption, not by attacking the machine bosses, but by printing unbiased records of crooked councilmen and School Directors."

On the day following the *North American*'s first installment in its "gallery" of "crooked" ward school board members, the principals of fifty Philadelphia public schools and several department heads at Central High School (one-third of whom were PEA members) published an "Appeal to the Citizens of Philadelphia." Unwilling to remain silent about the "deplorable administrative conditions under which the public school system of this great city must operate," the principals called for "the only effective reform possible, a complete reorganization of the system of control for the public schools of Philadelphia." After setting out their grievances in detail, and arguing that "it is the system that is at fault, not the men who operate it," the principals suggested a method for achieving reorganization.

> We believe, therefore, that all public agitation of the question should be directed to the great end of securing for Philadelphia through legislative enactment a thoroughly modern system of school control. Furthermore, the system should not be changed by reckless or haphazard methods. Just as the selection of a route for the Panama Canal or the plan for our own new water supply was determined by the advice of skilled engineers, so should men of established reputation for their broad knowledge and practical experience in the successful operation of modern school systems be consulted in the formation of a plan to place our schools upon this higher plane of administrative efficiency. This is the unquestioned right of the children of our city.

The principals appealed for an educational commission to draw up a new reorganization bill. The Board of Managers of the Teachers' Association, spurred by the dramatic move of the principals, unanimously agreed to support the demand for a commission. "The vice of the Philadelphia system," according to the President of the Association (who was also a long-time PEA activist), "is, in brief, that while we have grown into a great city, we have maintained a village organization. All of the other great cities of the United States have passed through a similar stage of administrative development." One week later, the Council of Representatives of the Teachers' Association also agreed to support the Appeal. But the membership of the Association at large never expressed its opinion on the Appeal, for a resolution at the Council of Representatives meeting for a referendum was overwhelmingly defeated.

Meanwhile, the Committee of Seventy prepared a City Party ticket for the February municipal elections, and the regular Republican organization, anxious to protect its appeal as much as possible—given another threat to its tenure of office—publicly announced its support for both an educational commission and [a] reorganization of the schools. Confronted with the third organized cry for "honesty and efficiency" in as many decades, a cry that had consistently cost them the mayoralty, the Durham organization found it especially expedient to join the fight for the abolition of the ward school boards. And, as the central city organization had been working for a decade to strengthen its control over the ward organizations, its ability to control the Philadelphia delegation to the House of Representatives in Harrisburg was considerably stronger than it had been in 1895. As the editor of the *Press* had written during the battle over the 1895 bill, "a majority [of the Philadelphia delegation] would vote for the abolition of the local school boards, because as a rule they are a source of great annoyance for candidates for the Senate and House. Candidates for the Legislature are compelled to go into these fights simply to maintain their political hold in the district, and it would be a relief to a great many of them could the measure prevail."

The Board of Public Education responded to the Appeal and to the support by the leaders of the Teachers' Association by appointing a five-man commission to prepare an Assembly bill to carry out reorganization. Three members of the commission had worked with the PEA for reform: Henry R. Edmunds, as a sympathetic nonmember while he was president of the Board of Public Education; lawyer William W. Justice, as an active member (he later became honorary president of the PEA); and Martin G. Brumbaugh, University of Pennsylvania Professor of Pedagogy and former Commissioner of Education for Puerto Rico, as vice-president. The Republican Party organization was represented by David H. Lane, and the other member, William H. Lambert, was President of the Board of Charities and Correction. Anxious to get the bill to the legislature by March 1, Lane advised the newspapers that "we seek to be enlightened but we should invite [to public hearings] only those specially equipped."

At the public hearings held by the commission on January 28, the members of the PEA, the Civic Club, and the Teachers' Association presented the plan outlined first in 1885 and refined in 1904 by Charles W. Eliot as the model the commission should follow in drafting the bill. The expected opposition from the ward school boards, now organized into a School Directors' Association, never materialized; its representative at the hearings informed the commission that its views would be made known through private correspondence. On March 1, as planned, Senator John M. Scott introduced the bill. At that point, the School Directors' Association played its hand by suggesting a substitute bill providing for an elected rather than an appointed board, allowing the ward school boards to continue hiring teachers, and leaving the financial specifications of the school system intact. Taking advantage of Durham's absence on a Florida vacation, the Directors' Association appealed to his lieutenants, Senator McNichol and the

Vares, to support the substitute bill. But Durham and David H. Lane, having already convinced Governor Pennypacker to approve an appointive board, and hard pressed by the Committee of Seventy for supporting the white slave trade, for stuffing ballot boxes, and for covering up police corruption, were unwilling to renege. Durham returned from Florida and quelled the potential revolt.

Both the Senate and the House favored the commission bill—the bill, in the words of the editor of the *North American*, "for the modernization of Philadelphia's school system"—and it passed the Senate 38 to 1 and the House 178 to 0 on April 11. Modernization removed power over the city's public schools from the 540 elected members of the ward school boards and placed it in the hands of the twenty-one appointed members of the Board of Public Education. Before the reorganization, the forty-two members of the central board had represented the forty-two sections of the city; now, twenty-one members represented the city as a whole. Modernization stripped the ward school boards of power, left them intact only as boards of visitors, and placed control of the schools in the hands of cosmopolitan and efficiency-minded upper-class businessmen and professionals, whose legislative decisions would be carried out by dispassionate, university-trained, educational experts according to the impersonal criteria of bureaucratic social organization. Power over teacher selection and construction and maintenance of schools shifted from the predominantly middle- and lower-class ward school boards to the upper-class central school board and the administrators in their offices at the Board of Public Education. The neighborhood loyalty and local orientation of the ward school boards that had encouraged the hiring of teachers who were "one of ours" disappeared, to be replaced by hiring practices based on the scientific and empirical indices that could be utilized in standardized civil service examinations. Reform signaled the end of the diversity of styles of instruction and the multiplicity of criteria of evaluation that had followed logically from curricula and supervision patterned according to norms rooted in the class, nationality, race, or religion of a ward. The new system brought curricula patterned according to the laws of educational psychology and a supervisory staff loyal to their superior and, beyond him, to the national corps of professional educators. Reform swept away the personalistic orientation characteristic of most ward school board members that excused occasional chicanery and dishonesty as "human nature," that regarded as normal to the social order the *quid pro quo* bargaining and factionalism of city ward political systems. In the place of such traditionalism stood impersonal educational administrators "above politics," whose rewards would come strictly from within the organization of which they were a part, and who would relate to their public in strictly defined capacities according to clearly defined rules.

To the PEA and the Civic Club, the passage of the bill, despite the compromises it contained, meant a considerable advance toward the creation of a school system in Philadelphia capable of meeting the demands of a modern age. They applauded what they saw as the most important features of the reorganization: centralization of power in the Board of Public Education over all city schools; concentration of executive work in the hands of educational experts rather than in the hands of committees of laymen; destruction of decentralization. The reformers admitted that their program for modernization was nearly complete with the passage of the 1905 Reorganization Act. Considering the extent to which the Reorganization Act radically altered the Philadelphia public school government and administration, the educational modernization laws easily qualify as the most revolutionary of the reform measures passed during "Philadelphia's Revolution" of 1905.

The Emergence of the Prep School
James McLachlan

The grand educational want of America at this present time," President James McCosh of Princeton told the National Educational Association in 1873, "is a judiciously scattered body of secondary schools, to bring on our brighter youth from what has been so well commenced in the primary schools, and may be so well completed in the better colleges." It was, in some respects, the same question that had concerned . . . reformers fifty years before: the problem of assuring a steady supply of well-prepared students in order to maintain or raise an institution's standards. It would be a major preoccupation of leaders in higher education through the last three decades of the nineteenth century.

If often on an uncertain course, over the three decades after McCosh spoke the American university would develop into much its present form. Despite their pretensions, before the Civil War American universities had been, at best, little more than good academies, with a professional school or so attached. But, by World War I, they rivaled and sometimes surpassed the institutions they were modeled on—the German universities of the nineteenth century. The great universities were built under the direction of a new breed of American, the academic entrepreneur. The Carnegies, Rockefellers, and Morgans had their counterparts, in the academic world, in university presidents like Charles W. Eliot of Harvard, William Rainey Harper of Chicago, Daniel Coit Gilman of Johns Hopkins, Andrew D. White of Cornell, and many others. Their roles bore about as much relation to those of the antebellum college presidents as did the role of the great corporation builder to that of the antebellum mill owner. From collegiate begin-

From *American Boarding Schools* (New York: Charles Scribner's Sons, 1970), pp. 189–218. Reprinted by permission.

nings—or, in some cases, from nothing—they created institutions that resembled, in influence, personnel, variety of services, and sometimes wealth, the contemporary industrial corporation. And, like the corporation president, the university president found it necessary to seek out new sources of supply for his operation.

McCosh, a Scottish philosopher who had assumed Princeton's presidency in 1868, scoured all Europe for educational models that might prove useful for the United States. Although the German system of secondary education was excellent, he thought it inappropriate to the United States. The "endowed schools of England"—or public schools—were also excellent. "A first-class English School," McCosh said, "if it does not impart much general knowledge, contrives, by its open-air exercise and the manliness of its school-life, to prepare youths for acting their parts in this world, and the high studies have sharpened the intellects of many, and produced a refinement among a select few such as you will scarcely find in another country." The difficulty with the English system was that it was only for the "select few." In "the utter want of provisions made for giving a higher-class education to the children of the poor, there is no advanced country in the world so deficient as England." If the English system was inappropriate to the United States, so were the schools of Ireland and Scotland. But the situation in the United States seemed almost desperate: "Wide regions, even in some of the most advanced states, are without not only a high school to give higher instruction to the middle and lower classes, but even without an academy." The country's "natural" gentlemen were going undiscovered; the Jeffersonian dream of "raking twenty geniuses from the rubble annually" was not being fulfilled:

[T]here is a vast amount of talent lost to the country, in bright boys, fitted to do good in the higher walks of life—in literature, in science, in statesmanship or the church—being obliged to devote their life to manual occupations. I hold that in the secondary school is the main means of calling forth talent in every country. It seizes the most promising boys of the primary schools and sends them up to college, or into the higher walks of life, where they have the means of distinguishing themselves and benefiting their country.

What was the solution? McCosh suggested, first, as Jonathan Edwards had done over a hundred years before, that wealthy individuals endow academies. "It would be far more to his credit for a man to have his name associated with academies such as Exeter and Andover, than to be handed down to posterity as the founder of some weakling college, ever ready to die, called Smith's College, or Jones's Scientific Institute, or Robinson University." Such schools might help fill the gap, but they would be of necessity scattered and sporadic. Drawing upon the recent example of the Freedman's Bureau, McCosh recommended another method, what he called "state and city endowments." Schools could be set up all over the country, as in Germany, open to rich and poor alike, well organized and well supervised. What McCosh was proposing, essentially, was a thorough and broadened public high school system, the path the United States would take in succeeding decades.

Others had dealt with the problem before, and others would afterward, but McCosh's 1873 speech occasioned a long and somewhat heated debate in his audience. The essential themes that emerged would occupy American educators for the next three decades: Should secondary education be publicly or privately supported? Should public high schools prepare students for college or be terminal institutions, or both? It would be better, said James Wickersham, superintendent of the Pennsylvania common schools, to "increase the number of high schools than of academies or seminaries—every town build up a high school . . . , so providing classical, mathematical and scientific instruction. This we have in hand now in Pennsylvania. If other states do the same, we do away with the old academies." An academy principal, the Reverend Charles Hammond of Monson, Massachusetts, objected. High schools belonged to the system of "popular education" and could not prepare boys for college as academies especially organized for the purpose could. "Not one boy in fifteen hundred ought to see the inside of college," he stated flatly. "What would a community be if everybody went to college? [Cheers.] Men are born into the world to get a living, and do their work, and act their destiny. That destiny is, not to go to college, except for a certain number." Joseph White, another Massachusetts man, challenged Hammond. Local high schools, he said, provided many boys with a college preparation who could never have received it at a distant and expensive academy.

President Charles William Eliot of Harvard made the lengthiest reply to McCosh's speech. The mass of the population, he declared, would not support tax-financed college preparatory schools. The work of the public high schools was to "train their pupils in English, in mathematics, in classics a little, up to their seventeenth year. A small per cent go to college. From academies almost all go to college." Toward McCosh's scheme for large-scale government aid to the public schools, Eliot had nothing but horrified scorn. One drop of aid would be

> a drop of poison. It demoralizes us, and weakens the foundation of our liberty. It interferes with the carrying-out of our destiny—the breeding of a race of independent and self-reliant freemen. I hope no words will go out from this Association which can be held to sanction, in any way or shape, a request from the government for education. I know of no more mischievous, insidious enemy to a free republic than this habit of asking help in good works which we ought to attend to ourselves.

Eliot was both an American and a nineteenth-century liberal; McCosh, being neither, had no such fears of governmental aid. Eliot, McCosh replied, "said tradesmen object to paying money to educate the minister's son and the lawyer's son. But what *we* say is: You pay money to open schools to which your own son may go. We want schools such that there shall be no poor boy in the country who shall not have within a few miles of him such a school as will enable him to go on to the highest place."

McCosh's view would, in the long run, prevail. Over the next five decades, American secondary education was drastically reorganized to meet the needs of a new, industrial society. In 1870, for instance, there were only about 80,000 students in the secondary schools of the United States, schools that were still mainly academies. The 16,000 secondary school graduates of 1870 made up only about 2 per cent of all the seventeen-year-olds in the country. Most of these students went on to college. By 1910, however, there were over 1,100,000 secondary school students in the United States, around 15 per cent of the fourteen to seventeen age group. In the space of just forty years, American secondary education had undergone a drastic reorganization, from the predominantly classical, elitist, semiprivate academy to the mass clientele of the job-oriented, egalitarian public high school.

Historians of education have usually described the growth of American secondary education as a unilinear institutional development: from Latin grammar school to academy to public high school. It was in the years from about 1870 to 1920, they would say, that the public high school became the predominant institution for a secondary education in the United States. If one were thinking in terms of centuries, this picture would be adequate; but, on closer examination, American secondary education in these years presents no such simple picture: A careful survey of these years reveals a splintering and proliferation of various institutional forms rather than any simple, unilinear development. As the structure of American society grew more complex, so did the structure of American secondary education.

In 1870, there were only about 500 public high schools in the United States. In Massachusetts alone, in 1876, there were still at least 57 secondary schools that the state board of education could classify as academies. Despite the large number of academies, however, an astute observer might have forecast the future: In the same year, at least 190 public high schools were in existence in Massachusetts, at least two-thirds of them offering the same type of "English" education as the academies, and, more important, about one-third a college preparatory course. By 1895, 41 per cent of students admitted to American colleges and universities (especially those of the Middle West) were prepared in public high schools. By 1910, there were at least 10,000 public high schools in the country; only a little over 11 per cent of secondary school students were being educated in private schools. However, while clear in retrospect, for contemporaries the road to the comprehensive public high school was a long and complex one. It was in just these years—the years of the decline of the academy, the growth of the public high school, and the emergence of the modern university—that the private family boarding school showed its most rapid increase. Aside from Exeter, Andover, St. Paul's, and St. Mark's, most of the more prominent boarding schools were founded in this period. The Lawrenceville School was refounded in 1883, Groton in 1884, the Taft School in 1890, Hotchkiss in 1891, the Choate School and St. George's School in 1896, the

Middlesex School in 1901; Deerfield was reorganized in 1903; and the Kent school was founded in 1906. There was, obviously, some connection between the successful founding of these schools, the decline of the academy, the rise of the public high school, and the emergence of the university.

The connection might be outlined briefly, as follows. Until the Civil War, American secondary education was largely oriented toward the colleges; academies offered terminal "English" courses, but their main interest was, as often as not, a college preparatory course. The colleges drew their students either from the academies, private proprietary schools, or their own college preparatory departments. The system was adequate to meet the requirements of the nation's relatively small groups of professionals and wealthy, to train them in the same way, to impart to them much the same body of knowledge that had formed the curriculum for gentlemanly education in the West since the Renaissance. However, with industrialization and the reorganization of society that it entailed, this system no longer proved adequate. An industrial society needed a large number of trained workers with technical skills for mechanical, clerical, sales, and other occupations. While the colleges responded by grafting the specialized training of the university to their traditional liberal arts course, or by doing away with the latter entirely, the academies were slowly strangled by the growth of the comprehensive public high school, whose goals diverged more and more in these years from producing a liberally educated man to producing a narrowly, technically trained citizen. The last stand of the traditional liberal educators was made by the National Educational Association's college-oriented Committee of Ten. Their 1893 Report on Secondary School Studies, as a recent critic has claimed, "would [have held] the child to a prolonged exposure and thorough mastering of the few subjects that a remote college decreed that he had to study"; in other words, to the traditional ideal of the liberally educated man. A major setback to traditional liberal education in the public schools was signaled by the 1918 publication of the *Cardinal Principles of Secondary Education* by the National Educational Association's Commission on the Reorganization of Secondary Education. These principles were, in the above writer's words, "student-oriented, life-centered, and socially directed"—an appropriate preparation for the anonymous worker in a mass society, devised by men who would soon be calling themselves "progressive."

The decline of the academy in the last decades of the nineteenth century meant that there was no longer an institution specifically geared to prepar[ing] students for college. The public high school was as yet unproven; in fact, according to some contemporary critics, the whole public school system was an utter disaster. Most of its pupils were "unable to read intelligently, to spell correctly, to write legibly, to describe understandingly the geography of their own country, or to do anything that reasonably well-educated children should do with ease." Doubtless an extreme view, but it expresses well the attitude of many toward the public high school. The well off and well educated were often distressed by the heterogeneous nature of its student body and its increasingly egalitarian social goals. Above all, they appear to have been distressed by the public high school's low academic standards and sheer educational ineffectiveness. Part of this was due to the emergence of teaching as a profession and the subsequent bureaucratization of public education systems. The experience of Boston may serve as a model for other American cities. As Michael Katz has described the situation there, the withdrawal of lay reformers from concern with the public schools in the 1850's "had left school systems open to capture by the professionals, who, quickly seeing the advantages of bureaucracy, had acted with dispatch to build large, hierarchical, differentiated, uniform and rigid organizations, which, in the 1870s, a new generation of lay reformers suddenly discovered with horror." An acrimonious and debilitating conflict between lay reformers and the new professionals ensued. The reformers lost, and the day of the impersonal urban educational bureaucracy dawned. By the 1880's, many well-to-do, college-educated Bostonians viewed the public high schools with disgust and sought alternative institutions for their sons. Many college and university leaders felt, with President Eliot, that public high schools were incapable of training many students to the level [that] a first-rate university should require of its applicants. For a steady supply of well-prepared students, they often turned instead to—in fact, actively encouraged the foundation of—family boarding schools.

Early in the 1890's, for instance, President Timothy Dwight and others concerned with securing well-prepared students for Yale managed—with a certain amount of what can only be called ruthlessness—to have the Hotchkiss School in Lakeville, Connecticut, established. In 1885, Benjamin Hotchkiss, a native of Salisbury, Connecticut, had died in Paris after accumulating a considerable fortune as a pioneer munitions manufacturer. Despite the fact that Hotchkiss had been in the process of divorcing her to marry his French mistress, his widow Maria searched about for a suitable memorial to her errant husband. Neighbors suggested a hospital; Maria herself wanted to macadamize every road in the township. Instead, even though she was said not to be "particularly fond of boys," she found herself endowing a school for them.

President Dwight and others concerned with Yale's welfare had heard of Maria's bumbling attempts at philanthropy, rushed to Lakeville, and, by a bit of artful moral armtwisting, persuaded her to endow a college preparatory school for boys. On reading the legal documents, Maria was outraged. "I have no interest whatever in a school for the pampered sons of rich gentlemen," she reportedly declared. "If this is not to be a public school, with its facilities open to boys of all classes, I shall have nothing further to do with it!" However, she was mollified when perpetual free tuition for six boys from the area was assured.

With Maria's gifts of land and $200,000 in bonds—and a tuition of $600 a year—the Hotchkiss School (briefly called "Yale Junior") opened in October, 1892. Its first headmaster, E. G. Coy, was brought from the Phillips Academy at Andover, where he had taught Greek for over twenty years.

Andover had long been a Yale feeder-school, and Hotchkiss's traditions would be decisively shaped by the traditions of Andover and Yale.

Relations between the founder and the school were strained from the beginning. One of Maria's desires, the school's historians write, "was to make Hotchkiss a small high school serving the needs of the neighborhood. Mr. Coy, backed by the board members from New Haven and his faculty, was determined that Hotchkiss should be a boarding school in the tradition of Andover, Exeter, and Groton [actually quite dissimilar traditions], a school serving the nation." Maria's further support of the institution was grudging; she left it nothing in her will, and quite possibly on muddy spring days thought wistfully of macadamized roads. But President Dwight and Yale were well satisfied; of the thirty members of Hotchkiss's class of 1896, twenty-eight were preparing for New Haven. Dwight had assured Yale for many years to come of at least one sure source of students prepared to its standards. If the $600 tuition meant that they were very often the sons of (comparatively) "rich gentlemen"—well, that was unfortunate, but at least they would have no difficulty paying the college tuition.

Some years earlier to the south, in New Jersey, another college president, with much the same needs and ambitions as Dwight, had followed a similar, though not quite so dramatic, course. Not long after assuming his post at Princeton, President McCosh found that one of the major problems facing him was in attracting a large enough number of properly prepared students to the college. When there was a slight decline in enrollments in 1872, he became seriously alarmed. What was the matter? It was the lack of "feeding schools" in the middle states. "In New England," he explained to his trustees, "the colleges draw the majority of their students from schools endowed by the States, or by the towns, or by private benevolence. We have no such schools in New Jersey, in Pennsylvania, in Maryland, in Delaware." A father in the middle states who wanted to prepare his son for Princeton would naturally be attracted to one of the famous New England schools, like Andover or Exeter. There were dangers for Princeton in this situation. "From the day the youth enters the school," McCosh said, "he hears of no other college [than] Harvard, of its professors, of its students, of its games and generally of its vast superiority over all other colleges. It would require more courage than can be expected of a boy to resist this influence, and in the nine cases out of ten the boy destined for Princeton goes to a New England college, where the religion of his father's household is entirely ignored." Princeton's friends, McCosh advised, could do the college no higher service than to endow preparatory schools.

Like Dwight, McCosh found a legacy. He was overjoyed when the trustees of the estate of John C. Green, a long-time benefactor of Princeton, began plans, in 1878, to purchase the old academy in nearby Lawrenceville and endow it as the Lawrenceville School. Though dead three years in 1878, Green would certainly have approved of what his legatees were doing with his immense fortune. He himself had given about $1.5 million to Princeton (of which his great-great-great-grandfather, Jonathan Dickinson, had been first president, and his great-great-grandfather, Caleb Smith, first instructor) in his lifetime, and would have taken particular satisfaction in the Lawrenceville plan. Green was born near Lawrenceville, then the hamlet of Maidenhead, in 1800. In 1810, he went off to the new academy that had been chartered there only two years before. He left the academy at Maidenhead at sixteen for New York City, where he entered the firm of N. I. and G. Griswold, which was involved in the China trade. His career followed the usual Horatio Alger pattern—he married his employer's daughter and prospered. In 1833, he joined Russell and Company, the most influential American merchant house in the Far East, and increased his fortune by dealings in silks and opium. He returned to the United States in 1839 with what was an immense fortune for the time. He increased it through investments in banking and railroads; when he died, in 1875, he was reported to be worth over $5 million. Green and his brother, Henry Woodhull Green, chief justice and later chancellor of New Jersey, were both trustees of Princeton College and the theological seminary there.

Before his death, Green had discussed the possibility of starting some sort of secondary school to assist Princeton. Knowing intimately Princeton's problems in securing adequately prepared students, his legatees decided to follow this course. In 1879, they bought the property of Green's old academy (now the Lawrenceville Classical and Commercial High School) for $25,000 from Samuel Hamill, the proprietor for almost forty years. Intending to transform it into a first-rate college preparatory school, they entirely obliterated the old academy. As a historian of Lawrenceville has written, "the change was complete and entire; it was a new school that came into existence on the John C. Green Foundation." Not until after 1899, under its second headmaster, Simon J. McPherson, would the Lawrenceville School make any attempt to claim relationship to the older academy—and its possibly nostalgic and generous alumni.

At first, the legatees thought of doing little more than enlarging and strengthening the old academy. But, as time passed and their ideas matured, this plan faded entirely. The new Lawrenceville, in personnel, plant, government, and spirit, would owe nothing to the old. A group of trustees, all connected in some way with Princeton, were brought together: the legatees; Dr. Hamill; Barker Gummere, a Trenton lawyer; the Reverend Charles A. Aiken of the Princeton Theological Seminary; and William M. Sloane, professor of history at Princeton. The trustees' first step, in the words of Professor Sloane, was "to seek the best headmaster where he could be found, with entire disregard of local prejudice."

One of the trustees, Charles E. Green, went to President McCosh to inquire about a suitable man. McCosh recommended a fellow Scotsman, James Cameron Mackenzie, the thirty-year-old principal of the Harry Hillman Academy in Wilkes-Barre, Pennsylvania, for the post. Mackenzie was born in Aberdeen, Scotland, in 1852 and brought to Wilkes-Barre—an area where many Scots had settled—by his mother about 1858. Until he was twelve, he had, at most, only one term of formal schooling. However, he became a clerk in the local bookstore and educated himself. Deciding to teach in the public schools, he entered the Bloomsbury State Normal School. This soon seemed inadequate; in 1870, at eighteen, he made his way to New Hampshire and entered the Phillips Exeter Academy, from which, with the help of scholarships and odd jobs, he managed to graduate in 1873. He then returned to Wilkes-Barre, took a job in a local private girls' school, and entered Lafayette College, from which he graduated, a member of Phi Beta Kappa and valedictorian, in 1878. He was asked to join the faculties of Grinnell and Columbia colleges but, instead, stayed in Wilkes-Barre as head of the girls' academy. He received his Ph.D. from Lafayette in 1882 and, in the same year, was asked to come to Lawrenceville. The trustees felt that their headmaster, even if not an ordained minister, should have some theological training, so Mackenzie, besides making plans for the new school, spent the year 1882–83 taking courses at the theological seminary and teaching Latin and Greek.

The Lawrenceville trustees appear to have been almost completely undecided about the exact type of school they were to found; they knew they wanted to establish a secondary school that would help Princeton, but that was all. "We have written to Mr. McKenzie [*sic*]," one trustee informed another, "to come down and have a conference as to the best mode of conducting the school. Keeping school is out of my line." Mackenzie himself was somewhat at a loss: "I am at considerable disadvantage in not knowing more of your purposes," he wrote the trustees as he attempted to make a comprehensive plan for the proposed school. Nevertheless, in October, 1882, he was able to report to the trustees that, "after visiting, pursuant to your instructions, the leading and representative preparatory Schools of the United States, conferring with their faculties, after corresponding with prominent educators, and after mature reflection, I desire to submit for your consideration the following suggestions touching the plan of boarding boys and the number and style of buildings for the proposed School at Lawrenceville." James Mackenzie's plan for Lawrenceville would be followed for over two decades in remarkable detail; more than anyone else, he was responsible for the school that ultimately emerged from Princeton's needs and John C. Green's bequest.

Among the many schools Mackenzie visited before making his plans for Lawrenceville were St. Paul's, the Phillips Andover Academy, and his own secondary school, Phillips Exeter. He also discussed the proposed school with a number of college men. As far as academic work went, the picture Mackenzie pieced together from the various schools was gloomy:

> It is admitted by the heads of the "Great Schools" that none of them are doing what ought to be done in the preparatory work. Andover, Exeter, East Hampton, St. Paul's and Adams each deplore some marked inability by reason of defective appointment or deficient endowment. Each one had some *sub rosa* confession of shortcoming. In not one can a good preparation for a high standard Sc[ientific?] Sch[ool?] be had. In not one are the modern languages properly or

ably taught tho' this fact is deeply deplored by the faculties. Natural Science fares no better. The same is true in England.

The problem of academic standards, however, was relatively easy to solve: Attract a good faculty by offering above-average salaries. More important to Mackenzie (most of his report is devoted to the subject) was the manner in which the students would live. State-supported juvenile reform schools excepted, his plan for this was, so far as I can discover, unique in the United States at the time. "I recommend," he told the trustees

> the "separate home" plan of boarding. These homes should be built at convenient distances from a main school building; should be large enough to hold a teacher and his family and not more than 25 boys; and should be under the immediate care of the teacher and his wife to organize and maintain a marked home life and supervision. . . . There should be a dormitory for the more matured in character and those of limited means who could not pay the necessary charges of the homes.

Such a plan would have definite advantages; it would work best, Mackenzie advised (possibly thinking of his own impecunious youth):

> were it possible to appropriate a sum sufficiently large to aid those in need. Its adoption would contemplate, in our case, a uniformity in the price of board at the different homes and at the dormitory; and further, a distribution of the boys, not according to means to pay board, but according to class or residence in the place. This, if effected, would render the dormitory a place of honor, as only those who could be trusted would be permitted to live there. Every new boy would be put in a Home for the first year at least. During this time his teachers could reform him if he needed reforming, or dismiss him if he were incorrigible. Some parents would prefer residence in a Home during the entire school course; others would prefer the dormitory; while others still would prefer, and see advantage in, spending part of the time in one, and the rest of the time in the other, place. The dual plan of boarding would incorporate all that is excellent in any plan, and it has the immense advantage of adaptability to meet emergencies. A boy could be remanded to a Home, if he were found unworthy of the constructive confidence reposed [in] him by placing him in the dormitory.

Mackenzie went on to spell out exactly the details and problems of his plan: the difficulty to be anticipated in attracting a proper faculty, the precise rates of board, the buildings that should be constructed, and so forth. All the educators he had spoken to envied him the opportunity Lawrenceville presented, he said. "Excepting Dr. Coit," he reported, "I believe I am correct in saying all the prominent Schools of New England would adopt the above scheme were they where we are now. Each independently practically suggested what I herein proposed." Mackenzie had presented his plan; the future of the school now depended on what kind of . . . endowment the legatees would make. Mackenzie had not inquired on this subject earlier, he said, preferring rather that the matter should open upon us gradually and basing confidence upon gentlemen whose experience in the management of a great college has doubtless revealed the essential conditions of a school that shall do for the Middle States, and orthodox, education what Exeter and Andover have done and are doing for New England and "Go as You Please" education. We must be well endowed after the "plant" is paid for. Garfield was right in declaring that a great university for him would be a log cabin, a rude bench with Mark Hopkins on one end and himself on the other. But Mark Hopkins can be obtained and held only by liberal, "ample" endowments.

The trustees eventually provided about $1 million for the construction of the school (it was designed by Peabody and Stearns of Boston, and its grounds were laid out by Frederick Law Olmsted) and $250,000 in endowment funds. While Lawrenceville may have been the best-endowed school in the country at the time of its founding, the tuition was set at a very high level: $500, the same as St. Paul's at the time. And, as at Round Hill or St. Paul's, a high tuition meant a preselected student body; only the well-to-do could afford to send their sons to Lawrenceville, though the trustees did make provisions for a certain number of scholarships.

Mackenzie gathered together a distinguished faculty, probably the best of any secondary school of the time. Lawrenceville offered three four-year courses of study; a classical and a scientific [course], which would prepare boys for college or scientific school, and, in the style of the old academies, a terminal English course. In 1893, the English course was dropped, and Lawrenceville became completely a college preparatory school. In 1904, another year was added to the course at the beginning, making Lawrenceville a five-year school.

Members of the faculties of both Andover and Exeter had predicted to Mackenzie that there would be considerable pressure for admission once the school got under way. They were correct: The new school opened in the fall of 1883 with 112 boys—only 12 of whom had been students at the old academy. The new buildings were completed in 1885; in that year, 138 boys from eighteen states were enrolled. By 1894, there were over 300 students and a faculty of 16; by 1898, 362 students and a faculty of 22. By then, the student-faculty ratio was down to about 13:1, which compared favorably with St. Paul's 8.5:1 in the same year.

A novel claim appeared in Lawrenceville's publicity releases and in contemporary newspaper reports on the school. "The Lawrenceville School is to be on the model of the English schools at Rugby and Eton," trustee Caleb Green told a New York *Tribune* reporter, "with such modifications as a careful study of the educational methods in vogue here may suggest." Lawrenceville would be "a combination that will include the best features of the American and English preparatory school systems," the New York *Sun* reported; it would incorporate the best of "the famous schools of New England—Exeter, Andover, and St. Paul's—with the well known characteristics of England's best schools," said the New York *Evening Post*. While

George Shattuck had been impressed by the English schools twenty-five years earlier, Lawrenceville's conscious claim that it would be, in part, directly modeled after them introduced a new note to the history of the family boarding school—American Anglophilia.

A natural, and considerable, Anglophilia had always been present in the United States. To Joseph Buckminster, Britain had been that "island of the blessed"; in the 1830's, Francis Grund, a former teacher at Round Hill, noted that young Bostonians could still talk, as their grandfathers had done, of England as "home." A rising young American like Charles Sumner might feel, on a visit to England in 1839, that "he was coming home—coming, as it were, to his father's hearthstone." Before the Civil War, however, American Anglophilia had been qualified by a defensive nationalism; during the war, the attitude of the British Government toward the Union weakened even the most fervent Anglophile's attraction to England. But, by the 1870's—in fact, about the time of the Centennial Year of 1876—old antagonisms had been almost forgotten. The image of Imperial England and its culture began to pervade and shape the social and cultural aspirations of thousands of Americans. The reasons for late-Victorian and Progressive Anglophilia are complex and difficult to assess—among others, the resolution of important diplomatic conflicts, the growth of racist "Anglo-Saxon" thought, foreign immigration to the United States, and the search for a usable American past. In any case, as we saw earlier, by the 1880's Lord Bryce detected a cult of what he called "Anglomania" in the United States. Lawrenceville's claim to be modeled, in part, on the English public schools was in keeping with the spirit of the age. The difficulty lies in determining precisely which aspects of the English public schools Lawrenceville actually copied.

James Mackenzie's experience was limited to American schools; what he learned of English schools he learned through reading or conversation. The one element in his plan for Lawrenceville that no earlier American school appears to have used was his "separate home" plan of boarding—the planned grouping of twenty-five to thirty boys with a master and his family in a house owned by the institution. This was precisely the system that Edward Thring had introduced at English Uppingham some thirty years earlier. Since no other variation from established American practice was introduced at Lawrenceville, one can only assume that this is what was meant by references to the "best features" of the English schools in Lawrenceville's early literature. However, Mackenzie's heavy emphasis on the school as a family or a home was in the direct tradition of nineteenth-century American educational thought. In some respects, Lawrenceville was a revival of the spirit of Round Hill or the Flushing Institute, from which St. Paul's, with its large size, dormitory life, and overroutinization, had drifted away. Mackenzie's plan also restored, in a formal, institutionalized manner, the conditions of the earliest American academies, at which students—ideally—had boarded with, and been regulated by, selected families of the town. In a way, the Lawrenceville School was an artificially reconstituted, late-eighteenth-century village—a little educational Utopia, carefully isolated from the great world, in which familial nurture could be carried on free from outside distractions and temptations.

Recognition came to Mackenzie and the school he had created at Lawrenceville almost immediately. President Eliot of Harvard visited it in 1886 and (excepting bathing facilities) pronounced it good. By 1894, Nicholas Murray Butler of Columbia could recommend it to a foreign educator as "the best equipped of the endowed secondary schools of America." President McCosh had more reason than anyone to be pleased. "The magnificent endowment at Lawrenceville," he told his trustees in 1884, "is the most important contribution that has been given to our college of late years." As early as 1886, he could report that twenty boys prepared at Lawrenceville had entered Princeton that year. As Dwight would do for Yale a few years later, McCosh had secured for Princeton a steady source of students prepared to its satisfaction.

Although private Northeastern universities actively encouraged the foundation of family boarding schools, they were by no means solely dependent upon these schools for students, nor did [their] graduates . . . ever constitute a majority of their freshmen classes. For instance, in the 1870's, Harvard—as it had done in the 1820's—drew the largest proportion of its students from private sources. However, *within* the private sector, over the succeeding decade, the freshmen prepared at private *boarding* schools would show, as a group, the most rapid rate of increase, as the following table indicates (percentages have been rounded off):

Preparation of Harvard Freshmen in Selected Years

	1826		1874		1883		1884	
	No.	%	No.	%	No.	%	No.	%
Public high and Latin schools	11	42	60	36	77	30	76	32
Academies	11	42	33	19	72	26	57	23
Private proprietary day schools	1	4	13	6	36	13	48	15
Private boarding schools	3	11	4	2	23	8	31	12
Individuals	1	4	52	31	46	17	31	12

Even though, between 1874 and 1884, the number of students prepared at private boarding schools increased by about 600 per cent, they still amounted to only about 12 per cent of the freshman class of 1884. (Note that academies are *not* counted as boarding schools.) Although comparable figures are lacking, at Yale the proportion of students drawn from private boarding schools seems to have grown at a more rapid pace than at Harvard over the years. By 1907, for example, almost 40 per cent (85 of 219 students) of the Yale freshman class was drawn from nine of [the] fourteen schools, while only about 20 per cent (45 of 219 students) came from public high schools. (The rest of the freshmen were drawn from at least 52 different, largely private day, schools in every part of the nation.) Despite the rise of the public high school, in 1909 the better private universities of the Northeast were still drawing, as they always had, the majority of their students from private sources—78 per cent at Princeton, 65 per cent at Yale, and 47 per cent at Harvard, as compared to 9 per cent at the University of Michigan or 8 per cent at the University of Wisconsin. Within this private group, however, the *boarding* school contingent seems to have grown the most in proportion to those from other types of schools. And, with all due weight given to scholarships, because of the expensive tuitions most of the students from the private boarding schools would necessarily have . . . been the sons of the rich.

Reliance on the family boarding schools for well-prepared students placed many Northeastern universities in an awkward position and altered drastically the tone of a hitherto rather simple social milieu. At Harvard, her historian writes, "about 1890 the Episcopal Church schools, together with Milton Academy and one or two Boston private schools, secured the social leadership." Neither family, race, nor wealth counted as much as graduation from certain schools, he claims. What was important "for a Harvard student with social ambition [was] to enter from the 'right' sort of school and be popular there." Yale's historian has noted that, at the turn of the century, "a growing distinction between the well-to-do prep-school men and the rest" of the students began to be apparent in the college, as "the rich and socially ambitious all congregated in a private dormitory." Yale's Western alumni began to complain that "the best preparatory schools were all in the East and only the rich could afford them." And, at Princeton, "around the turn of the century there came an increasing influx of boys of wealth from private preparatory schools, such as the Hill, Lawrenceville, Andover, Exeter, and St. Paul's. In less than a decade the proportion of Presbyterians among the undergraduates dropped from two-thirds to less than one half, the number of Episcopalians doubled, and President Patton was heard to boast that he was head of the finest country club in America." Actually, it is unlikely that Patton called Princeton a *country* club. Few country clubs existed in his day; the country club as a suburban institution and would not begin to influence the colleges until the 1920's. Patton is more likely to have called Princeton one of the finest *men's* clubs in America. In the 1880's and 1890's, the future Ivy League colleges were beginning to reflect the social patterns of the "wealthy inhabitants of large cities," whose sons they were more and more attracting. And, among these students' fathers, the metropolitan gentleman's club was becoming a central institution. That the sons should reproduce the fathers' social patterns when they reached college was hardly surprising.

As we saw earlier, an ever increasing proportion of prep-school and college graduates became businessmen in the decades after the Civil War. Educational leaders of the period were as emphatic on the necessity of well-educated men in "banking, transportation, manufacturing, mining, large-scale farming, and engineering" as those of the preceding two generations had been. "A young man who is going into business had better take an academic course . . . if he has any mind to train," declared President Eliot of Harvard. "That is an indisputable proposition, and there is no use in discussing it."

While eager and willing to provide for and to educate the natural aristocrat in any line of endeavor, American educators were decidedly ambivalent about the artificial aristocrat. But what of the heirs of the successful businessman? What role was left for the son? "Inherited wealth," said President Eliot, as befitted a nephew of Andrews Norton and George Ticknor, "is an unmitigated curse when divorced from culture." The sons of the rich, then, must be educated. But no college should—or would—depend entirely upon such students. Harvard, President Eliot told a former Overseer [Charles Francis Adams, Jr.], must "be open equally to men with much money, little money, or no money, provided they all have brains. I care no more than you for young men who have no capacity for an intellectual life. They are not fit subjects for a college, whether their parents have money or not. I am inclined to think that you would be more tolerant than I of the presence of stupid sons of the rich." Only the *intelligent* sons of the rich were to go to college, then. But where did this leave the family boarding schools, which Eliot and other college educators were assiduously encouraging, and which were sending more and more of their alumni to college? President Eliot, for one, was quite definite about their intellectual quality: "It seems to me to be a great disadvantage to St. Paul's School at Concord, or to the Groton School," he told Adams, "that it is, as a matter of fact, a school for none but rich men's sons. It is a disadvantage because a school so composed is sure to be a poorer school than one which is resorted to by a better class of boys. It is simply impossible for St. Paul's or Groton to maintain a high intellectual standard. It would be just so with Harvard College if it became exclusively the resort of rich men's sons."

Since he lent his support to Groton and was quite happy to accept at Harvard thirty-two of its first forty-one graduates, there seems, at first, something disingenuous about such remarks on Eliot's part. Particularly since he went on to add that "at this moment graduates of the public schools do better in college than the graduates of the private and endowed schools; and they are well-nigh sure to do better in after life, simply because they have won more personal power of work." But Eliot was not being hypocritical; it was just that his liberalism, acquired in the mid-nineteenth century, was inadequate to encompass the changes that occurred in American society in the four or five decades before 1904. To Eliot, the best society was the open society, in which all careers were open to the youth of talent and industry. Harvard existed, in large measure, to transform these natural aristocrats into gentlemen. But this did not mean that Harvard should ignore the artificial aristocrats. Since they started with several strikes against them, they, perhaps even more than the natural aristocrats, needed to be educated. In large part, Eliot's uneasiness and inconsistency [were] inspired by the fact that there were simply so many *more* "rich men's sons" than there had been in his youth, and that so many of them seemed to want to go to Harvard.

Like all revolutions, the Industrial Revolution in America brought power and wealth to new men. While there were not twenty millionaires in the United States in the 1840's, by 1892 there were over four thousand. This was not an overnight development, but had begun with industrialization itself; a new artificial aristocracy of wealth had been apparent in cities like New York since the 1830's. As early as 1853, in his *Potiphar Papers*, the editor, George William Curtis, had satirized the ostentatious and awkward attempts of the Fifth Avenue *nouveaux riches* to create a viable style of life for themselves. The young gentleman who had lived at Brook Farm, sat at Emerson's feet, and helped Thoreau build his shelter at Walden was to feel all his life that "to scale society is only to climb a golden stair. The more gold, the more distinction." The Civil War accelerated the accumulation of larger and larger fortunes in the hands of more and more families. "There was a great increase in ostentation of life in the city," the published George Haven Putnam wrote of New York just after the war, "and there came into existence a division of society that could be called plutocratic." Putnam expressed well the feelings of men of established, modest wealth toward the newly rich of the 1860's. Inflation, he thought, had given people with fixed incomes a

> much smaller return in purchasing power or in securing the necessities of life, that for all practical purposes [their] income was seriously curtailed. Through the change in currency values, thousands of retired merchants, women, and others, no longer able to take advantage of business opportunities, were reduced to comparative poverty. These were the people who had constituted a large portion of the book-buying community. The *nouveaux riches*, who had made money out of shady contracts or through speculations in pork, could not easily be reached by the publishers of standard literature.

Though hardly illiterate, in the scale of their fortunes and scope of their operations men like Jay Gould, John D. Rockefeller, Cornelius Vanderbilt, or Leland Stanford did constitute a new element on the American scene. The style of life of the newly rich of late-Victorian America particularly grated on the sensibilities of men of established position. "When Americans who have become rich by trade or speculation," said one alumnus of the Flushing Institute in the 1880's, "assume the position, and [a]ffect, to the best of their blundering ability, the customs of an aristocratic class, it must be with utter lack of both memory and common sense." Historians have agreed with such judgments. Why, one has asked, "did the business leaders from San Francisco to Bar Harbor have to live in their houses with libraries, billiard rooms, art galleries, several rooms in which to eat, at least one of which had to be two stories high and paneled to the ceiling, buildings sometimes equipped with small theatres and perhaps even a chapel capable of holding a considerable congregation?" The answers are varied and complex (it was certainly more satisfying than sitting in a cottage and playing with one's money), but at least one was the wish to prove oneself a true gentleman. After all, it had been an American tradition, from Westover and Mt. Vernon on, to assert one's status in a great house. And: English nobles had great houses; should not their American counterparts have them too? The newly rich of late-Victorian and Progressive America showed a lack of neither memory nor of common sense.

One thing, at least, seemed clear to contemporaries: Natural or artificial, America now possessed an aristocracy. "However democratic a nation may be in spirit and character," the popular English author Thomas Hughes told Americans in 1879, "and in its political and social constitution and organization, the time must come when it will breed a gentry, leisure class, aristocracy, call it by what name you will." The United States, Hughes thought, had now reached that stage. For many educated Americans of established position, the question was whether . . . American aristocrats also constituted a class of Christian gentlemen and scholars. One contemporary, Frederick Law Olmsted—journalist, landscape architect, and executive secretary of the influential United States Sanitary Commission during the Civil War—thought that they might. Like Joseph Buckminster fifty years before, he had a scheme for uniting wealth, virtue, and intelligence. In Olmsted's case, it was the Union League Club of New York, which he hoped to see become "a club of true American aristocracy, the legitimate descendents and armsbearers of the old dukes of our land; of our law-givers, [Union] loyalists. . . . We wish also to establish the fact that there is an 'aristocratic class' in New York, which in this respect is not European." Olmsted suggested three distinct types of members to achieve the club's immediate aims during wartime and to continue its existence during peacetime. The first group, or hard core of the organization, should be the men described above, New Yorkers of colonial stock, "who had by character and ability risen to social, professional, and commercial eminence." The second group was to be composed of intellectuals, mainly artists and scientists; while, for its third segment, the club was to scour the city for promising younger men, "especially those rich young men of whom I see so many now who don't know what their place is in American society." To others, however, it seemed important to catch all "those rich young men" even younger in order to transform them into a true American aristocracy. Thomas Hughes had a suggestion: Why not introduce a system of boarding schools like the great public schools of England? After all, Hughes continued, "in the case of nations of the same race, and so nearly identical in character and habits as the people of the United States and the English, it may reasonably be assumed that a system which has borne such fruits in the one is at least worth the careful examination of the other."

Immediate and vigorous exception was taken to Hughes's suggestion. The English public schools, one educational journal replied, "were good schools for the sons of the wealthy alone." It could not "assent to Mr. Hughes's belief either in the 'inevitable growth' in America of an exclusive aristocratic order, nor in the impossibility of so improving our common-school system as to render it 'thoroughly satisfactory' to all reasonable and patriotic persons, citizens of a republic, not of a monarchy." Although neither Hughes nor his critics seemed to be aware of them, in St. Paul's and St. Mark's such schools already existed; through Round Hill, the Flushing Institute, and St. James's, thousands of well-to-do and well-educated Americans were already familiar with them. While hardly opposed to the improvement of the common-school system, such families were not willing to trust their sons to them. Who were these families?

St. Paul's founder, George Shattuck, had married Anne Henrietta Brune of Baltimore, the sister of two of his schoolmates at Round Hill. The marriage linked Shattuck and his descendants with the Brunes of Baltimore, [with] the newly rich Morisons of New England, and with a branch of the Eliot family. But the intermarriages of the Boston Brahmins are perhaps too familiar. Consider the family connections of another Round Hill alumnus, Samuel Ward III of New York. On his banker father's side, Sam Ward was descended from various governors of Rhode Island; on his mother's side—Julia Rush Cutler—from Francis Marion, the South Carolina "Swamp Fox" of Revolutionary fame, and from Benjamin Rush of Philadelphia, a signer of the Declaration of Independence. One of Sam's sisters married the American sculptor Thomas Crawford; another (Julia Ward) married the famous humanitarian Samuel Gridley Howe. Intellectually brilliant, socially charming, and financially unstable, Sam himself married Emily Astor, daughter of William Astor, a son of John Jacob I. Through Emily's mother, the marriage tied Sam to the Livingstons and other old Knickerbocker families of New York. Various other connections linked Ward to scores of families from Georgia to Maine, from New York to San Francisco; he could travel from city to city and stay only with cousins. Sam Ward's situation was not unique. By the 1870's, ties of blood united scores of wealthy American families, particularly in the older urban centers of the East. A touch in Savannah on one strand of this web of kinship could cause vibrations in Philadelphia, New York, Baltimore, Boston, and other cities. Although the great industrial and financial fortunes of the late nineteenth century dwarfed those of Federalist and early-Victorian America, when newly wealthy Americans of the postbellum years looked for models for an appropriate style of life, they naturally referred first to the longer-established families—and only later to foreign models. Thus, it was only natural that Sam Ward's Savannah cousin, Ward McAllister, should assist Sam's (comparatively) newly rich in-law, Mrs. William Astor, in her social wars. (On a frivolous level, this was precisely the sort of union Frederick Law Olmsted urged for the membership of the Union League Club.) And it was only natural that Round Hill's Sam Ward should see two of his nephews, John Jacob Astor II and F. Marion Crawford, attend St. Paul's School. The family boarding school was well established among the rich of antebellum America. Its expansion in the pastwar years was due, in some measure, to the adoption by the newly rich of long-established styles of life and social and cultural goals. Such social adaptation also accounts, to some degree, for the increase in the number of rich students at Northeastern universities in the same period. Higher education was valued not only for its own sake but as a status indicator for those who often cared little for its content. It is no wonder that educational leaders such as Eliot felt ambivalent about the family boarding schools and the students they were drawing from them.

There was more to the proliferation of family boarding schools after 1880 than the needs of the universities, traditional respect for education, status striving, or the adoption of older styles of life by the newly rich. In the two decades after the Civil War, urbanization for the first time became a controlling factor in American life. Americans had always felt ambivalent about their cities. Across the continent, they founded and promoted city after city. At Harvard, the moral philosopher Francis Bowen taught his students that "cities and towns are the great agents and tokens of the increase of national opulence and the progress of civilization." But, from the founding of Yale in 1701 to avoid the temptations of wicked Boston, to Thomas Jefferson's animadversions on urban corruptions, to Nathaniel Hawthorne's recommendation that cities be purified by periodically burning them to the ground, suspicion of, and abhorrence toward, the city had been an equally familiar theme. In the 1870's and 1880's, the negative aspects of the city seemed dominant to many Americans. The industrial city attracted not only native American workers from rural areas but millions of immigrants from Southern and Eastern Europe. The rural American blended fairly easily into the population; the most conspicuous city dweller of late-Victorian and Progressive America was the foreigner. In some cities, he actually outnumbered the native Americans; for instance, in Chicago in 1890, the foreign-born population alone almost outnumbered the *entire* population of 1880. A native American such as Henry Adams was hardly alone in his feelings when he wrote that: "Not a Polish Jew fresh from Warsaw or Cracow, not a furtive Yacoob or Ysaac still reeking of the Ghetto, snarling a weird Yiddish to the officers of the customs—but had a keener instinct, an intenser energy, and a freer hand than he—American of Americans, with heaven knew how many Puritans and Patriots behind him, and an education that had cost a civil war." By 1880, scores of native-born Americans would have heartily agreed with the New Yorker who wrote that whole areas of his city had become "so degraded that hardly a Republican will reside there." In the light of such attitudes, it would hardly be surprising that a 1903 survey of family boarding schools would state quite bluntly that they were being founded, in part, because of parents' feelings that "in certain localities the companions of the boy in all but the higher grades of day school are, from their nationality, objectionable personal habits, or what not, undesirable."

It was the day, too, of the scandals of the Grant Administration, of the corruption of innumerable city governments such as New York's under Boss Tweed. The new political machines were based, in large measure, on the immigrant vote, which was secured by providing special favors in a time before organized social welfare agencies had developed. Boss Tweed himself distributed $50,000 to the poor of his own ward on Christmas day of 1870, and gave $1,000 to each of his aldermen to buy coal for the needy. He could well afford it: In 1870 alone, the Tweed Ring pulled in a million dollars a month from graft on New York's public works program.

The effects of such corruption on public education were widespread and so strong that, in 1874, a committee of the National Educational Association reported that a major drawback of the public schools was "one which afflicts our whole system of state schools. It is the interference of gutter politicians with these matters, about which they know nothing at all. Pandering to the prejudices of the rabble, for the sake of votes, they perpetually criticize and quarrel with every effort to elevate our schools, and so annoy able and sensitive teachers that they are driven out of the field and it is then confined to such incompetent hands that its course of study must be lowered or they cannot teach it." It was little wonder that many parents refused to entrust their sons to the public schools.

By the end of the 1880's, deteriorating urban conditions and rising tax rates, partially the result of political corruption based on the immigrant vote, had become so widespread that an acute British visitor, James Bryce, noted that "there is a strong tendency for rich men to migrate from the city to its suburbs in order to escape the city collector." This movement of the well-to-do to the suburbs was particularly strong between 1870 and 1900, the years in which the majority of [the] fourteen schools were founded. What was happening to the Boston area was probably typical of many other contemporary American cities. As Boston expanded, Sam Warner has discovered, "the settlement line of the wealthy was always the farthest out from the center of the city, the largest in area, and the smallest in number of people." Before he was imprisoned, even Boss Tweed of New York established himself on a huge country estate in Greenwich, Connecticut. In these protosuburban areas, "farming still went on and old villages remained, but sizable quantities of land were taken up by the wealthy either for estates or as streets of large suburban homes." And, of course, the new suburbanite or estate dweller had the same need to educate his children as the earlier farmer had had. Theodore Sizer has observed that, with the growth of the city in the 1880's, "the academy failed because it was fundamentally a rural institution, a school uniquely appropriate for a population thinly spread." But a region of estates or of scattered suburban streets could not support a high school, public *or* private. Thomas Hughes offered suburban parents a solution. "However good your common-school system may be," he wrote, "you cannot have a thoroughly satisfactory school, so far as instruction is concerned, except in great centers of population; . . . [and] a large portion of the class in question [the rich] live too far from the great centers to make use of the best common schools, without sending their boys for long periods from under their own roofs. Some system of boarding schools, therefore, must be established."

It was. Family boarding schools multiplied, their ranks joined by old academies that survived by transforming themselves into boarding schools. The same impulse that had sent so many urban children to Round Hill in the 1820's intensified tenfold in the 1880's. In 1884, the founders of the Groton School would state frankly that one of their motives was the "rapid growth of large cities." In the 1880's, many well-established urban private day schools found, like Boston's Noble's Classical School, that parents "were beginning to send their sons away to such boarding schools as St. Paul's, St. Mark's, and Groton." The successful private day school would be careful to point out that it was situated, like one Philadelphia school, in "a central position in one of the best sections of the city, and . . . at the same time, removed from the undesirable surroundings and associations of the business centres." But the family boarding schools flourished, meeting the needs of the new suburbanites as well as those of their well-to-do cousins who remained in a "silk-stocking" district of the politically corrupt city. They were country schools that were as much, paradoxically, the product of the growth of the industrial city and immigration as were the bureaucratic and rigid urban public high schools.

By the time of America's entry into World War I, the fourteen schools listed in our introduction as the core group of prep schools were well-established and familiar American institutions, representative of a far larger group of schools. They were very expensive schools. In 1916, seven of them charged an average tuition of about $950 a year. Altogether, in the same year thirteen of them had a combined enrollment of 3,540 students and a total faculty of 320, for a student-faculty ratio of about 11:1. In 1915, eight of the schools had sent 449 students on to college. The largest was the Phillips Academy at Andover, with 562 students; the smallest was the Middlesex School, with 123 students. On the basis of their history and traditions, they could be roughly divided into three groups. In the first were the direct descendants of the eighteenth-century academies—Andover, Exeter, and Deerfield. These schools were comparatively inexpensive, drew their students from a broader social spectrum, and imposed a less Victorian regimen than did the others. In the second group were the Episcopalian church schools—St. Paul's, St. Mark's, Groton, St. George's, and Kent. Generally, they drew their students from a rather restricted clientele of rich urban families, imposed an almost obsessively minute regulation on the life of their students, and had in common, naturally, a heavily religious orientation. In the last group were the nondenominational boarding schools —Lawrenceville, Hill, Choate, Taft, Hotchkiss, and Middlesex. They drew their students from much the same group as the Episcopalian schools and consciously attempted to strike a balance between the freedom of the academies and the heavily paternalistic discipline of the church schools. In 1916, all the schools had two objectives of equal, though often conflicting, importance: to prepare their students for entrance to college and to build character. To a greater or lesser degree, they all believed that the best institution through which to fulfill these aims was the family boarding school.

By 1916, their image, for better or worse, would be fixed for the greater part of the twentieth century: the son of a St. Paul's rector of 1916 summed up the commonly held picture well. He described the schools as "self-sufficient and insular communit[ies], providing for [their] rather narrow clientele just what was expected—a conservative, gentlemanly preparation of body and mind for the Ivy League Colleges and for support of the economic, political and religious status quo." So far as this picture goes, it is accurate. But it does not go far enough.

The family boarding schools of the 1880's and 1890's were founded in response to many motives and would be shaped by a complex of often conflicting ideological and social traditions and pressures: among others, by a reaction against the rigidity of the emerging urban school bureaucracies; by the admission standards of the new universities; by the needs and aspirations of the urban and suburban rich; by much the same Victorian notions of childhood innocence and isolation as had molded St. Paul's and St. Mark's; and, not the least, by many parents' undefined hope that they provided the "best" education available for their sons.

The emergence of the private boarding school in significant number at the end of the nineteenth century was only one indication of an increasingly complex society. As the American public school system developed, it would be tied to the seemingly egalitarian neighborhood school concept, a concept that has often masked the reality of American education. Lawrence Cremin, however, has suggested that "the common school in its classic form was essentially a northern and western phenomenon and that it reached its apotheosis in rural and small-town America west of the Alleghenies. It thrived best where there was already a reasonable homogeneity of race, class, and religion, and where communities were not so large as to permit the development of substantially dissimilar ghettos. Wherever social or physical instances did become great, as in the South or in the larger cities, the public school tended to be less 'common.' " In other words, almost from the beginning there has been a built-in social and economic segregation in urban American public schools. The private preparatory school was but one manifestation of an America that was becoming more socially and cu' turally pluralistic.

Urban Reform and the Schools: Kindergartens in Massachusetts, 1870–1915

Marvin Lazerson

ORIGINS AND IDEOLOGY

In the decades after the Civil War, no individual did more to popularize the kindergarten in America than Elizabeth Palmer Peabody. First acquainted with the new institution for childhood through Mrs. Carl Schurz in 1859, . . . Peabody spent the next thirty-five years of her life proselytizing for the emancipation of the child. The kindergarten, she believed, was not simply a method of education but a movement of mystical significance. Her advocacy was an "apostolate," kindergartening a religion, a "Gospel for children." Like Froebel, Peabody spoke of absolutes and universality. She dealt with Truth, the Child, the Home, Family, and Motherhood, and offered to stem the hedonistic tendencies of childhood. All children, Peabody and her associates believed, were self-centered. In their earliest years, they discover their bodies, senses, and power to act. Their mothers' tenderness heightens their impulses toward selfishness. They demand immediate satisfaction. Without an agency external to the family in which socialization among peers and to society's mores occurs, childhood would thus ultimately become self-destructive. It was here that the kindergarten became necessary, allowing the child "to take his place in the company of his equals, to learn his place in their companionship, and still later to learn wider social relations and their involved duties." "A kindergarten, then," Peabody wrote, "is children in society—a commonwealth or republic of children—whose laws are all part and parcel of the Higher Law alone."

Since the kindergarten's primary goal was socialization, children could not be allowed to run free. In the garden of children, the trained kindergartner helped the child develop by carefully removing obstacles to natural growth and by providing nourishment. As the gardener must know plants, the kindergarten teacher had to understand children, bringing together the natural instincts of motherhood with special training in child development. "The mother," one speaker at a National Education Association meeting declared, "as handmaid of the Lord, will recognize in the consecrated kindergartner a fellow-worker in the garden of the Lord." The kindergarten thus stood as an extension of ideal Motherhood, an institution that would

From *The History of Education Quarterly*, Volume 11, Number 2 (Summer, 1971), pp. 115–37. Used by permission.

effect the transition between the individualistic education of the home and the social necessities of the broader society.

Although socialization was frequently discussed, what the term actually encompassed varied. On the one side stood the emancipation of the child from traditional and insensitive restrictions, the enhancement of spontaneity and creativity. On the other, emphasis was given to uniformity and control. Early kindergartners often pointed to the former as their new institution's primary contribution, calling for love and understanding of the child, creative expression, youthful teachers, and the elimination of corporal punishment and parrotlike memorization. They advocated movement and activity for children who desired and needed both, introduced new play objects into the environment, and were willing to accept noise as a healthy corollary to happy play. "Of the two evils," Elizabeth Peabody wrote, "extreme indulgence is not so deadly a mistake as extreme severity."

But, while kindergartners urged emancipation, they also argued that their ultimate goal was order. The kindergarten was, after all, a "guarded company of children," and children could not be left "to a chaos of chance impressions." Individualism, with its potentiality for disorder and conflict, was another form of self-centeredness, vitiating the primary goals of kindergarten learning. "All government worthy of the name begins in self-government," Peabody declared, "a free subordination of the individual in order to form the social whole." The need for such socialization could hardly be underestimated. "The child is doubtless an embryo angel; but no less certainly a possible devil." Obedience, Mary Mann similarly concluded, was essential for order, and order "I regard as 'heaven's first law.'"

To produce this socialization, which channeled spontaneity into order, the kindergartners evolved a complex and highly structured methodology of play activities. Building on Froebel's assertion that play represented the highest and purest form of activity for young children, they created an ordered environment within which the child learned by doing. The child's own activity—spontaneous, natural, and satisfying his most basic needs for movement and self-mastery—became the mechanism for positive social growth. All play activities, however, were not equally valid. Music, song games, and marching, which called for great activity but kept children within a highly structured program and prevented "disagreeable romping," were fundamental. Formalized games helped the child internalize rules. As one kindergartner put it, "The ordinary child remembers to be good; the kindergarten child forgets to be naughty." Froebel's "gifts"—soft cloth balls, blocks, cubes, rings, triangles, spheres, and cylinders—introduced the child to geometrical forms and suggested the harmony and symmetry of life. Less important but still necessary in a well-run kindergarten were such utensils as paper, scissors, clay, pencils, and paint to elicit creative activity and help develop manual dexterity. Small gardens offered the child an object lesson in organized natural growth. Above all, early kindergartners warned, avoid the overuse of books, let the child learn the use of objects before the words of adults.

These views of childhood education received impressive support in the closing decades of the nineteenth century from a new emphasis upon early habit formation and from the emerging child-study movement. Although earlier Lockean ideas had laid the basis for an emphasis on childhood learning, not until the end of the nineteenth century did American educators generally acknowledge the importance of the early years in shaping adult behavior. To the kindergartners, this was an article of faith. The young child, they argued, was both malleable and perceptive. "The first seven years of the child's life," wrote Angeline Brooks, "Froebel saw to be the most important for purposes of education; for, as he said, during that time tendencies are given and the germs of character are set." Having found that the child's social and moral character could be shaped at an early age, the kindergartners also asserted that the influences would be lifelong. In 1886, the *Journal of Education* simply concluded that "In the first 7 or 8 years of a child's life it will probably be settled whether he is to be swayed by superstition or intelligence, whether he is to live terrorized by fear or buoyed up by hope and courage." Under these circumstances, the kindergarten appeared vital.

Further support for the kindergarten appeared as a by-product of the child-study movement, particularly the ideas formulated by G. Stanley Hall. President of Clark University, indefatigable organizer, prolific author, editor, and public speaker, Hall played, in the years prior to World War I, a seminal role in the fields of child and adolescent psychology. To the kindergartners, he was the "father of the child-study movement," the individual who made of childhood "a gospel." Hall provided a scientific rationale for Froebel's views that education was evolutionary and developmental, that human growth was a process of stages, and he urged the public to allow children to express their needs and peculiarities. His injunction that teachers and parents "get out of Nature's way and allow her free scope, and avoid excessive checks and inhibitions," was readily echoed by the kindergartners. His calls for teachers to know their children confirmed what early childhood educators already knew. The extraordinary breadth and proliferation of his studies and those inspired by him made child study a national topic of discussion. It was thus not surprising that, in 1880, when Hall sought to study children entering the first grade in Boston's public schools, he should be financed by Boston's leading supporter of kindergartens, Mrs. Quincy Adams Shaw, or that four of Mrs. Shaw's kindergarten teachers should act as investigators.

"The Contents of Children's Minds," the 1880 study, propelled Hall to the forefront of the child-study movement, and it revealed some of the reasons Hall's early theories found such ready support from the kindergartners. Determined to take an "inventory of the contents of the minds of children of average intelligence on entering the primary schools" of Boston, Hall formulated questions that "should lie within the range of what children are commonly supposed or at least desired or expected, by teachers and by those who write primary text-books and prescribe courses of instruction, to know." The findings were shocking. City children existed in almost total ignorance of the commonplaces of life: 80 per cent of the children were ignorant of beehives, 54 per cent of sheep, 87 per cent of a pine tree, 40 per cent of a pond, 92 per cent of a triangle. Such alarming results, however, contained some positive affirmations of the kindergarten. Children who had been to the charity kindergartens, where "superior intelligence of home surroundings can hardly be assumed," did substantially better than the other children. Most primary teachers found children from the kindergartens better fitted for school work, though often more restless and talkative. Perhaps most revealing was the relationship between Hall's standards of intelligence and the activities of the kindergarten. The test items were heavily weighted toward rural imagery, and consciously so. "As our methods of teaching grow natural," Hall believed, "we realize that city life is unnatural, and that those who grow up without knowing the country are defrauded of that without which childhood can never be complete or normal. On the whole, the material of the city is no doubt inferior in pedagogic value to country experience. A few days in the country at this age has raised the level of many a city child's intellgience more than a term or two of schooltraining could do without it."

These views paralleled basic assumptions of the early childhood educators. Kindergartners conceived of the city as an artificial environment antipathetical to natural growth and sought, in the "children's garden," a surrogate for urban life. Nature walks, small gardens, and freedom to play, which were assumed to be the life-style of the rural child, were essential ingredients of the kindergarten, while the strenuous play activities of the countryside found their parallel in the marching and games. The wood carving, sewing, drawing, sand and mud manipulation that Hall thought fundamental to growing up intelligently were re-created in a variety of forms in the children's classes. Most kindergartners, then, could find Hall's assumptions and his study of the "contents of children's minds" gratifying. Not merely had kindergarten children outdistanced the others, but the general solution advocated by the child psychologist pointed directly to the expansion of their institution.

KINDERGARTENS AND SOCIAL REFORM

While the ideology of the early kindergarten movement stressed its universality, its applicability to all children, the first kindergartens catered to the affluent. The earliest practitioners were cultured women whose daily associations were with individuals of wealth. Even when Boston established a publicly supported kindergarten in the early 1870's, "circumstances made it necessary," former Superintendent of Schools John Philbrick later wrote, "to locate it among the better class of population."

But, despite this initial indentification with the affluent and cultured, the kindergarten received its most important support in late-nineteenth-century Massachusetts as an institution of the urban slum. In the 1880's and 1890's, the social problems of the city came under more intensive investigation and received more publicity than ever before. Heightened concern for the slum helped spawn a new view of poverty that looked at the results of economic hardship rather than simply condemning them as a cause of social ills. Americans began to define poverty in terms of insufficiency and insecurity and no longer as desirable or necessary. The belief that poverty was debilitating paralleled assertions that its evils—disease, want, disrupted families—could be eradicated by the social measures of an aroused public, by a reorganizing of the environment in which the poor lived. Simultaneously, the child and his home, not simply as symbols of the child-study movement, but as special objects of social amelioration, received new attention. Children's aid organizations sprouted and flourished. Volunteer charity workers reported that "labor among the children" was the most important feature of their work. "Here [in the homes of the children], by means of books, games and pictures, the visitors can bring brightness and activity instead of dreariness and idleness. The comfortable and interesting home will be the best safeguard against outside temptations."

Not all educators adopted this new view of urban poverty; few were as articulate. But the kindergartners and those who supported them found the attitudes and the goals of the social welfare movement congenial. The kindergarten's antiurban bias accentuated the horrors of the slum and provided a vantage point from which to view poverty. Kindergarten advocates argued that healthy family life could not occur in the slums, that children of the poor were "uncared for." The urban street and home seemed environments of terror. Mary Mann, usually a sympathetic observer, was reported to have characterized slum children as "little savages from three to five, the pests of the street, their mouths full of profane and obscene language." In the immigrant ghetto—by the late nineteenth century in Massachusetts, poverty and immigrants were deemed synonymous—an institution adaptable to children, willing to recognize their need for activity and play, while introducing order to their lives, appeared vital if society [were] to avoid adults bred in anarchy. The kindergarten, the editor of *Century Magazine* declared, was "our earliest opportunity to catch the little Russian, the little Italian, the little German, Pole, Syrian, and the rest and begin to make good American citizens of them."

Between 1880 and 1900, similar expressions revolving around the preschooling of the urban poor came from almost every educational leader in Massachusetts. In Lawrence, the superintendent of schools in 1881 recommended public support for kindergartens in the less fortunate areas of the city. Lynn's superintendent pleaded for just one kindergarten especially adapted to "little ones from homes of the poor and the uncared for." The school committee in New Bedford, arguing for kindergartens, believed that "the great majority of children who do not attend school between five and seven are unfortunately those of foreign parentage, and, as a rule, often of the most ignorant kind. They are the very children who should be in school at the earliest permissible age, as they, as a rule, are the first to leave school to go to work." In 1897, the new superintendent of schools in Haverhill summarized the prevailing ideology:

> In my opinion the Kindergarten should be established not for the benefit of those children who come from homes of culture and refinement; but on the contrary, it should receive those children that have had little, if any, good home-training. If it were established in such a portion of our city, and were properly conducted, it would furnish a happy transition from those homes and the unwholesome influences of street life to the healthful schoolroom surroundings.

These views were not isolated phenomena. They reflected a growing sense of urgency about the relationship of education and schools in slum life, manifest, to some extent, in almost all the educational innovations of the late nineteenth century. Schooling and social welfare were becoming synonymous as individuals desperately sought to correct the dysfunctional institutions of the urban environment. In their efforts, educational change was seen both as a way of improving the schools and of ameliorating broader urban social problems. Not surprisingly, then, school reform received much of its impetus from social settlement workers and philanthropists engaged in reshaping the urban environment. To these individuals, the kindergarten was a unique institution, distinctive in its approach to child development and a means of entering the home and neighborhood. To the social reformers, the kindergarten was more akin to the settlement house than to the school, and they joined with the early formulators of the kindergarten ideology to keep kindergarten education distinct from the narrow pedagogy and academic goals of the regular school classroom.

In the late nineteenth century, the settlement was seen as an agency for melting families into a neighborhood. The kindergartens would participate in that work primarily by harmonizing and socializing individual families. Proposing a club for little children along kindergarten lines, one settlement worker wrote, "They would be easy to manage, and would give us an entree into the homes of the mothers." Settlements and kindergartens gave the highest priority to taking the child off the streets by providing him with attractions unattainable on them. Both viewed the poor, particularly the immigrant poor, with a mixture of sympathy and contempt. Kindergarten teachers, the Pittsfield, Massachusetts, *Sun* wrote in 1898, would explain their methods and objects, teach the games and songs to mothers, thus allowing mothers to play with their children at home. And, "if the mothers happen to be poor, ignorant, uncultivated women, as so many are who have children in the public or free kindergartens, the kindergartner does real missionary work in the talks she can give on hygiene—proper food and clothing and neatness in every way." Mothers' meetings, kindergartner Nora Smith argued, for those "hard-worked, unlettered women" whose children attended the charity kindergarten classes, should be social gatherings in spotless rooms containing flowers, light refreshments, and cloth-covered tables. "It will be," she wrote, "a cosmopolitan audience thus gathered together in any of our free kindergartens, and somewhat uncongenial in its elements, comprising, as it does, Italians, Germans, French, Irish, Scandinavians, Hebrews, Africans, a few native-born Americans [possibly], and perhaps even some wanderers from Syria or Armenia." Indeed, even the settlement house itself might be considered a "kindergarten for adults." "The settlement may not have intentionally preached the doctrines of Froebel, but it has practiced them in every phase of its work. In the playground, the children's club, the vacation school, nay, in the very settlement itself, one may read the philosophy of the kindergarten writ large."

A striking manifestation of the kindergarten as urban reform was the philanthropic kindergarten activities of Mrs. Quincy Adams Shaw. Daughter of famed Harvard scientist Louis Agassiz, stepdaughter of Radcliffe College's first president, Elizabeth Cary Agassiz, and wife of a copper-mining heir who claimed three of Massachusetts' most distinguished names, Mrs. Shaw epitomized the socially concerned philanthropist. In the last year of her life, she wrote her children that she had "had too much—you will all have too much—and it will require great effort with God's help to determine 'to give' rather than 'to hold.'." Considered the richest woman in Boston and the city's "greatest woman philanthropist," Mrs. Shaw was a major sponsor of settlement houses, a strong supporter of women's rights, and founder and president of the Boston Equal Suffrage Association. Many of the educational innovations of the period—sloyd (a Swedish method of woodworking), industrial education, and vocational placement bureaus—received their initial support from her proselytizing and financial activities. Of all her concerns, however, none so involved her interest and money as the kindergarten and day nurseries, believing that "the bringing up of children is the vital question of life—the great problem of the race."

Mrs. Shaw was probably converted to kindergarten work by Elizabeth Peabody during the 1860's. In 1870, when Peabody's school appeared ready to close for lack of funds, Mrs. Shaw provided additional financing and, shortly thereafter, helped open a charity kindergarten in Boston's North End, followed by two similar ones in suburban Jamaica Plain and Brookline. Within a decade, she was supporting three such ventures in and around Boston, spending more than $200,000 on them between 1882 and 1889. Even after her kindergartens were incorporated into the Boston public school system in 1888, she continued her philanthropy, providing funds for training courses for kindergarten teachers, Christmas parties, and an assortment of related activities.

The most famous of Mrs. Shaw's charity kindergartens were undoubtedly those in Boston's densely populated, immigrant North End. In this district, housing twenty-five nationalities in 1900, most recently arrived from Eastern Europe, wrote Francis Parker, a former supervisor of primary schools in Boston, "hundreds of parents turn their children out into the streets in the morning to care for themselves, while they, by selling fruit, grinding organs, begging, or even worse, strive to eke out a miserable existence." To meet the needs of these children, two charity kindergartens had been established in the early 1870's, "to collect," its sponsors wrote, "some of the neglected children who swarm in the streets, while yet too young for the primary schools, and give them facilities for intellectual and moral training at an age most tender and sensitive to every surrounding influence."

It is unclear how long these schools remained in existence, but, by 1880, Mrs. Shaw had helped establish at least three separate kindergarten classes, receiving permission from the Boston School Committee to hold two of them in rooms of a local public school. That is, from their inception, the philanthropic kindergartens were provided with some facilities by the public schools. All furnishings, heat, teachers, and assistants were paid for by Mrs. Shaw, the classes catering to children between twenty-two months and five years of age. Physical needs were met first: each child was greeted by daily face washing, his clothes cleaned, and milk and bread provided. The kindergaretn room, one observer of a North End class wrote, "is warm and cheery; bright pictures hang on the walls; on one blackboard is a crayon sketch of swans floating on still waters; on another are notes and words of simple songs; on the shelves at one side of the room is a company of dolls, while various childish treasures are scattered here and there within easy reach of tiny hands." The activities of these classes in the heart of the immigrant ghetto had a certain bizarre quality to them. Children marched and sang about a "little birdie"; they learned that wooden balls come from "the great, tall trees," and talked about pussy willows, the sun, and walks in green fields. Committed to memory were such verses as:

> I'm an oriole, I'm an oriole,
> My nest hangs on high
> Where the breezes are singing
> Their sweet lullaby.
> They rock in their cradle,
> My birdies and me,
> And we are as happy,
> As happy can be.

But the North End kindergartens were more than play spots dedicated to introducing rural imagery into the life of the ghetto child. Both Mrs. Shaw and her supervising teacher, Laliah Pingree, were devoted to reaching the neighboring homes. Mothers were invited into the classes; parents' gatherings were held in the evenings to explain kindergarten methods and to suggest improvement in child care. The kindergartners placed great faith in the belief that the habits children learned while under their care would pervade the slum home. Forced to overcome apathy among parents toward the new classes, kindergarten teachers systematically and consistently visited the homes of enrolled and prospective pupils, teaching only half a day for this purpose. Kindergartners were enthusiastic about such tales as Lucy Wheelock's "A Lily's Mission," in which two "ragged, dirty children" bring a flower home to their dingy tenement apartment. The mother has failed to keep the house clean; the father is out drinking. Overjoyed at seeing the flower, the mother places it on a window sill only to discover that dirt prevents any sunlight from shining through the window to the flower. With the window clean, sunlight reveals the filth of the apartment, which is then quickly cleaned; mother washes and dresses, and father, overcome by his new environment upon his return home, vows to give up the bottle. Such tales revealed only the most spectacular of powers attributed to the kindergarten as an instrument of reform. "The interest manifested in the children and families," Laliah Pingree wrote of Mrs. Shaw's kindergartens, "does much to encourage the parents to do something for the children themselves, and to make them more responsible for them. The impression made upon the mothers by the patience and gentleness of the teacher is a deep one." Pointing to the need to instruct slum parents, Pingree told of the kindergarten child who, after being struck by her mother, declared, "God did not give you those to strike me with; he made them to do nice and good things; my [kindergarten] teacher said so." To the philanthropists and settlement workers, the kindergarten thus emerged as a crucial wedge to bring order to the child's growth and to his life at home, on the street, and in the classroom. Through the child, the adult poor would be instructed in the mores of the dominant society. As the kindergarten moved from the organizations of charity to the public schools, it would retain that ideology of reform, but not for long.

INSTITUTIONALIZATION AND COMMUNITY

Tied to, and invigorated by, the settlement houses and philanthropists, the kindergarten soon found its way into the public school systems of urban Massachusetts. By 1914, seven of the ten largest cities and twelve of the twenty largest had public kindergartens. In almost every case, they developed out of a philanthropic base and, particularly in the first years of the transition from charity to public education, continued their allegiance to the ideals of social philanthropy and their commitment to the kindergarten as distinctive from the regular school classroom. Almost invariably, the first kindergartens under public auspices focused on the peculiar needs of the slum child, and upon the role kindergartens could play in elevating the home and neighborhood, while preparing the child for the elementary grades. Ultimately, however, the incorporation of early childhood training into urban school systems represented a withdrawal from the broad goals of community reform. An emerging consensus developed among educators and philanthropists that all education, whatever its social justification, should be centered in the schools, that social change occurred best through classroom practices. In Massachusetts, this would lead, in the decades after 1900, to a gradual narrowing, rather than broadening, of social commitments, a turning away from urban reform. For reasons of economy and theory, public kindergartens began to eliminate mothers' meetings and home visits, while their supporters on the eve of World War I spoke less about reforming and elevating the family and about social amelioration than they did about smoothing the child's progress in grade school and separating him from his social background. The processes of transfer from philanthropic to public, and the need for an institutional rationale acceptable to the professional educator, worked a subtle but nonetheless radical transformation in the philosophy of the kindergarten.

The transition from philanthropic to public occurred first in Boston, and it was there that the initial continuity between schooling and social reform was most clearly apparent. Although the city had briefly experimented with a public-supported kindergarten in the 1870's, preschooling before 1887, remained almost exclusively a philanthropic–social settlement activity, dominated by Mrs. Shaw. During the mid-1880's, however, rising costs forced Mrs. Shaw to cut back her commitments, and she and her associates began pressuring the Boston School Committee to finance its own kindergartens. Receiving strong support from Superintendent of Schools Edwin P. Seaver, Mrs. Shaw agreed to turn over her program to the city, thereby enlarging charity into a broader public responsibility. The rationale for accepting this responsibility emerged in two areas, one involving the relationship of preschooling to social reform, the other focusing on early childhood education as a prerequisite for future school success. The former reflected a direct transfer of philanthropic ideals to public education. In an immigrant, working-class city like Boston, few families could be considered positive agents of socialization, and any improvement in family life depended upon bringing children into more adequate institutions. Calling for the adoption and expansion of kindergarten classes as a regular feature of the Boston public schools, Superintendent Seaver declared, the kindergarten "affords a much-needed protection from the injurious influence of the street." "For those unfortunate children—and there are many—who suffer from parental carelessness, indifference, ignorance, or poverty, the kindergarten measurably supplies what the home does not—kindly nurture in the virtues and graces of a more refined and elevated democratic life." Simultaneously, the kindergarten also seemed an effective way of getting children ready for further schooling. This view was best summarized by an experienced teacher who had taught primary school for thirty years—beginners for about twenty years. She had received ten or twelve children each year from kindergarten for about ten years. Their training "in habits of neatness, cleanliness, order, self-reliance, and prompt obedience," she wrote, was "a great saving of time to the primary teacher." They had also "formed habits of observing closely, and using their hands properly." All their faculties" were "so cultivated that no time" was "lost in preparing them for Primary School work." Those children who belonged to cultivated families, she continued, might not need kindergarten training, "but it is almost a necessity for the majority of children under our charge."

Inherent, then, in the Boston School Committee's adoption of the kindergarten, a step taken in 1888, were these two interrelated themes: community reform as epitomized by the social settlements, and school achievement defined by adequate preparation for primary grades. Both themes depended upon a consensus among philanthropists, reformers, and educators that urban social life had failed, that the children of the city needed a special institution if they were to learn proper habits of behavior. While community reform and school achievement initially seemed complementary, however, public education would be hard-pressed to achieve either among the poor, and educators would soon be choosing schools rather than community as their central concern.

The dominant role philanthropy and philanthropic ideals played in establishing kindergartens in Boston also appeared in other Massachusetts cities. In Cambridge, kindergartens were initiated by Mrs. Shaw in the late 1870's. A decade later, she and other philanthropists convinced the Cambridge School Committee to incorporate their charity classes into the public schools. As occurred in Boston, philanthropy continued to play a role in the classes even after their adoption by the public system. Mothers' clubs, evening receptions for fathers, and home visits by teachers all designed to improve family life remained integral to Cambridge's kindergarten program through to the end of the century. This blurring of public and philanthropic similarly occurred in Fall River, where, as late as 1912, Mrs. Spencer Borden was supplying furniture, materials, and all other equipment to the public school system's five classes. Even in the wealthy Boston suburb of Brookline, considered by an observer in the 1890's to possess "one of the most unique school systems in the country," charity overtones persisted. Discussing educational activities in the town, Superintendent of Schools Samuel Dutton noted that the Brookline Education Society and Child Study Association brought "cultured women" together with "those less favored" to explain the care of children. Dutton, one of the most articulate and active exponents of innovation among the state's professional educators and a propagandist for widespread kindergarten education, remained committed, like other educators, to the particular applicability of such classes to "all neglected children and those whose breeding and environment are likely to result in criminal habits."

If Massachusetts' major cities thus drew upon philanthropic initiative to establish kindergartens as part of their public school systems before World War I, the élan and vitality that marked the movement's early years, especially the commitment to community reform, suffered a noticeable decline in the decade and a half after 1900. Despite continuing assertions that kindergartens were essential for children of the ghetto, despite affirmations of their importance to all children, despite a resolution by the Massachusetts Teachers' Association in 1895 and proposed legislation in 1909 that all cities and towns with populations over 10,000 have public kindergartens, and despite the activities of individual superintendents of schools, public classes showed only moderate growth. While the number of children enrolled in public kindergartens increased from about 3,000 to 14,000 between 1890 and 1900, annual enrollment climbed to only 18,000 by 1914, with Boston and Worcester, the state's largest cities, accounting for half the latter figure. Whereas Massachusetts, in 1898, accounted for 8.8 per cent of all kindergarten-registered children in the United States, its proportion gradually dropped to 5.4 per cent by 1912. Even where public kindergartens were established, they sometimes catered to as few as 6 per cent of the eligible population (ages four to six), although Boston's 22 per cent, Cambridge's 31 per cent, Springfield's 61 per cent, Holyoke's 23 per cent, and Worcester's 28 per cent were outstanding among the larger cities.

The most obvious question arising from these statistics is why the lessening of commitment. Many educators continued to affirm the kindergarten's importance in implementing proper habits of behavior, in educating urban parents, and as an introduction to early school life; yet the movement's enthusiasm waned, and its implementation slowed. In part, this reflected heightened concern with costs. Many cities and towns, already heavily taxed to support elementary and high schools, and particularly burdened by overcrowded classrooms, found kindergartens an unjustifiable luxury. Between 1889 and 1909, while enrollment in the Boston kindergartens climbed, the city paid about $20 a year for each pupil. By 1914, however, expenditures had increased to $27 a pupil. Cambridge found itself in a similar situation when instruction per kindergarten pupil increased from $14.78 (1890), to $19.33 (1898), to $27.15 (1908), and, finally, to $39.77 (1915), as compared to expenditures per primary school pupil of $12.92, $13.94, $16.11, and $24.46 for the same years. Expenses in Fall River went from $12.37 in 1904–05 to $21.65 per pupil in 1913–14, while Lowell, which cut its kindergarten enrollment between 1904 and 1914, found that its expenditures per pupil continued to increase. Although these rises reflected a general trend in school costs, kindergartens remained more expensive than the lower primary grades. As distinctive institutions, they demanded special treatment, and to varying degrees they got it. In a study of twenty American cities in 1911, the Boston Finance Commission found that five of the seven Massachusetts cities analyzed averaged fewer pupils per teacher in kindergarten than in the elementary schools, and in some cases the difference was dramatic.

Lessening commitment to the kindergarten, however, represented more than a reaction to high and rising costs. Cities were invariably involved in choosing educational innovations or expanding their educational services; kindergartens could have received more priority than they did. "More fundamental [than costs]," David Snedden, State Commissioner of Education, wrote in 1915, was ". . . whether the aims and the field of the kindergarten have been defined to the satisfaction of educators." "It is widely assumed that the chief value of the kindergarten is to compensate for deficiencies of home environment." Such an assumption, the Commissioner claimed, implied that educators knew what the ideal environment for healthy growth was, and that the "compensatory functions" of the kindergarten provided such an environment. If this were so, why did the "cities having conditions of environment least favorable to the normal growth of children [viz., the immigrant-industrial cities] have usually the fewest kindergartens?" In effect, Snedden argued, kindergarten advocates asserted they offered an ideal environment to overcome home and neighborhood conditions, without proving their case to the public. But there was more to the criticism, for implicit in the argument was a sense that the essential failure of kindergarteners had been their attempt to establish their institution distinct from the primary grades, the unwillingness of kindergarten advocates to see their programs as simply the beginning of the regular school process. "Children of English-speaking parents living in good environments," Snedden wrote, could most afford to delay their school work until the age of six, either by remaining at home or engaging in the play activities of the kindergarten. Children of the slums, however, especially the non-English-speaking, needed early exposure to a more rigorous school atmosphere, one that combined certain kindergarten methods with systematic primary school training.

This issue, the conflict between essentially structured and formalized learning versus "play" learning, effectively undercut appeals for kindergartens as distinctive public institutions. Within the kindergarten movement itself, the distinctions that had developed between the needs of all children and those peculiar to children of the poor, the differences between early childhood schooling for children from healthy homes and those from the urban slums, were reflected in controversy over kindergarten methods. As Snedden implied, once educators differentiated among categories of children, methods and goals had to be modified. Those who remained committed to the universal child and Froebel's methods therefore came under constant criticism by kindergarten reformers, who demanded programs adapted to such categories as the child's nationality, class, age, approximation to normality, physical handicaps, environmental background, and material and social development. Conflict within the kindergarten movement itself over the extent to which young children should be differentiated undercut expansion of preschooling programs.

Concern over costs and confusion among kindergartners as to the true nature of their institution soon led Massachusetts educators to focus on the relationship between primary and kindergarten education, evolving a compromise situation that effectively curtailed the latter's distinctiveness, and helped terminate the philanthropic commitments to social amelioration. The establishment of subprimary classes, or, in less defined form, the absorption of the kindergarten by the lower primary grades, had particular appeal to those concerned with the slum child. "When . . . children live in crowded quarters," Commissioner Snedden wrote, "and especially if the language of the home be foreign, or else poor English, a twofold gain results from admission at five to a so-called subprimary class. The school will provide for a few hours each day a better environment than the street, and a moderate amount of systematic training will give to the pupil such command of English and training in school behavior in general as to enable him, after entering the first grade, to keep pace approximately with more favored classmates."

The processes that made the kindergarten simply an adjunct of first grade occurred throughout the state, but the most pertinent example can be found in the immigrant industrial city of New Bedford. There, rapid population growth—from 40,000 to 96,000 between 1890 and 1910—and large numbers of foreign-born, reflecting the enormous expansion of the city's cotton textile industry, placed great pressures upon the city's school system. In the lower grades, where a majority of the children, by 1913, came from homes of non-English-speaking parents, conditions were exceedingly bad. It was to these children of New Bedford's immigrant mill population that the first kindergartens in the city were directed.

In 1894, under the auspices of the City Mission, an aid station for the poor, two charity classes were set up in the mill and immigrant north and south ends of the city. Within two years, pressure developed for public sponsorship of the classes, now accepted as necessary "for children whose home advantages were not of the best." After a minor skirmish between the city council, which refused to allocate funds, and the School Board, three kindergarten classes were established, under conditions, however, that manifested a significant deviation from earlier philanthropic conceptions. The new classes were not to be distinctive institutions but "should conform somewhat to the plan or organization which rules in all other grades of the schools if they are to become a permanent part of the school system." As was true of primary school teachers, kindergarten instructors were required to conduct two sessions daily, each containing 50 different pupils, although, as a concession to the particular necessities of the kindergarten, two teachers were assigned to every 100 pupils. Teachers' home visits, small classes, and an educational and social ethic distinct from that of the primary schools received little recognition. New Bedford thus initiated its public kindergarten program with virtually no concern for the social reform measures that had previously dominated much of the movement.

Even with these modifications, New Bedford's educators were unhappy. None of the three kindergartens was meeting its quota of 100 pupils per day, making the program more expensive per pupil than originally intended. "I am a firm believer in kindergartens," Superintendent William Hatch wrote at the end of the first year's experiment, "and I have so expressed myself before; but I also firmly believe economical questions must have proper consideration in school administration. The cost of kindergarten under the one-session plan [with afternoons devoted to home visits and mothers' clubs] is too great to warrant their maintenance on that plan. If there is not sufficient appreciation of this class of schools on the part of the parents of the city to support the double plan, as much as I should dislike to see kindergartens abandoned here I should feel it my duty to advise their discontinuance." Five years later, in 1902, attendance continued considerably below expectations. With two teachers in each school, Hatch claimed, kindergarten instructors averaged only 14 pupils contrasted to a primary school teacher's 40–50. Reflecting growing community concern over school costs, the superintendent contended that the kindergartens created more problems than they solved. While he believed "it would be an excellent thing if most of the children of our schools could have the advantage of the kindergarten," New Bedford's schools were already over-crowded with increasing costs already "causing more dissatisfaction."

The controversy finally came to a head between 1904 and 1909, when a compromise effectively eliminated kindergartens. In the former year, Super-intendent Hatch enlarged his criticism from economic to theoretical grounds, claiming that children should not be in school before the age of six and suggesting that earlier attendance had no discernible effect on school per-formance. With the city in the midst of an economic depression the follow-ing year, the School Board narrowly voted, in June, 1905, to continue the kindergartens, although it recognized that they were expensive and insuffi-ciently patronized. Nine months later, however, the Board reversed itself and moved to abolish the classes—an action that aroused a storm of protest among prominent individuals in the city. At a special public hearing, a citizens' group, headed by the founders of the charity kindergartens of the 1890's, declared: "In an industrial city like ours we believe it essential to begin the education of hand and mind of the child at the earliest possible time. We therefore petition your Honorable Board to continue the kinder-gartens we have already and to establish others where they are needed." Kindergarten supporters claimed that New Bedford's industrial community urgently needed the classes. The Reverend Paul R. Frothingham, who had started the city's second kindergarten in the immigrant northend, declared: "There are some cities where the kindergarten is not so necessary as in New Bedford, cities where all the people are well-to-do, where there are small families, and the parents are able to provide for their children. But in a great industrial center, with large families and crowded conditions, a kin-dergarten, I believe, plays a very important and necessary part." Indeed, the issue was so important that Frothingham called for the elimination of Latin and Greek from high school rather than drop kindergartens.

Under intense pressure—the School Board received petitions from boards of directors of the Orphans' Home, Mothers' Club, Woman's Club, and City Mission, all representing prominent New Bedford citizens, as well as petitions from several of the mill corporations—the School Committee en-gaged in a tactical retreat. In June, 1906, two and a half months after the stormy open hearing, the Board voted eight to seven to retain the public kindergartens and, within six months, had added a fourth class in the south end. The 1906 decision, however, did not settle the controversy. Con-fronting a situation in which more than 50 per cent of the children entering first grade did not understand English or could do so only with difficulty, the School Board moved to establish half-time subprimary classes for five- and six-year-olds. These classes would continue the game activities of the kindergartens but would also introduce the children to the routine of school life. No child under the age of seven would be allowed to enter school after the first two weeks of classes unless he was qualified to do so, thus forcing all newly arrived, non-English-speaking children into the subprimary classes. In effect, New Bedford had found that isolating the immigrant child was an effective way of educating him, but that this could best be done by introducing him to the "routine of school life," rather than by establishing distinctive, socially involved kindergartens.

New Bedford was not an exceptional case. It and seven other of Massachusetts' twenty largest cities had either eliminated or never established public school kindergartens before 1914. More important, a number of other cities that had maintained such classes were, by the second decade of the twentieth century, eliminating the kindergarten as a distinctive institution, moving away from its earlier conception as a unique environment for children with socially amelioristic goals. The subprimary movement prominent in New Bedford had received strong support from the state's commissioner of education. The emancipatory goals of creative play and expression within a structured environment and the humanization of early childhood education had become confused with the need to bring order and discipline to the slum child. Preparation of the child for the primary grades was becoming the kindergarten's *raison d'être,* combining English-language instruction with an emphasis on traditional learning and curriculum. What Francis Parker had called "the most important, far reaching educational reform of the nineteenth century" was ceasing to be conceived of as an environment in itself and as a supplement to the child's environment and, instead, was assuming a position as a pre-elementary class whose major function was to remove the child from his home environment and lead him into the schools as quickly as possible.

This tendency was not totally novel. Rather, it represented a subtle change in emphasis that, in turn, resulted in the radical transformation of the kindergarten as an urban institution. Antagonism to the slum child's background had always existed within the kindergarten movement and, indeed, provided a major impetus to its growth. A "social quarantine" movement had even become prominent at the turn of the century, calling for a "strict quarantine for the innocents [i.e., 'children of the street and of wretched homes'], where the kindergarten influence and gentle training . . . may overcome the moral starvation from which they suffer, and develop in them human potentialities for goodness." But such views had always co-existed with, and even been dominated by, philanthropic and settlement goals that had seen the child as a means to larger social reform. The mothers' meetings, social gatherings, child-care talks, home visits, and a host of other activities had effectively enlarged conceptions of child schooling. Now, in the first two decades of the twentieth century, Massachusetts' cities began to eliminate or de-emphasize these as regular features of the kindergarten. Cambridge instituted a one-year experiment in double teaching sessions for each kindergarten teacher in 1911, necessitating "the dropping of much of the visiting to the homes of the children as well as the mothers' meetings." Worcester believed that kindergarten teachers had to be trained for the primary grades as well as for their particular kindergarten roles. Boston's Finance Commission undoubtedly offered the most extreme proposal: all-day kindergartens in foreign districts with all four-year-olds attending as the only means of preparing the children for their first grade work. These public pronouncements, however, only partially reflect the changing conceptions of the kindergarten. As revealing was the absence of discussion about the social responsibilities of early childhood educators. Whereas superintendents of schools had once affirmed the key roles kindergartens would play in slum districts, between 1910 and 1914 such discussion practically ceased. Where children of the poor were mentioned, it was now almost invariably in the context of non-English-speaking immigrants who needed aid in being propelled through the school and into the work force, rather than in terms of helping reform the larger society of which they were a part. As they became institutionalized in the urban public school, kindergartners moved from the delicate balance they had earlier proposed between freedom and order, emancipation and discipline, to a clear and overriding commitment to control. Slum children, removed from the guiding restraints of healthy, orderly family life, growing up in the anarchic environment of the street, needed, above all else, discipline, needed to be prepared for the strict environment of the primary grades. By the time of America's entry into World War I, Massachusetts' educators had resolved the tension that had existed in the kindergarten movement between focusing on the child or using the child for the larger setting. They had turned from the child in the slum home to the slum child in school—a far easier and cheaper means of education—and, in the process, they were ceasing to believe that positive benefits could be derived from a focus on the former.

Immigrant Social Aspirations and American Education, 1880–1930

Timothy L. Smith

Statistics for literacy and school attendance in the federal census of 1910 suggest that immigrant families showed as much—or more—zeal for education as those in which the parents were native Americans. Not just in the South, where the school system was weak and the former slave population

Reprinted from *The American Quarterly*, Volume 21, Number 3 (Fall, 1969), pp. 523–43, by permission of The University of Pennsylvania, publisher, and the Author. Copyright, 1969, Trustees of The University of Pennsylvania.

large, but in every section of the country, the percentage of children of foreign or mixed parentage aged six to fourteen who were enrolled in school closely approximated that for children of native Americans. And the literacy of the immigrants' offspring was uniformly higher, even in the populous Middle Atlantic and North Central states, where newcomers from Central and Southern Europe were many, and traditions of education among the Yankee population strong. The relative preponderance of first- and second-generation immigrants in public school teaching underlines the point. In 1908, in Duluth, Minnesota, 10 per cent of 460 teachers in the kindergarten and elementary grades were themselves immigrants, and the fathers of another 42 per cent were foreign-born. Such figures help explain why those who campaigned to restrict immigration on the argument that newcomers were illiterate cited statistics only for the foreign-born themselves, ignoring the achievements of their children. Woodbridge M. Ferris, Governor of Michigan during the copper strike of 1913–14, appealed soon after for a great expansion of night school programs for immigrants from Central and Southern Europe on the grounds that their desire for education far outran the provisions the community was making for them. During the year-long strike, he noted, the children enrolled in the public schools of the polyglot Marquette peninsula recorded an average attendance of 97 per cent, a result that an army of truant officers could not have achieved if the parents had lacked enthusiasm.

Apparently, not only parents but also the single men who joined them in forming, after 1890, the new Italian, Greek, Slavic, Finnish, Hungarian, and Jewish ethnic associations displayed a remarkable commitment to education. When, for example, in 1889 Protestant women in Rochester, New York, opened an Italian mission, ninety men enrolled at once in the English class that met three nights a week. The attendance by the year's end averaged seventy, though the total Italian population of the city that year was barely five hundred. Peter Roberts noted, in 1904, that ambitious young Slavs in the anthracite-mining towns of eastern Pennsylvania crowded out the night schools that private agencies conducted there, after they learned that the public ones could enroll only persons under twenty-one years of age. By 1910, a former Polish peasant, who had begun life in America as a Michigan farmhand thirty years before, was operating a printing firm in Toledo, Ohio, which issued every year more books than any publishing house in Poland. John Jurin, a coppersmith's apprentice from Croatian Slavonia, was unable to read or write his own language when he came to Chicago on the eve of World War I. Members of a Croatian dramatic club helped him, first, to become literate in his native tongue and then taught him English. He wound up editor of the newspaper that the club published during the 1930's, earning his living all the while at his trade. Stoyan Christowe, a Bulgarian who came from a Greek village to St. Louis at about the same time, soon fled the inferno of jackhammers and hot rivets that he encountered on his first job, but he did not forget the advice of an older immigrant that he study English. "I applied myself to it with the diligence of a scientist," he wrote later. He pored over the dictionary and the grammar and read newspapers and magazines continually. "I never threw away a package, a can or a box without reading whatever labels were pasted upon them," Christowe said. "The words that were unfamiliar to me I wrote on small square pieces of paper in red or green pencil. These I tacked to the walls of the bunk until every available inch of space was covered. In whatever direction I looked I saw words."

Intensified concern for schooling seems to have been an integral part of the social experience of migration from Central and Southeastern Europe at three important junctures: on the eve of departure from the homeland villages, when some chose to go and some to stay; in the first years after settlement in America, when the lessons to be learned were many and the rewards were large for those who learned them quickly and well; and, thereafter, among the residents of the former Old World villages, where letters from those who stayed overseas as well as the example of others who returned helped the peasant class to understand the role of education in personal, communal, and national advancement. The records also indicate that the laymen and clergymen who established programs of parochial education in Roman Catholic, Greek Catholic, Eastern Orthodox, and Protestant immigrant congregations linked their efforts closely to the social aspirations that had drawn the newcomers from the villages far away.

Behind the concern for learning lay three interlocking motives. The one most explicit in their literature and also most deeply rooted in Old World experience was simply the desire to earn a better living and, if possible, to gain both riches and fame. The second, and the one that seems to have been most prominent in religious congregations in America, was the need to shape a structure of family and communal life that would fit the requirements of mobile and urban existence. The third was specifically ethnic: the quest of a definition of national identity that would fulfill the sense of duty to their homeland or to their people that memory inspired and still not contradict their new allegiance to America.

The most obvious factor in the educational awakening on both sides of the Atlantic was the migrating peasants' desire to make money, and so to get ahead. Italian or Slavic workers who came intending to stay in America, and who brought over their wives or sweethearts as soon as they had gotten a foothold, were keenly aware of hardship. They often protested their exploitation by native Americans or by [their] countrymen who had arrived earlier. Nevertheless, they knew their condition was vastly improved over the poverty they had experienced in Calabria, Dalmatia, Carniola, or the Carpathian mountains. As for the "birds of passage," Romanian old-timers who came from Bukovina or the Banat intending only temporary employment here recall that each man's slogan on departure was "a thousand dollars and my ticket home."

Both the permanent and the temporary migrants realized that to learn to speak and read English was to make their investment of time, expense and emotion gilt-edged. The earliest volumes of virtually every Slavic newspaper that religious or secular organizations published in America carried lessons in English, announced the publication of simple dictionaries or grammars, and exhorted readers to learn the new tongue as a means of getting and holding a better job. The night school movement, for which public officials and industrial executives generally took credit, began in many cities under the auspices of immigrant associations themselves. Polish farmers who took over poorer farmsteads in the Connecticut Valley around Hadley, Massachusetts, after 1900 acknowledged that monetary values prompted them to flock to evening classes, and to require faithful attendance by their younger children in the public schools. Even in the anthracite country, where the availability of employment for twelve-year-olds caused a sharp drop-off of attendance above the primary grades, Peter Roberts' tabulation showed that 55 per cent of all the children enrolled in the two public elementary schools in Mahanoy City were of Slavic parentage. Proportionate enrollment was similar in five nearby mining towns, despite the fact that several thousand Slovak and Polish children in the region attended parochial day schools.

The early parochial schools, moreover, stressed the learning of English quite as much as the preservation of Old World culture. The 70,000 pupils attending Polish Roman Catholic schools in Chicago, in 1901, studied religion and Polish language and history in their parents' native tongue, but the language of instruction in geography, American history, bookkeeping, and algebra was English. The first Hungarian and Slovak Roman Catholic congregations in Cleveland employed English-speaking Benedictine nuns as teachers; the priest or some interested layman came in periodically to instruct the youngsters in Magyar or Slovak. Roberts noted that Slavic Roman Catholic priests in the anthracite country often limited parochial education to the first three or four grades, because they were unable to secure instructors of their faith and nationality who could teach the children in English. Laymen insisted on an adequate program of secular instruction. A Milwaukee Polish editor declared, around 1907, that many of his readers had begun to discover that their parish schools were doing a poor job, and were demanding improvements. "With the exception of those where the priest himself" was "a sincere educator," he charged, children were getting superficial instruction in reading, writing, arithmetic, geography, and history. Moreover, the memorization of the catechism and of dogmatic formulas was, he said, "far from being really religion." The editor advised the public school authorities that, if they would add Polish language to their curriculum in Slavic neighborhoods, many parents would send their children to public school.

The fact that the so-called new immigrants arrived in largest numbers from Central and Southeastern Europe during the same decades when the progressive movement in American education was placing much heavier emphasis upon vocational training, helped to confirm their utilitarian attitude toward schooling. Religious and fraternal leaders encouraged that attitude by recounting the economic aims of the parallel reform that was taking place at the same time in their Old World homelands. In the Kingdom of Hungary, for example, the law of 1868, though ineffective in those northern countries from which most Americans came, made school attendance obligatory for children aged six to twelve, added geography and natural science to the elementary curriculum, and required in each public school some rudimentary training for the occupation that a majority of the parents followed. After 1902, the state required children aged twelve to fifteen who were gainfully employed to attend continuation classes in various trades a part of each day. By 1911, commercial, technical, and agricultural high schools in Hungary enrolled 102,000 students, and a law that became effective that year required the establishment of apprentice schools in all communities in which as many as fifty youngsters were working in shops or factories. From the year 1880 onward, the Kingdom of Serbia endeavored to prohibit by law the classical curriculum traditional in European secondary schools and promoted, instead, the German-style *Realgymnasium*. Similarly, in industrial northern Italy, Will S. Monroe observed, in 1905, "a marked tendency to correlate the training in the elementary schools with the civic, social, and industrial needs of the future." The course of study in primary grades generally included history, geography, civics, nature study, drawing, singing, and gymnastics, he reported, just as in contemporary progressive American elementary schools. Domestic science was obligatory for girls in the upper grades, as was either manual training or agriculture for boys.

Most of the benefits of such legislation in Central and Eastern Europe, however, reached only children reared in larger towns. The exception was Finland, where an immense expansion of public education between 1880 and 1910 touched the whole population. The state required schooling for boys and inaugurated programs of manual training in both rural and urban districts. Literacy became so general that the church was able to require it as a prerequisite for marriage. The results were evident in the fact that [fewer] than 2 per cent of Finns arriving at American ports between 1899 and 1907 were illiterate. By contrast, Emily Greene Balch observed, as late as 1909, that, in backward Croatian counties like Lika-Krbava, . . . whence many of the Americans of that nationality came, the public schools enrolled only one-third of the children who were supposed to attend, and the proportion of boys to girls was four to one. There, however, as in the New World, the priests in village parishes were often the leaders of local movements to establish or improve the system.

A direct relationship appears to have existed between the degree to which individuals had taken advantage of their educational opportunities at home and the decision to migrate. For, despite their rural origins, the literacy of Slavs arriving in the United States was generally higher than that of the total population in their homelands. In the state census of 1900, the inland Croatian provinces that were under Hungarian rule reported that 53 per cent of the adult men and 38 per cent of the women were able to read. In coastal Dalmatia and Istria, which were under Austrian government, only

30 per cent of the men between thirty and fifty years of age could read, and just under half of the boys aged ten to twenty. Both sets of figures included urban and rural populations, of course. Yet, 63 per cent of the Croatians and Slovenians who debarked at United States ports in 1900 could read, a figure that compares favorably with that of 72 per cent for the Jews. Similarly, 72 per cent of the Slovak immigrants that year were literate. At home, only their westernmost county, located nearest to Moravia, could boast that high a figure, whereas the overwhelming majority of migrating Slovaks were from the eastern counties, where the literacy rate ranged sharply downward, to as low as 33 per cent. Of course, the immigrants of all nationalities were chiefly young adults, the age group most likely to have benefited from recently expanded village school programs. Nevertheless, they seem either to have come from the families in their neighborhoods who saw the value of an education and sent their children to school, or else to have prepared themselves for their overseas adventure by learning to read and write.

Once the migratory movement became an established pattern, letters from fathers and husbands overseas, as well as educational leadership by those who returned, helped homeland peasants to see more clearly the link between education and economic advancement. A Croatian village leader who lived near Karlovac, south of Zagreb, told Emily Greene Balch, in 1908, that one could tell a returned emigrant on sight. "He carries himself more independently, he works better, he is more interested in education," her informant declared. In Zagreb, Croatia's capital, an organization composed partly of returned emigrants established, in 1921, a vocational and technical high school called *Hrvatska Radiša*. With the assistance of substantial contributions from their countrymen in North and South America, the leaders set out to give young men planning to migrate to America proper training in a skilled trade. The institution soon grew into the largest technical school in Croatia and helped produce a reservoir of skilled labor for the industrial development that was soon under way in Zagreb itself.

On a return visit to Italy in 1908, Antonio Mangano studied the effects of emigration on the towns of his native Calabria. He remembered that, when he was growing up, only six boys of his age group in a town of 15,000 had received any schooling at all, despite national laws that, for decades, had prescribed an elementary education for each child. In the intervening years, however, emigration had accomplished what laws could not. The initial impulse, Mangano said, was a simple one. When fathers or sons in America sent letters home with money enclosed, an illiterate family had to depend upon the *padrone* or some local official to read and answer them, thus giving the whole town knowledge of their private business within hours of the arrival of the mail. The obvious solution was to have the brightest child learn to read. As time went on, Mangano continued, fathers working overseas saw the wider advantages of education and sent home orders that all their children should be sent to school. In towns such as Toritto, which had sent many emigrants to America and where the percentage of illiteracy in former years had been as high as 90 per cent, Mangano found schools crowded to overflowing. In nearby Grummo, however, where the same economic conditions prevailed, but . . . whence few had emigrated, only a small proportion of the children were in school. Meanwhile, Albanian emigrants representing perhaps two-fifths of the population of San Demetrio, another town in southern Italy, sent home from New York gifts sufficient to establish a museum of natural history and a physics laboratory at the lyceum there. The citizens of the town proudly maintained what they called *Il Collegio Albanese,* and fought successfully to keep it free from church control.

On both sides of the Atlantic, then, the experience of migration required priests and laymen, parents and children, to adjust to urban and industrial conditions. For those who undertook the venture, money, education, and respectability formed a trinity of controlling aspirations that we have too long associated with the term . . . "Protestant ethic." The successful immigrant's value system seems, on closer inspection, to have been simply a new combination of preferences that shrewd peasants had shared for generations, and which Orthodox, Catholic, and Jewish, no less than Protestant, faith managed to sanctify.

A second major social aspiration that helps to explain the extensive educational interests of immigrants from Central and Eastern Europe was their desire to establish and preserve a new order of family and communal life. The small-family unit in America at first stood free of the kin-group system that prevailed in Old World villages, but it did not stand alone. The immigrant family simply drew sustenance from an improvised rather than an inherited community—usually a religious congregation, although sometimes an anticlerical ethnic association replaced the old village as the web of communal life. The new bonds were psychic rather than geographic, and their organizational forms were in every case voluntary, oriented to the future, and, therefore, generally receptive to social change. The leading laymen in a congregation were usually heads of families, not bachelors. The officers were often the first successful businessmen—tavernkeepers, coaldealers, travel agents, and the like—in whose households emotional security and a hopeful outlook prevailed.

Priests who were directly responsible for parochial education in these communities were not all mere guardians of tradition. Father Paul Tymkevich, pastor of a Ruthenian Greek Catholic congregation in Yonkers, New York, formed, around 1900, a cooperative association that erected a model tenement house for 39 families, complete with a tavern on the ground floor. Then, he instituted, in his own home, a boarding school for older boys from the anthracite country. He sent them to the Yonkers public high school for their general education and, after hours, gave them instruction in the faith, language, and traditions of their fathers. Tymkevich told Miss Balch that, although his people had gained economically by coming to America, their customs did not fit them for life in the city. "The first step in civilization is to acquire habits," he said, "and where can they acquire them? On the streets? In the saloon?" What they needed most, he believed, was educated leaders from among their own ranks, "to form themselves upon, to give them a standard of ambition." At about the same time, Ivan Ardan, another Greek Catholic Ruthenian pastor, encouraged the establishment of self-improvement clubs in the larger towns of the anthracite country. One of them maintained, by 1904, a library of three hundred volumes. Generally, under the supervision of the priests, these clubs aimed to "qualify Slav immigrants for the duties of citizenship."

In the study of immigrant acculturation, the attention that scholars have paid to Jewish examples has raised the proper question but produced a distorted answer. The question is: How did positive faith in education as a means of personal gain become dominant in young families, where the crucial shaping of childhood attitudes had to take place? The answer has been that Jews who came to North America enjoyed a special combination of favorable circumstances. Sex ratios among adults were more balanced, leaving fewer unattached males in each community; whole families tended to migrate together; a proportionately much higher number intended, on their first arrival, to settle permanently here: Jewish group life was by tradition essentially ethnic, rather than nationalistic, reflecting more a religious and cultural than a political ideology; and, finally, their religious tradition was, even in the anthropological sense, a literary one; for, in the lowliest Galician *shtetl,* the man of prestige was the one who knew the Book.

But like a devotion to family life, often in a religious setting that idealized literary culture, prevailed among immigrants of other Central European backgrounds as well. Certainly, the group life of those of Orthodox and Greek Catholic faith, whether they were Romanians, Ruthenians, Greeks, Serbians, or Slovaks, was anchored in a distinctively literary religion. The Bible held an important place, but even more important were the words and the music of the Divine Liturgy, which laymen memorized in all the various forms it assumed for the successive seasons of the Christian year. Moreover, significant numbers of husbands and wives of all nationalities migrated together in the early years, declaring by that fact their intention to settle permanently here. The marriage records of the congregations they established indicate that a continuous stream of girls began arriving soon after from homeland villages to become wives of the bachelor lads who were numerically preponderant in the pioneer group. These first families of Hunkytown and Dagoville became, within each nationality, the "American" models for those of their countrymen who came over later.

Protestant and Roman Catholic congregations also nurtured the growing commitment to education. Associations of Slovak, Lithuanian, and Polish laymen often organized schools to teach both English and their native language and culture long before priests arrived from the Old World. A primary objective of the earliest Hungarian Reformed congregations, established in Pittsburgh and Cleveland with the help of American Presbyterian and Reformed home mission funds, was to educate their children in the religious and national traditions of their homeland and in American ways, as well.

Immigrants of Greek Catholic faith, whether they called themselves Rusins, Ruthenians, Ukrainians, Carpatho-Russians, Slovaks, or Hungarians, almost invariably sent their children to public schools, as did the Eastern Orthodox Serbs, Romanians, and Russians and the Lutheran Finns. All these, however, insisted upon frequent and sometimes daily attendance at the church for catechetical instruction, precisely as Orthodox Jewish parents sent their youngsters from public schools to the synagogue in the late afternoon or on Sunday.

An optimistic outlook characterized family life in all these religiously oriented ethnic communities. As among the Jews of Galicia, Slovakia, or sub-Carpathian Ruthenia, so among Slavs, Magyars, Italians, Greeks, and Finns, the decision to migrate had been a personal one. It brought men and women to America whose family traditions as well as individual dispositions inclined them to seize the main chance with faith and hope, at whatever sacrifice of the traditions they had known or the familiar associations they had enjoyed. An immigrant priest in New York City told Emily Greene Balch that Slovak brides in small mining or factory settlements of the West often matched their husbands' income by keeping boarders. As their children reached school age, however, the parents usually gave up the extra income and moved to the city to assure their youngsters good schools and kindergartens. As late as 1922, Jerome Davis found that, although single men still comprised the majority in Russian and Carpatho-Russian neighborhoods in Jersey City, nearly all the women kept boarders or else did outside work in order to help with the expenses of their children's education. He visited a family living in a one-room tenement whose two older youngsters were making good grades in public school, although the parents were illiterate and "the cost of food and clothes for the children, who wanted to be dressed as well as the others, . . . made saving impossible." Peter Roberts believed that the occasional outbursts of criminal behavior among the offspring of immigrants stemmed from the frustration of the "desire to excel," of the "intensive longing" for better things that fathers had passed on to their sons.

The notion of persistent conflict over educational goals between immigrant parents and their children during the early years of the settlement of each group in America finds scant support in the several kinds of testimony I have been able to read. The contrary, rather, seems more typical. The highly unbalanced sex ratios that at first prevailed among these groups may have provided the stress necessary to break down the tradition of patriarchal domination and to secure rapid acceptance of the more democratic and child-centered family ideals that characterized urban America. The husband had typically emigrated first. He found a job, saved the money to pay back what he had borrowed for passage, then sent home a ticket for his wife or sweetheart, or for a girl picked out for him by someone in his old village. In the process, of course, he learned the ABC's of urban life. When, at last, he met his long-awaited companion at the railway station, he often took her directly to buy a complete outfit of American clothes. Then followed an evening at the tavern and a day at the church or synagogue, where she met his friends, most of whom were single. In the following weeks, he showed her how to operate a stove, to open windows and door-latches, and to regulate the gas lights of an urban tenement; and he taught her enough English to communicate with postmen, streetcar conductors, and push-cart peddlers. He was unquestionably the leader, then, as "American" husbands were, and so felt little pain at the surrender of the tradition of formal mastery. His wife, for her part, accepted willingly the burden of keeping boarders, sensing, at once, the vast improvement in her position as compared with that of her homeland cousins, who still must toil in the fields from dawn to dusk. For she was now the indispensable manager of a successful business venture and, the competition in a predominantly bachelor society being what it was, the object of her husband's romantic love. As time passed, such parents cultivated together dreams for their children's future and, along with their priests or other communal leaders, took pride in seeing the youngsters acquire the traits necessary to success in the new land. The child-centered family thus became as characteristic among immigrants from Central Europe, I think, as among Anglo-Saxon Protestants.

An essential psychological element in the success of many of the children was the fact that their real world, the one where they felt both the security and identity that flow from a structured system of values and relationships, was the private one of the family, the ethnic association, and the religious congregation. Here, a youngster knew he belonged. In the youth auxiliary of the *bratsva,* or ethnic lodge, he found his true brothers. And surrounding him were men and women who noted with pride his every success. The society outside, by contrast, was an arena, not a community. A bright young man practiced in the arts of marginality could manipulate its elements impersonally, to his own advantage, without feeling any of the native-born Protestant's compulsion to impose upon it the structure of values that, in his private world, he found to be relevant and true.

The adjustment to urban and secular society of the son of the villager who had been born in Lika-Krbava, therefore, may have been easier than that of the son of one from Waterville, Vermont. Perhaps the recent popularity, among intellectuals of white, Protestant, and Anglo-Saxon backgrounds, of the notion that alienation and conflict were the central aspects of immigrant history represents more a projection of their own experiences than the real situation among Italians, Greeks, Slavs, and Jews. I believe that the error, if it is one, has persisted because historians of secular commitment but of Jewish ancestry—sons and grandsons of immigrants whose sense of alienation is a cultural heritage centuries old—have given it such frequent and thoughtful exposition.

A third important factor that quickened the impulse to education among

Americans from Central Europe was their half-conscious groping toward a bipolar sense of national identity, one that embraced cultural pluralism in the New World while supporting movements for national independence at home.

The use of education to enhance group status in polyglot America was apparent from the outset. Organizations such as the National Slovak Society, the Slovenian Catholic Union, the Finnish temperance societies, and the Polish National Alliance insisted at their founding that one of their principal aims was to prepare their members for American citizenship. Father Joseph Buh, pioneer Slovene priest on the Minnesota Iron Ranges, in an editorial he wrote in 1895 with the title "Let Us Be Proud—About What?" declared that American Slovenes must develop scholars from among their own youth if they wished to enhance their nationality's status in the land they had adopted. A year later, the "Polish Educational Society" of Milwaukee called a mass meeting at Kosciusko Guard Hall to protest derogatory statements before the United States Congress, which was considering legislation to restrict the immigration of illiterate persons. "Polanders as a nation are great friends of education," their memorial declared. Their activities in America included "organizing educational societies, supporting numerous newspapers and magazines, attending lectures delivered in their own language, and building and providing for schools for their children." In Rochester, New York, Louis J. Vannuccini, a future high school teacher, proposed, in 1905, the organization of the "Italian Civic and Educational League," which united the lay societies of several parishes in furthering the general interests of the nationality and in promoting education. Meanwhile, a "Lithuanian Education Society" flourished in Brockton, Massachusetts. The group erected a building dedicated exclusively to housing the classes in English and citizenship, the travelogues, and the discussions of job opportunities in various American industries that Yankee do-gooders had initiated among them some years earlier.

Whether its purposes were primarily religious or political, each immigrant brotherhood eventually organized an auxiliary society for young people. The Slavs usually called theirs *sokols* (falcons), in imitation of European pan-Slav organizations of that name. The lay leaders of the First Greek Catholic Union, for example—a mutual benefit insurance society formed in 1892 among Ruthenians and Slovaks from the northeastern counties of Old Hungary—performed many of the functions of a bishop, including educational ones. They assigned pastors to congregations, issued ABC books, readers and catechisms, and founded, before World War I, both a weekly newspaper and a monthly magazine for their flourishing *sokol*. Later, they issued a substantial periodical for children, as well.

Group interaction, whether by imitation or competition, nourished such national pride and so spurred on the growing educational concern. Finnish Lutherans wished their children to surpass the Swedes and Danes in public school, and they often did. German Catholics built their own secondary schools and supported Catholic colleges such as St. John's University, at Collegeville, Minnesota, in direct competition with the Irish. Poles and Czechs withdrew from German congregations and lodges so as to further the advancement of their own people, as well as to preserve their native languages and traditions. Slovenes and Slovaks strove thereafter to equal the cultural accomplishments of the Czechs, and [the] Lithuanians, who at first had often worshipped with the Poles, drew apart for a competition in which both sides scored points through educational achievement. When intensely anticlerical organizations adopted socialist platforms, as happened in the Slovene National Benefit Society, the Jewish workers' circles, and the Finnish workers' clubs, they renounced parochial in favor of public schools but promoted, after hours, an ethnic as well as a class-conscious education for their members' children.

Among the Italians, as with German and Polish Roman Catholics, national consciousness was often too strong to permit them to send their children to the "Irish" parish schools. Educational traditions were so weak among immigrants from southern Italy, however, and their numerous congregations were so small, that the development of their own parish institutions was retarded. The leading Italian editor in Chicago, Oscar Durante, complained, in 1893, that other nationalities were "dishonoring" his countrymen for their failure to send their children to school and "make them good American citizens." Shortly thereafter, the Chicago Board of Education received from a Committee of the United Italian Societies of Chicago a request to remove Durante from his position as truant officer because he had not been able to prevent many parents from keeping their children out of school. In a bitter response, the editor said the committee had only contributed further to the low social esteem in which the American public held his countrymen. Meanwhile, he and other leaders of north Italian extraction "promoted and seconded the movement in favor of the compulsory education law" in order to force the Calabrian and Sicilian *Contadini* to send to school the swarms of children whom they had previously "allowed to go wild on the public streets." Alessandro Mastrovalero, editor of another Chicago newspaper, *La Tribuna*, and a former resident at Hull House, became the Italian truant officer in 1897. For a decade thereafter, both in that office and through the columns of his newspaper, Mastrovalero championed liberalism and nationalism in Italy and promoted public education for Italians in the United States. In response, Italian priests in Chicago and elsewhere intensified their efforts to promote parochial schools. They received steady encouragement from the Italian consulate and much help from the Scalabrini Society, an order of missionary priests with headquarters at Florence. By 1906, one-fourth of the 330,000 Italian children who were attending school in Chicago were in parish institutions.

The connection between this interweaving of education and of national pride in America with what was going on at the same time in the Old World, particularly among the subject nationalities of the Austro-Hungarian Empire, was apparent to all close observers. Peter Rovnianek, president of the National Slovak Society and editor of the Slovak daily in Pittsburgh, attributed the remarkable advance of his people in the United States to the fact that, here, "they had been able to combine schools with their churches," without interference from a hostile government. After the division of administrative responsibility between Vienna and Budapest in 1867, Austrian authorities encouraged native Slovenian and Polish culture in Carniola and Galicia but were unable to keep the Poles from frustrating their similar intentions for the Ruthenians in Galicia. Ukrainian nationalists, acting with strong support from Greek Catholic priests, thereupon organized among the Ruthenians a network of village educational societies that promoted both a literary and a political awakening. The Kingdom of Hungary, meanwhile, set out upon a policy of artificial and forcible assimilation of its Slovak, Ruthenian, Romanian, Serbian, Croatian, and Jewish minorities through the Magyarization of the educational system and the control of access to professions, business, and the civil service. The government made the Magyar tongue mandatory in secondary instruction and steadily increased its control of church schools operated by members of subject nationalities, though it gave scant support to education of any sort in the Carpathian and Transylvanian highlands.

As the nineteenth century came to a close, national awakenings throughout the Hapsburg Empire were bound up more and more with struggles for religious and educational autonomy. Slovak, Slovene, Serbian, and Croatian cultural societies, called *Maticas* (Queen Bees), began to cultivate more intensively their countrymen in America. They solicited subscriptions to periodicals and almanacs and sought direct financial and political aid. Their leaders pled for the preservation of Slavic culture in the churches, schools, and mutual benefit societies of the New World, on the grounds that these were the only sanctuaries that were surely beyond the reach of Magyar or Polish domination. During the early 1890's, *Matica Slovenska*, forbidden to operate from its Slovak center at St. Martin, in northern Hungary, established headquarters in exile at Cleveland, issuing pamphlets and almanacs to its members in both the Old World and the New. A coalition of Serbian and Croatian political parties, formed in Dalmatia, in 1905, promised that the two peoples would "work shoulder to shoulder as blood brothers in national political questions," especially in public school issues. Both declared their aim to be "that the names Croatia and Serbia occupy a position of honor" there, that textbooks would stress the history of both peoples, and that all students should learn both Latin and Cyrillic scripts. Oscar Jászi declared, after World War I, that the steadily increasing Magyar effort to choke off national self-expression among the minority peoples and to deny them the right "of speaking their own idioms in the schools, the churches, the administration, and before the tribunals," had driven the Slavs into separatist movements, and so helped dismember the empire. Recently, however, Peter Sugar has demonstrated that conflicting currents of political and religious loyalty and of economic interest within each nationality made the masses of peasants and many of their leaders prefer a resolution of their grievances within a culturally plural empire.

The emigrants overseas, however, were able to accept the divergence of the two ideologies of pluralism and nationalism and to cultivate both of them, precisely because their political loyalties embraced two worlds. Their American platform was pluralism, even when they championed separatism at home.

During World War I, as students of Central European history well know, the nurseries of nationalism that Slovaks, Ruthenians, and South Slavs maintained in Pittsburgh and Cleveland bore fruit at last. T. G. Masaryk, architect of the modern state of Czechoslovakia, visited the United States early in 1918 and worked out agreements with Slovak leaders in the newly formed Czechoslovak National Council as well as with Ruthenians in the First Greek Catholic Union. These called for political autonomy of the two peoples in the new republic and the use of their own languages in the schools and in public offices. A Pittsburgh attorney, Gregory T. Zlatkovic, returned to his native Carpathian mountains, dreaming of leading a political and cultural awakening among the Ruthenian villagers who had so long suffered from the educational privation that Magyar rule had imposed. Zlatkovic's political plans came to naught, but the event helped stir the Carpatho-Russians, as by then they were often called, to accept the help of the Czech civil servants, who, during the next two decades, sought to provide them with a respectable educational system. A similar event occurred in Albania. During World War I, Orthodox Bishop Fan S. Noli, a Harvard graduate who had become the political and spiritual leader of the Boston Albanians, returned to his homeland determined to bring about both an educational and agricultural reform. He served for a time as prime minister of the country, importing schoolbooks and other educational materials printed on the presses of the Boston Albanian newspaper and intended originally for use in American parishes.

The cultivation of the sense of nationality through church and fraternal educational programs in America thus fulfilled two divergent purposes, though the immigrants themselves did not find them contradictory. America was, in their eyes, above all a land of many cultural traditions. Freedom, for men who had long struggled for it in the Austro-Hungarian and Russian empires, meant not only opportunity for personal advancement but liberty to maintain the cultural life of their ethnic group as well—in short, cultural pluralism. Nationalism, in the sense of a political commitment to establish an independent homeland for their people, was focused almost entirely on the Old World. Native Americans and Jews who disclaimed Zionism have rarely understood the capacity of religion to hold in balanced tension these two diverging goals of immigrant ethnic groups. Parochial education, like most of the other cultural and social programs that the new citizens from Central and Southeastern Europe carried on, was, from their point of view, a nursery of two patriotisms, to both of which the immigrants were fondly attached. Woodrow Wilson was one of the few who perceived this fact. He and his political successors, Al Smith, Franklin Roosevelt, and John Kennedy, were able to act upon that perception in many fields and so to bring the vast majority of new immigrants into the mainstream of American politics.

These aspirations, then—the economic, the communal, and the civic—propelled immigrants from Central and Southern Europe toward [a] growing concern for education, both within their ethnic associations and [with]in the public and parochial schools. Quite as much as any coercion from compulsory education acts or any pressure from professional Americanizers, the immigrant's own hopes for his children account for the immense success of the public school system, particularly at the secondary level, in drawing the mass of working-class children into its embrace. By their presence, and by their commitment to these several ambitions, the first generation of immigrant children prompted educators, in administrative offices as well as classrooms, to a thousand pragmatic experiments geared to the interests and the needs of their students. Self-styled patriots and scholars devoted to the special value of the liberal arts later found the results displeasing, though for different reasons, of course. But the event contributed heavily to the national consensus about progressive reform in both school and society that has dominated American social ideals throughout the twentieth century.

5. Blacks and the Schools

Northerners have found it easy to be self-righteous about black education in the South. In the early nineteenth century, Southern states made it a crime to teach slaves to read or write; at the same time, Northerners were busily erecting public school systems that were to embrace everyone. Though valid, this statement neglects the antiblack racism that was dominant in the North. Northerners neither welcomed blacks to the places where they lived nor believed them to be equal, and their educational practices reflected these attitudes.

In the South, the question of whether blacks should be educated was part of a general uncertainty about the effects of literacy and schooling. The Southern laws making it illegal to teach slaves to read or write were the strongest American manifestation of a traditional European conservative viewpoint. Education, in this opinion, was dangerous, for literacy bred political consciousness and discontent. In the North, this fear of learning, never so strong as in the South, gave way almost completely to a different conception of education, stressing that the outcomes of literacy were social order and stability. The notion 'that the education of the lower orders was prerequisite to a peaceful, acquiescent society was, in fact, a major contribution of early American educational theory, culminating in the writings of Horace Mann and Henry Barnard. Whereas a half-century earlier Thomas Jefferson had argued that education was an activating force, a weapon with which people would guard their interests against the overweening ambition of their leaders, Horace Mann and Henry Barnard saw education as a conservative force, a way in which society's leaders could ensure that ordinary people would learn appropriate beliefs and behaviors.

The relevance of this shift for the education of blacks as well as of working-class whites hardly can be overemphasized. It formed the ideological basis on which public systems of education were built and by which they have since been justified. Once this point of view was accepted—in the North, early in the nineteenth century; in the South, well after the Civil War—the question became not whether to educate but how. In the case of blacks, acceptance of the need to educate did not carry with it a commitment to equality or integration. Segregated schools persisted in the North for decades, despite challenges in some cases by blacks and their white supporters.

The history of black education (indeed, the history of white education as well) is generally written from the top down, to use a current phrase. Thus, we learn of reformers' attitudes toward the working class, or we study the attitude of whites toward the provision of education for blacks. But little is written about the opinions of the people at whom educational efforts were directed; we know very little about the educational attitudes of working-class whites or of blacks. The problem is that the poor, black or white, have left few diaries, letters, speeches, or other written records that can tell us directly how ordinary people felt. But they have left a great deal of evidence from which their attitudes can be inferred quite reasonably. This evidence often takes the form of numbers; it may consist of information about individuals found in the volumes of census enumerators, or in records of birth, marriage, and death found in churches, or in tax records. By using these records imaginatively and carefully, it is possible to reconstruct the structure of families, the details of social structure, and some of the typical behavior of various sorts of people. Through this discovery of the actual circumstances and experiences of ordinary people, it is possible to infer what they thought and felt. Imperfect as this process is, it nonetheless is the most direct way to look at history from their point of view.

The use of quantitative information about ordinary people should enable historians to clarify two important, controversial issues. The first is the impact of the slave experience on black people. Did slavery leave the black family disorganized and dampen its concern with the education of its children? One way to approach this problem is to compare the behaviors of black ex-slaves, freeborn blacks, and other groups. The use of manuscript censuses and related sources makes this possible. The other issue is the degree of similarity in the experiences of blacks and immigrants. Sometimes the argument is made that the experience of blacks will repeat that of immigrants. Immigrants, in this contention, made use of the educational system to boost themselves out of poverty and into the mainstream of society; in time, blacks can do the same. There are good reasons that can be advanced, without much research, for supposing this line of argument to be simplistic and untrue. But its thorough testing requires a comparative analysis of black and immigrant experience, which can be done reliably and thoroughly only through the use of quantitative evidence about the life histories of the people.

The selections in this section touch upon most of these issues. In the first, Leon Litwack carefully documents the educational handicaps faced by blacks in the North before the Civil War, making it abundantly clear that segregation, discrimination, and the unequal distribution of funds, all reflecting an underlying racism, put blacks at a tremendous educational disadvantage. The second selection, by Theodore Hershberg, is a sample of the information that will be made available by his Philadelphia Social History Project, perhaps the most important study of nineteenth-century America now under way. His essay compares the family structures, economic circumstances, and school attendance of ex-slave and freeborn blacks in antebellum Philadelphia. Colin Greer, in the third selection, considers the relation of education and social mobility in the experiences of blacks and immigrants, primarily in the twentieth century, and points to fundamental differences in the histories of the two groups. Finally, August Meier and Elliott Rudwick document an early twentieth-century case of black protest over educational segregation. Their essay demonstrates both the degree of racism that remained in twentieth-century Northern cities and the capacity of blacks to organize and sustain a prolonged and peaceful protest movement. It shows, too, that educational segregation has been a deep concern within the black community since long before the recent civil-rights movement gave it national prominence.

Education: Separate and Unequal
Leon Litwack

Education was one of the foremost aspirations of the Northern Negro. "If we ever expect to see the influence of prejudice decrease and ourselves respected," a Negro national convention resolved in 1832, "it must be by the blessings of an enlightened education." This sentiment was repeated throughout the antebellum period. Through education, the Negro hoped to improve his economic status, produce his own literary and scientific figures, and break down the barriers of discrimination. However, the Negro's quest for educational opportunities, partly because he hoped to accomplish such goals, prompted some strong and frequently violent protests in the North. The possibility that Negro children would be mixed with white children in

From *North of Slavery: The Negro and the Free States, 1790–1860* (Chicago: University of Chicago Press, 1961), pp. 113–52. By permission of the Publisher.

the same classroom aroused even greater fears and prejudices than those that consigned the Negro to an inferior place in the church, the theater, and the railroad car. This, indeed, constituted virtual amalgamation.

Although some white schools admitted Negroes, especially before 1820, most Northern states either excluded them altogether or established separate schools for them. As early as 1787, Boston Negroes petitioned the legislature to grant them educational facilities, since they "now receive no benefit from the free schools." Forty years later, the first Negro newspaper repeated this complaint. "While the benevolence of the age has founded and endowed seminaries of Learning for all other classes and nations," it declared, "we have to lament, that as yet, no door is open to receive the degraded children of Africa. Alone they have stood—alone they remain stationary; while charity extends the hands to all others."

The means employed to exclude Negroes from the public schools varied only slightly from state to state. In New England, local school committees usually assigned Negro children to separate institutions, regardless of the district in which they resided. Pennsylvania and Ohio, though extending their public school privileges to all children, required district school directors to establish separate facilities for Negro students whenever twenty or more could be accommodated. The New York legislature authorized any school district, upon the approval of a town's school commissioners, to provide for segregation. The newer states frequently excluded Negroes from all public education, but, by 1850, most of them had consented to separate instruction. In the absence of legal restrictions, custom and popular prejudice often excluded Negro children from the schools. For example, an Indianan noted, in 1850, that the laws provided no racial distinctions in the state school system, but "the whites rose *en-masse*, and said your children shall not go to schools with our children, and they were consequently expelled. Thus, then, we see that in this respect, there is a higher law than the Constitutional law." By the 1830's, statute or custom placed Negro children in separate schools in nearly every Northern community.

Proposals to educate Negroes invariably aroused bitter controversy, particularly in the new Western states. The admission of Negroes to white schools, opponents maintained, would result in violence and prove fatal to public education. Moreover, some contended that Negroes, "after a certain age, did not correspondingly advance in learning—their intellect being apparently incapable of being cultured beyond a particular point." When an Ohio legislative committee rejected a petition to grant Negroes a share of the education fund, it conceded that this might "at first appear unnatural, and unbecoming a charitable, high-minded, and intelligent community," but the security of the government depended upon "the morality, virtue, and wisdom" of its white citizens, and the school fund should thus not be confused with charity. Opponents also warned that equal educational privileges would encourage Negro immigration and antagonize Southern-born residents. On the basis of such a pretext, a California mayor vetoed appropriations for Negro schools as "particularly obnoxious to those of our citizens who have immigrated from Southern States." The city aldermen defended his action with a warning against placing the two races on an equal basis, "not withstanding the distinction stamped by Divinity between them."

Delegates to the state constitutional conventions debated various proposals to exclude Negroes from the schools. Westerners, fearing an increase in Negro immigration, voiced some especially vehement objections. "They are not by nature equal to the whites," an Iowan declared, "and their children cannot be made equal to my children, or those of my constituents." In 1850, an Ohio convention delegate opposed any measure, including education, that would tend to encourage Negro immigration or impede colonization. Nine years later, a Kansas Republican warned that he would immediately object to any Negro's attending school with white children. However, he opposed any legal bars, claiming that the "neighborhood could protect itself." Other Kansas convention delegates predicted that voters would reject the proposed constitution unless it explicitly prohibited racial mixing in the schools. As late as 1860, an Iowa congressman warned that no Northwestern state would countenance biracial education. Antebellum constitutional provisions and legislation confirmed his prediction.

*　*　*

The objections to classroom integration extended beyond the public schools to private academies and colleges. . . . Most Negro youths continued to attend segregated institutions or secured no education at all. White political leaders, including those who bitterly opposed Negro education, could thus contend that widespread illiteracy in the Negro population prevented any extension of the suffrage or other civil rights. "The colored people are . . . charged with want of desire for education and improvement," a Negro remarked in 1839; "yet, if a colored man comes to the door of our institutions of learning, with desires ever so strong, the lords of these institutions rise up and shut the door; and then you say we have not the desire nor the ability to acquire education. Thus, while the white youths enjoy all these advantages, we are excluded and shut out, and must remain ignorant."

Excluded from white schools, Negroes moved to establish their own educational institutions and enlisted the support of abolitionists, some white philanthropists, and several state legislatures. By 1860, a number of private ventures had been attempted, with varying success, and nearly every Northern state had provided for a Negro public school system.

*　*　*

After 1831, the revived abolitionist movement gave substantial support and encouragement to Negro education. The constitution of the American Anti-Slavery Society cited the importance of the "intellectual, moral, and religious improvement" of Negroes, and William Lloyd Garrison praised Negro efforts to obtain adequate educational facilities. Convinced "that faith without *works* is death," Cincinnati abolitionists, prompted by Theodore Weld, provided instruction for the Negro community through the establishment of a regular adult school, Sabbath and evening schools, Lyceum lectures, and Bible classes. "Everything goes on here as we could wish," a Cincinnati abolitionist wrote in 1834. "Our colored brethren are animated with hope. A calm determination to alter their conditions is firmly fixed in every breast. Elevation, moral, political and religious, fires their mind." The schools, he added, had aroused no overt opposition. Other communities attempted to duplicate the work of the Cincinnati abolitionists but were less successful.

Exclusively Negro schools did not necessarily meet with popular favor. The identification of abolitionism with the cause of Negro education provided whites with a convenient excuse for resisting such institutions.

* * *

Two classic incidents in the Negro's struggle for education involved attempts to institute schools for their benefit in New Haven and Canterbury, Connecticut. In both cases, townspeople vigorously protested the establishment of any school that might attract Negroes from other states or threaten the property values and peace of the town. The participation of prominent abolitionists in these projects further enabled the opposition to hide its racial prejudices behind slogans of patriotism, racial purity, and national unity.

* * *

It was but a short distance from New Haven to Windham County. There, in the quiet and picturesque Connecticut countryside, stood the village of Canterbury. In 1831, Prudence Crandall, a young Quaker schoolmistress, established in Canterbury a successful and popular girls' boarding school. Miss Crandall's welcome proved to be short-lived, however, for, one year later, she agreed to admit a Negro. This immediately aroused the town, brought protests from the white parents, and resulted in the withdrawal of most of the students. The schoolmistress thereupon made a hasty trip to Boston and New York, where she consulted with William Lloyd Garrison and other leading abolitionists about the expediency of opening her school exclusively to Negro girls. On March 2, 1833, [the] *Liberator* announced the establishment of "a High School for young colored Ladies and Misses" and published a list of "sponsors" that included virtually every prominent Negro and white abolitionist leader in the North. Garrison praised the projected school but warned Miss Crandall that she now faced possible "reproach and persecution." For once, at least, Garrison had understated the case.

Canterbury responded to news of the proposed school with meetings, delegations of protest, bitter attacks on abolitionism, and warnings that terrible consequences might follow. Such a school would depreciate property values; local Negroes would claim an equality with the new arrivals, and these, in turn, would demand equality with the whites; the town had to resist this obvious abolitionist plot, this invidious attempt "to foist upon the community a new species of gentility, in the shape of sable belles." The town's elected officials reiterated these charges in a letter to the American Colonization Society: "We might ask the citizens of any town in New-England, wherever situated, would it be well for that town to admit the blacks from Slave States, or other States, to an unlimited extent? Once open this door, and New-England will become the Liberia of America."

Against a background of increasing tension, a Canterbury town meeting, convened on March 9, voiced its "unqualified disapprobation" of the proposed school and appointed a committee to persuade Miss Crandall to abandon her project in view of "the injurious effects, and incalculable evils" that would follow. At the same time, certain "responsible" townspeople offered to purchase her newly acquired house upon condition that the school be discontinued. Two of Miss Crandall's friends appeared at the meeting on her behalf, but the chairman refused to recognize them. Afterward, Andrew T. Judson, town selectman, Democratic politician, and an officer of the local colonization society, explained that Negroes could never rise above their menial condition and proposed that they be colonized in Africa, where they could civilize and Christianize the natives. In the meantime, he asserted, "that nigger school shall never be allowed in Canterbury, nor in any town in this State."

The Quaker schoolmistress and her abolitionist backers refused to abandon the school. "I have put my hand to the plough," she declared, "and I will *never no never* look back." She hoped that public sentiment might change and, in the meantime, cautioned the temperamental Garrison to handle the prejudices of Canterbury "with all the mildness possible," since severe attacks would only further inflame the inhabitants. The abolitionists, however, spared few words in rushing to Miss Crandall's defense. This had become not only a moral issue but a test of strength; defeat would create a dangerous precedent and prove a major setback to the entire abolitionist movement. She "must be sustained at all hazards," Garrison wrote. "If we suffer the school to be put down in Canterbury, other places will partake of this panic, and also prevent its introduction in their vicinity. We may as well, 'first as last,' meet this proscriptive spirit, *and conquer it.*"

The school opened in April and attracted students from Philadelphia, New York, Providence, and Boston. Meanwhile, the town adopted a new form of opposition—harassment. Stores denied necessary provisions to the school; townspeople insulted the students in the streets and filled the school's well with manure, forcing Miss Crandall to import water from her father's farm two miles away; the village physician refused to treat the pupils; the churches admitted them only under degrading circumstances; civil authorities threatened to invoke an old vagrancy law against them; and another town meeting appealed to the state legislature for appropriate measures.

Connecticut's legislators, responsible only to a white electorate, acted quickly. On May 24, they formally agreed that an increase of the Negro population would not serve the best interests of the state and thus adopted a law that prohibited the establishment of "any school, academy, or literary institution, for the instruction or education of colored persons who are not inhabitants of this state," and which forbade anyone to instruct, harbor, or board such persons without the approval of local authorities. The state had dealt a mortal blow to Miss Crandall's school for Negro girls. Indeed, the town bells and cannon greeted the news in Canterbury. "In the midst of all this," a student wrote the next day, "Miss Crandall is unmoved. When we walk out, horns are blown and pistols fired. . . . The place is delightful; all that is wanting to complete the scene is *civilized* men." In Boston, the *Liberator* cried: "GEORGIA OUTDONE!!"

In the face of this overwhelming legal and extralegal pressure, Miss Crandall refused to close her school. Local authorities thereupon arrested her on charges of violating the new law. The controversy had thus been transferred to the courts. "Consider me your banker," Arthur Tappan wrote from New York. "Command the services of the ablest lawyers. See to it that this great case shall be thoroughly tried, cost what it may." On August 23, the schoolmistress stood before the Windham County Court. Although the judge instructed the jury that "the law was constitutional and obligatory on the people of the State," it failed to agree on a verdict and was discharged. Two months later, Chief Justice David Daggett presided at a second trial. His charge to the jury anticipated much of the Dred Scott decision. First, he dismissed the defense's contention that the law violated the privileges-and-immunities clause of the federal constitution. The "plain and obvious" meaning of that provision, he declared, was "to secure to the *citizens* of all States, the same privileges as are secured to our own, by our own State laws." Second, he ruled that Negroes were not citizens. "God forbid," the Chief Justice declared, "that I should add to the degradation of this race of men; but I am bound, by my duty, to say, they are not citizens." This time, the jury found Miss Crandall guilty, but an appellate court reversed the conviction on a technical defect in the information.

Meanwhile, the villagers subjected the school to continuous harassment. Visiting Canterbury in August, 1834, an English traveler remarked that the school "had become more odious to its enemies in proportion to their failure in trying to put it down with or without law." It had been frequently stoned, and an unsuccessful attempt had been made to burn it down. Finally, on September 10, 1834, the siege ended. Miss Crandall abandoned the school and departed for Illinois.

Three years later, Theodore Weld met the chairman of the legislative committee responsible for the "Black Law" of 1833. "I could weep tears of blood for the part I took in that matter," he told Weld. "I now regard that law as utterly abominable," but, at the time, "my prejudices . . . were so violent as to blind me to the dictates of common humanity and justice." Consequently, he headed a repeal petition to the legislature that charged that the law was impolitic, unjust, and unconstitutional. In May, 1838, the state senate repealed the law by a unanimous vote, and the house concurred with only four dissents.

Despite abolitionist fears, the New Haven and Canterbury defeats failed to establish any real precedent. Most communities consented, some reluctantly, to the establishment of Negro schools. But this did not necessarily advance the cause of education. Segregated schools afforded Negro children a poor educational environment; such schools invariably resulted in inferior facilities and instruction and prompted frequent protests from both Negroes and white school officials. "What are the advantages to be derived from an instruction in these schools," a Negro newspaper asked in 1827, "compared to those of a higher and more elevated nature? What are the incentives held out to a lad of colour? Are there higher schools to stimulate him to greater exertions? Is he placed, and considered, an equal with other boys in schools of the same rank?" Trustees expected little from Negro students, the newspaper found, for their color alone usually elicited praise from school visitors, when the same performance from white youths "would pass unnoticed, and be considered as a thing of course."

Negro classes frequently met in ill-equipped and poorly ventilated buildings. . . . In Rochester, New York, where Frederick Douglass led the attack on separate schools, a committee appointed by the board of education noted that, although the city taxed both Negro and white property "to build commodious school houses," Negro children found themselves excluded and "grouped together in some 'Rented Rooms,' in darkness and ignorance, there to seek education with all the attending disadvantages."

Negro schools also encountered difficulties in securing competent teachers.

* * *

In addition to substandard teaching conditions, Negro schools generally provided only the most elementary curriculum. To a large extent, this limitation reflected the exclusion of Negroes from most professional pursuits and the prevailing belief that the average Negro's intellectual capacity debarred him from advanced studies. The trustees of the New York African Schools, for example, discouraged higher education for Negroes by informing parents that there was "no disgrace incurred by the pursuit of any honest calling, however humble," and that it was "the duty of everyone to do all the good in his sphere in which Providence has placed him." Too many Negro parents, David Walker argued in 1829, evaluated their son's education in terms of a neat handwriting and considered spelling and grammar immaterial: "If it only looks beautiful, they say he has as good an education as any white man—he can write as well as any white man, etc." Most of the blame, however, could be placed on the schools. For example, Walker continued, a Negro student had told him that the white instructor forbade his class to study grammar and explained that the school committee permitted such training only in the white schools. The New Haven Board of Education admitted, in 1860, that few Negroes graduated with a sufficient knowledge of arithmetic to enable them to be clerks or to conduct independent businesses. In summing up the state of Negro education, a Negro national convention charged, in 1847, that the instruction of Negro youth "has been shamefully limited," consisting only of "rudimental notings, and superficial glancings. . . . In comprehensiveness it has never yet made any pretensions, to profundity not the most distant approach. . . . In very deed it has not reached the dignity, and the elevation of education."

In the face of a growing demand for integrated schools, Northern boards of education finally took steps to improve the existing separate institutions. By the 1850's, considerable progress had been made in the quality of both the instruction and the classrooms. But the Negro, too, had advanced, and his fight for equal rights could no longer countenance the existence of segregated schools.

Although Negroes hoped for eventual integration, many of them agreed, in the meantime, to send their children to separate schools. Seizing upon such support, segregationists charged that Negroes originated these distinctions and desired their maintenance. Boston school officials, for example, pointed out that separate schools had been established "at the urgent and repeated requests of the colored people themselves," and that Negroes regarded such schools "as a great privilege, and the only means by which their children could receive the benefits of education." In nearby Providence, the president of Brown University noted that segregated education "works well," and that the Negro residents preferred it to integration.

Some Negroes defended segregation. During the attack on Boston's Negro school, an officer of that institution justified it as "the greatest advantage to the colored people" and declared that its abolition would be "unjust, inexpedient and injurious." Separate schools, he asserted, afforded Negroes the opportunity to refute charges of inferiority by producing scholars superior to those of the best white schools. The abolition of such schools would lead whites to infer "that when equally taught and equally comfortable, we are ashamed of ourselves, and feel disgraced by being together." In Hartford and Providence, Negroes petitioned for separate schools after once enjoying "equal" advantages with whites. In New York, however, Negroes simply preferred segregated education to no education whatsoever. "The choice of the [lesser of] two evils," a prominent New York Negro leader, school director, and teacher wrote, prompted him "to improve the colored schools in this city—believing them to be only better than no schools at all."

In many cases, antipathy toward biracial education and the mistreatment of Negroes, where admitted with whites, required or encouraged the establishment of separate schools. For example, Negro petitioners in Rochester, New York, asked for a separate school on grounds that "the literary and moral interests of the coloured scholar can scarcely prosper" in the present integrated system. The Negro student found himself "reproached with his colour; he is taunted with his origin; and if permitted to mingle with others in the joyous pastimes of youth, it is of favour, not by right." In 1807, a

Salem, Massachusetts, minister declared that "pride" prevented the presence of Negroes in the existing school for poor children, and called for separate instruction. In Connecticut, both races once attended the same schools, but frequent insults and humiliations prompted Hartford Negroes to ask for separation. School authorities admitted similar problems in other areas. "To escape intolerable persecution and contempt," two Boston school officials observed, Negroes "were once glad to be herded together by themselves."

Increasingly after 1830, Negro spokesmen denounced segregated schools as unequal and inferior and demanded integration . . . The growing demand for integration prompted abolitionists to reconsider their own efforts to establish an exclusively Negro manual-labor college. In view of the willingness of more white colleges to admit Negroes, an abolitionist leader asked William Lloyd Garrison, in 1834, if it would not be preferable to patronize those institutions rather than build new ones, since "the object we aim at, the destruction of caste, will be the sooner gained." Two years later, an abolitionist convention resolved not to countenance the establishment of separate schools.

* * *

Although confined nearly everywhere to separate public schools, Negroes gradually gained admittance to white colleges. The first Negro college graduate, John Russwurm, attended Bowdoin College, Maine, and subsequently helped to edit the first Negro newspaper. By 1860, twenty-eight Negroes had earned degrees from recognized colleges, and many others had been admitted.

In most cases, the opening of colleges to Negroes occasioned little controversy. Dartmouth College at first denied entrance to a Negro applicant, but student petitions helped to reverse the trustees' decision in 1824 and thereby established a permanent school policy. Harvard's president, Edward Everett, announced, in 1848, that a Negro applicant would be judged solely by his qualifying examinations, "and if the white students choose to withdraw, all the income of the College will be devoted to his education." The admission of Negroes to these two leading institutions undoubtedly influenced others to follow suit.

In the 1830's, two Ohio colleges—Western Reserve and Oberlin—opened their doors to Negroes. The Oberlin decision, however, evoked some furious protests. . . . Perhaps the most interesting experiment in biracial education was performed in McGrawville, New York. Founded in 1849 by the American Baptist Free Mission Society, New York Central College admitted both races and sexes, appointed a Negro to the faculty, adopted the manual-labor system of education, and abjured the use of tea, coffee, alcohol, and tobacco. The school's partial dependence on state support occasioned some bitter protests and legislative debates, including the charge that it promoted a "mottled conglomerate of insanities"—miscegenation, women's rights, abolitionism, and socialism.

* * *

By the eve of the Civil War, several other colleges had agreed to the admission of Negroes. Among them were Amherst, Rutland, Oneida Institute, Union College, Princeton, and various medical colleges and theological seminaries. This did not necessarily indicate the existence of exclusion policies at the remaining institutions. The inferiority of Negro education on the lower levels seriously hampered preparation for college instruction and limited the number of qualified applicants. This fact convinced Negro leaders that they had to press even harder for improved elementary and secondary education. "The colleges of New England and the West, which are opened to us, do not meet the needs of our people," a Negro convention complained in 1847, "because . . . there is no previous opportunity offered for that early, almost childish culture, which is absolutely necessary to the formation of true high scholarship; and for which white children possess superabundant faculties." By 1850, many Negro leaders concluded that only integrated schools could afford this necessary preparation.

Through convention appeals, petitions, court suits, and editorial campaigns, Negroes maintained a constant agitation in the 1840's and 1850's for the abolition of school segregation. "The point which we must aim at," Frederick Douglass wrote, "is to obtain admission for our children into the nearest school house, and the best school house in our respective neighborhoods." Integrated schools would not only afford Negro children a better education; they would strike a fatal blow at racial segregation and create an atmosphere in which Negroes could work more effectively for equal political and social rights. Indeed, Douglass told New York Negroes that the attainment of equal school privileges should take precedence over immediate political demands, such as the suffrage.

* * *

The Negro-abolitionist attack on segregated schools achieved its greatest success in Boston. By 1845, Massachusetts Negroes had won virtual political and legal equality, and they could send their children, without discrimination, to the public schools in Salem, New Bedford, Nantucket, Worcester, and Lowell. Only Boston maintained segregation, and there, Negroes launched the most concerted attack on Northern "caste" schools. White abolitionists, convinced that segregation impaired the effectiveness of their antislavery pleas, joined the campaign. "It is useless for us to prate of the conduct of South Carolina," a segregation foe declared in 1845, "so long as we maintain—*illegally* maintain—a practice here which at least incidentally sanctions it." Endorsing this sentiment, the Massachusetts Anti-Slavery Society resolved, in the following year, that "the friends of the cause" residing in communities that still practiced educational segregation should immediately inform Negroes of their legal rights and "afford them all possible aid in securing the full and equal enjoyment of the public schools."

Negroes and abolitionists directed their attack at Boston's Primary School Committee, since it assumed responsibility for the classification and distribution of students. In petitions to that body, Negroes charged that school segregation injured the best interests of the community and resulted in needless expense, neglect, and low standards of scholarship and instruction. Replying to these charges, the Committee issued lengthy reports in 1846 and 1849, both of which condoned segregation on grounds that varied from the degrading aspects of racial mixing to the observation that the Pilgrim Fathers had not been depressed by their separation from the Indians, "in whose country they were but strangers and sojourners." Distinctions established by the "All-Wise Creator," the Committee charged, separated the two races, negated any legislation, and rendered "a promiscuous intermingling in the public schools disadvantageous" to both Negroes and whites. To substantiate its arguments, the Committee claimed that integration had failed in several Massachusetts communities, while separate schools had already demonstrated their superiority in Philadelphia, New York, and Providence. Where attempts had been made to mix the two races, teachers reported that Negro children kept pace with the whites in instruction involving "imitative faculties" but quickly fell behind when progress depended on "the faculties of invention, compassion, and reasoning." In any case, the Committee asked, why should Negroes object to school segregation when they themselves always met together in separate churches and social affairs? "It is as though they thought that a white skin was really better than a dark one; and that the society of all who wear it was more reputable, more to be coveted, than they of a sable tint. In a word, it is as if they were ashamed of themselves."

Even assuming the correctness of integration, the Committee felt that any attempt to implement it would be disastrous "under the present state of public feeling and sentiment." White children would refuse to associate with Negroes; conflicts and disagreement would arouse tempers and lead to possible violence; white parents would withdraw their children rather than permit them to mix with Negroes; and Negro parents would refuse to send their "ill clad" children to a school "where not only color, but dress and station, would be so strongly contrasted." The Committee cited the testimony of a local Negro that integration would bring "poor and ill-educated colored children . . . into disadvantageous competition and association with the more advanced and wealthy white children." This, he warned, would result in "sneers, insults, assaults, jeers, etc."; the Negro children would be set off by themselves—"and what is the difference between an exclusive class and an exclusive school?" Finally, the Committee concluded, legislation could neither regulate social customs nor force children, Negro or white, "to associate with, or be 'crumbled up' among, any class of people, except those to whom it may be mutually agreeable."

Vigorous dissents accompanied each of the Committee's reports, and they included favorable testimony from integrated school officials and teachers. Referring to the anticipated parental opposition, the Committee's minority members felt that it would probably be less than that being exerted against the admission of the more numerous Irish children. In any event, the mingling of white and Negro children could hardly be more objectionable than the usual meeting of their parents at the polls, in the courts of justice, and in the daily pursuits of labor. Segregated schools not only required additional and needless expense, they exercised a damaging effect on white youths. "We deem it morally injurious to the white children, inasmuch as it tends to create in most, and foster in all, feelings of repugnance and contempt for the colored race as degraded inferiors, whom they may, or must, treat as such. This is the standard of morals and humanity which these schools teach our children, who are thus led to attach to color alone, sentiments and emotions, which should arise, if at all, only in view of character." Integration, on the other hand, could help to destroy racial prejudice; for, where Negro and white children shared "the same bench and sports, there can hardly arise a manhood of aristocratic prejudice, or separate castes and classes."

While the *Liberator* assailed the majority reports as "flimsy yet venomous sophistries," Boston Negroes denounced the Primary School Committee's decision and prepared new appeals and methods of attack. Some local newspapers, in the meantime, predicted violence in the wake of any attempt to integrate the public schools. "Law or no law," the Boston *Post* warned, "our citizens of the west end will not suffer the infusion of forty or fifty colored boys and girls among their own children." Constant harassment faced any integrated school; whites would abandon "the finest edifices in the city" and permit them to become Negro schools rather than integrate them; all this because a few "rabid enthusiasts" were not satisfied with "a system which was working prosperously, in all love and harmony."

After nearly four years of agitation, Benjamin Roberts, a Boston Negro, decided to test the legality of the Primary School Committee's power to enforce segregation. In 1849, he brought suit in the name of his daughter under a statute that allowed any person illegally excluded from the public schools to recover damages from the city. Four times a white primary school had refused to admit his daughter; consequently, she now passed five such schools on her way to the Negro primary school. Charles Sumner, subsequently an antislavery leader in the United States Senate, took the case of the five-year-old plaintiff. Peleg W. Chandler, a recognized authority on municipal law, appeared for the city of Boston, and Chief Justice Lemuel Shaw presided. The stage was thus set for an eloquent and crucial legal debate. "On the one side is the city of Boston," Sumner declared, "strong in its wealth, in its influence, in its character; on the other side is a little child, of a degraded color, of humble parents, still within the period of natural infancy, but strong from her very weakness, and from the irresponsible sympathies of good men. . . . This little child asks at your hands her *personal rights*."

Sumner turned to history, political theory, philosophy, literature, and legal precedents to demonstrate that the state constitution, legislature, and courts, as well as "the spirit of American institutions," recognized no racial distinctions. Segregated schools violated the principle of equality by recognizing "a nobility of the skin" and "hereditary distinctions." Efforts to justify such schools as affording separate but equal facilities constituted a "mockery." Although the quality of instruction might not differ in some cases, "a school, exclusively devoted to one class, must differ essentially, in its spirit and character, from that public school . . . where all classes meet together in equality." Segregation injured both races; it instilled the sentiment of caste in the minds of white youths while it discouraged the aspiring Negro and widened his separation from the rest of the community. "The Helots of Sparta were obliged to intoxicate themselves," Sumner remarked, "that they might teach to the children of their masters the deformity of intemperance. In thus sacrificing one class to the other, both were degraded—the imperious Spartan and the abased Helot." Racial prejudice, Sumner concluded, had found its last refuge in the segregated school. On behalf of a Negro child and the "civilization of the age," he appealed to the court to abolish it.

The city's attorney declined to discuss the merits of segregation but confined his argument largely to a legal defense of the powers of the Primary School Committee. Chief Justice Shaw, delivering a unanimous decision, upheld the Committee's power to enforce segregation. Since Boston provided for the instruction of Negro children, it had discharged its duty. As for the contention that separate schools perpetuated caste distinctions, Shaw replied that the law had not created and could not alter the deep-rooted prejudice that sanctioned segregation. The importance of the decision transcended the local struggle for integration. Shaw's legal defense of segregated schools on the basis of the "separate but equal" doctrine established a controversial precedent in American law.

Rejected by the Primary School Committee and the courts, Boston Negroes turned to legislative appeals and formed the Equal School Rights Committee. Five years after the Roberts case, they won their initial success when the city's committee on public instruction recommended to the mayor and aldermen that separate schools be abolished. In view of the favorable action of other Massachusetts communities, the committee hoped that Boston would at least be the first large American city to integrate its public schools. On March 17, 1855, a legislative committee submitted a bill to prohibit racial or religious distinctions in admitting students to any public school. The legislature approved the bill, and the governor signed it on April 28.

* * *

The Boston victory encouraged Negroes and abolitionists in other states to step up their agitation. Rhode Island Negroes secured a favorable legislative-committee recommendation in 1859, but the proposed bill lost by two votes. In Philadelphia, Negro leader Robert Purvis protested "the proscription and exclusion of my children from the Public School" by refusing to pay his school tax, but integration efforts failed. In some states, Negroes appealed directly to the judiciary. The Ohio courts, however, ruled, in 1850 and 1859, that public policy required segregated schools; for, "whether consistent with true philanthropy or not . . . there . . . still is an almost invincible repugnance to such communion and fellowship." An Indiana court upheld segregation in 1850, "because black children were deemed unfit associates of whites, as school companions." By 1860, some small and scattered communities agreed to integration, but the larger cities, including New York, Philadelphia, Cincinnati, Providence, and New Haven, hoped to stem increasing agitation by correcting existing abuses and making the Negro schools equal to those of the whites.

The growing admission of Negroes into white schools and colleges did not immediately eradicate old prejudices. The life of a Negro in an overwhelmingly white school was not always pleasant. Some communities admitted Negroes to the public schools but seated them separately and frequently punished white offenders by forcing them to sit with the Negroes. A Negro attending a Massachusetts private academy, where a "majority" claimed to be abolitionists, reported that he could neither live in the same house with the whites nor be admitted to the dinner table until they had been served. When Frederick Douglass's daughter entered Seward Seminary in Rochester, school authorities assigned her to a room separate from the whites and appointed a teacher to instruct her. Douglass protested the school's action and withdrew his daughter. The principal told him that perhaps prejudice would subside after a few terms, and she could then be accorded equal privileges. College life, a Negro convention reported, frequently imposed "peculiar restraints" on Negroes, for it placed them in the midst of many hostile and few sympathetic colleagues. Social pressures prompted some students to be friendly with Negroes on campus but ignore them elsewhere. A Salem, Massachusetts, Negro thus testified that, although white children treated him well in school and even invited him to some of their parties, "they did not seem to know him" on the street. Confirming this reaction, Charlotte Forten, later a prominent Negro abolitionist and teacher, recorded in her diary (kept when she was a student at a New England school) that her white colleagues treated her cordially in the classroom but feared to recognize her in public.

For many Negro students, campus and off-campus life constituted two separate worlds. Although Northern whites finally recognized the Negro's right to an adequate education, they maintained, outside the classroom, racial barriers that virtually nullified the benefits of that education. "To what end are these poor creatures taught knowledge, from the exercise of which they are destined to be debarred?" asked an instructor in a New York Negro school. "It is surely but a cruel mockery to cultivate talents, when in the present state of public feeling, there is no field open for their useful employment. Be his acquirements what they may, a Negro is still a Negro, or, in other words, a creature marked out for degradation, and exclusion from those objects which stimulate the hopes and powers of other men."

* * *

Free Blacks in Antebellum Philadelphia: A Study of Ex-Slaves, Freeborn, and Socio-economic Decline

Theodore Hershberg

Afro-American history in general has received a great deal of attention from historians in the past decade. The same cannot be said about the history of black Americans who were free before the Civil War. Studies published since Leon Litwack's *North of Slavery* have considered racial discrimination in the legal tradition, the relationship between race and politics, the establishment of black utopian communities, and the role of blacks in the abolitionist movement. With a few exceptions notable in the earlier studies of the free Negro by Luther P. Jackson and John Hope Franklin, the literature lacks a solid empirical base, a sophisticated methodological and theoretical approach, and a focus on the black community itself. There exists an important need for new studies of the family and social structure, of the development of community institutions such as the church, school, and beneficial society, of migration and social mobility.

Antebellum Philadelphia offers the historian an important opportunity to study each of these topics. The free-black population of the city had its roots in the eighteenth century. Its free-black population in 1860, more than 22,000, was the largest outside of the Slave South and second only to Baltimore. All-black churches, schools, and voluntary societies were numerous. The National Negro Convention Movement met for the first time in Philadelphia in 1830, and the city hosted such meetings frequently thereafter. Many of the leading black abolitionists, such as James Forten, Robert Purvis, and William Still, were Philadelphians. Most significantly for the historian, the data describing all facets of this history are extant. The black history collections and the papers of the Pennsylvania Abolition Society at the Historical Society of Pennsylvania and the Library Company of Philadelphia are even richer for the antebellum period than the Schomburg Collection of the New York Public Library.

* * *

A CONTEXT OF DECLINE

The decision of the Pennsylvania Abolition Society in 1837 to take a census of Philadelphia's free-Negro population was made for both a specific

Copyright © 1971 by Peter N. Stearns. Reprinted from *The Journal of Social History*, Volume 4, Number 4, pp. 333–56, by permission of the Editor.

Census: Pennsylvania Abolition Society, 1838

| | Total Households | | | | Male-Headed Households | | | | | |
	All Freeborn	Ex-Slave HH's	Ex-Slave HH HD's	Ex-Slave HH Heads Bought Selves	All Freeborn	Ex-slave HH's All	Ex-slave HH's Free HD's	Ex-Slave HH Heads All	Manumitted	Bought Selves
Variables										
Churchgoers										
Nonchurchgoers	17.8%	9.3%	5.4%	3.2%	18.5%	10.5%	13.5%	4.8%	7.1%	3.7%
White churches	5.5%	5.1%	5.7%	7.5%	5.2%	4.3%	4.1%	4.6%	3.8%	5.1%
Baptist	8.7%	10.3%	11.4%	12.9%	8.1%	11.0%	10.0%	12.7%	13.9%	12.8%
Methodist	70.7%	76.5%	74.1%	76.3%	71.1%	75.1%	77.7%	70.6%	70.9%	75.6%
Episc.	7.0%	4.8%	4.7%	2.2%	8.1%	4.6%	0.4%	5.1%	3.8%	2.6%
Presbyt.	7.6%	5.3%	6.7%	5.4%	7.8%	5.8%	4.7%	7.6%	7.6%	5.1%
Cath.	4.1%	1.1%	1.3%	1.1%	2.6%	1.3%	0.9%	2.0%	2.5%	1.3%
Misc.	1.9%	2.0%	1.7%	2.2%	2.3%	2.2%	2.4%	2.0%	1.3%	2.6%
School										
HH child attnd	27.6%	29.2%	29.0%	35.4%	29.7%	35.9%	35.3%	37.2%	36.5%	38.3%
HH child not attnd	22.5%	25.4%	15.9%	22.9%	25.2%	28.3%	32.2%	20.1%	17.6%	24.7%
Child attnd	55.0%	67.1%	71.7%	71.2%	54.9%	61.4%	55.7%	72.7%	75.0%	70.8%
Ben. Soc.										
HH w/members	56.4%	56.1%	60.8%	64.6%	52.0%	57.7%	53.8%	65.2%	62.3%	69.1%
Members	27.1%	27.0%	35.1%	32.4%	25.5%	26.2%	22.6%	34.5%	34.6%	33.0%
Occ. Cat.										
White collar	4.0%	5.4%	8.2%	4.9%	4.2%	5.4%	4.4%	7.0%	7.3%	5.1%
Skilled	17.6%	16.6%	18.8%	20.7%	17.5%	15.6%	14.2%	18.4%	17.1%	20.3%
Unskilled	78.4%	78.1%	73.1%	74.4%	78.3%	79.0%	81.4%	74.6%	75.6%	74.7%

and a general purpose. The specific purpose was to defeat the move, already under way in Harrisburg, to write into the new state constitution the complete disfranchisement of Pennsylvania blacks. The general purpose was to "repel" those who denounced "the whole of the free colored people as unworthy of any favor, asserting that they were nuisances in the community fit only to fill alms houses and jails."

The strategy employed to accomplish these ends reveals a good deal about the faith that the abolitionists had in hard fact and reasoned argument. The data from the census were presented to the delegates at Harrisburg and to the public at large in the form of a forty-page pamphlet summarizing the findings.

The pamphlet argued that disfranchisement should be defeated because the free-Negro population made a worthy contribution to the well-being of the entire community. Blacks paid considerable taxes and rents, owned property, were not disproportionately paupers and criminals, cared for their own underprivileged, and, finally, put money as consumers into the income stream of the general economy. The facts contained in the published pamphlet, therefore, "gave great satisfaction affording the friends of the colored people strong and convincing arguments against those who were opposed to their enjoying the rights and privileges of freemen."

Though unsuccessful in the specific purpose—blacks were disfranchised in Pennsylvania until 1870, when the Fifteenth Amendment was adopted—the Abolitionists and Quakers undertook further censuses in 1847 and 1856. As in 1838, these later censuses were followed with printed pamphlets that duly noted the discrimination and problems facing free Negroes and counseled patience to the "magnanimous sufferers," as they referred to their Negro brethren. The general tone of the pamphlets, however, was *optimistic* and pointed to important *gains* made in past decades. The over-all optimism, however, proved unfounded when the actual manuscript censuses were submitted to computer analysis.

The "friends of the colored people," unfortunately, had been carried away by their admirable purpose. It was one thing to document that free Negroes were not worthless, that they could indeed survive outside of the structured environment of slavery, and even that they could create a community with their own churches, schools, and beneficial societies; but it was quite another thing to argue that the people and the institutions they created actually *prospered* in the face of overwhelming obstacles. It is not so much that the Abolitionists and Quakers were wrong as that they went too far. And, in so doing, they obscured a remarkable deterioration in the socioeconomic condition of blacks from 1830 to the Civil War.

Beginning in 1829 and continuing through the ensuing two decades, Philadelphia Negroes were the victims of half a dozen major antiblack riots and many more minor mob actions. Negro churches, schools, homes, and even an orphanage were set on fire. Some blacks were killed, many beaten, and others run out of town. Contemporaries attributed the small net loss in the Negro population between 1840 and 1850, in large part, to riots.

Census: Pennsylvania Abolition Society, 1838

Variables	Total Households (3,295) (12,084 Persons)				Male-Headed Households (2,361) (9,609 Persons)					
	All Freeborn	Ex-Slave HH's	Ex-Slave HH HD's	Ex-Slave HH HD's Bought Selves	All Freeborn	Ex-slave HH's All	Ex-slave HH's Free HD's	Ex-Slave HH Heads All	Ex-Slave HH Heads Manumitted	Bought Selves
Total HH's	2489	806	314	96	1760	601	394	207	85	81
Total persons	8867	3217	1013	358	6966	2643	1852	791	312	327
Fam. size	3.88	4.27	3.84	4.12	4.06	4.40	4.70	3.99	3.80	4.72
(w/o singles)										
Two-par. HH (%)	77.0	79.8	79.3	90.5	99% of all male-headed households with 2 or more persons were two-parent households.					
Wealth Cats.										
$0–20 (%)	23.9	19.6	17.5	10.4	21.8	16.3	19.0	11.1	16.5	6.2
$21–40 (%)	21.1	19.6	19.7	11.5	18.6	18.1	19.5	15.5	16.5	8.6
$41–90 (%)	17.8	15.1	14.6	11.5	16.7	14.0	14.7	12.6	12.9	11.1
$91–240 (%)	18.6	21.1	18.8	25.0	20.9	23.0	22.6	23.7	24.7	28.4
$241+ (%)	18.6	24.6	29.3	41.7	22.1	28.6	24.1	37.2	29.4	45.7
Ave. TW	$252	$268	$295	$388	$257	$317	$284	$380	$388	$409
Ave. PP* all HH's	$176	$175	$191	$223	$181	$204	$180	$249	$269	$252
Ave. RP all HH's	$76	$93	$105	$164	$69	$113	$103	$131	$119	$157
Ave. RP owners only	$987	$730	$567	$527	$768	$770	$1017	$564	$776	$472
% RP owners	7.7	12.8	18.5	31.2	9.0	14.6	10.1	23.2	15.3	33.3
Ave. rent	$48	$50	$47	$53	$53	$55	$55	$54	$49	$56

TW = Total Wealth   PP = Personal Property   RP = Real Property   HH = Household
* There is little observable difference between the ave. PP for all HH's and the ave. PP for owners only: 95%–100% of all HH's owned PP.

In the same decade, white population grew 63 per cent. While it is important to maintain the perspective that the antiblack violence occurred within a larger context of anti-Catholic violence, this knowledge must have been small comfort to Philadelphia Negroes.

A victimized minority, one reasons, should organize and bring *political* pressure on local government officials. But black Philadelphians after 1838, as we have seen, were denied even this remedy. Disfranchisement of all Negroes, even those citizens who owned sufficient property to vote in all elections during the previous twenty-three years, was all the more tragic and ironic because, at the same time, all white males in Pennsylvania over the age of twenty-one were specifically given the right to vote.

In addition to the larger, less measurable forces, such as race riots, population decline, and disfranchisement, after 1838 black Philadelphians suffered a turn for the worse in wealth, residential segregation, family structure, and employment.

The antebellum black community was extremely poor. The total wealth —that is, the combined value of real and personal property holdings—for three out of every five households in both 1838 and 1847 amounted to $60 or less. This fact, it can be noted in passing, precludes the use of simple economic class analysis in determining social stratification in the black community. The distribution of wealth itself, moreover, was strikingly unequal within the black population. In both 1838 and 1847, the poorest half of the population owned only one-twentieth of the total wealth, while the wealthiest 10 per cent of the population held 70 per cent of the total wealth; at the very apex of the community, the wealthiest 1 per cent accounted for fully 30 per cent of the total wealth.

Between 1838 and 1847, there was a 10 per cent decrease in per capita value of personal property and a slight decrease in per capita total wealth among Philadelphia blacks. Although the number of households included in the 1847 census was 30 per cent greater than in 1838, the number of real property holders fell from 294 to 280, and their respective percentages fell from 9 to 6 per cent. There was, in other words, despite a considerable increase in the number of households, both absolute and percentage decrease in the number of real property holders.

Another way of highlighting the decline is to create roughly equal population groups, rank them by wealth, and determine at what point in the rank order blacks ceased to include owners of real property. In 1838, owners of real property extended through the wealthiest 30 per cent of the ranked population; in 1847, they extended less than half as far. In 1838, moreover, it required a total wealth holding of between $200 and $300 in order to own real property; by 1847, an individual required a total wealth holding twice as high before he could purchase land or own a home.

This statistic is complemented by a measurable rise in residential segregation over the decade. Disfranchisement (perhaps as valuable to us as a symptom of contemporary feelings about Negroes as it was a cause), a decade of race riots, and a general backlash against abolitionist activities, all contributed to the creation of a social atmosphere in which it was considerably more difficult for even the wealthiest of Negroes to acquire real property. It is tempting to conclude quite simply that rising.racism meant that a far higher price had to be paid in order to induce a white man to sell land to a black man. Stating such a conclusion with complete confidence, however, requires further *comparative* research in order to determine if, instead, this phenomenon applied equally to all ethnic groups—that is, a period of generally appreciating land values.

The actual measurement of residential segregation depends upon the use of a "grid square"—an area roughly one and one-quarter blocks square—and is a vast improvement over far larger geographical entities, such as districts or wards. Each Negro household was located on detailed maps and its precise grid square recorded. All variables about each household, then, are observable and measurable in small, uniquely defined units.

Residential segregation is measured in two dimensions: (1) the *distribution* of the household population—that is, the number of grid squares in which Negro households were located; and (2) the *density* of the population—that is, the number of Negro households per grid. Residential segregation was rising in the decade before 1838, and it increased steadily to 1860. Between 1838 and 1847, average density increased 13 per cent in all grid squares inhabited by blacks; more importantly, however, the percentage of households occupying the most dense grid squares (those with more than one hundred black households) increased by almost 10 per cent. Between 1850 and 1860, the average density changed very little, but the trend toward settlement in the more dense grids continued. By 1860, the number of households occupying the most dense grid squares reached more than one in four, an increase of 11 per cent over the previous decade and the high point between 1838 and 1880. During the Civil War decade, residential segregation fell off but rose again from 1870 to 1880 as migration from the South swelled the Negro population of Philadelphia to 31,700, an increase of 43 per cent over both the 1860 and 1870 totals.

Data from the Abolitionist and Quaker censuses, the U.S. census of 1880, and W. E. B. Du Bois' study of the seventh ward in 1896–97 indicate, in each instance, that two-parent households were characteristic of 78 per cent of black families. That statistical average, however, belies a grimmer reality for the poorest blacks. There was a decline in the percentage of two-parent households for the poorest fifth of the population from 70 per cent in 1838 to 63 per cent ten years later; and, for the poorest half of the black population, the decline was from 73 per cent to 68 per cent. In other words, among the poorest half of the community at mid-century, roughly one family in three was headed by a female.

An unequal female-male sex ration no doubt indirectly affected family building and stability. Between 1838 and 1860, the number of black females per 1,000 black males increased from 1,326 to 1,417. For whites, in 1860, the corresponding figure was 1,088. Between 1860 and 1890, the sex ratio for blacks moved in the direction of parity: 1,360 in 1870, 1;263 in

1880, and 1,127 in 1890. The age and sex distribution throughout the period 1838–90 indicates that the movement away from—and, after 1860, back toward—equal distribution of the sexes was due to a change in the number of young black males in the 20–40 age bracket. Changes in this age bracket usually result from two related factors: occupational opportunities, and in- and out-migration rates. The remarkably high excess of females over males throughout the period probably reflects poor employment opportunities for black men (while the demand for black female domestics remained high), accompanied by net out-migration of young black males. The gradual improvement of industrial opportunities for young black males after 1860, accompanied by net in-migration of increasing numbers of young black men, reduced the excess of black females. The sociological consequences of such an imbalance in the sex ratios are familiar: illegitimacy, delinquency, broken homes, and such. In light of these statistics, it is surprising that the percentage of two-parent households was as high as it was.

More important for our purposes, however, is another measure of the condition of the entire black population often obscured by the debate over the matrifocality of the black family, focusing as it does on narrow statistical analysis of traditional household units. How many blacks were living outside of black households? How many were inmates of public institutions? How many were forced not only to delay beginning families but to make lives for themselves *outside* the black family unit, residing in boarding houses as transients or living in white homes as domestic servants?

The data indicate that there was a slow but steady rise in the percentage of black men and women who found themselves outside the black family. Between 1850 and 1880, their numbers nearly doubled. By 1880, six thousand persons—slightly [fewer] than one-third of the adult population (inmates, transients, and servants combined)—were living outside the normal family structures. One out of every five adults lived and worked in a white household as a domestic servant. That so many Negroes took positions outside their traditional family units is testimony to the strength and pervasiveness of the job discrimination that existed at large in the economy; that this occurred within a context of widening occupational opportunities for whites, a benefit of increasing industrialization and the factory system, makes it even more significant. In 1847, [fewer] than one-half of 1 per cent of the black male work force was employed in factories. And this came at a time, it should be remembered, when thousands of Irish immigrants were engaged in factory work.

Blacks were not only denied access to new jobs in the expanding factory system, but, because of increasing job competition with the Irish, they also lost their traditional predominance in many semiskilled and unskilled jobs. The 1847 census identified 5 per cent of the black male work force in the relatively well-paying occupations of hod carrier and stevedore. The following letter to a city newspaper, written in 1849 by one "P. O.," attests to the job displacement:

That there may be, and undoubtedly is, a direct competition between them (the blacks and Irish) as to labor we all know. The wharves and new buildings attest this fact, in the person of our stevedores and hod-carriers as does all places of labor; and when a few years ago we saw none but blacks, we now see nothing but Irish.

"P. O." proved perceptive, indeed. According to the 1850 U.S. census, the percentage of black hod carriers and stevedores in the black male work force fell in just three years from 5 per cent to 1 per cent. The 1850 census, moreover, reported occupations for the entire country and included 30 per cent more black male occupations than the 1847 census; nevertheless, the absolute number of black hod carriers fell sharply from 98 to 28 and stevedores from 58 to 27.

A similar pattern of increasing discrimination affected the ranks of the skilled. Blacks complained not only that it was "difficult for them to find places for their sons as apprentices to learn mechanical trades," but also that those who had skills found it more difficult to practice them. The "Register of Trades of the Colored People," published in 1838 by the Pennsylvania Abolition Society to encourage white patronage of black artisans, noted that 23 per cent of 656 skilled artisans did not practice their skills because of "prejudice against them." The 1856 census recorded considerable deterioration among the ranks of the skilled. The percentage of skilled artisans not practicing their trades rose from 23 per cent in 1838 to approximately 38 per cent in 1856. Skilled black craftsmen were "compelled to abandon their trades on account of the unrelenting prejudice against their color."

Job discrimination, then, was complete and growing: Blacks were excluded from new areas of the economy, uprooted from many of their traditional unskilled jobs, denied apprenticeships for their sons, and prevented from practicing the skills they already possessed. All social indicators—race riots, population decrease, disfranchisement, residential segregation, per capita wealth, ownership of real property, family structure, and occupational opportunities—pointed toward socio-economic deterioration within Philadelphia's antebellum black community.

EX-SLAVE AND FREEBORN

Among the 3,300 households and 12,000 persons included in the 1838 census, about one household in four contained at least one person who, though free in 1838, had been born a slave. Living in these 806 households were some 1,141 ex-slaves, or 9 per cent of the entire population.

What was the condition of the ex-slave relative to his freeborn brother? Were ex-slaves in any way responsible for the socio-economic deterioration just described? Contemporaries perceived two very different effects of direct contact with slavery. "Upon feeble and common minds," according to one view, the slave experience was "withering" and induced "a listlessness and an indifference to the future." Even if the slave somehow managed to gain his freedom, "the vicious habits of slavery" remained, "worked into the very grain of his character." But for others "who resisted . . . and bought their own freedom with the hard-earned fruits of their own industry," the struggle for "liberty" resulted in "a desire for improvement" that "invigorated all their powers and gave energy and dignity to their character as freemen." An analysis of the data permits us to determine whether both groups were found equally in antebellum Philadelphia, or whether one was more representative of all ex-slaves than the other.

The richness of detail in the census schedules allows us to make several important distinctions in the data describing the ex-slave households: We know which of the 806 households were headed by ex-slaves themselves— 314—and how these 40 per cent of all ex-slave households were freed—if, for instance, they were "manumitted," or if, as they put, they had "bought themselves."

We are dealing, then, with several ex-slave categories: (1) 493 households in which at least one ex-slave lived, but which had a freeborn household head; I shall refer to this group as free-headed, ex-slave households; (2) 314 households in which at least one ex-slave lived, but which had an ex-slave household head; I shall refer to this group as ex-slave-headed households. In this second group of ex-slave-headed households, I have selected two subgroups for analysis: (a) 146 ex-slave household heads who were manumitted, and (b) 96 ex-slave household heads who bought their own freedom.

Cutting across all of these groups is the dimension of sex. The census identified household heads as males, females, and widows. There was a strong and direct relationship between family size [and] wealth [on the one hand] and male sex [on the other], so that the largest families had the most wealth and the greatest likelihood of being headed by a male. Because there was also a strong and direct relationship between sex and almost all other variables, with males enjoying by far the more fortunate circumstances, it is important to differentiate by sex in comparing the general condition of the ex-slave groups to that of the freeborn population. Ex-slaves differed from their freeborn neighbors in a variety of significant social indicators:

Family Size. The family size of all ex-slave households was 10 per cent larger than households all of whose members were freeborn: 4.27 persons as compared to 3.88. Families of ex-slave households headed by freeborn males, and those families headed by males who bought their own freedom, were 20 per cent larger—4.70. The instances in which freeborn families were larger occurred only where female and, to a lesser extent, widow ex-slave households were involved. (This, by the way, is the general pattern in most variables; in other words, ex-slave females and widows more closely resembled their freeborn counterparts than ex-slave males resembled freeborn males.)

Two-Parent Household. Two-parent households were generally more common among the ex-slaves. Taken together, two-parent households were found 80 per cent of the time among ex-slaves, while the figure for the freeborn was 77 per cent. A significant difference, however, was found in the case of ex-slave household heads who bought their own freedom. In this group, 90 per cent were two-parent households.

Church. For two basic reasons, the all-black church has long been recognized as the key institution of the Negro community: First, an oppressed and downtrodden people used religion for spiritual sustenance and for its promise of a better life in the next world; second, with the ability to participate in the political, social, and economic spheres of the larger white society in which they lived sharply curtailed, Negroes turned to the church for fulfillment of their secular needs.

Important in the twentieth century, the church was vital to blacks in the nineteenth. Philadelphia Negroes were so closed off from the benefits of white society that church affiliation became a fundamental prerequisite to a decent and, indeed, bearable existence. For this reason, nonchurch affiliation, rather than poverty, was the distinguishing characteristic of the most disadvantaged group in the community. Nonchurchgoers must have enjoyed few of the benefits and services that accrued to those who were affiliated with a church in some manner. The socio-economic profile of nonchurchgoers is depressing. They fared considerably less well than their churchgoing neighbors in all significant social indicators: They had smaller families, fewer two-parent households, [and] high residential density levels; and they were disproportionately poor. Their ratios for membership in beneficial societies and for the number of school-age children in school was one-fourth and one-half, respectively, that of the larger community. Occupationally, they were decidedly overrepresented among the unskilled sectors of the work force.

In this sense, then, the percentage of households with no members attending church is a more valuable index of general social condition than any other. Eighteen per cent of the freeborn households had no members attending church; for all ex-slave households, the figure was *half* as great. Although ex-slave households were one in four in the community at large, they were [fewer] than one in ten among households with no members attending church. The ratios were even lower (one in twenty) for ex-slave-headed households and lowest (one in thirty) for ex-slaves who bought themselves.

About 150 households, or 5 per cent of the churchgoing population of the entire community, attended 23 predominantly white churches. These churches had only "token" integration, allowing a few Negroes to worship in pews set apart from the rest of the congregation. Ex-slaves of all groups attended white churches in approximately the same ratio as did the freeborn—one household in twenty.

The churchgoing population of the entire community consisted of 2,776 households distributed among five religious denominations: Methodists (73 per cent), Baptists (9 per cent), Presbyterians (7 per cent), Episcopalians (7 per cent) and Catholics (3 per cent). Methodists worshipped in eight and Baptists in four all-black congregations scattered throughout the city and districts. Together, they accounted for more than eight of every ten churchgoers. The various ex-slave groups were found an average of 11 per cent more frequently among Methodists and 30 per cent more frequently among Baptists.

In any case, Methodists and Baptists differed little from each other, and to describe them is to characterize the entire community: poor and unskilled. Within each denomination, however, a single church—Union Methodist and Union Baptist—served as the social base for their respective elites. And, while ex-slaves attended all of the community's all-black churches, it was in these two churches where the ex-slaves were most frequently found. The ex-slave members of these two churches shared the socio-economic and cultural characteristics of the community's elite denominations, the Episcopalians and the Presbyterians; and it should not be surprising, therefore, to find ex-slaves of all groups underrepresented in each of these last two denominations.

Beneficial Society. Next to the church, in value to the community, were the all-black beneficial societies. These important institutions functioned as rudimentary insurance groups that provided their members with relief in sickness, aid during extreme poverty, and burial expenses at death.

There were over one hundred distinct societies in antebellum Philadelphia. They grew out of obvious need and were early manifestations of the philosophy of "self-help" that became so popular later in the nineteenth century. Almost always, they were affiliated directly with one of the all-black churches. The first beneficial society, known as the "Free African Society," was founded in 1787. A dozen societies existed by 1815, fifty by 1830, and 106 by 1847.

Slightly more than 50 per cent of freeborn households were members of the various societies. Making good the philosophy of "self-help," half a century before Booker T. Washington, the societies found ex-slaves more eager to join their ranks than freeborn blacks. Each group of ex-slaves had a higher percentage of members, especially ex-slave-headed households (61 per cent), ex-slaves who purchased their own freedom (65 per cent), and the males among the latter group (70 per cent).

Membership in beneficial societies varied significantly by wealth and status. Ranking the entire household population in thirty distinct wealth categories revealed that, beginning with the poorest, the percentage of membership rose with increasing wealth until the wealthiest six categories. For this top 11 per cent of the population, however, membership in beneficial societies declined from 92 to 81 per cent. Among the wealthiest—and this applied equally to ex-slaves—there was less need for membership in beneficial societies.

Education. One household in four among the freeborn population sent children to school. For ex-slave households, the corresponding figure was more than one in three. Ex-slave households had slightly fewer children but sent a considerably greater percentage of their children to school. For freeborn households, the percentage was 55 per cent; for all ex-slave households, 67 per cent; and, for ex-slave-headed households, the figure rose to 72 per cent. To the extent that education was valuable to blacks, the ex-slaves were better off.

Location and Density. Small groups of ex-slaves clustered disproportionately in the outlying districts of Kensington, Northern Liberties, and Spring Garden. Twenty-five per cent of the entire black population of Philadelphia, they comprised about 35 per cent of the black population in these areas. Most ex-slaves, however, lived in the same proportions and in the same blocks as did the freeborn population.

More interesting than the pattern of their distribution throughout the city, however, was the level of population density in which they lived—that is, the number of black neighbors who lived close by. To calculate the number of black households in a grid square of approximately one and one-fourth blocks, three density levels were used: 1–20, 21–100, and in excess of 100 households per grid square.

The less dense areas were characterized by larger families, greater presence of two-parent households, less imbalance between the sexes, and fewer families whose members were entirely nonnatives of Pennsylvania. In these areas lived a disproportionate greater number of wealthy families and, among them, a correspondingly overrepresented number of real property owners. Here, white-collar and skilled workers lived in greater percentages than elsewhere in the city, and unskilled workers were decidedly few in both percentage and absolute number. The major exceptions to the distribution of wealth and skill came as the result of the necessity for shopkeepers and craftsmen to locate their homes and their businesses in the city's more densely populated sections.

Ex-slave households were more likely than freeborn households to be found in the least dense areas (one in four as compared with one in five). Conversely, ex-slave households were less likely to be found in those areas with the greatest density of black population.

Wealth. The parameters of wealth for Negroes in antebellum Philadelphia have already been described. The community was impoverished. Poverty, nevertheless, did not touch all groups equally. In terms of average total wealth, including both real and personal property, free-headed, ex-slave households differed little from the freeborn population. In considering the ex-slave-headed household, however, differences emerge. Average total wealth for this group was 20 per cent greater; for males in this group, 53 per cent greater; and, for males who freed themselves, 63 per cent greater.

The most significant differences in wealth by far occurred in real property holding. One household in thirteen, or slightly [fewer] than 8 per cent among the freeborn, owned real property. For all ex-slave households, the corresponding ratio was one in eight; for ex-slave-headed households, one in five; for males who were in this group, one in four; and, most dramatically, for males who purchased their own freedom, one in three owned real property. To these ex-slaves, owning their own home or a piece of land must have provided something (perhaps a stake in society) of peculiarly personal significance. Distribution of wealth, to view the matter from a different perspective, was less unequal for ex-slave households, particularly ex-slave household heads. The poorest half of the freeborn and ex-slave-headed households owned 5 and 7 per cent, respectively, of the total wealth; for the wealthiest quarter of each group, the corresponding figure[s] [were] 86 and 73 per cent; for the wealthiest tenth, 67 and 56 per cent; and, for the wealthiest one-hundredth, 30 and 21 per cent. Over-all wealth distribution, in other words, while still skewed toward pronounced inequality, was more equally distributed for ex-slave household heads in the middle- and upper-wealth categories.

Occupation. The final area of comparison between the ex-slaves and the freeborn is occupation. Analysis of the data using the same classification schema for Negroes as for white ethnic groups confirms an earlier suspicion that, although such schemata are necessary in order to compare the Negro to white ethnic groups, they are entirely unsatisfactory tools of analysis when social stratification in the Negro community is the concern. Despite the fact that the Negroes who comprised the labor force of antebellum Philadelphia described themselves as engaged in four hundred different occupations, a stark fact emerges from the analysis: There was almost no occupational differentiation!

Five occupations accounted for 70 per cent of the entire male work force: laborers (38 per cent), porters (11.5 per cent), waiters (11.5 per cent), seamen (5 per cent), and carters (4 per cent); another 10 per cent were employed in miscellaneous laboring capacities. Taken together, eight out of every ten working men were unskilled laborers. Another 16 per cent worked as skilled artisans, but fully one-half of this fortunate group were barbers and shoemakers; the other skilled craftsmen were scattered among the building-construction (3.2 per cent), home-furnishing (1.3 per cent), leather-goods (1.2 per cent), and metal-work (1.2 per cent) trades. Less than one-half of 1 per cent of Negroes, as pointed out in another context, found employment in the developing factory system. The remaining 4 per cent of the labor force were engaged in white-collar professions. They were largely proprietors who sold food or secondhand clothing from vending carts, and should not be considered as "storeowners."

The occupational structure for females was even less differentiated than for males. More than eight out of every ten women were employed in day-work capacities (as opposed to those who lived and worked in white households) as domestic servants: "washers" (52 per cent), "day workers" (22 per cent), and miscellaneous domestics (6 per cent). Fourteen per cent worked as seamstresses, and they accounted for all the skilled workers among the female labor force. Finally, about 5 per cent were engaged in white-collar work, which, like the males, meant vending capacities in clothing- and food-selling categories.

It should come, then, as no surprise that there were few distinctions of significance in the occupational structure of the ex-slaves and freeborn work forces. The differences in vertical occupational categories find male ex-slave household heads more likely to be in white-collar positions (7 per cent as opposed to 4 per cent for the freeborn), equally distributed in the skilled trades, and slightly less represented in the unskilled occupations (75 per cent as opposed to 78 per cent). Within the horizontal categories, there were few important differences. Male ex-slave household heads were more likely than the freeborn to be employed as porters, carpenters, blacksmiths, preachers, and clothes dealers.

In summary, then, we find the ex-slaves with larger families, greater likelihood of two-parent households, [and] higher affiliation rates in church and beneficial societies, sending more of their children to school, living more frequently in the least dense areas of the county, generally wealthier, owning considerably more real property, and being slightly more fortunate in occupational differentiation. By almost every socio-economic measure, the ex-slave fared better than his freeborn brother. While ex-slaves were distributed throughout the socio-economic scale, they were more likely to be part of the community's small middle class, which reached into both the lower and upper strata, characterized more by their hard-working, conscientious, and God-fearing life-style than by a concentration of wealth and power.

AN URBAN PERSPECTIVE

On the basis of the data presented, it is possible to state two conclusions, offer a working hypothesis, and argue for the necessity of an urban perspective. First, the relatively better condition of the ex-slave, especially the ex-slave who was both a male and who bought his own freedom, confirms the speculations of a few historians that the slave-born Negro freed before the Civil War was exceptional: a uniquely gifted individual who succeeded in internalizing the ethic of deferred gratification in the face of enormous difficulties. More striking was the fact that the socio-economic condition of the great majority of ex-slaves was not markedly inferior to that of the freeborn. That ex-slaves were generally better off than freeborn blacks, however, should not suggest anything more than relative superiority; it does not imply prosperity and should not obscure the generally impoverished and deteriorating condition of the black community. Second, because the remaining 91 per cent of Philadelphia's antebellum black population was freeborn, the dismal and declining socio-economic circumstances of that population cannot be attributed to direct contact with the "slave experience." Direct contact with slavery was undoubtedly a *sufficient* cause of low status and decay; it most certainly was not a *necessary* cause.

In a very important sense, the first conclusion has little to do with the second. The latter is not arrived at because those who had direct contact with slavery fared better in the city than those who were born free. The second conclusion is not based upon a recognition that slavery was less destructive or benign (although, in some aspects, it certainly could have been so), but, rather, that the antebellum Northern city was destructive as well. It is significant to understand that slavery and the discrimination faced by free Negroes in the urban environment were both forms of racism, which pervaded the institutions and informed the values of the larger white society.

The comparison of the freeborn and the ex-slave was undertaken in an effort to learn more about the question that students of the black experience want answered: What was the effect of slavery on the slaves? In the case of antebellum Philadelphia, the ex-slaves may not be representative of the slave experience. If they were, however, our insight would necessarily be limited to the effect of the mildest slavery system as it was practiced in Maryland, Delaware, and Virginia.

De-emphasizing direct contact with slavery does not imply that the institution of slavery, and the debasement and prejudice it generated, did not condition the larger context. The indirect effect of slavery cannot be underestimated. The proslavery propaganda provided the justification not only for the institution but for the widespread discriminatory treatment of the free Negro both before and long after emancipation.

Yet, on the other hand, one must not allow this understanding, or an often overwhelming sense of moral outrage, to lead to a monolithic interpretation of the effects of the slave experience. Stanley Elkins's treatment of slavery may be in error, but few historians doubt that his urging of scholars to end the morality debate and to employ new methods and different disciplines in the study of slavery was correct and long overdue.

There is no historically valid reason to treat the slave experience as entirely destructive or entirely benign; nor, for that matter, does historical reality necessarily fall midway between the two. It may be more useful to study the problems that blacks faced at different times and in different places in their history and make the attempt to trace their historical origins, rather than to begin with slavery and assume that it represented, in all instances, the historical root. Some of the problems faced by blacks may more accurately be traced to the processes of urbanization, industrialization, and immigration, occurring in a setting of racial inequality, rather than to slavery.

One of the most significant contributions to black history and sociology in recent years presents data that suggest the postslavery, possibly urban, origins of the matrifocal black family. In groundbreaking essays on the Negro family after the Civil War, Herbert Gutman has demonstrated convincingly that traditional interpretations of slavery and its effect on the black family are seriously misleading. Examining "the family patterns of those Negroes closest in time to actual chattel slavery," Gutman did not find "instability," "chaos," or "disorder." Instead, in fourteen varied Southern cities and counties between 1865 and 1880, he found viable two-parent households ranging from 70 to 90 per cent.

It is significant to note that, of the areas studied by Gutman, the four lowest percentages of two-parent households were found in cities: Natchez and Beaufort, 70 per cent; Richmond, 73 per cent; and Mobile, 74 per cent. The urban experience was in some way responsible for the weaker family structure—and for a whole set of other negative socio-economic consequences, all of which are found in the Philadelphia data.

Yet, the city is more than a locale. Slavery itself underwent major transformations in the urban setting. Sustained advances in technology, transportation, and communication made the city the context for innovation; and the innovation, in turn, generated countless opportunities for upward mobility for those who could take advantage of them. And here was the rub. Blacks, alone among city dwellers, were excluded not only from their fair share but from almost any chance for improvement generated by the dynamics of the urban milieu. That the exclusion was not systematic but, by and large, incidental did not make it any less effective. The city provided an existence at once superior to, and inferior to, that of the countryside: For those who were free to pursue their fortunes, the city provided infinitely more opportunities and far greater rewards; for those who were denied access altogether (or for those who failed), the city provided scant advantages and comforts. There were few interstices.

The data presented in this essay point to the destructiveness of the urban experience for blacks in nineteenth-century Philadelphia. To proceed, data comparing the black experience to that of other ethnic groups are necessary, and they are forthcoming. Although much research remains, it is possible to offer a hypothesis. The forces that shaped modern America—urbanization, industrialization, and immigration—operated for blacks within a framework of institutional racism and structural inequality. In the antebellum context, blacks were unable to compete on equal terms with either the native, white American worker or the thousands of newly arrived Irish and German immigrants. Philadelphia Negroes suffered in the competition with the Irish and Germans and recovered somewhat during the Civil War and Reconstruction decades, only to suffer again, in much the same circumstances, in competition with the "new" immigrant groups, this time the Italians, Jews, Poles, and Slavs who began arriving in the 1880's. Best characterized as a low-status economic group early in the century, Philadelphia's blacks found themselves a deprived and degraded caste at its close.

Students of black history have not adequately appreciated the impact of the urban experience. In part, this is due to several general problems: to the larger neglect of urban history; to unequal educational opportunities, which prevented many potential black scholars from the study and other students from publication; to difficulties inherent in writing history "from-the-bottom-up"; and to present reward mechanisms, which place a high premium on quickly publishable materials involving either no new research or shoddy and careless efforts.

There are, however, other and more important considerations, with no little sense of irony. The moral revulsion to slavery prevented development of alternative explanations of low status and decay. In the immediate post-slavery decades, and throughout the twentieth century, blacks, and then white allies, took refuge in an explanation used by many abolitionists before them, namely, that slavery and not racial inferiority was responsible for the black condition. They were, of course, not wrong; it was rather that they did not go far enough. It was, and still is, much easier to lament the sins of one's forefathers than it is to confront the injustices in more contemporary socio-economic systems.

Although August Meier and Elliot Rudwick titled their well-known and widely used text *From Plantation to Ghetto,* and, with the little data available to them, subtly but suggestively wove the theme of the impact of urban environment through their pages, scholars have been slow to develop it in monographic studies.

The Philadelphia data from 1838 to 1880 enable one to examine this theme in minute detail. Although 90 per cent of the nation's black population in 1880 was Southern and overwhelmingly rural, the key to the twentieth century lies in understanding the consequences of the migration from the farm to the city. The experience of Philadelphia Negroes in the nineteenth century foreshadowed the fate of millions of black migrants who, seeking a better life, found different miseries in what E. Franklin Frazier called the "cities of destruction."

If we are to succeed in understanding the urban experience, we must dismiss simplistic explanations that attribute all present-day failings to "the legacy of slavery" or to "the problems of unacculturated rural migrants lacking the skills necessary to compete in an advanced technology." We must understand, instead, the social dynamics and consequences of competition and accommodation among different racial, ethnic, and religious groups taking place in an urban context of racial discrimination and structural inequality.

Immigrants, Negroes, and the Public Schools

Colin Greer

Concern over the failure of the American Negro to become a part of the postindustrial society has found vigorous expression within the framework of the traditional American faith in public education. Now that it is totally unprofitable for the nation to support a large reserve unskilled labor force, self-interest has reforged an old alliance with altruism in a concerted effort to free the Negro from welfare dependency.

Political and social energy has been spent in an increasingly more determined effort to effect change in precisely that area where the roots of future national and ethnic progress are believed to lie: namely, in the classroom, where reading achievement promises a lifetime of better jobs. The civil-rights movement is generally recognized as being of signal import in rewriting the *de jure* status of the ex-slave, but this change has come slowly, and the typology of "cultural deprivation" describes the deficits of that tardiness and finds alarmingly far-reaching debilitation stretching from plantation to city tenement.

Of late, the perspective of quasi-historical comparison has been employed to stress the similarities between the newly urbanized immigrant at the turn of the century and his present counterpart, the newly urbanized Negro. The myth has emerged that the miracle of the American melting pot had been accomplished with the school acting as prime agent in the process; and, if public education could do it for the immigrant, then why not for the Negro? For some, this myth provides the basis for an invidious comparison; for others, it offers reassurance in the power of the American city to assimilate widely diverse groups, particularly through a heavy investment in the public schools. However, comparisons that span fifty years of industrial explosion misrepresent the dynamics of foreign-born accommodation into the fabric of American society. The misrepresentation has grown as a product of longstanding fear of the foreigner and the economic need of him, combined with the apparently successful accommodation of ethnic diversity in the modern nation. As a result, it is wishfully expected, despite totally different circumstances, that the Negro should be able to respond to the readiness of white America to accept his change in status.

The only period for which such historical comparisons can be meaningfully undertaken is at the turn of the century, when both foreign-born immigrant and Negro migrant left the farm and the tradition-bound struc-

From *The Urban Review,* Volume 3, Number 3 (January, 1969), pp. 9–12. Reprinted by permission.

tures of their past in unprecedented numbers. They came to the Yankee North to find economic and social breathing space amid its growing urban centers. Although we have been accustomed to regard the Negro's exodus from the Southern states as a function of the greater and lesser migrations that followed World War I and the cessation of large-scale foreign immigration, it should not be forgotten that there were almost 100,000 Negroes in New York in 1910, and that they were largely a migrant population. Philadelphia and Chicago, too, contained increasingly Negro populations after 1880. After all, the nation was on the move cityward and the Negro was a part of it. By 1910, only Washington, D.C., had a larger urban Negro population than New York, and the Negro's movement northward aroused the concerned notice of a number of contemporary observers. But foreign immigration repeatedly reached floodlike proportions, and the Negro migration remained relatively small.

Nonetheless, a significant number of Negroes were attempting to set a foot on the very industrial ladder the immigrant was mounting, and amid the same deplorable conditions of urban poverty and tenement squalor. With varying degrees of speed, the diverse foreign ethnic groups successfully clambered aboard the ongoing society, became a part of it and proceeded to grow with it and adapt to its demands (though at very different rates for each group). In this period of early industrial investment, the Negro remained on the periphery; as strikebreaker and menial service worker, he became the "slave of industry," not a partner in it. Economic dependence and familial dislocation took on a new relevance and has continued to deny him the gradual preparation for the demands of the technological, highly literate society we are now so anxiously inviting him to join.

In the momentous years at the turn of the century, the assumption of Anglo-Saxon superiority and a demanding machine economy led to a tremendous investment in the efficacy of an open door on immigration—contingent, always, on the ability of the melting pot to melt. On a structural level, it never really did; but, as a general behavioral conformity became established, urbanization was easily mistaken for Americanization. The factory, the union, and the promise of material well-being (real or vicarious) laid important ground rules for this level of cultural unity, just as they played their part in expanding the urban condition itself.

Nevertheless, the twin threads of melting pot magic and public school alchemy, despite periodic divergences, started in unity and reunited in a tremendous faith in the ostensible success of both. The public school has consistently maintained a hallowed place in the process. Before the fear for internal security that surrounded the World War I years, and the "Red Scare" phenomenon that followed close upon its heels, social critics and educational reformers made clear that they trusted the effectiveness of the school system in the nation's cities. As one immigrant herself put it, "[T]he public school has done its best for us foreigners and for the country, when it has made us into good Americans." A federal commissioner of education expressed his wonder at the "marvelous" job done by the schools. To Jacob Riis, faith in the real and symbolic power of the "flag flying over the schoolhouse" seemed more than justified. Below the surface, however, and not too far below, the reality was very different.

New York's Superintendent Maxwell called in vain for public response to the problems of immigrants. Settlement house workers tried desperately to fill the gap while waging a campaign to broaden the commitment of public education. With the outbreak of war in Europe, xenophobes lamented the failure of the schools to assimilate, and schoolmen reacted anxiously to the fact of ethnic diversity. (More recently, under changed circumstances, the continuing diversity would be used as evidence of an America made vital by the strains of "pluralism.") Suddenly, in 1916, the U.S. Office of the Interior ran a series of conferences to discuss the role of education in the acculturation of foreigners. Programs were developed to bring schooling into factories to reach those who had no time at the end of the working day. By 1918, the president of New York's Board of Education agreed with the many who complained that the schools had failed miserably in dealing with the problems of heavy foreign immigration.

New York's Board of Estimate commissioned a comprehensive study of the city's public schools in 1911. The $50,000 that the study cost was spent in response to Superintendent Maxwell's feverish attempts to persuade the Board of Estimate that the schools must take a fuller responsibility for the city's school-age children. Paul Hanus of Harvard University conducted the survey and, found, as successive studies continued to find, that the schools with the largest immigrant members were totally unprepared to deal with the rapidly multiplying needs that confronted them.

Contemporary public and private welfare records show that all evils characteristic of an unemployed urban lower class today were disastrously well known to a high proportion of immigrant families caught in the disrupting pressures of poverty and squalor and the flutterings of the business cycle. Of 12.5 million families in the United States, 11 million had an annual income below $380. . . . When jobs were not available to the men of a family for a long period of time, the woman and child might be deserted or forced to become breadwinners. It was these conditions that Lillian Brandt, like many of her settlement house colleagues, found when she reported the dire effects of urban poverty on the immigrant family. According to the Hanus survey and reports of school superintendents, from 1904 to 1922 between 32 and 36 per cent of public school pupils were "average" and making "slow progress" in any given year. Schoolmen regularly pointed out that school failure was a district problem; "excessive retardation," they claimed, was the perennial correlate of lower-class life. Statistical method varied, so that improvement was now affirmed and now denied; but, on the whole, the rates of school failure were astronomical. In the opinion of the state Department of Education, however, New York City's record was considerably better than "elsewhere" in the nation.

While almost all school pupils, immigrant and native-born, were dropouts, school dropouts were employable most of the time. (Fewer than 10 per cent of the school population graduated from high school in 1915.) Indeed, it was for this very reason that the majority of "new" immigrants made their homes in urban centers. Both the immigrant and his children found employment in expanding "manufacturing and mechanical pursuits." Compulsory education beyond fourteen years of age referred only to those without "permanent employment." When higher education finally opened up, it was as a result of completion rates in elementary and high schools—the percentage of high school graduates who attain some college and college entrants who graduate has not increased greatly, even by 1960 figures. George Counts reported, in 1922, how few and how socially select were the children who continued their education to the high school level, making it clear that American education was still much more involved in the production of healthy, minimally literate labor. In the same year, New York City's school superintendent, William Ettinger, set about "Facing the Facts," the same facts, in the system he supervised. This Survey Committee found progressive failure in the high school grades. A 1927 . . . study of truancy in the city echoed the findings of a similar study carried out in 1915, in which Elizabeth Irwin described the high incidence of truancy (and truant employment) in a West Side section of Manhattan "noted for its large proportion of broken homes." Public education had broadened its efforts to care for the health needs of its charges, but few of them found the specifically educational effort relevant to their place in society. Typically, school success came after the establishment of an indigenous ethnic stability (e.g., ethnic business and political organizations grounded in the community) and the subsequent need of a high school diploma education to advance it.

Data compiled for the 1920 census, the last before the door on European immigration was slammed tightly shut, show clearly that the years of schooling attained by native whites of native parentage is separated from the years attained by those of foreign parentage by a similar proportion, which separates the adult employment rate of the former group from the latter. In fact, the level of employment is in proportion to the rate of school retention beyond compulsory attendance age and breaks down with a revealing differential even between native-born of foreign parentage and the foreign-born. For example, foreign-born groups, as a whole, showed a level of adult unemployment smaller only than that of the Negro, while bearing, at the same time, the greatest proportions of 15-, 16-, and 17-year-olds out of school.

Most of the students who now drop out *would never have been* in high school fifty years ago. Students remained in grade school until acceptable standards or school-leaving age [was] attained. Public education was the rubber stamp of economic improvement; rarely has it been the bootstrap. The economic value of an education has been at once a cause and a consequence of its scarcity.

During these years, manpower was the important factor; the factory and the union, rather than the school, were the assimilating agents. In 1909, a Greek-language newspaper told its readers to "become citizens and join labor unions." In Manhattan, only 47 per cent of the school population was even registered at the high school level. The secretary of the city Census Board informed Hanus that the elementary school graduate and the elementary school dropout were generally to be found in "blind alley" occupations in the factory and the shop.

Economic stability for an ethnic group preceded its entry onto the broader middle-class stage via education. The correlation between school achievement and economic status was so high that, in school surveys carried out in the Midwest during the 1920's, it became necessary to separate Scandinavian Americans from other "ethnic" Americans, because the school performance of their children so outdistanced other foreign Midwest groups. And census figures reveal that the degree of economic security among farm-holding Scandinavians (and storekeeping Jews—surprisingly high even in 1920) was much greater than among more characteristically wage-laboring groups. As Theodore Saloutos points out, the Greeks, too, were among the first to make this transition.

There is a hard core of reality behind the story that depicts the entry of the Eastern European Jewish immigrant into small business enterprise[s] and then of his son into the university and the professions. The "business" quality of the ethnic community is not itself the vital ingredient: The key factor is more probably the indigenous grounding of the unit within the ethnic boundary—the establishment of an ethnic middle class before scaling the walls of the dominant society. In this perspective, one is less ready to mythologize the role of the public school.

While school dropouts were generally employable, the Negro, for the most part, worked sporadically and as a reserve force. If the immigrant was vulnerable in his lower-class status, it was usually the individual, not the group, who was throttled by swings of the economic pendulum. For the Negro, caste, through color, added a much more pervasively ethnic dimension to the rigors of lower-class life.

As one might expect, the marginal place of the mass Negro was accurately reflected in the educational arena. With no evidence of any considerable economic progress, and with a history of circular justifications for Negro inferiority, the Negro was eminently suited to being placed outside the general faith in both the melting pot and the public school. Despite the Hanus survey and the conditions that made it necessary, the complaints of school personnel led the school system to undertake a study of its "Colored School Children" during the very time when the Hanus findings were being reported. There were [fewer] than 8,000 Negro school children in a school population of more than 700,000; yet a separate study seemed to be justified. Both reports found the rates of truancy and retardation in the city to be outrageously high. Among the populations surveyed in the two reports, school retardation was discovered to be progressive: The child was performing less adequately at the end of his school career than at the beginning. Hanus placed the blame on the combination of inappropriate family preparation among immigrants, the exploitation of children by parents, and the totally inadequate conditions with which the school was prepared to meet its new responsibilities. At least 33 new school buildings were needed; provisions were long overdue for about 2 per cent of the school population that could be classified as mentally defective; and ungraded classes were immediately required to accommodate 15,000 children. Frances Blascoer, who conducted the study of "Colored School Children," after having agreed with the Hanus observations and acknowledging the particular prejudice that made the school that much more painful and ineffective for the Negro child, reported that the Negro's unique educational problems demanded a rather different educational treatment. She advised the Negro to give up hope of the factory floor and develop a small, separate, and self-employing ghetto economy.

While one may be tempted to acknowledge Miss Blascoer's recommendations as pertinent to the Negro's need for independence and indigenous growth, she made it clear that, despite her sincere concern for the urban poor, this was a "child race" and, as yet, unready to compete in a highly "civilized" world. She castigated the Urban League for its efforts to train Negro social workers, because it was clear to her that the Negro worker would do only serious harm; the white worker alone must provide regenerative help. The Negro was advised to move away from the areas of employment that left him standing as a blatant scar, the very areas through which real industrial progress was being made. Blascoer's vision for the school went no further than the economy that excluded the Negro so extensively, instead of using the school as a way of leading to Negro mobility. The separate definition of Negro failure in school may be seen as a symbol of the failure and the animosity that underlined his life within the city and as an accurate measure of the school's extremely limited power to cope with broad social issues.

The Hanus and Blascoer surveys were carried out during a time when several of the nation's other cities were examining their school systems. The first decades of the century found schoolmen across the country searching for greater "efficiency" in dealing with greatly increased populations. Philadelphia, too, looked Janus-like, with one face toward the system as a whole and another toward the Negro. With a sophistication that must, at the very least, make for unease in the mind of the modern educator, Philadelphia's study of Negro school children showed sympathetic understanding of the problems that beset the ex-slave: Perhaps the issue was really one of basically different cultures. Very possibly, the Negro performed laudably by measures other than those used to judge the "superior" (*my* quotes, *their* tone) white race. Apparently, different measures were applicable and, in a sense, justified, because, with whites, school failure had meaning in the economic market place; with blacks, it bore no relevance to the improvement of their place in society.

Comparisons such as those I criticized at the outset as pseudo-historical tend to ignore the push and pull of events at any given time. Abstracted from time, sociological parallels may confuse rather than clarify. We should realize that urban Negroes, at the turn of the twentieth century (and those who followed), were confronted by very different conditions than were the foreign immigrants at the turn of the century. The gap between Negro and European immigrants, as groups, has steadily widened, so that the difference in their respective rates of social and economic progress has been intensified by changing economic demands and by the appropriateness of the tools with which the lower classes, at any given time, have met those demands.

The school system that served the expanding industrial society has changed little in the interim. What *has* changed is that success in school has become essential to security and status. Big-city public schools have never, in fact, done the job they are now expected to do. In the face of today's urban poor, nostalgia for 1910 is at best a tempting but suspiciously convenient method of presenting facts.

Early Boycotts of Segregated Schools: The Case of Springfield, Ohio, 1922-23 *

August Meier and Elliott Rudwick

Recent agitation over *de facto* segregation in Northern cities is not simply a product of the civil-rights revolution of the 1960's. Actually, it is a continuation of the struggle against Jim Crow schools that many Negroes . . . waged throughout the nineteenth and twentieth centuries.

During the antebellum period, those Northern communities that offered Negroes an elementary education generally created separate schools. Negroes sought integrated education by petitioning the public authorities, conducting litigation in the courts, and working to secure antidiscrimination legislation. In the most famous of these campaigns, Boston Negroes, having failed in their appeals to the Massachusetts judiciary, transferred their efforts to the legislature, which, in 1855, made it illegal to refuse a Negro

* This article was based primarily upon research in the local daily Springfield newspapers and the major black weekly in Ohio, the Cleveland *Gazette;* the annual reports of the Springfield Board of Education; records in Clark County, Ohio, Courthouse; the NAACP Archives in the Library of Congress; and interviews with two residents of Springfield who participated in the protest and boycott against the segregated schools.

Reprinted from *The American Quarterly,* Volume 20, Number 4 (Winter, 1968), pp. 745-58, by permission of The University of Pennsylvania, publisher, and the Authors. Copyright, 1968, Trustees of The University of Pennsylvania.

child admission to his neighborhood school. Ohio Negroes were less successful. The Black Laws of 1829 excluded them from public schools entirely. Not until 1848 was legislation passed creating public schools for Negroes, and then they were segregated schools, for which the state never provided adequate financing.

After the Civil War, other Northern Negroes followed the example set by those in Massachusetts and took the initiative in securing the passage of laws barring public school segregation in most of the Northern states. In Ohio, agitation and litigation by Negroes and their friends proved unsuccessful for two decades, and the colored schools remained clearly substandard institutions; finally, in 1887, the legislature, pushed largely by the militancy of both blacks and whites in the Western Reserve, passed the Arnett Bill, requiring mixed schools. Although the statutes were often flouted in areas bordering the South, Negroes in most major Northern and Western cities attended integrated schools by the opening of the twentieth century. In the wake of the Great Migration of Negroes to the North that began during World War I, however, numerous boards of education actively promoted policies that resulted in racial segregation, and Negro opposition generally proved incapable of reversing the trend.

Not only is protest against school segregation in the urban North very old, but the use of what today we call "nonviolent direct action" also has a long, if sporadic, history. As early as 1865, Chicago Negroes initiated a boycott that led the board of education to eliminate Jim Crow schools soon after they had been established. Two years later, Buffalo colored people, for a couple of weeks, staged a school sit-in and boycott, which ended in failure. At the turn of the century, Alton, Illinois, and East Orange, New Jersey, witnessed prolonged, though unsuccessful, boycotts in response to the inauguration of Jim Crow classes. In the 1920's, the boycott technique was used again in a handful of communities during the wave of proscriptive regulations enacted by Northern school boards. Of this group of boycotts, the longest and most dramatic occurred in Springfield, Ohio.

Prior to 1887, when the state legislature repealed the law authorizing educational segregation, Springfield had three Jim Crow schools. In response to the 1887 statute, the school board integrated the pupils and summarily dismissed all the Negro teachers. Records at the turn of the century show that, although about half of the colored children were concentrated in three schools, there was not a single institution in the entire city that did not have some Negro students.

Two segments of the Springfield population, one white and the other Negro, however, favored and, from time to time, agitated for the resegregation of the schools. In 1898, it was reported that "a few misguided Afro-Americans who profess to be lovers of the race are seeking to re-establish the separate school system in our city, in order, they say, to get [Negro] teachers." Four years later, a group of white mothers protested to the board of education, alleging that their children were outnumbered by Negroes in the Fair Street school. School integration was maintained, however, until

1922, even in the face of a prejudiced milieu that produced the Springfield race riots of 1904 and 1906.

Some Springfield whites averred that the riots were caused by an increase in the Negro population. Census figures, however, indicate that its growth was negligible until the Great Migration that began with World War I, when the vast demand for unskilled labor brought many Negroes from the South to Springfield and other Northern cities. In the decade 1910–20, the Negro population climbed from [fewer] than five thousand to somewhat more than seven thousand—an increase of 40 per cent. Actually, this gain was small in absolute numbers, and the white population also rose rapidly, with Negroes forming around 11 per cent of the city's population in both years. The whites' impression of a sizable increase in the Negro population was, of course, heightened by the tendency of the migrants to settle in the southwestern portion of the city served by the Dibert (later the Fulton) elementary school. There, the proportion of Negroes in the student body rose from about 35 per cent at the turn of the century to about 45 per cent in 1912–14, and to 62 per cent in 1920–21. This white awareness of a "Negro influx" helped to bring on a third riot in 1921, and renewed efforts to resegregate the schools.

Early in 1920, the board of education, in anticipation of the opening of three new schools in 1922, redistricted the school zones. A report later published by the National Urban League noted that, soon after this action of the board, the school superintendent, George E. McCord, interested a few, selected Negroes in the establishment of separate schools. According to the League, "These Negroes represented a wide diversity of personal interests: some with political aspirations, some cherishing the notion of independent educational development, and some with the more immediately practical hope of employment as teachers either for themselves or for their children." Mrs. John Collins, Mrs. Forest Speaks, and Mrs. Jane Lee, three socially prominent Negro ladies who wanted to teach and were fully qualified applicants, informed by the board of education that it could not hire them because there were no Negro schools, thereupon obtained the signatures of over three hundred colored women to a petition urging the creation of a segregated elementary school. The petition was presented to the board by Mr. Forest Speaks, a clerk at a local printing company and state grand secretary of the Negro Oddfellows. A group known as the Progressive Civic League countered with its own petition, signed by twelve hundred people who urged the board to select all teachers in the "regular way," without discrimination or segregation. The Springfield branch of the NAACP held a mass meeting to discuss the question and appointed a committee to take steps against the move to establish segregated schools. The committee was composed of the physician Dr. Richard E. Peteford, who had served as branch president for the year 1918–19, and two attorneys: George W. Daniels and Sully Jaymes, the president of the Great Lakes District Conference of the NAACP. In a statement addressed to the superintendent and board of education, these men applauded the idea of hiring Negro teachers but voiced their fear that the request might "be used as an excuse to fasten upon this community that outrageous, un-American, undemocratic and unchristian [sic] institution of Separate, Segregated and Jim-Crow Schools," to the "possible temporary financial and political benefit" of "a few self-serving people," but an "everlasting moral detriment to . . . the entire community."

In May, 1922, by a vote of three to two, the board decided to make Fulton an all-Negro elementary school. Fulton was situated in an old, middle-class neighborhood, which contained many Negroes, but which, in the recollections of old residents, was also "full of whites," a situation that suggests that it was not unusual at that time for Negroes to have white neighbors. The school also served an adjacent subdivision popularly known as "Needmore," so named because it was an impoverished ghetto inhabited chiefly by recent Southern migrants. There was more need of decent housing, paved streets, and sidewalks here than in any other part of town. Some of its residents were so poverty-stricken that they took sheets of tin from a neighboring city dump to construct their hovels. The board planned to create a segregated institution at Fulton by transferring all the white pupils and filling their places with Negroes from other schools.

Meanwhile, for the first time in almost forty years, the school board had authorized the employment of Negro teachers. By the end of August, it had secured twelve Negro teachers and a principal, R. W. Bullock, a graduate of the Presbyterian institution, Knoxville College, Knoxville, Tennessee. Although it had been argued that the separate school would provide employment for Springfield Negroes, only two local persons were appointed. One was Jane Lee, who had helped circulate the petition for a separate school.

The board justified its actions in the name of the expressed will of the Negro community and cited the support of the two leading Negro clergymen—Elmer W. B. Curry, of the Second Baptist Church, and T. D. Scott, of the North Street African Methodist Episcopal Church. Both pastored churches that, in the words of an old Springfield resident, "catered to all the educated and cultured Negroes in the city." In these two churches were the few professionals, the skilled laborers, and "those who worked in service for the very wealthy whites."

The leadership of both the supporters and the opponents of separate schools appears to have been drawn primarily from these two churches. The local NAACP branch was also led by the elite of the community and was likewise split on the issue of school segregation. In the face of the cleavage, the NAACP was practically immobilized for effective protest. Old residents recalled that the branch had "turned pink tea," that "every time there was a crisis here, we couldn't get the local NAACP to help us," that "as a working organization the NAACP went flop."

The NAACP's national office, it is true, was very much interested in the case and encouraged the local branch to support actively the protest effort. Reviewing the matter in a report to the national board of directors some months later, the executive secretary asserted that, in May, 1922, the local branch had presented a petition against the segregation plan, signed by nine hundred Negroes of the Fulton School District; that, late in September, 1922, an attorney speaking at a mass meeting had pledged the NAACP's assistance in the fight; and that the national office had sent field staff members to Springfield to lend what aid they could. Nevertheless, effective protest action was clearly organized outside of the NAACP, and, all in all, the local branch seemed incapable of making itself relevant to the situation in Springfield. Characteristically, a 1922 meeting consisted of the reading of a paper on "The Disarmament Conference and What It Means to All American Citizens." This is all the more surprising because, among the branch's officers were four outstanding leaders in the protest movement: the physician T. W. Burton, the dentist Clarence F. Keller, attorney George W. Daniels, and, most notably, the branch president, Sully Jaymes.

In part, the split in the Negro community over the school segregation issue appears to have been associated with a political cleavage. In spite of the fragmentary evidence that survives concerning Negro participation in local politics at the time, two things, at least, are clear. One is that, as will be shown below, the Clark County Republican leadership was segregationist in its attitude. The second is that Negroes with political aspirations in Republican-dominated Springfield took their cues from the white Republican chieftains and were, therefore, obliged to support the proposal for separate schools.

Two of the leading Negro politicians of the city, both of whom held quasi-political patronage jobs, were George W. Eliot, school board janitor and president of the Center Street YMCA, and Olie V. Gregory, librarian of the Springfield Bar and Law Library Association. Both were unwilling to talk out against the segregation at Fulton because of their political loyalties. Forest Speaks, the Oddfellows leader who had promoted separate schools, and the two elite ministers, Curry and Scott, were also political types who spoke for the Republicans. It is not possible today to ascertain the rewards that these Springfield leaders personally received from their political connection. Yet, as Ralph Bunche has pointed out, it was a common pattern at that time for Negro religious and fraternal leaders to be closely allied with the Republican Party and to receive for their support small favors, such as an occasional minor job and small amounts of money, and political patronage.

On the other hand, the leaders in the protest against school segregation —men like Daniels and, especially, Jaymes—were Democrats and advocates of the view that Negroes should be "independent" and "divide their vote," rather than remain unswervingly loyal to the Republicans, who had deserted them. It would appear likely that, just as the standpatters were identified with the local Republican machine, so many of the leaders and participants in the protest movement were supporters of the Democratic

Party. Moreover, Democratic strength among the protesters grew in the course of the controversy. Since Negroes were generally Republican in this period, very likely it was the prejudiced attitudes of the local Republican influentials that caused this sharp political cleavage in the Negro community.

With the Springfield NAACP immobilized because of the split within the Negro community, the Negroes who wished to combat the plans of the school board accordingly established the Civil Rights Protective League about the middle of July. In fact, the appeal for aid made to the NAACP national office came from this group rather than from the NAACP branch. The League's leaders were a distinctly elite group of Negroes. The president was Charles L. Johnson, reputedly the relative of a prominent local white businessman, and manager of the Champion Chemical Company plant. The dentist, Dr. Keller, was vice-president of the League. Other important leaders were James W. Leigh, a coal and ice dealer; Mrs. Arthur Riggs, whose husband was a chemist at the Champion plant; David Wilborn, an undertaker; Charles Green, a postman; and attorneys Daniels and Jaymes. Some laboring-class people were also active in the League: Mrs. Minnie Clark, its recording secretary, was listed in the City Directory as a helper's wife. Of thirty-two members arrested in November, 1922, during a picketing incident, ten were in the professional and business class, three others were also in white-collar occupations, two were college students, nine were skilled workers, and eight were in the unskilled laboring class.

Among the ministers, the League's staunchest support came from the Reverend Pleas P. Broughton of the Mt. Zion Baptist Church, a "hell-fire" church whose members were mainly recent Southern migrants [with] limited schooling, living in "Needmore." The Reverend Mr. Broughton opened Mt. Zion for the League's weekly meetings. At the first mass meeting there, a "deafening applause" greeted the suggestion of David Wilborn, the undertaker, that preachers who refused to take Sunday collections for the League "should be run out of town." League president Johnson condemned conciliatory Negro leadership, telling the audience that Negroes in Dayton and Columbus lost their battles to prevent school segregation because "their leaders threw them down." The assembled citizens of the Fulton district voted not to send their children to the school when it opened on September 5, and they agreed to set up a picket line in order to increase the boycott's effectiveness. The League's strategy was to use this form of what would now be called "direct action" as a device to force the school segregation issue to the attention of the courts. In an effort to involve the courts, the leaders promised legal aid to boycotters arrested for violating the compulsory attendance law, and Johnson even stated that, if the school authorities failed to prosecute the boycotting parents, the League would file a taxpayers' suit compelling the board to obey the state law. It was also announced that three attorneys would handle the legal work: George W. Daniels, Sully Jaymes, and A. N. Summers, formerly a judge on the State

Supreme Court. Judge Summers had been identified as a friend of the Negroes from the time he had first run for city solicitor in 1885 on a ticket that included two Negroes running for township office. *

Superintendent McCord at first warned Negroes against using pickets to keep children from school, and he promised that the state truancy law would be strictly enforced. League officials defiantly distributed handbills announcing, "If you don't want jim crow schools, keep your children home." When school opened on September 5, pickets surrounded Fulton, and, though estimates varied, press reports made it clear that [fewer] than half [of] the colored students attended that day. League leaders recorded the names of children crossing the picket line and planned home visitations. Johnson begged truant officers to arrest parents who participated in the boycott. By the end of the first week, the League was publicly branding its Negro opponents as traitors to the race. Picket lines of over fifty persons greeted the Negro teachers with such signs as "THEY TEACH IN JIM CROW SCHOOLS," and "WE WILL NOT SELL OUT FOR A JOB." A contingent picketed the home of the Reverend Mr. Curry. When the police chief refused to grant a permit for a parade at the school, League members defiantly marched nearby with their banners. At a mass meeting celebrating the success of the first week of the boycott, Johnson claimed that about 75 per cent of the Fulton children remained absent—a figure in substantial agreement with that of the school superintendent.

At the start of the second week of picketing, the League opened headquarters in an abandoned Baptist church directly opposite the Fulton School and made arrangements to serve hot lunches to the pickets. At the weekly mass meeting held on September 14, Johnson reminded the League members that, regardless of the sacrifice, integration was essential, since it was crucial for Negro and white children to "get to know each other." He recalled that, to end Jim Crow schools in 1887, Negroes had sacrificed Negro teachers, and, in 1922, they were prepared to do it again: "If we cannot have colored teachers except in segregated schools we do not want them at all." The next mass meeting drew a capacity crowd that overflowed into the street and contributed $103.50 toward legal expenses.

For over two months, the school board failed to prosecute those who kept their children out of school. Reluctant to summon the boycotting parents into court, it tried to undermine the movement by placing pressures on the poorest and most vulnerable of the boycotting parents. Before the end of September, League leaders reported that the loyalties of some parents in the "Needmore" area wavered after the school board's business manager visited their homes. Accordingly, League representatives went from house to house countering his arguments. On one occasion, two League workers called upon a poor widow whose children continued to attend school despite her promise to keep them out. In the middle of their talk with the lady, the Reverend Mr. Curry's son appeared with a gift of a sack of flour—and this occurred at the very time that the minister was disclaiming participation in the controversy. The following month, protest leaders charged that the Springfield Social Service Bureau had denied assistance to a needy widow for insisting that she would keep her four children out of the illegal Jim Crow school.

Morale remained high, and few children attended the school, despite these covert pressures from local authorities. Even in the rain and mud of late October weather, from ten to fifteen demonstrators, mostly women, lined the street daily and watched the Negro teachers drive up to school in city automobiles and be escorted inside by the policeman on duty there. When Principal Bullock left for Kentucky to visit his sick mother, a committee of "lady-pickets" was at the railroad depot to see him off, urging him not to return.

Prominent visitors from out of town, like Harry C. Smith, editor of the Negro weekly Cleveland *Gazette* and a former state senator, and R. B. Barkus, grand chancellor of the Negro Knights of Pythias of Ohio and special counsel in the state attorney-general's office, encouraged the demonstrators in their activities.

Since it was an election year, League leaders tried to use the Negro vote as a weapon in their struggle. They sent questionnaires to Republican candidates asking if they belonged to the Ku Klux Klan and if they believed in separate schools. William Copenhaver, chairman of the Clark County Republican executive committee, and father of H. C. Copenhaver, one of the school board members who voted for the segregated schools, informed a Negro leader that whites were running the city, and that it was the Negro's place to vote for the Republicans but not to question their policy in regard to the race's interests. League officials sponsored a boycott of a Republican rally, and Charles L. Johnson declared, "If necessary we should defeat the entire county ticket." Although state Republican leaders indicated concern about Negro dissatisfaction, there is no evidence that local party officials were disturbed.

From the beginning, however, the League had placed its chief hope in litigation. Anxious to get the case into the courts, where they were confident of victory, in September Charles Johnson and James Leigh filed suit in the court of common pleas, requesting that the board be enjoined from keeping white students out of Fulton. On October 30, Judge Frank W. Geiger granted a temporary injunction, but the board made no efforts to reassign the white children. With the injunction going unenforced, and no other progress evident, by November signs of sagging morale became clear to League leaders, who envisioned disintegration of their movement if the controversy were not settled before the arrival of winter weather. Moreover, school authorities continued to refuse to arrest parents for the truancy of their children. Thus, more dramatic steps seemed required to compel a real confrontation in the courts. On the morning of November 7, therefore, the demonstrators arrived at the school, one hundred and fifty strong, prepared to block the entrance of the teachers, even at the risk of arrest. When the automobile arrived with Bullock and several teachers, the crowd surged into the street, and some pickets jumped on the running board. In the melee, a few rocks were thrown, and it was reported that one hit Bullock and the policeman on duty. More police arrived, and the crowd broke up. But no pupils whatsoever reported for school that morning. Next day, thirty-two persons, including several leaders of the League, were arrested.

Other arrests followed, for the board now took sterner measures and intensified its campaign of intimidating lower-class parents by threatening them with prosecution for the truancy of their children. Five parents—all unskilled working-class people—were charged in magistrate's court with violating the compulsory attendance law. The courts, however, took a more sympathetic view than did the school authorities. On November 28, the case against Laura Jackson, a Negro laundress, was dismissed after she testified about her unsuccessful efforts to register her children at a school other than Fulton. The magistrate took the remaining cases under advisement, awaiting the decision on the lawsuit that the League had instituted for a permanent injunction against the school board. A couple of weeks later, proceedings against Waldo Bailey, a laborer accused of rioting and assaulting the teachers in the November 7 demonstration, resulted in an even more significant victory for the Civil Rights Protective League. Defense attorneys admitted that Bailey had jumped on the car but denied that he had committed an assault. The jury found him not guilty and subsequently the police prosecutor dropped the other cases.

The picketing and the boycott continued throughout the fall and winter of 1922–23. Negroes claimed that, of more than two hundred and fifty Negroes assigned to the school, daily attendance never exceeded fifty. Meanwhile, the proceedings on the Negroes' request for an injunction against the school board were taking their course. In testimony submitted in January, school officials denied that they had established segregation at Fulton, claimed that white children were, in fact, enrolled as pupils there, and contended that race had nothing to do with the assignment of teachers.

On January 31, 1923, Common Pleas Judge Frank N. Krapp, who had defeated Frank Geiger in the November election, granted a permanent injunction restraining the local school board from transferring children on the basis of race or color to or from the Fulton school. Krapp dismissed the board's contentions as "pure sophistry." He declared that, except for the first day of the school year, when three white children appeared at Fulton, not a single white child attended, and that neither the superintendent nor the board of education expected any to enroll. Krapp offered the board two alternatives: 1) Close Fulton until the start of the following school year, and meanwhile transfer the pupils to other schools; or 2) reopen Fulton immediately, giving all children the choice of attending there or any other school. The judge ruled that, to prevent hardship, the white children who formerly attended Fulton could remain where they were for the remainder of the school year, but he stressed that, beginning in the fall, no school assignments were to be based on race. The board ignored his specific directives and simply authorized its attorney to appeal the decision. Negroes discovered that the principals of nearby schools were still refusing to admit Fulton children.

In May, the board began deliberations about the Negro teachers at the Fulton school. All were graduates of colleges or normal schools and had some previous teaching experience before coming to Springfield. The board regarded their work as "very satisfactory." Nevertheless, the superintendent postponed recommending their reappointment. By the end of the summer, with no decision from the appellate court and with Fulton therefore scheduled to reopen on an integrated basis, McCord dismissed every one of the Negro teachers and replaced them with whites. Almost a quarter of a century would elapse before any Negroes were again hired as teachers in the Springfield public schools.

Two weeks after Judge Krapp's ruling, leading officials in the school system were implicated with the Ku Klux Klan. On February 14, the Springfield Police Department raided the Klan's local headquarters and confiscated its membership rolls. Listed among the 681 names were several teachers; the school board architect; two school board members, including H. C. Copenhaver, son of the chairman of the Republican executive committee of Clark County—and Superintendent McCord. Some issued denials; others remained silent. McCord, who had permitted a Ku Klux Klan meeting in the local high school auditorium a week before the exposé, at first called it "one of the prettiest frameups I have ever seen." A week later, however, he not only admitted membership in the Klan, but added, "I'm mighty glad of it. I think it is the best 100 percent American organization in the country today."

Although the Klan supported the pro-McCord slate in the school board election of 1923, the Negroes were unable to make the Fulton school controversy a campaign issue. Neither McCord's connection with the KKK nor his role in the Fulton controversy hurt his prestige as much as the fact that, for his own political reasons, he had fired several popular white teachers. It was these dismissals that made him the "main issue" in the school board election of 1923. Thus, the Fulton school matter was not a significant campaign issue. Indeed, although the board candidates endorsed by the Klan were defeated by over 3,500 votes, the KKK emerged victorious in contests for the city commission and the post of police judge.

Shortly after the election, McCord resigned under pressure as superintendent, and the board of education authorized its attorney to withdraw the Fulton case from the Appellate Court. It is not known to what extent the new board of education abided by Judge Krapp's decision. In its annual reports, the board no longer supplied information about school boundaries and the number of Negro pupils. Interviews with Springfield Negroes suggest that whites residing in the Fulton district were soon able to transfer their children to other schools, while Negroes were denied that privilege. By 1936, the board's Annual Report once again contained data on race and boundary lines. At that time, the neighborhood was still a mixed one.

Nevertheless, the Fulton school district, its borders substantially changed, was 97 per cent Negro.

Thus, despite the support of the courts, despite the exposure and defeat of the Klan candidates for the school board, the Springfield educational officials were able by various tactics to retain essentially the system of segregation. As in other places—like Alton, Illinois, in 1908, East Orange, New Jersey, in 1906, and Dayton, Ohio, in 1926—where the boycott was also employed as a device to resist the introduction of school segregation, the victory of the Springfield Negroes was an empty one.

In retrospect, the defeat of the Springfield demonstrators would appear to have been almost inevitable. Given the increasingly racist social context in which they lived, even a more unified Negro community could not have stemmed the rising tide of segregation that accompanied the Great Migration of Negroes to the Northern cities. The Negroes' position was further weakened by their political impotence and the hostility of the leaders in the party that had traditionally assisted them. The remarkable thing is not that school segregation was successfully introduced in Springfield during the early 1920's, but that some Negroes were able to resist this effort as effectively as they did.

6. The Fate of Educational Reform

There is a benign view of American history. It sees in the twentieth century the emergence of a solid consensus about the need for liberal reform. Begun by the Progressives, set back perhaps in the aftermath of World War I and the mindlessness of the 1920's, the liberal consensus triumphed definitively in the New Deal, which represented the end of serious opposition to the use of the state to promote social welfare. The steady amelioration of social problems has marked the triumph of liberal theory, and we can look forward to even greater improvements in the lot of the poor, the aged, the sick, and the ignorant.

During the last several years, a less optimistic and more critical view of twentieth-century history has surfaced. Revisionist historians have attacked virtually all aspects of the argument sketched above. To them, the dominant theme in the twentieth century has been the attempt to adapt existing power relations to the development of a corporate industrial society. The prominence of the expert and of bureaucratic forms of organization characterizes the attempt to ensure orderly, efficient social development. In this view, reforms have represented not so much humanitarian social change as a way of maintaining the system by reducing the friction caused by unruliness, unhappiness, disease, and other social ills. Liberal reforms, revisionists argue, have neither lessened social stratification, significantly changed the distribution of wealth, nor redistributed power.

Educational history only recently has begun to reflect these revisionist themes about the nature of twentieth-century reform. However, the dissenting view of American history raises a number of serious questions about the nature and role of educational reform. At one level, there is the problem of progressive educational thought. Should Dewey, to take one example, be regarded as a champion of liberating reform, or was his writing compatible with the emphasis on order and control that historians are finding in the social thought of other liberals? The same kind of question can be asked of actual educational innovations. Does one view the introduction of industrial education, for example, as an attempt to provide a new and relevant form of educational experience or as an attempt to ensure a stream of properly trained workers for the lower slots in the occupational hierarchy?

The interpretation of the recent history of educational reform is of the utmost contemporary importance. One of the most difficult questions for current reform is the degree to which educational purposes and results can be changed within existing structures. If educational structures (the way in which schools are organized in relation to each other, controlled, financed, and administered) are basically sound, reform becomes a matter of dealing with specific problems, such as curriculum, teacher training, pedagogy, and pupil-teacher ratio. But, if the structure itself is the source of the problem, then what must be changed is the very form of education; reform, in this view, must mean the fundamental alteration of educational structure through the redistribution of power and resources. The information on which to choose between these points of view lies partly in historical experience. If one adopts the more benign, liberal view of recent American history, it follows that all the necessary changes in education can be made without altering its fundamental structure. On the other hand, if one views modern education as shaped, like other modern institutions, to fit an industrial, corporate society, reform must mean a recasting of basic features.

The articles in this final section address these themes. In particular, three of them directly approach the problem of liberal interpretations of reform. In the first, Clarence J. Karier presents a bold and significant view of the weaknesses of twentieth-century liberalism, especially as reflected in the work of John Dewey and naive assumptions about the relation of science to social progress. David K. Cohen and Marvin Lazerson, in their description of twentieth-century educational history as an adaptation of schooling to large-scale corporate capitalism, point out contradictions and evasions inherent in liberal ideology, especially in beliefs about the relationship of schooling to social problems and about the contribution of meritocracy to equality. Their thesis is reinforced by the perspective on progressive education in the next selection, Daniel Calhoun's brilliant exploration of the mechanisms through which the adaptation of people to an urban environment has been fostered throughout American history. In the last essay, I try to show how the foremost statement of the liberal-reform position on contemporary education, Charles Silberman's *Crisis in the Classroom,* represents an evasion of uncomfortable questions about both past and present.

Liberalism and the Quest for Orderly Change

Clarence J. Karier

As conflict in American culture increases and the idea of revolution is no longer dismissed as some absurd anarchist dream but increasingly entertained by men of more moderate persuasion, more and more voices can be heard echoing a common warning. The warning is this: The new left must either temper its attacks on the military, corporate, and educational establishment in this country, or we will all suffer the wrath of a fascist nightmare. Put in these terms, the new left is made responsible for the coming American fascism. The usual analysis proceeds with the notion that the attack on the liberal center from both the right and left weakens and eventually destroys democratic institutions. The process begins with the left questioning the mythologies that sustain bourgeois society, thus threatening the security of those in power, and ends with a repressive fascist order. In this sense, the more the left agitates, the more the fascist right can be expected to grow. There are few political and social analysts in this country who seriously doubt the possibility that, given an open confrontation, the fascist[s] would win. Virtually every observer seems to predict that a socialism of the right, not the left, would emerge. It is interesting that, in times of severe crisis, most liberals can be relied upon to move to the right rather than to the left of the political spectrum.

There are, of course, a number of problems with the above analysis. It is clear that this analysis is created by liberals who see themselves as the guardian[s] of a kind of middle-class democracy, who abhor conflict and violence, and who take pride in endorsing reasoned intelligent change. Espousing the moderate humanitarian virtues of the enlightenment, these liberals see themselves as victims of extremist thought and action on both the left and right. Such an analysis, in effect, justifies the liberal's capitulation to fascist power. It was, after all, the agitation of the left that forced the liberals to support the fascist solution for law and order in the streets and the universities. Thus, the liberals are quick to point out that the responsibility for the destruction of democratic institutions lies with their

From *The History of Education Quarterly,* Volume 12, Number 1 (Spring, 1972), pp. 57–77. Used by permission.

intemporate brothers on the left and not with any failure or perhaps fatal flaw in liberal philosophy. Although such an analysis is heavy on justification, it is relatively light on explanation. It does not, for example, explain how, despite the strong, pragmatic, liberal influence in American social, political, economic, and educational institutions for the past half century, the problems of race, poverty, and militarism have been exacerbated rather than alleviated. Such an analysis, furthermore, does not help us to understand just why it is that, when the chips are down, liberals can be expected to move to support a fascist order rather than an equalitarian revolution.

Without suggesting a scapegoat view of the past, it might be fruitful to re-examine critically some of the key tenets of the twentieth-century liberal's faith. A more critical view of that faith might reveal some of its major sources of weakness as well as a more realistic assessment of its strengths. Such an analysis might also shed some light on current problems. If, for example, we had fully appreciated the liberal's commitment to expert knowledge over populist opinion, or his desire for unity, order, and universalism over respect for idiosyncratic needs of individuals and groups, we might have more realistically anticipated, or at least understood, his stand on such confrontations as Ocean Hill–Brownsville.

The roots of the current crisis in American culture lie deeply imbedded in both the social and intellectual history of the last one hundred years. In a very real sense, the crisis is a result of both the success and the failure of the enlightenment philosophy of progress. The collective side of that philosophy, with its scientifically organized technology and computer-managed bureaucracy, has become a reality; on the other side, however, individual freedom, dignity, and well-being have not fared so well. Caught up in collective institutional progress, the individual has become a means rather than an end to social order. Both the philosopher of nineteenth-century classical liberalism, John Stuart Mill, and the philosopher of twentieth-century liberalism, John Dewey, were centrally concerned with this issue. Both agreed, in principle, that the enlightened society must strive to achieve the greater happiness of the greater number. They disagreed, however, on how this was to be achieved. While Mill maintained a mistrust of state power and discussed freedom in terms of freedom from government interference, the new liberals reversed this process and saw individual freedom tied to a positive use of state power. In this context, positive liberalism means more than just the opposite of negative liberalism. The use of unchecked state power to control the future through shaping the thought, action, and character of its citizens could ultimately lead to a totalitarian polity. The basic assumptions of many who espoused the philosophy of positive liberalism were succinctly put by Isaiah Berlin in his *Four Essays on Liberty* when he said:

> First, that all men have one true purpose, and one only, that of rational self-direction; second, that the ends of all rational beings must of necessity fit into a single universal, harmonious pattern, which some men may be able to discern more clearly than others; third, that all

conflict, and consequently all tragedy, is due solely to the clash of reason with the irrational or the insufficiently rational—the immature and undeveloped elements in life—whether individual or communal, and that such clashes are, in principle, avoidable, and for wholly rational beings impossible; finally, that when all men have been made rational, they will obey the rational laws of their own natures, which are one and the same in them all, and so be at once wholly law-abiding and wholly free.

To be sure, not all positive liberals held all these assumptions. They were, however, implicit in the thought and action of most.

Whether it was the negative freedom of Mill or the positive freedom of Dewey, each, in his own way, became a philosophic justification for the dominant economic organization of the period. By the time John Dewey assumed the role of philosophic leader in America, the laissez-faire idea, which characterized much of the nineteenth-century economic rhetoric, was beginning to be replaced by the theme of a managed corporate economy, more characteristic of the twentieth century. As capital began to be organized at the end of the century in new and unique ways, the corporate state of the twentieth century was born. Classical liberalism, with its philosophic justification of a competitive economy, private property, individualism, and freedom from state interference, gave way to the new liberalism that espoused controlled economy, state planning, group thought, and managed change.

Behind this ideological change from a laissez-faire liberalism to a state-welfare liberalism existed social, political, and economic conflict of a violent nature. Violence was not new to frontier-minded America, nor was it new to the immigrant worker desperately trying to survive in a competitive industrial society. What was new, however, was the emergence of the corporate mass technological society and, with it, the rise of a middle-class liberalism that eschewed violence, conflict, and rugged individualism. The new liberals criticized the ends (private profit) but not the means (scientifically organized technology) of the emerging corporate society. They repeatedly expressed their faith in the rational knowledge of the expert and rejected the irrationalism of the masses. Fearing the potential for violence and chaos implicit in the uncontrolled immigrant masses of our urban ghettoes, the new liberal turned increasingly toward the development of nonviolent but coercive means of social control.

The new liberals directed the nation's social thought and action toward an acceptance of a compulsory state in which the individual would be "scientifically" shaped and controlled so as to fulfill the nation's destiny. Such a compulsory state would as easily require compulsory schooling as military service. Rejecting both the classical liberal's rhetoric concerning individual autonomy as well as his "robber baron" practices, many new liberals turned to some form of state socialism. In the process, he turned to the social science expert for knowledge that would control and shape that state. The rhetoric of the new liberalism, whether in politics or education, reflected a key concern for more effective and efficient means of social control in order to eliminate conflict and to establish the harmonious organic community. Some of these men looked to a highly romanticized version of the nineteenth-century American village as a source of community. Others opted for a future in which scientific intelligence might rule out bloody conflicts and overt coercion as a means of social control. The new "science" of psychology applied to the schooling of the masses could be used to prevent revolution by committing the children of the disinherited to the larger more universal social order through a process of internalizing the shared goals and ideal of the controlling middle class.

The immigrant was often viewed as a threat to social order. By 1900, America was a land of strangers. Approximately half of the population was foreign-born or children of foreign-born. The real threat came when the flow of immigration abruptly shifted from Northern Europe to Southern Europe. By the closing decades of the nineteenth century, the Northern European immigrant was viewed by the white Anglo-Saxon Protestant community as relatively safe; while the Southern Europeans were viewed as an acute threat to the mores of America. The stranger in the land had to be Americanized so as to protect the "American way."

Traditional Protestant theology offered little solace to those who felt the dangers to social order. After Darwin and the higher criticism of the Bible, little intellectual vitality remained to support the credibility of theological, doctrinal disputes. What remained, however, was the moral capital of a pious Protestant past and a missionary zeal to convert the heathen in our own midst. Missionary work needed to be done, not only in Africa and the Far East, but in Hell's Kitchen in New York City and on Halsted Street in Chicago. The new immigrants had to be made safe for the streets of New York and Chicago, so that a better, more efficient American might emerge. The Social Gospel, whether preached by Walter Rauchenbush in Hell's Kitchen or by Jane Addams at Hull House, all had a similar ring. The immigrant had to be educated for his own "good," and that "good" was defined by the mores of the new liberal.

The religion of the settlement houses and the urban ministries reflected the collapse of theological Protestantism and the rise of a secularized, socially conscious Protestant Christianity made relevant to a rising middle class. Those men and women reared in the earlier faith and who, in the twilight of their youth, found themselves searching for more creditable meaning to their lives usually turned to a secularized Protestant moral value system as the basis for their new, progressive, reformist faith. Jane Addams, speaking before the Ethical Culture Society's summer session at Plymouth, Massachusetts, proclaimed that the settlement house movement embodied the true spirit of Christ in the world. Similarly, John Dewey expressed his belief that the teacher in his concern for the "formation of the *proper* social life," and the "maintenance of *proper* social order," and the "securing of the *right* social growth: is the prophet of the true God and the usherer in of the true kingdom of God." Both were translating their personal values into a new religion of humanity. Most spokesmen for progressive education in America were fundamentally moralists, working in the interest of the hegemony of an emerging middle class. To Dewey, as to many who followed him, science and technology were the new theology. All was tied to a quest for "The Great Community" where men would ultimately learn, as Dewey put it, to "use their scientific knowledge to control their social relations."

Political progressivism was bent not on the destruction of capitalism but, rather, on rationalizing and stabilizing the system. Stability, predictability, and security were the expected consequences of a controlled, rational process of social change. Federal control and regulation of labor, management, and the consumer market became the trademark of the political progressive movement. Through the efforts of such liberals as Jane Addams, John R. Commons, Charles W. Eliot, Samuel Gompers, and others in the National Civic Federation, labor, management, and government were brought into a cooperative working relationship. The triumph of political progressivism meant the rise of the new managerial class to positions of power in the newer reform-type city governments, as well as in the growing bureaucratic structures of both the state and federal systems. By World War I, the corporate state emerged, embodying many of the values of both the political and educational progressives. World War I brought political and educational progressives even closer together in common cause. Although most twentieth-century liberals believed that one could best serve the interest of the individual through involvement in a larger corporate society, it is not at all clear that liberal thought and action have always served the interest of the individual in any sense other than that which happened to coincide with the needs of the corporate society. John Dewey set the problem for the twentieth-century liberal fairly succinctly when, in discussing "What America Will Fight For," he said:

> Politics means getting certain things done. Some body of persons, elected or self-constituted, take charge, deciding and executing. In the degree in which a society is democratic this governing group has to get the assent and support of large masses of people. In the degree in which the things to be done run counter to the inertia, bias and apparent interests of the masses, certain devices of manipulation have to be resorted to. The political psychology of the older school, that of Bentham and Mill, taught that in a democratic state the governing body would never want to do anything except what was in the interests of the governed. But experience has shown that this view was overnaive. Practical political psychology consists largely in the technique of the expert manipulation of men in masses for ends not clearly seen by them, but which they are led to believe are of great importance for them.

Rejecting this "practical political psychology" as both inefficient and ineffective in achieving broader social aims Dewey went on to call for a more "business-like psychology" that would consist of "intelligent perception of ends . . . and effective selection and orderly arrangement of means for their execution." In this way, the road could be kept open for the possibilities of "world organization and the beginnings of a public control which crosses nationalistic boundaries and interests." In the closing days of the war, Dewey pointed with pride to the intelligent mobilization and management of the nation in crisis. He then looked to the future with hope that the same intelligence might be applied in developing a "New Social Science" that would help shape the new order in the future along similar lines.

The major impetus of progressive reform, whether political or educational, was to make the system work efficiently and effectively and to do so by using the compulsory power of the political state to achieve that end. The thrust of progressive reform was, indeed, conservative. In this way, many socialists were also, in effect, conservative. They were conservative in their quest for efficiency [and] orderly change, and in their desire to maintain the system. For example, John Dewey, in his "Confidential Report" to the War Department during World War I, was centrally concerned with the manipulation of Polish affairs, so that we would not lose our cheap labor supply after the war through emigration. As Dewey said:

> The great industrial importance of Polish labor in this country must be borne in mind and the fact that there will be a shortage of labor after the war and that there is already a movement under foot (which should be carefully looked into) to stimulate the return of Poles and others of foreign birth in Southeastern Europe to their native lands after the war. With the sharp commercial competition that will necessarily take place after the war, any tendencies which on the one hand de-Americanize and on the other hand strengthen the allegiance of those of foreign birth to the United States deserve careful attention.

Although Dewey considered himself a socialist, these were not the concerns of a radical socialist but, rather, one of a management, welfare-state socialist interested in the development and maintenance of the system. To be sure, Dewey's values did not coincide with the values exhibited by the National Association of Manufacturers, which represented the smaller entrepreneurs, but the thrust of his values with respect to order, conflict, and social change was not far from that of the National Civic Federation, which supported progressive social legislation in the interest of the new, emerging corporate society. John Dewey was committed to the economic growth and progress of that society, even though such progress might require manipulation of Polish workers. From this perspective, one can also account for his intense dislike and distrust of Papal Catholics as opposed to Protestant Catholics, as well as his condescending attitude toward ethnic differences, which appear throughout the report. Ethnic and religious differences were viewed as a threat to the survival of the society and had to be overcome through assimilation. Dewey, as well as other liberal reformers, was committed to flexible, experimentally managed, orderly social change, which included a high degree of manipulation.

The war brought some of the strengths and weaknesses of the new, pragmatic liberalism to the fore. The central weakness, as Randolph S. Bourne so aptly put it, was that, in times of crisis, the really fundamental value upon which the pragmatist rested his case was survival. Pragmatism, he argued, is a philosophy for those who are inclined to calculate consequences so as to survive. Faced with what appears as insurmountable opposition, the pragmatic liberal can be expected to compromise his value in the name of survival and effectiveness. Thus, Dewey argued that the "pacifists wasted rather than invest[ed] their potentialities when they turned so vigorously to opposing entrance into the war." So, too, those Russians who resisted the politicizing of the schools along Communist lines were criticized by Dewey as the "more unhappy and futile class on earth." The good pragmatist, he thought, should not waste his "influence" on lost causes. In this sense, Dewey was a good pragmatist. He never seriously challenged the power sources within American society. His nonviolent socialist views would threaten few in power. In fact, much of his philosophy of nonviolent, reasoned, and orderly change (albeit toward a kind of welfare-state socialism) was adopted by those who directed and managed the corporate industrial state. His work in such organized efforts as NAACP, AAUP, and Teachers' Union was symptomatic of his pragmatic quest for limited objectives within the established system. As Bourne saw it, pragmatism was not a philosophy for all seasons but, rather, one more appropriate for "peaceful times," when critical decisions did not have to be made and compromises were easy. The tendency of the pragmatist confronted with power was to compromise from a base line of survival, and, thus, expediency governs. If the self was never to be sacrificed, then what would remain was a philosophy of accommodation to the most powerful. Bourne's stinging analysis of John Dewey's pragmatism still remains a serious critique of the progressive liberal tradition in America. If Bourne's analysis is correct, and if, during times of crisis and in times of confrontation with power, the liberal can be expected to opt for the more powerful side in order to survive, then it does follow that, given a confrontation of left and right, and if the political right is stronger, the liberal will often be found supporting the right. It may be that crisis and power are the twin Achilles' heels of pragmatic liberal philosophy in America.

Although liberals are not fascists or Communists, their quest for orderly change within a managed society led some of them at times to become enthusiastic about certain characteristics of emerging totalitarian societies. Just as Dewey became enthusiastic about the role the Soviet schools were playing in the creation of a new Soviet Union, so, too, other liberals were impressed with Italian corporate fascism as a grand experiment in social engineering. Herbert Croly, for example, warned critics of fascism to "beware of outlawing a political experiment which aroused in a whole nation an increased moral energy and dignified its activities by subordinating them to a deeply felt common purpose." Italian fascism was warmly received among such well-known American liberals as Charles Beard, Horace Kallen, Herbert Croly, and Lincoln Steffens (1926–30). This reception was prompted by more than a simple desire to have the "trains run on time." While Beard was impressed with the flexibility of the fascist state and its freedom from "consistent scheme," others were more impressed with the ability of that state to act decisively by subordinating outworn "principles to method" and law to order. For many, corporate fascism seemed to satisfy the need of the corporate society for unity, order, efficiency, collective meaning, social engineering, and experimentation as well as freedom from the older rationalistic liberal philosophies that tended to value individual liberty over state authority. It was not until the early 1930's that these liberals began to see the consequences of the fascist experiment in terms of political refugees. At that point, they reversed their opinion about fascism. Historically, we have tended to treat this sympathetic treatment of fascism by pragmatic liberals as an "accidental flirtation," or perhaps an aberration in which normally rational men got carried away with the *Zeitgeist* of the time. If we had critically analyzed pragmatic liberal thought within the context of the corporate state, we might have understood the fascist flirtation as a logical and reasonable extrapolation of certain characteristics of liberal thought. If we considered the liberal's need for social experiment and reconciliation of opposites, we might further have understood why Charles A. Beard looked upon Benito Mussolini's fascist Italy as working out "new democratic direction," and why he might conclude that:

> Beyond question an amazing experiment is being made here, an experiment in reconciling individualism and socialism, politics and technology. It would be a mistake to allow feelings aroused by contemplating the harsh deeds and extravagant assertions that have accompanied the fascist process (as all other immense historical changes) to obscure the potentialities and the lessons of the adventure—no, not adventure, but destiny riding without saddle and bridle across the historical peninsula that bridges the world of antiquity and our modern world.

The role of the liberal within American society was essentially that of the knowledgeable expert dedicated to the survival of the system through growth. The liberal educational reformer, just as the liberal political reformer, was, in effect, a flexible conservative. To be sure, Dewey sharply disagreed with the mechanistic conservatism of men like David Snedden, Edward L. Thorndike, and Charles A. Prosser. His own commitment, however, to flexible experimental change would contribute to the survival of the system. In this sense, Dewey's experimentation in education, as well as most of twentieth-century progressive education, can be viewed as conservative.

The liberal philosophy that Dewey put together during his Chicago years (1894–1904) was really the ideological center for much of the progressive tradition in American education. At Chicago, in close working relationship with Jane Addams, Ella Flagg Young, and Francis W. Parker, Dewey put his ideas to a practical educational test. By the time he opened his Laboratory School in Chicago, certain concerns were already foremost in his mind. Abstract theology held little meaning. To Dewey, the spirit of God was in man, and only through a more authentic community could that truth be set free. The community was the sacrament through which the divine in man could be allowed to grow. For Dewey, the end of education was "growth." The concept "growth" itself is an organic concept that implied man's continuity with nature and his transactional dependence on environment. His search, while at Michigan, Chicago, and Columbia, was for organic unity and community. For Dewey, the good community was more than a rural face-to-face model taken from a Vermont community. His community would include the experimental, the scientific, and the technical and would necessitate a new man, who found his individualism realized in the emerging corporate community. The older individualism that saw the self as the center of the universe was passing away. Collective, cooperative intelligence was the key to understanding the new technology as well as the new individualism.

Drawing on both his Hegelian and Herbartian past, Dewey saw history as critical in understanding the present and shaping the future. As Dewey later put it, "The past is of logical necessity the past-of-the-present, and the present is the past-of-a-future-living present." The past was "a lever for moving the present into a certain kind of future." It is significant that Charles Sanders Peirce criticized Dewey and his Chicago school for their confusion of logic with history. If, for example, one were to delete all of Dewey's discussion of the history of various problems in *Democracy and Education,* little would remain for the serious student of experimental philosophy. Man's destiny was not predetermined by his history but, rather, by the way men use their history. Dewey was using history with a particular "end in view." In addressing parents and teachers in his Laboratory School (1897), Dewey explained why history was so important a subject in his school:

History is introduced at a very early period and is conducted on the principle that it is a means of affording the child insight into social life. It is treated, therefore, not as a record of something which is past and gone, but as a way of realizing what enters into the make-up of society and of how society has grown to be what it is. Treated thus, as a mode of insight into social life, great emphasis is laid upon the typical relations of humanity to nature, as summed up in the development of food, shelter, habitation, clothing and industrial occupations. This affords insight into the fundamental processes and instruments which have controlled the development of civilization and also affords natural and frequent opportunities for adjusting the work in history to that in manual training on the one side and to science on the other.

In Herbartian-like fashion, Dewey constructed his Laboratory School history to help the child "gradually to shape his expression to social ends, and thus make them, through his growing control, more and more effective in the corporate life of the group." The enrollment of Dewey's school consisted primarily of middle- and upper-middle-class children. Following his historical perspective, the social studies curriculum emphasized social unity, cooperative living, and the rational, orderly, progressive development of technology from the spinning wheel to the modern, industrial, corporate society. The violent, bloody history of the Indians, blacks, and immigrants, as well as the labor conflicts of the previous decades, [was] peculiarly missing in the school's history of the progressive evolution of American technology. Thirty years later, while reflecting on his "Chicago Experiment," Dewey said, "historical material was subordinated to the maintenance of community or cooperative group in which each was to participate."

Although Dewey, in 1936, described the use of historical materials in his "Chicago Experiment" as designed to maintain community, during the same decade he also advocated the use of historical materials to change community. However, what Dewey seemed to generate earlier at Chicago was a kind of middle-class history that eschewed conflict and violence and supported the organizational thinking of the new managerial class. Even though Dewey vacillated and at times called for a more critical use of the past, it was unfortunately the former kind of uncritical history that generally came to dominate much of the social studies curriculum of the American public schools.

The schoolroom was to be a miniature community. Just what kind of community was critical. Dewey's school had to be an idealized abstraction. As long as the larger community had unworthy aspects to it, the schoolroom would be selective with regard to enhancing those social values that Dewey prized. As much as Dewey desired an experimental school, he knew that ultimately such a school could be relevant to society only in an experimental community. Although he found fault with Plato's limited conception of individual potentialities, his own reconciliation of individuality and social coherency was largely Platonic. "True" individualism and "true" community were for Dewey, as for Plato, one. Just as in Plato's *Republic* all men were to be educated according to their natural talents so as to maintain order and virtue, so, too, in Dewey's *Democracy and Education* all men were to be educated in order to realize their individual talents and yet develop "a personal interest in social relationships and control, and the habits of mind which secure changes without introducing disorder."

While all might participate in Dewey's conception of democracy and education, the function of knowledge and the expert was a powerful determiner of social policy. In 1897, Dewey said, "The school, accordingly, is endeavoring to put the various lines of work in charge of experts who maintain agreement and harmony through continued consultation and cooperation." Thirty years later, he consistently argued, "It is more than probable that the only genuine solution of the question of the place of social guidance and indoctrination in education will be found in giving a central place to scientific method as the key to social betterment." If Plato had his logic, Dewey had his scientific method. Dewey, in accordance with the new liberal ideology he helped construct, turned not to the masses for social guidance, but rather to the knowledgeable expert. This ideology ultimately led to the rise of a kind of bureaucratic meritocracy that talked about democracy and education without seriously contesting the power elite who controlled the system.

The problem of relating a progressive school to the main currents of the emerging technological society was a continuing problem for Dewey. If the school was relevant and, at the same time, experimental, then only in an experimental society could educational reform occur. Only in such a society could one get an "organic" relationship between school and society. Dewey once defined democracy as "A society which makes provision for participation in its good of all its members on equal terms and which secures flexible readjustment of its institutions through interaction of the different forms of associated life is in so far democratic." What was meant by "on equal terms" remained ambiguous enough to allow Dewey to see democracy wherever he saw an involved social experimental group. So, it was that, when he visited the Russian schools, he found

> . . . the children much more democratically organized than are our own; and to note that they are receiving through the system of school administration a training that fits them much more systematically than is attempted in our professedly democratic country, for later active participation in the self-direction of both local communities and industries.

Dewey's inadequate conception of political democracy led him to look at a totalitarian society organizing its population educationally to participate in the bureaucratic system at various institutional levels and call it democratic. What impressed him most about this system was that, unlike his Chicago Laboratory School experience, the progressive educator could be true to himself and teach in unison with the shaping forces of the larger Soviet community. As he put it, "The Russian educational situation is enough to convert one to the idea that only in a society based upon the cooperative principle can the ideals of educational reformers be adequately carried into operation." He was impressed with the organic unity that existed between the school and Soviet society, as well as the use of social behaviorism that was employed in using the school as a vehicle for entering and shaping family life. In viewing Russian education, Dewey had some difficulty distinguishing propaganda from education. He said:

> The present age is, of course, everywhere one in which propaganda has assumed the role of a governing power. But nowhere else in the world is employment of it as a tool of control so constant, consistent and systematic as in Russia at present. Indeed, it has taken on such importance and social dignity that the word propaganda hardly carries, in another social medium, the correct meaning. For we instinctively associate propaganda with the accomplishment of some special ends, more or less private to a particular class or group, and corre-

spondingly concealed from others. But in Russia the propaganda is in itself of a burning public faith. One may believe that the leaders are wholly mistaken in the object of their faith: but their sincerity is beyond question. To them the end for which propaganda is employed is not a private or even a class gain, but is the universal good of universal humanity. In consequence propaganda is education and education is propaganda. They are more than confounded; they are identified.

Propaganda became justified as education when it served a universal good. Dewey later suggested that certain kinds of propaganda were "obnoxious" to him personally but then went on to say that "The broad effort to employ the education of the young as a means of realizing certain social purposes cannot be dismissed as propaganda without relegating to that category all endeavor at deliberate social control." Dewey's impressions of the Soviet schools are revealing, not so much in what they tell us about the schools themselves, but as they shed light on what Dewey, the philosopher of American liberalism, meant by democracy, freedom, and the organic unity between school and society.

Dewey had long ago rejected the classical conception of individualism and its political corollary of a free market place of conflicting ideas. The traditional notion of democracy, dependent on conflict of parties and public discussion, according to Dewey, had passed. In *Liberalism and Social Action*, Dewey talked of the collapse of both the capitalistic system and laissez-faire democracy. Neither had much in common with scientific method. He said:

> The idea that the conflict of parties will, by means of public discussion, bring out necessary public truths is a kind of political watered-down version of the Hegelian dialectic, with its synthesis arrived at by a union of antithetical conceptions. The method has nothing in common with the procedure of organized cooperative inquiry which has won the triumphs of science in the field of physical nature.

Rejecting confrontation politics, Dewey turned to science and what he termed a method of intelligence. The solution was to be found in the new *scientific* socialism, not in a democratic socialism (democratic in the older sense of the term). The new theology, for Dewey, had become science and technology. In a way, it had become a creator of new values and ends. As he put it, "Take science (including its application to the machine) for what it is, and we shall begin to envisage it as a potential creator of new values and ends."

Just as the older theology called for a new Adam, so, too, Dewey's unbounded faith in science and technology led him to call for a new man. Such a man must work well within the corporate system, where, almost in Orwellian fashion, positive freedom would mean control. Freedom for Dewey meant rational control over future possibilities; as he put it, "Control is the crux of our freedom." This kind of freedom over future possibilities would be maximized when the "great society" would become the "great community." Only thus would a true public exercising a maximum degree of freedom and control come into being. Such a public would assert its "general will" in Rousseauian fashion where "force is not eliminated but is transformed in use and direction by ideas and sentiments made possible by means of symbols." Ideas, sentiments, and words become the force vehicles of social control in Dewey's great community. One side of his search for the great community had its precursors in Rousseau, Emerson, Royce, and Walt Whitman; while another side was rooted in Lester Frank Ward, Albion Small, and Herbert Croly. As Dewey put it, "Democracy will come into its own, for democracy is a name for a life of free and enriching communion. It had its seer in Walt Whitman. It will have its consummation when free social inquiry is indissolubly wedded to the art of full and moving communication." The age-old problem of educating the man or the citizen would be resolved when the great society became the great community, and the new man, indeed the one-dimensional man, would become a living reality. This new community was one in which men would, "systematically use scientific procedures for the control of human relationships and the direction of the social effects of our vast technological machinery." The solution to social conflict, for Dewey, remained the intelligent use of education for social control. The direction that such control should take, he believed, could be determined by scientific method.

Dewey's benign faith in the scientific method and technology remained undaunted. Perennially optimistic, he believed there was a way of humanizing American social institutions, be it industrial or educational. He saw the possibility in the progress of science and technology toward what he called a "humane age." The experimental method, he believed, was "the foe of every belief that permits habit and wont to dominate invention and discovery, and ready-made system to override verifiable fact." With a somewhat romantic view of the scientific community in mind, he went on to suggest that not only are science and technology revolutionizing our society, but that science carries with it the germ of a more open society. He said:

> No scientific inquirer can keep what he finds to himself or turn it to merely private account without losing his scientific standing. Everything discovered belongs to the community of workers. Every new idea and theory has to be submitted to this community for confirmation and test. There is an expanding community of cooperative effort and of truth. . . . Suppose that what now happens in limited circles were extended and generalized.

The problem, here, is that, although theoretical science may be open-ended, technology concerned with serving particular social institutions may not be so dedicated to truth or an open community of discourse. On the contrary, a social institution dedicated to survival may find it expedient to sacrifice truth. The new liberalism of Dewey and others failed at this critical juncture. Perhaps, in some ideal world where all men were governed by "rational self-direction," Dewey's idea of science might be applicable. In the world of twentieth-century power politics, however, most scientists and technologists became hired men of the industrial, militarized society. It is significant that neither Dewey nor the many educators who followed him preaching the gospel of science in education paid much attention to the social environment in which modern science and technology were born and bred—i.e., Prussian Germany. Instead, the rhetoric of American educators abounds with the association of freedom and democracy with scientific method and technology. Dewey made a significant contribution to this mythology. Repeatedly, he treated technology as either a positive or a neutral tool and seldom ever seemed to sense or show serious concern with the negative and limiting consequences of the technological system itself. More fundamental, however, he failed to realize that neither democracy nor individual freedom had any necessary inherent connection with science and technology. It could, however, have a very intimate connection with his passion for unity, order, and systematic, rational change, as well as his high regard for the knowledgeable expert. These were all characteristic of his new liberal ideology. These constructs, moreover, remained fairly constant from his Chicago Laboratory School days until late in life, when he favorably reviewed Karl Mannheim's book *Man and Society* (1940), in which Manheim called for elites to plan the new social order. Dewey's faith in science, knowledgeable elites, and scientific social planning remained firm. By 1943, R. Bruce Raup, George E. Axtelle, Kenneth D. Benne, and B. Othanel Smith published *The Improvement of Practical Intelligence*, which attempted to create a method of social dialogue through which collective planning might occur. Dewey's response to this work was that he believed it to be too subjectivistic, and that, furthermore, values for social planning could be arrived at through an objective science. Two decades later, Daniel Bell, following in the footsteps of John Dewey, published *The End of Ideology*, in which he asserted that the new social order will be planned by an ideology-free social scientist, charting the course of a future civilization.

Just a century after Comte had prophesied the emergence of a positive, objective science of man and values, liberals such as Dewey and Bell heralded the development of an objective science of human values. Bell had correctly surmised that this was, indeed, the end of ideology. It was also the culmination of one of the most significant ideologies in the first half of the twentieth century—liberalism itself. If human values could be objectively determined and predictably controlled by the social science expert using systems analysis in the cybernated world of the future, then little need existed for that once burning faith that called for rational, progressive change. To be sure, the "games" that engaged the "think tank" experts seemed a pallid substitute for the philosophic discourse in which the liberals had engaged for the past century; nevertheless, they were still a logical extension of liberal thought and action. Just as many nineteenth-century liberals found themselves justifying "robber baron" capitalism, so, too, many twentieth-century liberals found themselves justifying the military-industrial establishment. This, however, could be expected. The twentieth-century liberal was in many ways the articulate spokesman for that managerial middle class that actively participated in the creation of the militarized society in the post–World War II period.

Perhaps, if we had fully appreciated the liberal's commitment to the survival of the system through evolutionary, orderly change, we might have understood why so many were impressed with early fascist and Soviet experiments in human engineering. It might also have been easier to understand why the "liberal"-dominated Committee for Cultural Freedom (1939) opted for McCarthy-like solutions to the problems of Communist teachers in the schools fully a decade ahead of the McCarthy era. Nor would it seem unusual that Sidney Hook would be one of the founders of the American Committee for Cultural Freedom (1951), an offspring of the CIA supported Congress for Cultural Freedom. Finally, if we had an accurate historical analysis of the role the liberal has played in the development and maintenance of the corporate state, we would not have been so repeatedly surprised along the road from Berkeley to Attica to find a liberal mind behind the hand on the policeman's club or trigger.

In education, the liberal supported the creation of a mass system of schooling dedicated to filling the need of society for a citizen capable of adjusting to the necessities of an industrial system. Such a society required citizens who respected the authority of the knowledgeable expert and who believed the mythologies that sustained bourgeois culture. Despite the equalitarian rhetoric, educational liberals most often, in practice, supported an education directed from the top down. In this respect, they repeatedly stood for the professionalization of the expert-teacher and the use of improved technique to enlighten the ignorant masses. "Enlightenment," for most, implied education for social control.

With Dewey and other liberals, words such as freedom, democracy, and individualism took on new and different meanings. The philosophy of John Dewey and most liberals who attacked the ancient dualisms could readily lead to a one-dimensional view of reality, where opposites appeared blurred. Freedom, for example, became control. Dewey's conception of *Democracy and Education* bypassed the politically potent power questions and, instead, moved toward a cultural participatory perspective that assumed an increasing acceptance on the part of the masses of the scientific method as the "key to social betterment." Cultural participation, however, was no substitute for political and economic power. In spite of the fact that Dewey, in *Liberalism and Social Action*, called for a greater militancy, the behavior of liberals in the past decades has been best characterized as acquiescence in the face of political, economic, and military power. Perhaps Isaiah Berlin put his finger on the problem when he suggested that "virtue is not knowledge, nor freedom identical with either." Liberals tended to confuse all three. They sought social change without conflict and violence, by placing their faith in science and technology as a "creator of human values," and turned to a mass system of education that would impart those values to the children of the immigrant. In the process, education of the individual was sacrificed for the greater need [of] social control and security. As a consequence, large numbers of people were ultimately not educated to be critical individual citizens but trained to seek security and comfort in the symbols and mythologies manipulated by Madison Avenue social science experts. Political office came to be as salable as soap and the people the pawns of "expert policy decision-makers." In this way, neither science nor technology was effectively employed to enhance democracy (rule by the people) but, rather, became an effective tool of the powerful in controlling the social system. Perhaps the liberal faith in science and technology is not an adequate substitute for a philosophy of man.

During times of crisis, this weakness in the liberal ideology is exposed. Whether it was Dewey calling for a more effective manipulation of the Polish immigrant during World War I, or . . . President Johnson manipulating public opinion so as to escalate the Vietnam war, liberals in crisis usually, directly or indirectly, supported the existing power structure. They were, in fact, *Servants of Power*. If, indeed, the unfortunate time shall come when the left confronts the right in open confrontation, little doubt should remain where many liberals will stand.

Education and the Corporate Order
David K. Cohen and Marvin Lazerson

During the last fifteen years, mounting conflict over the nature and function of schools has generated heightened concern over education and an unprecedented awareness of school failure. Few would now proclaim, as Angelo Patri did in 1927, that "the schools of America are the temples of a living democracy." A new history of American education reflecting these social conflicts has emerged. It focuses on the development of city school bureaucracy and professionalism, the education of European immigrant and black children, and inequality of educational opportunity. Yet, despite the broadened scope of historical research on education, the new work remains disparate. In this paper, we try to take the next step by suggesting several unifying themes and outlining a framework for understanding the development of education in the United States in this century.

In our view, this history has to be understood in the framework of the schools' adaptation to large-scale corporate capitalism and the conflicts

From *Socialist Revolution,* Volume 2, Number 2 (March–April, 1972), pp. 47–72. Copyright 1972, *Socialist Revolution.*

this engendered. Infusing the schools with corporate values and reorganizing them in ways seen as consistent with this new economic order has been the dominant motif. Education has been closely tied to production—schooling has been justified as a way of increasing wealth, of improving industrial output, and of making management more effective. The schools' role has been to socialize economically desirable values and behavior, teach vocational skills, and provide education consistent with students' expected occupational attainment. As a result, the schools' culture became closely identified with the ethos of the corporate workplace. Schooling came to be seen as work or the preparation for work; schools were pictured as factories, educators as industrial managers, and students as the raw materials to be inducted into the production process. The ideology of school management was recast in the mold of the business corporation, and the character of education was shaped after the image of industrial production.

But the schools' adaptation to advanced corporate capitalism has not been accomplished without conflict. While the corporate society seemed to require schools that socialized students for work and evaluated their success in economic terms, the counterargument, that education should be playful and evaluated only on intrinsic and noneconomic criteria, has grown progressively more insistent. Industrialization drew and held a multitude of immigrants to the cities, but the public schools promulgated an essentially native version of American culture. From the outset, some newcomers reacted against schooling that barely recognized them, and sought alternative schools to legitimize and preserve their cultures. The corporate society required an academic meritocracy that selected students on the basis of ability and educated them accordingly. The great inequities in this selection system were a function of the students' presumed occupational destination and could not be squared with prevailing ideas of equality.

These conflicts still pervade the school system: schooling as work against education as play; cultural diversity against assimilation and nonrecognition; academic merit against equality. These tensions are a product of the schools' adaptation to large-scale corporate capitalism and cannot be understood apart from its evolution.

THE INDUSTRIAL SYSTEM OF SCHOOLING

The leading idea of the corporate capitalist system of schooling was that education was an economic activity. Schooling was justified as a way to expand wealth by improving production. Skill and behavior training were stressed; students were selected for occupation strata based on ability and matched to occupations through counseling and training. *Education was fashioned into an increasingly refined training and selection mechanism for the labor force.* These ideas were reflected in the formulation of a Michigan educator in 1921:

We can picture the educational system as having a very important function as a selecting agency, a means of selecting the men of best intelligence from the deficient and mediocre. All are poured into the system at the bottom; the incapable are soon rejected or drop out after repeating various grades and pass into the ranks of unskilled labor. . . . The more intelligent who are to be clerical workers pass into the high school; the most intelligent enter the universities, whence they are selected for the professions.

Such ideals had important implications for the conception and organization of schooling. If schools were the primary occupational training and selection mechanism, then the criteria of merit within schools had to conform to the criteria of ranking in the occupational structure. *The schools' effectiveness then could be judged by how well success in school predicted success at work.* The criteria for these predictions were work behavior and academic ability.

From the late nineteenth century onward, educators' concern with student behavior was justified in terms of training for work. In 1909, the Boston School Committee described the program of instruction in an elementary school given over to "prevocational" classes—a school for children expected to become factory workers:

Everything must conform as closely as possible to actual industrial work in real life. The product must be not only useful, but must be needed, and must be put to actual use. It must be something which may be produced in quantities. The method must be practical, and both product and method must be subjected to the same commercial tests, as far as possible, as apply to actual industry.

Typically, school officials stressed that classroom activities should inculcate the values thought to make good industrial workers—respect for authority, discipline, order, cleanliness, and punctuality—and the schools developed elaborate schemes for grading, reporting, and rewarding student behavior. "One great benefit of going to school, especially of attending regularly for eight or ten months each year for nine years or more," argued A. E. Winship, editor of the *Journal of Education*, in 1900, "is that it establishes a habit of regularity and persistency in effort." "Indeed," Winship claimed, "the boy who leaves school and goes to work does not necessarily learn to work steadily, but often quite the reverse." Going to school was better preparation for becoming a good worker than work itself!

If schooling was conceived as a preparation for work, it was only natural to organize it on the model of the factory. School superintendents saw themselves as plant managers, and proposed to treat education as a production process in which children were the raw materials. It was equally natural to evaluate schooling in terms of economic productivity. If education was work, then its success or failure could be measured by income returns to schooling. This tendency to use market criteria in evaluating education flowered around the turn of the century: Between 1880 and 1910, scores of studies of income returns to education appeared. Superintendents, plant managers, and teachers' associations published reports that sought to show that the more education students received, the greater their later earnings would be. This was reflected in the schools' internal evaluation systems, as grades and school retention were justified as strategies for raising later earnings.

The ability criterion was no less important. The notion that adult success depended on school achievement came to have the status of religious dogma. As Ellwood Cubberley revealed in 1909, this idea is closely linked to the view that, as the level of technology in production rises, workers require more education:

> Along with these changes there has come not only a tremendous increase in the quantity of our knowledge, but also a demand for a large increase in the amount of knowledge necessary to enable one to meet the changed conditions of modern life. The kind of knowledge needed, too, has fundamentally changed. The ability to read and write and cipher no longer distinguishes the educated from the uneducated man. A man must have better, broader, and a different kind of knowledge than did his parents if he is to succeed under modern conditions.

The idea that knowledge is power dates back to the scientific revolution; but, here, Cubberley was articulating a new version. It was not simply that knowledge was power, but that technological training was the key to personal success.

These ideas were powerfully reinforced by the results of early testing research. The U.S. Army World War I tests, for example, showed a clear correlation between measured intelligence and occupational attainment. This was generally presumed to prove that the occupational structure was meritocratic, allocating people to occupations on the basis of innate intelligence. Early test results also showed that people who completed more years of school had higher I.Q.'s—from which it was inferred that, "on the average, the stage in the school system attained by the average individual corresponds roughly with his capacity . . . the amount of education is pretty closely related to the degree of natural intelligence." These results gave an enormous boost to the notion that students who ranked high in school would later have high-ranking jobs. If people were poor, these tests seemed to prove that it was because they were stupid. It occurred to few (least of all the pioneers in testing) that people might test "stupid" because they were poor—that the tests might be biased to favor certain classes and social strata.

Whatever the merit of these inferences, they did provide a powerful thrust for educational testing. If smarter people got better jobs, then it was essential to make the ability criterion in I.Q. and achievement tests operational. Armed with such instruments, educators could separate students on the basis of a projection to adult status and thus tailor educational offerings to occupational expectations. The tests quickly came to be seen as the surest way to classify students and to organize schools for their work in occupational preselection. Cubberley maintained, in his introduction to Lewis Terman's *The Measurement of Intelligence*, that "the educational significance of the results to be obtained from careful measurements of intelligence of children can hardly be overestimated. Questions relating to the choice of studies, vocational guidance, schoolroom procedures, the grading of pupils, [and] promotional schemes . . . all alike acquire new meaning and significance when viewed in the light of the measurement of intelligence."

Educational testing grew rapidly during the two decades after World War I. Between 1921 and 1936, more than five thousand articles on testing appeared in print; a 1939 list of mental tests reported 4,279 and six printed pages of bibliographies on testing. By then, almost every major school system had a full program of achievement and I.Q. testing and a research bureau to administer the tests and interpret the results. A new subprofession, educational psychology, had been established, complete with separate graduate training programs, distinct departments with education schools, different degrees, and professional journals. School psychology had become a quasi-independent career line within the schools, integrated into the administrative structure from local schools to the central research bureaus. Of one hundred fifty large cities surveyed in connection with a White House Conference on vocational education, called by President Hoover in 1932, three-quarters were using intelligence tests to classify and assign their students for instruction.

Occupationally diversified curriculum was the corollary of testing. Curricular differentiation began before the testing movement, but testing provided a powerful reinforcement and rationale for it. The increasing differentiation of work in an urban corporate economy, the demand of business and industrial leaders for appropriately trained and disciplined workers —and, at the same time, the desire to protect educational standards for nonworking-class children—gave rise to diverse curricula before the theory of meritocracy was developed. Under the pressure of these forces, the older curriculum had begun to give way at the turn of the century—years before the testing movement emerged—and was being replaced by a multiplicity of course offerings geared to the major strata of job categories. The National Education Association's 1910 *Report of the Committee on the Place of Industries in Public Education* summarized the rationale for educational differentiation:

1. Industry, as a controlling factor in social progress, has for education a fundamental and permanent significance.
2. Educational standards, applicable in an age of handicraft, presumably need radical change in the present day of complex and highly specialized industrial development.
3. The social aims of education and the psychological needs of childhood alike require that industrial (manual-constructive) activities form an important part of school occupations. . . .
4. The differences among children as to aptitudes, interests, economic resources, and prospective careers furnish the basis for a rational as opposed to a merely formal distinction between elementary, secondary, and higher education.

The last point is important, for the inventory of differences among children clearly reveals the class character of educational differentiation. Working-class children should not only get a different sort of schooling but also should get less. Industrial elementary schools, prevocational programs, and junior high schools all were offered as ways of assuring that working-class children would stay in school and receive appropriate training. At the same time, Cleveland's school superintendent, for example, argued that working-class children would neither continue their education beyond the compulsory minimum nor learn very much if they did stay. He proposed that their schooling be limited to the elementary years, with a curriculum that imparted basic literacy, good behavior, and rudimentary vocational skills.

Later, as the high schools became less and less the preserves of children from advantaged families, curricular differentiation was necessary to maintain differences in educational opportunity within the same period of schooling. Differentiation centered more and more on curricular differences within secondary schools. At the turn of the century, special business and commercial courses already had been established in the high schools; by the second decade, many cities had created vocational, business, and academic curricula. The school board president in the Lynds' *Middletown* summarized the change succinctly, in the mid-1920's: "For a long time all boys were trained to be President. Then for a while we trained them all to be professional men. Now we are training boys to get jobs."

The differentiation of educational offerings ran across the grain of established ideas about equality in education. As in so many things, Cubberley characterized the situation bluntly in 1909:

> Our city schools will soon be forced to give up the exceedingly democratic idea that all are equal, and our society devoid of classes . . . and to begin a specialization of educational effort along many lines in an attempt to adapt the school to the needs of these many classes. . . . Industrial and vocational training is especially significant of the changing conception of the school and the classes in society which the school is in the future expected to serve.

Some educators insisted that differentiation implied no change in the reigning ideas of equal opportunity, but a greater number tried to reconcile differentiation and its implications for equality. The NEA juxtaposed "equality of opportunity as an abstraction" to the idea that education should be based on "the reality of opportunity as measured by varying needs, tastes, and abilities." Although such formulations were offered to support differentiation of educational offerings along class lines, this was rarely seen as inconsistent with the idea that "education should give to all an equal chance to attain any distinction in life." The reconciliation lay in the ready identification of ability with inherited social and economic status, an idea that the early testing movement reinforced. In theory, at least, there was no tension between the differentiation of school offerings and the academic meritocracy.

The appeal of the meritocratic idea extended far beyond a rationale for curricular differentiation. Educators and social reformers at the turn of the century were disturbed by the accumulation of a large, heavily immigrant, industrial proletariat in the cities; they feared the prospect of class warfare and found in educational opportunity a ready formula for remedy. Schools would provide a mechanism whereby those who were qualified could rise on the basis of ability. Even the greatest skeptics about the influence of environment on ability—E. L. Thorndike, for example—agreed that the schools should provide avenues for mobility based on selection of talent. And liberals maintained that schools ought to remedy deficiencies that the environment inflicted upon children. Frank Carleton, for example, wrote, in 1907, that the schools should reduce crime and dependency by providing special education for disadvantaged children. If schools compensated for environmental deficiencies, they would improve children's chances for success in later life.

This faith in the transforming power of education has been the basis for compensatory education and social welfare programs since the late nineteenth century. Schooling was conceived as an engine of social reform, a mechanism whereby injustice could be remedied by distributing rewards on the basis of talent rather than inheritance. It was an idea peculiarly suited to corporate liberalism. The redistribution of social and economic status promised through schooling was neither an attack on property nor an effort to weaken the class structure. Rather than eliminating inequalities in social status or wealth, schooling would insure that these were consistent with qualification instead of birth. *The great appeal of social reform through education was that all issues of distributive social justice were translated into matters of individual ability and effort in school and market place.*

These developments did not occur all at once, nor was the new system of schooling monolithic. As Michael Katz has pointed out, many educators who sought to model their schools on industrial lines seemed to have little idea of how industrial corporations worked. And efforts to make the curriculum correspond to the occupational structure did not mean that educators knew, or tried to find out, what labor skills were actually needed. As production utilized increasingly advanced technology, the schools slowly followed suit—just as now the old model of the schools as factories is beginning to change, as man-power needs change. But the commitment to the ability criterion, testing, guidance, and differentiated schooling has only been accentuated. While the character of work is changing, the schools' role as the primary labor training and selection mechanism continues.

TENSIONS IN THE NEW ORDER

In the course of the schools' adaptation to large-scale corporate capitalism, conflicts emerged in three areas. One centered on the system's essential educational values—extrinsically rewarded work—and the school culture this encouraged. Although the ethos of work has been dominant, the notion that education should involve play and intrinsic rewards has become increasingly prominent. A second involved the schools' role in political and cultural socialization, and the conflicts this provoked between successive groups of urban immigrants and the schools. These have been manifest in struggles over school governance and curriculum and in the rejection of public education in favor of alternative educational institutions. Finally, tension occurred between the ideology of class structure—academic meritocracy—and the ideas of equality presumed to govern public education.

Work and Play. The tension between these two conceptions of social activity increasingly permeates advanced industrial societies; it extends from the character of productive activity to the quality of pedagogy. In education, the notion of play contains several elements. It suggests a learning environment and process that, in its pure form, stresses self-expression, independence, and spontaneity. Several ideas underlie this. One is the view that learning is best if it is not compelled but occurs freely through "natural" interactions—in games, in social intercourse among children and adults, and in the reach of intermittent curiosity. Another is the assumption that the ethos of education should be arranged so as to protect children from the rigors of work—instead of instilling the disciplines of the workplace, schools should avoid routine, compelled, and occupationally oriented learning. The advocates of play in education have reflected diverse political and pedagogical viewpoints, sometimes stressing academic learning and, in other cases, emphasizing affective education or socialization. Some have justified play as an initial and more efficient method for producing good workers, but usually there has been hostility to extrinsic, market-oriented criteria of educational merit. Typically, the advocates of play in schooling are found in the "child-centered" wing of American education.

The idea of education as play received its first major institutional expression in the kindergarten movement at the turn of the century and later in the nursery school movement. Upper-middle- and upper-class advocates of early childhood education opposed their notion of school as play to the more disciplined forms of schooling then current. Their young charges were to learn through games, songs, stories, and other forms of casual interaction; direct compulsion and outright discipline were to be avoided. Although they sought to harmonize this with the work ethic by claiming that play was a better preparation for work than rigid discipline and by asserting that play was the child's natural work, the advocates of kindergarten education were unable to avoid conflict with the established public schools. The kindergartens were often considered undisciplined: Some educators argued that kindergarten children came to school poorly prepared, either to learn or to behave properly. While the notion that preschool education should be playful gradually became accepted by early childhood educators, it continued to find itself in conflict with public school personnel.

With the progressive movement in education, the idea of schooling as play was more widely diffused, and attempts were made to bridge the work-play conflict. Rejecting dualism in any form, John Dewey believed that work and play were part of a continuum, differing only in terms of "time-span" and the rigor of commitment to a specified goal. "In play," he argued, the "activity is its own end, instead of having an ulterior result." Play was "free, plastic"; it meant keeping "alive a creative and constructive attitude." Yet, Dewey could harmonize work and play only by rejecting prevailing notions of work. He contended that work in an industrial society, "especially in cities," was "anti-educational," because it took its definition from the needs of the economy rather than individual or social needs. To offset this, schools should function with an "absence of economic pressure," allowing students to build upon individual and social experience. In school, activities "are not carried on for pecuniary gain but for their own content. Freed from extraneous associations and the pressure of wage-earning, they supply modes of experience which are intrinsically valuable; they are truly liberalizing in quality." Although Dewey would oppose the child-centeredness of later play advocates, his call for a learning process that began with the experience of the learner gave an added emphasis to intrinsic learning.

Other educational reformers also juxtaposed learning from experience to learning by rote or from books. They sought to infuse the curriculum and pedagogy with spontaneity and free expression. The extreme incarnation of playful education was the child-centered school. In these schools, two commentators on the child-centered movement wrote in 1928, children "dance . . . sing . . . play house and build villages; they keep store and take care of pets; they model in clay and sand; they draw and paint, read and write, make up stories and dramatize them." Education in the child-centered classroom was designed to produce "individuality through the integration of experience." The ideal was expressed by one five-year-old, who said of her painting, "It looks the way you feel inside." To the traditional notions of order, regimentation, and vocationalism, the child-centered school opposed spontaneity, freedom, and self-expression.

It would be wrong, however, to counterpose the movement to bring "warmth" and spontaneity into the classroom to the process of the schools' adaptation to corporate capitalism. The educational reformers often had little impact on public education. The best examples of reform were usually found in private schools for middle-class children. This more "natural" schooling process fits in nicely with the trend in middle-class child-rearing ideas, away from repression and externally imposed discipline, toward greater freedom; and happiness in learning seemed to be linked with higher levels of achievement. It also fit in with the decline in the ethic of asceticism, the increase in leisure time that followed rising productivity in industry, and the promotion of a new ethic of consumption during the 1920's. Later, particularly in the period after World War II, with the growth of a larger labor force engaged in social control and services, the playful style has begun to find its way into public education.

The urban school-reform movement has increasingly gravitated in this direction, as Leicestershire styles of schooling emphasizing naturalness, freedom, and experiential learning have grown in influence. Educational theoreticians have, for the first time, adopted a stance of conscious opposition to the notion of school as externally disciplined work. Holt, Denison, Leonard, Illich, and Friedenberg attack not only the discipline and work ethos of the public schools but also the extrinsic rewards to which schooling is presumed to lead. They distinguish education from schooling, identifying education with freedom, natural authority, and learning-on-the-hoof; any discipline that does not arise immediately from the subject matter or the student-teacher relationship is rejected as illegitimate. They have called the entire authority structure of public education into question by rejecting the market values on which it rests. This is precisely the major change of the last decade: The polarity between work and play in education has become an overt issue of policy rather than a persistent conflict of pedagogical styles.

The source of the conflict between work and play lies in the changing character of productive activity. The increasingly technological nature of production has created a demand for a more highly trained and differentiated labor force, engaged not only in goods production but also in the production of culture, socialization, and welfare. Among the new strata of workers, labor has become more technological, cerebral, and mobile and has created more room for leisure. Not only must the training period of such a labor force be extended, but the kind of training must be changed. An emphasis on "creativity" replaces a pure emphasis on discipline. Play as an educational ideal becomes opposed to work, insofar as it encourages creativity.

Play is, then, closely linked to the changes in the character of urban middle- and upper-middle-income groups and the emergence of these new occupational strata as a cultural aristocracy. Schools organized to satisfy the educational values of these strata also have distinct "class" character: They often are exclusive, and, more important, they represent an effort to escape or deny the ethos of the industrial system and its traditional asceticism. The free schools—like the styles of their pupils' parents—reflect not only differences in taste but a freedom and a leisure that the distribution of wealth denies to the lower- and lower-middle-income groups. Nonetheless, these new groups have become important agents of political and social change.

The development of corporate capitalism toward increasingly technological forms of production carries with it vast changes in the life-styles and occupational needs of middle-income groups. If our analysis is correct, these developments carry with them values antithetical to earlier conceptions of education. The educational style of the urban upper-middle-income groups stands in increasing opposition to the central values of the established system of schooling. While the discipline of that system is still dominant, there have been enough changes to achieve an irretrievable legitimacy for play. The continued growth of the welfare-socialization-culture industries and the development of technological industrialism will only increase the pressure to treat schooling as a form of play and pleasure.

Culture and Political Tensions. Cultural differences between urban immigrants and the schools were a second point of conflict. Industrialization attracted immigrants to the cities and held them there, producing a deluge of non-English-speaking families at the turn of the century, especially in the East. The response was twofold: Efforts were made to use the schools as vehicles of intensive and rapid socialization—preparation for citizenship and work—and the movement to centralize urban school government was accelerated.

American educators had always assumed that the public school was essential to cultural unity, but, at the turn of the century, that idea received intensive application. Immigrants were inculcated with the values of the dominant culture through evening schools—often compulsory for the non-English-speaking—language instruction, civics, and American history, the celebration of patriotic holidays, and countless informal ways. Specially designed textbooks taught immigrants cleanliness, hard work, and how to apply for a job and naturalization papers, and informed them that rural, Protestant America epitomized the best in American life. Evening-school teachers in Lawrence, Massachusetts, were told to convince the foreign-born of the efficacy of schooling: "Try to make them feel that they are coming to school not because they are obliged to, but because they wish to, because they know America means Opportunity . . . and the Opportunity now knocks at their door."

Americanization programs were also established outside the schools. In the International Harvester Company plants, immigrants learned English through such lessons as:

> I hear the whistle. I must hurry.
> I hear the five-minute whistle.
> It is time to go into the shop. . . .
> I change my clothes and get ready to work. . . .
> I work until the whistle blows to quit.
> I leave my place nice and clean.

Yet, if a variety of institutions sought to integrate the newcomer, the public school was almost universally considered the primary agency of assimilation. "The American school," educators and public agreed, "is the salvation of the American republic."

How immigrants responded to this Americanization process is unclear. Were language instruction and the curriculum's social content points of tension? Did immigrants go to evening schools? Did particular immigrant groups relate to the public schools in different ways? The evidence is mixed. Some historians and contemporary writers report great enthusiasm for public education as a vehicle of assimilation and social mobility. Mary Antin found her first day at school "the apex of my civic pride and contentment": "To most people their first day at school is a memorable occasion. In my case the importance of the day was a hundred times magnified, on account of the years I had waited, the road I had come, and the conscious ambitions I had entertained." On the other hand, there was substantial conflict at both the state and municipal levels and between immigrant nationalities over foreign-language teaching in the public schools. Some immigrant groups established educational institutions of their own—among Catholics, usually in the form of parochial schools, and, among Jews, as part-time educational alternatives. In the larger cities, there were numerous afternoon and weekend Jewish schools—many of them apparently in wretched condition—designed to transmit religious and cultural traditions.

Another source of conflict seems to have been the public schools' staff, although evidence on this is hard to come by. Teachers in immigrant neighborhoods often were antagonistic to the newcomers, and there is some evidence of resistance to accepting teaching positions in immigrant neighborhoods. Michael Gold, in his autobiographical novel *Jews without Money*, records the hostility of his teacher in a Lower East Side elementary school, calling her a "Ku Kluxer before [her] time," a woman tortured by having to teach in a predominantly Jewish school. And even those teachers not explicitly hostile to immigrants rejected their unfamiliar behavior and values. Rarely were pleas for pluralism in the schools heard from professional educators.

These conflicts were partly resolved by the process of ethnic succession to bureaucratic power in the city school systems. Although the process occurred at different times, even by 1909 it was fairly well advanced in some of the larger cities. At least in the large Eastern cities, the Jews and the Irish were solidly entrenched in the teaching force by the 1920's. In addition, conflict was muted by the second-generation immigrant identification with the dominant culture; as the children of immigrants entered urban school bureaucracies, they may often have rejected demands for ethnic pluralism.

The political response to the immigrants involved changes in the organization and control of urban school systems. As the Europeans inundated the cities, local schools were removed from ward and neighborhood control and given over into the hands of central boards controlled by the established city elites. This shift away from district control and ward-oriented politicians to centralized agencies was central to the Progressive movement in politics, and it drew heavily on the Progressive ideology of reform: efficiency, expertise, and nonpartisanship. But these ideas were also linked to bigotry and explicit class biases. School centralization in the interests of efficiency had the effect—and, in at least some cases, the intent—of removing power and influence over schooling from the hands of the poor and the culturally different.

Cubberley made this explicit in his rationale for replacing the ward system of school government with centralized school committees:

> The tendency of people of the same class or degree of success to settle in the same part of the city is a matter of common knowledge. . . .
> One of the important results of the change from ward representation

to election from the city at large, in any city of average decency and
intelligence, is that the inevitable representation from these "poor
wards" is eliminated, and the board comes to partake of the best characteristics of the city as a whole.

Cubberley gave the example of a city in which the board was divided between working-class and professional members and argued that this pointed
up the "constant danger" in the ward system: "The less intelligent and
progressive element would wear out the better elements and come to rule
the board." When he came to suggesting the sort of people who might best
serve on the new citywide boards, Cubberley was no less forthright:

> To render such intelligent service to the school system of a city as has
> been indicated requires the selection of a peculiar type of citizen for
> school board member. . . . Men who are successful in the handling
> of large business undertakings—manufacturers, merchants, bankers,
> contractors, and professional men of large practice—would perhaps
> come first. . . . College graduates who are successful in their busi-
> ness or professional affairs, whatever may be their profession or occu-
> pation, also usually make good board members. . . .

Opportunities for schooling were extended to immigrant children partly
to transform them into a stable, quiescent labor force. The school demanded
cultural homogeneity and extolled the virtues of work; work was viewed
not as a way of staying alive but as a pattern of behavior. *Placing people in
an industrial complex and making them dependent upon it—economically
and psychologically—forged a link between them and the system's prosperity.* It was toward this end that the cultural and political activities of
public education worked.

The parallels to the recent black struggle for control of education are
striking. In part, the current conflict represents an effort to establish a
legitimate black culture and control the instruments of its diffusion, but it is
also an effort to reconstitute more particularism in school government. Although there are many important distinctions, because of the very different
historical experiences of European immigrants and Negro Americans, the
structural features of conflict in education are strikingly similar. The schools
are still essentially WASP in their values—even with ethnic succession to
teaching and administration—and they have conceded little to racial, national, or class cultures. *Cultural diversity is still a matter of basic struggle
in education,* and groups seeking it have had to adopt alternatives outside
the public system.

Merit and Equality. In theory, the schools' relation to the social structure
has been egalitarian and reformist—to allocate status on the basis of achievement rather than inheritance, thereby providing a remedy for injustice. Historically, however, the extent to which the meritocracy actually worked, and
the value of merit selection and its implications for equality, have been in
dispute.

At the turn of the century, the issue centered on differentiating educational opportunities. Tension arose between the egalitarian principle that the state should treat all citizens equally and the meritocratic notion that equality meant status allocated by achievement. The first implied exposure of all students to a common curriculum, while the second involved allocating educational resources based on expectations of student's adult status. The established egalitarian ideology of public schooling seemed to demand the inculcation of common values, absorption of a common heritage, and exposure to the same school experiences. The notion of schools as an industrial meritocracy implied diversification, discrimination, and hierarchy. As the differentiation of school offerings spread, a new notion of equality emerged—equal school achievement for equal ability. Differentiation was justified as a way of organizing education to conform with social and economic realities, and this, in turn, was presented as a way of providing meaningful equality of educational opportunity. As the Boston school superintendent argued in 1908:

> Until very recently [the schools] have offered equal opportunity for all to receive *one kind* of education, but what will make them democratic is to provide opportunity for all to receive such education as will fit them *equally well* for their particular life work.

The idea was difficult to oppose, for the advocates of equality—the unified curriculum—were identified with tradition during a ferment of progressive reform. Their defense of common learning asserted the need for broad "mental training" at a time when influential psychologists like E. L. Thorndike were calling for training for specific ends. But, most important, the traditionalists seemed hostile to the educational needs of working-class and immigrant children entering the schools in large numbers. The diversifiers needed only to point to evidence of massive school retardation and dropouts to make their case; the choice was diversification and vocational orientation or continued inefficiency. As long as the alternatives were so limited, it is hardly surprising that differentiated educational "equality" met with such rapid acceptance.

For those who accepted this notion of equality, the success of the new system was measured by the extent to which students were actually afforded education on the basis of the announced merit criteria. From the outset, critics argued that the academic meritocracy involved considerable discrimination. George Counts, for example, argued, in 1922, that the differentiation of secondary educational offerings selected students on the basis of race, nationality, and class. His research showed that the inherited indicia of social status played an enormous role in determining entrance to secondary school, the likelihood of remaining in school, and the curricula pursued within schools. Counts concluded that

> . . . the inequalities among individuals and classes are still perpetuated to a considerable degree in the social inheritance. While the establishment of free public high schools marked an extraordinary

educational advance, it did not by any means equalize educational opportunity. Education means leisure, and leisure is an expensive luxury. In most cases today this leisure must be guaranteed the individual by the family. Thus, secondary education remains largely a matter for family initiative and concern, and reflects the inequalities of family means and ambition.

He maintained that public support for secondary education could not be justified as long as the selectivity was so badly biased by student's background. Either selection should be absolutely rigorous and objective, scientifically selecting an educated elite from all classes, or the same education should be made available to all without any selection. Counts maintained that the measurement technology was inadequate to support a really scientific system, although his opposition to selectivity was political, not technological. He favored the absolute universalization of secondary education.

The problem was that, while Counts got his wish—secondary education rapidly became virtually universal—this was accompanied by selectivity based on the measurement technology he regarded as inadequate. Although an impressive literature grew up that raised questions about the class and ethnic bias of the tests, their use to group and assign students increased. Although scores of studies of ability grouping failed to reveal any clear advantage for students in the practice, ability grouping became widespread. Although—as Counts pointed out in 1922, and critics of vocational education have pointed out since—curricular differentiation really helped little in job training or placement, the spread of differentiation continued. Since the 1920's, evidence has accumulated that children of the poor and the working class, and those from immigrant groups, were disadvantaged by grouping, differentiation, and intelligence testing. Whether educational progress was measured by curricular placement, school completion, or the tests themselves, those who were economically disadvantaged or culturally different usually came out at the bottom of the heap.

The chief implication of all this was reasonably clear: The schools' methods for measuring merit—especially the tests—were seriously biased by inherited status and culture. Evenhandedness and the application of "objective measures" could not provide equal chances for school success among groups of children who arrived in school with differing class and cultural backgrounds. But educators, researchers, and reformers have generally taken different views.

Most reformers have accepted the principle of merit selection because they saw education as a vehicle for promoting social reform through individual mobility. The notion that education was a means for deferring direct (redistributive) social change by displacing it onto individual achievement has been a central element in modern American liberalism. It rests on a desire to promote social justice without attacking the distribution or ownership of property. The consequence for education has been curious—the more evidence has accumulated that school success depended upon inherited economic and social status, the more the liberal reformers insisted that the schools should compensate for environmental differences among children. Such efforts have been tried increasingly over the past four or five decades, but there is scant evidence that they work any particular advantage for the children concerned. Nonetheless, every evidence of failure seems only to reinforce the idea that more compensation is required. Because of the liberal commitment to social reform through individual achievement, the development of school reform has been perversely related to the evidence: *The more it shows that school performance is profoundly conditioned by inherited status, the more insistent the demands for compensatory schooling have grown; there never has been much mention of directly reducing the underlying status inequalities.* It is testimony to the power of liberal ideology—and the class character of school-reform efforts—that evidence on the educational consequences of inequality produces efforts to improve the meritocracy, rather than efforts to reduce the inequality.

The reason for this is apparent: Since the underlying function of the school system is not challenged by the educational reformers, the only thing that can be done to make it more democratic is to eliminate the barriers facing the "brighter," or more ambitious, children of minority or low-income parents. The attempt has been made over the last several decades, and especially in the 1960's, to apply the principle of merit as fairly as possible (given the class purpose of public education), so that an occupational elite can be chosen from all groups in American society while class and social stratification remains intact. Equality in education will require the elimination of the meritocratic structure, but that reform cannot take place in an educational system whose purpose is to socialize children into a stratified class society.

The City as Teacher:
Historical Problems

Daniel Calhoun

Fifteen years ago, the songwriter John LaTouche turned the Odyssey on its head when he wrote the musical *The Golden Apple.* Instead of sending his returning veterans on an unfortunate tour of a primitive inland sea, he dropped them into a modern city, to experience the varieties of novelty

From *The History of Education Quarterly,* Volume 9, Number 3 (Fall, 1969), pp. 312–30. Used by permission.

and disillusionment. To the corrupting politician character who plotted these experiences, he gave the line "The city itself will be our strategem."

Ordinarily, of course, we don't see the city as quite so deliberate, so conspiratorial a kind of teaching strategy. Instead, we think of it as intruding into the learning process as a kind of Automatic Teaching Environment—poorly and chaotically programmed, but effective for all that. In one way or another, people have recognized this for a long time, if only in the traditional fear of the city as a place too morally corrupt for the educating of the young. But it has figured quite positively, too. The psychological demands of the city were recognized in 1824 by Josiah Quincy, the first mayor of Boston, when it was raised from the status of town to city. He described the qualities that were needed in citizens—efficiency, discipline, punctuality, order, regularity—and he stood ready to help shape the Boston schools in ways that would fit these qualities. Men of his generation recognized, too, that schools were *not* essential in this process: The quickness or cleverness of the unschooled juvenile vagrant became a cliché of social commentary. In our own generation, the most important example of this kind of thought has been a more scientific, empirical kind: the long series of studies, beginning especially with that of Otto Klineberg, on the effects of northward migration on the tested intelligence of Negro children. Although Northern city schools were certainly part of this process, the studies were not generally designed to separate school effect from whole city effect, and this lack of differentiation reflected a proposition that we take for granted—that the urban setting is itself educative, and that it may have far stronger effects than do any specific schools. In anything that we say about the training or modernizing of whole populations, we cannot talk comprehensively about the process if we talk about specific educational practices quite independently of the general environment. This seems obvious in principle, but it becomes difficult when it affects policy. Although I will be talking about its bearings on the working out of historical points of view, it involves also the question: Does investment in schooling always do as much to change the mentalities of people as does investment in the more general facilities that help to make urban life quick, close, and specialized?

If we had no procedure available here except the nebulous one of speculating about the effects of whole environments or whole media, we might not have much to work with, at least not much that could be communicated from one student to another. But there are complexities within the proposition, and those wrinkles make cultural criticism possible, even while they make it difficult.

First, even aside from the difference between ability and knowledge, investigators have been doing much on the different kinds of ability, and lately on the different kinds of experience that are associated with the growth of various kinds of ability. Whether we are talking about the distinction between intelligence and creativity, or that between convergent and divergent mental processes, or that between quantitative and verbal abilities, we are moving into an area where it is unrealistic to talk simply about the stimulating or quickening influence of an environment, without reference to the *kinds* of influence it has.

Second, much of any direct effect of environment on individuals works through an intimate setting, the family, that is not uniquely urban, even though it may take somewhat special forms in cities. A very large part of the detailed research that has been undertaken to determine which kinds of experience produce which kinds of intelligence has taken the varieties of child-raising attitudes as the independent variable. Some of this research has pointed also to kinds of urban micro-environment—meaning, often, the mother-centered Negro family—that are supposed to have effects on the development of ability. The fact that such particular findings are controversial and may come in for extensive modification does not need to obscure the general point that, when we begin to analyze the effects of the general environment on the particular environments individuals actually experience, we may find contradictions and exceptions that make it possible to build up a more precisely drawn picture.

And, third, there is a particular emphasis that has worked within some studies on cognitive style, an emphasis more than a finding, but one that suggests a real weakness in any reliance on large-scale environmental effects. Some workers have studied the phenomenon of "field-independence" —the tendency for individuals to perceive or assess objects more in terms of their absolute properties, less in relation to the surrounding contexts that may bias judgment. While the exact relation of this cognitive style to the more conventional categories of ability or intelligence has not been worked out in fully satisfactory ways, it clearly is at least an aspect of many kinds of developed ability. If I may take the risk of erecting an analogy upon a technical concept, this suggests that an ability to act independently of environment is an important aspect of intelligence—that is, of the very ability that we are trying to understand in relation to the urban environment. Something of this paradox we might have expected already, simply by noting how far the media (and the schools) have worked to detach individuals from the country and then to begin the process of moving them into the stimulating city life. And, just to complicate the analogy a bit more, we all know individuals who are emotionally dependent on the urban "field," and in whom that very dependence seems to encourage an effective intensity of response. Dependence on some parts of the environment, and for some parts of the life process, may promote independence in relation to other aspects of experience. What the individual actually experiences is a series of interlocking, or impinging, or nested, environments, whose interacting effect on him may be quite different—either more effectively liberating or more effectively binding—from that of any one setting within the array.

Quite aside from the old heredity-environment problem, which we may simply forget for the time being, the exact relations between urban environment and intelligence are riddled with complexities. The way that any group was carried along by the outside world must have been a chancy process. For purposes of argument, we may take it as given that the majoritarian

American population did undergo some kind of upward mental push during the course of urbanization, much as the Negro population has during periods of cityward migration. But this implies a historical question. Just how did that American population undergo its acceptance of urbanization in such a way that complexities were resolved in favor of heightened mental performance? Why were developing minds not bewildered into disorganization by the buzzing confusion of city life or crushed into rote performance by the demands of city pace?

The answer is that they relied on many different adaptive mechanisms, many different ways of representing the urban demand to themselves in such terms that it became acceptable. Often, these mechanisms were religious, although we can, for ourselves, redefine them in more general intellectual terms.

Quite early, some Americans began defining their own isolated, largely rural society as if it were inwardly urban. New England clergymen in the seventeenth century, anxious to preserve the intellectual tradition that lay back of them in England, supported social policies looking to compact settlement. Hardly modest, they designated their society as a "city set on a hill." Although, in fact, the churches in wealthier communities enjoyed special prestige and were sought after as parishes by ambitious clerics, the ideology of the society put all local churches at a parity—not that all were equally bucolic and pure, but that all, no matter how remote, were supposed to be able to sustain a complex, townlike culture and discipline. In New England, and in the parts of America that later derived from New England, the urban image was available as a symbolic home in a way that it never was to believing European peasants, even though the material life of the Yankee farmer did not differ much from that of the better-off peasants.

If Americans had a preset mental slot for city culture, they also entertained pre-established categories for the paradox that is suggested by the concept of field-independence. The doctrines about which men argued turned especially on the question of the relation between inward forces and environmental influences in determining how a man would look at the world. Some men adopted answers that gave primacy to inward or "gracious" influences; others adopted answers that freely conceded worthwhile force to events that happened in the external world (such as preaching). In a rough way, subordination to inward influences was strongest in the colonial years, while reliance on environment and action grew after about 1800; but the striking feature of the debate was that many who took part refused to profess either an uncomplicated subordination to grace (Antinomianism) or an uncomplicated confidence in environment (Arminianism). They were compelled to argue that God's grace, while absolute, *usually* works through the instruments of worldly culture; or that religious institutions, *while* powerful and inevitable, *nevertheless* work to produce souls whose ultimate grace is direct communion with God. The worldly means for improving men were there, but, if successful, they weaned men from themselves. And that freed condition was not just an end product; wherever the faintest whiff of Calvinism lingered, the elected saint had been such all along, had all along enjoyed the potential beauty of being Christian. And that beauty not only carried with it the joyous obligation to join in communion with brothers; it also carried an ability to perceive values as they actually are, not in terms of social convention.

This relation between authenticity and environment had an equivalent in the social mechanisms of religious revival. Call this, if you will, the conflict between itinerant revivalists and settled pastors. Men who represented the cause of authenticity intruded into the world of ordinary environmental influences with news from what they said was the real world. More and more, over the years, these outside intruders had organizational ties of their own, whether through home mission committees or through Methodist bishops. They were among the earliest representatives of complex, bureaucratic organization who were encountered by many Americans. If there were things about the coming city life that frightened Jeffersonians even while they fulfilled the symbolic hopes of Yankees, there were also reassurances for all but the sour-tempered; bureaucracy in the cause of authenticity was no vice.

In the event, the practical need to provide continuity to the work of the outside agitator helped to transform his personalistic, rather anti-intellectual behavior into a means for introducing bookish culture. If the revivalist did not linger at the communion table, the religious press did linger at the kitchen table. Partly in order to sustain morale during the intervals between revivals, that press burgeoned. For similar reasons, so did the publications put out by partisan politicians and by the spokesmen for other causes. As the stronger of these efforts acquired followings and survived, they took on much the same character as the commercial press. The way that they distributed opinions through the countryside resembled closely the way that the metropolitan newspapers came to dominate local opinion formation over wide areas. This change, which was largely accomplished during the early nineteenth century, meant a shift in the responsibility for social excitement, from stimulus brought by personal agents to stimulus brought by what we now call the media. The media, extending far beyond the cities as such, gave new meaning to the city symbolism that had long been potent on Yankee farms. Since this had apparently been necessary in order to sustain the work of personal excitement, the media as parts of urban environment became acceptable to people who might otherwise have rejected any influence so formal.

The intellectual content of this organized, urban life was often simplified in order that people might the more readily be initiated into its effective influences. In the twentieth century, the Progressive version of this simplification is a staple of educational history. Many of the most influential of Progressives held a contemptuous view of the capacities of the mass of students, and they were willing to set up "general" courses of study for these students in order to cement them as clients within the school system. But, in the nineteenth century, a considerably subtler transformation took place within the substance of the working culture (not just of the culture as taught), in ways that made that culture more accessible to large numbers of people. On the verbal side, the analytical bent of eighteenth-century preaching and political writing gave way to an emotional bent, so that the consumers of culture felt closer to the producers by means of sentimental identification; the classic case of this was the homiletic "personalism" expounded by Henry Ward Beecher. On the quantitative side, Americans adopted plain, visual models for complex engineering problems, so that solutions could be reached without more than elementary numerical calculations; the classic case of this was shipbuilding, which was, *at that time,* newly carried out through models, not through elaborate plans, and which became a semipopular spectator sport.

Finally, among the adaptive mechanisms that I would like to note here: Middle-class Americans have repeatedly taken up simple child-raising fads, fads that have been too one-sided to carry out in any but hysterical practice, but which have served to compensate for persisting problems in the induction of children and populations into urban society. As with the simplification of the content of culture, a more recent example may first be more familiar. From about 1890 to 1930, L. Emmett Holt and John B. Watson, followed by many others, spread an antiseptic regimen in the handling of children. Although their surface logic rested heavily on the fear of germs, they spoke for the cause of regularity and reason and early independence, against the evils of maternal indulgence. Since the families to which they spoke were those in which the father was likely to be a preoccupied professional (like Holt or Watson), they were offering a kind of rule-bound, bureaucratic antidote to maternal domination in the urban family. But this is exactly what had happened a century earlier, in a campaign against maternal indulgence conducted by educator-clergymen like John Witherspoon and Jacob Abbott. Seriously frightened at the absence of fathers from the ordinary life of city homes, these moralists had done a striking job of *almost* holding back the wave of sentimentalism that overcame American attitudes toward the family during the middle of the nineteenth century. It was probably impossible to run any family with the rigidity that an Abbott or a Holt asked; their advice was, in that sense, a kind of normative mythology. But it may well have helped to shore up the balance between disciplinary and indulgent forces within the family, at times when the pressures of new urban life were threatening to undermine the good intellectual effects to be had from a *balanced* approach to discipline and to the teaching of sex identity.

These several adaptive mechanisms that I have outlined amount, when stripped and combined, to two. First, the process by which people have accepted the intellectual possibilities of the city has often included a heavy reliance on myth—that is, on some emotionally serviceable misrepresentation of reality, or of the past, or of the way the mental world hangs together. Although men have sought the city and lapped at it hungrily, they could not take it undisguised. The intensity of its stimulation, the artifice of its disciplines, and the complexity of its demands have been too much for many people to accept without somehow pretending that the whole phenomenon has been more familiar, more naturally right, than it actually is. Second, much that has looked like regression or primitive anti-intellectualism in American life has actually worked to make complex processes more visible to the ordinary man and, thus, has broadened the base on which subsequent structures could be elaborated. It is true that the proponents of anti-intellectual programs have often seen them as absolute, not as provisional or transitional. The men in 1918 who urged progressive studies for secondary schools believed that such studies were just the right thing for the supposedly limited mentalities of American students. The limited goals of such men are neither more nor less alarming, in the long run, than the simplifying goals of the men who reduced much of nineteenth-century thought to a simple visual mode.

Yet, the urban environment has had an educative effect, independent of any effects of formal schooling. But the independence of that effect does not mean that it has worked through simple, inevitable means. It has imposed difficulties and challenges that men could often accept only by buffering their consciousness with indirection, with defense mechanisms, even with outright cultural lies. If, on looking back at that process, we think of it as a simple impact of environmental entity upon receptive minds, we are indulging in an equally gross metaphysical myth-making of our own. Environment, like that other abstraction, the gene, has worked through fine particulars. As part of those particulars, men have continually reconstructed and repictured the bits and pieces of the environment that came their way. Some of the steps in that assimilation have always been cultural lies. If we can build a complex, responsible account of how people accepted urban influences in the past, we may get into a better position to think about how people are adapting in the present.

On "Crisis in the Classroom"
Michael B. Katz

In his recent, widely publicized book, Charles Silberman has written a strangely comforting indictment of American education. The cause of the "crisis in the classroom," he would have us believe, is a simple failure to think clearly and honestly. Consequently, remedies for the schools' prob-

From *Interchange,* Volume 3, Number 1 (1972). Reprinted by permission of The Ontario Institute for Studies in Education, publisher.

lems do not require the replacement of present social or educational structures; they demand, rather, the introduction of sensible and humane reforms into institutions that now exist. Mr. Silberman, in fact, has little use for most educational radicals, and his book will stand as a classic example of the liberal reform approach to American education in the late twentieth century. Therein lie its strengths and weaknesses. As a catalog of educational horrors and a dissection of the weaknesses of several reform theories and practices, Crisis in the Classroom, though not original, is intelligent, clear, and compelling. As an analysis of the causes of educational failure, it is shallow and, even, evasive. Finally, as a program for change, Crisis in the Classroom is inadequate and, worse, misleading.

Crisis in the Classroom is the result of the Carnegie Corporation's Study of the Education of Educators, of which Mr. Silberman served as director. The Corporation's funding, Mr. Silberman reports, enabled him to spend three and one-half years in research and writing, assisted by an administrative staff of four. It is apparent that he used the time and resources available to him vigorously and responsibly, reading an immense quantity and variety of literature about education and visiting schools and schoolmen throughout the United States and England. The outcome is a book of more than 500 pages, written with the lively and graceful style that one would expect from an editor of Fortune, in which capacity Mr. Silberman also serves. The length of the book, its wealth of detail, its professional presentation, its sponsorship, its publicity: All of these factors lend to it an air of authenticity and, almost, a legitimacy. There is no doubt that it will be as widely read, considered, and influential as a book about education can be. For that reason, it is all the more important to explore with some care its adequacy as a diagnosis and proposed treatment for American education.

First of all, consider Mr. Silberman's indictment of American education, which, in its way, is as severe as most of the critiques offered in more radical contexts. Most of his criticisms have been made before by other observers, but it is useful to have the case against the schools gathered together and put before the general public in such a persuasive fashion. Mr. Silberman's first major indictment is that the schools fail, and indeed have always failed, to act as equalizers of opportunity. The rhetoric of social mobility notwithstanding, schools have done remarkably little to counteract racial, social, and economic inequities within American society. Their failure, in fact, has touched off "burning anger" (p. 69), especially on the part of "Negro Americans . . . Puerto Ricans, Mexican Americans, and Indian Americans . . . furious because the schools are not moving their children into the middle class rapidly enough."

Mr. Silberman's second major indictment against the schools is their repressive and spirit-breaking quality. Preoccupied with order and control, schools, he observes, operate on an assumption of distrust, which creates an antagonistic and authoritarian atmosphere. Students, deprived even of the freedom to go to the bathroom at will, become totally dependent upon authorities for direction, unable to assume any responsibility even if it is offered. They learn from the school that docility and conformity are the best strategies for survival. Mr. Silberman gives to these by now sadly familiar points special poignancy through interspersing his argument with spine-chilling vignettes drawn from his own observations within contemporary schools.

Throughout the twentieth century, school reformers, including those of the 1960's, have accomplished remarkably little, Mr. Silberman correctly observes. In fact, he is most acute as he analyzes the failures and weaknesses of a number of recent, widely proclaimed, but ultimately disappointing innovations: educational television, the new physics and related curricular reform movements, team teaching, the nongraded classroom, and computer-assisted instruction. In particular, his discussion of the latter—his effective debunking of the new myth that computers are the key to an educational revolution—is one of Mr. Silberman's most valuable achievements.

Of all educational institutions, Mr. Silberman argues that the high school is the worst:

> Because adolescents are harder to "control" than younger children, secondary schools tend to be even more authoritarian and repressive than elementary schools; the values they transmit are the values of docility, passivity, conformity, and lack of trust. These unpleasant attributes might be tolerable if one could view them, so to speak, as the price of a "good education"—good, that is to say, in academic terms. Such is not the case. . . . And the junior high school by almost unanimous agreement, is the wasteland—one is tempted to say cesspool—of American education. [p. 324]

The schools at all levels fail: They do not teach skills or produce knowledge in the conventional sense; they reinforce the handicaps of poverty and race; and they try to root out whatever traces of independence and individuality they can find in the personalities of their students. The weaknesses of teacher education, Mr. Silberman bluntly but fairly claims, compound all of these problems. Intellectually vapid, inheriting a tradition that neglects questions of purpose, nearly useless in a practical sense: Teacher education is a disgrace. Its quality is not helped by snobbish professors of liberal arts who offer their criticisms, but rarely their help, from a safe and jealously guarded distance. In fact, as Mr. Silberman points out, the liberal-arts professors are also in trouble. They, too, lack a clear sense of purpose and face growing public dissatisfaction with their work. Mr. Silberman is quite right to say that "the weakness of teacher education is the weakness of liberal education as a whole; if teachers are educated badly, that is to say, it is in large measure because almost everyone else is educated badly, too" (pp. 380–81).

If any people remain unconvinced that there is a crisis in education and that the schools are failing miserably (and, unfortunately, those people may still be a majority), Mr. Silberman's book should shatter their complacency and arouse their indignation. More important for those already indignant are questions that move beyond descriptivism. How are we to account for the awful situation that confronts us, and what are we to do about it? Here, as I have already observed, Mr. Silberman unfortunately has much less to offer the troubled and confused observer, consumer, or casualty of American education.

Mr. Silberman has a straightforward view of the cause of educational failure: "what is mostly wrong with the public schools is due not to venality or indifference or stupidity, but to mindlessness" (p. 10). "Mindlessness" Mr. Silberman defines as "the failure or refusal to think seriously about educational purpose, the reluctance to question established practice" (p. 11). According to Mr. Silberman, mindlessness pervades all of American society, accounting not only for its bad schools but for other major social difficulties, as well. We have simply been too preoccupied, too lazy, or too self-interested to think seriously and reflectively about the purposes of our activities and institutions. The lack of correspondence between the complexity of the problems Mr. Silberman describes and the reasons he gives for their continued existence is startling. To attribute the persistent failure of a major social institution to a 125-year fit of mindlessness appears almost tongue-in-cheek from an observer as acute, informed, and intelligent as Mr. Silberman.

However, his explanation has two functions, positive or negative, depending on one's point of view. First of all, it removes the hint of personal threat implicit at least in most social criticism. No one in particular is at fault for what has happened. We can all—educationist, parent, citizen—be comfortable in the knowledge that our motives and our intentions have not been blameworthy. Mr. Silberman is not attacking us; despite his portrait of our failure, he is really doing little more than giving us a strong exhortation to pull up our socks.

Second, and more seriously, attributing educational failure to mindlessness removes the blame not only from individuals but from the larger social and economic system in which schools operate. Unlike the educational radicals whom he criticizes, Mr. Silberman does not even hint, to paraphrase Paul Goodman, that the problem of education is that young people do not have a worthy society in which to grow up. There is no question in Mr. Silberman's view that schools can be made well without a major overhaul of the structures that surround and sustain them. It is not the requirements of industrial capitalism, the obsession with law and order on the cheap, or the persistence of class bias and racism that have produced educational disaster. It is simply mindlessness. It would be comforting to believe that Mr. Silberman is right.

Unfortunately, it would be difficult for anyone reasonably versed in the history and sociology of education to accept Mr. Silberman's explanation. For example, take the first of his charges against the schools: They do not equalize opportunity. They were never seriously meant to. Throughout American history, extensions of public education have given more benefit to middle-class or affluent people than to the poor. That was the case, for example, with the high school, which offered middle-class parents a chance to have the community, as a whole, pay for the education of their children. The alternative was relatively expensive private schooling. From the time of their founding in the middle of the nineteenth century until about 1930, high schools enrolled only a minority of eligible children; these were, insofar as one can tell, not very often the children of the poor. The poor, we sometimes forget, not infrequently saw through the rhetoric surrounding the high school and tried to delay or defeat its introduction; they were rarely successful. Today, perhaps, the greatest inequality exists in public higher education, which offers greater benefits to the affluent in the same way that the high schools did earlier in the century. Within schools, tracking systems —ways of separating students—developed with the explicit purpose of neatly channeling poor children into occupations similar in status to those of their fathers. My point is that these inequalities have not resulted from mindlessness. They have been quite deliberate. The inequality in the educational system, it is not unfair to say, is a reflex of the inequality in the social structure. Schools are now, and they have always been, reflections of class structure, which they have reinforced rather than altered. Thus, it was no accident, or example of simple mindlessness, when a white teacher told Malcolm X that he had better give up his hope of becoming a lawyer and be a carpenter instead. That, in fact, is the message that public schools have been designed to give the average lower-class boy, black or white.

The same sort of explanation must be offered for Mr. Silberman's second major indictment of the schools: their emphasis on docility. Here, the case is crystal clear, because it can be made from explicit statements in educational documents spanning a period from early in the nineteenth century until the present. People urged the introduction of systems of public education, including compulsory schooling, to socialize the poor. Educational history abounds with discussions of the dangers to law, order, and morality posed by unschooled lower classes. Educational promoters have argued, quite explicitly, throughout American history that the purposes of schooling should be more moral than intellectual; formation of attitudes, that is to say, has been of far greater importance than the development of intellectual or cognitive skills.

Mr. Silberman is quite wrong to imply that little thought has been given to educational purpose. School reformers have always considered the relation of the details of curriculum, pedagogy, and structure to larger social and educational objectives. The problem is that those objectives have usually stressed the inculcation of the virtues that, it has been thought, would ensure law and order at the lowest possible cost: restraint, reliability, punctuality, and docility. These are the qualities, as well, that employers have sought in their work force. When nineteenth-century schoolmen asked employers if educated laborers were any better than ignorant ones, the answers came back that they were, indeed, not because they knew much more, but because they were more acquiescent, more honest, and less likely to strike.

Mr. Silberman feels that the balance in American education has tipped too far toward the cognitive. On the basis of the evidence he presents—the preoccupation with order, control, and conformity at the core of the school experience—as well as on the basis of the historical record, it is not easy to accept that conclusion. It would be more appropriate to say that schools have been so deeply concerned with the affective, so committed to the primacy of attitude over intellect, that they have never paid sufficiently serious attention to cognitive skills, or to knowledge. Mr. Silberman's arguments, consequently, do not offer a new direction for American education. His stress on the need to emphasize the affective is a continuation of a very old tradition. The problem with that tradition, most starkly, is that poor people do not need another lesson in how to behave, even if that behavior is to be liberated rather than repressed. They need the knowledge and skills to move out of poverty. Affective schooling could become a particularly subtle form of "repressive desublimation," to use Marcuse's term. It could be a distraction rather than a benefit to people whose long-term interests would best be served by the redistribution of power and income. In this way, affective education could, without too much difficulty, serve the purposes of social control for which traditional repressive schools have suddenly become inadequate.

Mr. Silberman's diagnosis of mindlessness as the cause of educational failure underlies his prescriptions for educational change. "If mindlessness is the central problem, the solution must lie in infusing the various educating institutions with purpose, more important, with thought about purpose, and about the ways in which techniques, content and organization fulfill or alter purpose" (p. 11). This argument misses the point, which I have made above, that the problem with American schools is not their lack of purpose but their continued dedication to purposes that have reflected the inequities of American society and the less appealing aspects of American culture. It is curious, moreover, that a man as concerned as Mr. Silberman with educational purpose gives us no more than the most general indications of his ideas on the subject. What is missing, in particular, is an elaboration of his views on the connection between educational purpose—the kinds of things he would like to see schools teach children—and the society of which the school is a part. The question is particularly important because Mr. Silberman champions a particular kind of educational innovation, and it is important to know his reasons. What difference will it make to the serious social problems of American society if schools change in the way that he hopes? Are changes in education part of a pattern of more widespread social change that he sees happening? I find myself unable to determine more than Mr. Silberman's most general answers to these questions. His school reform takes place, as it were, in a social vacuum.

Mr. Silberman is a champion of the English infant schools. He stands in a long tradition of American educational reformers who have found abroad a cure for America's educational problems. Among the first, in fact, were the champions of English infant schools, which started in the late eighteenth century as a way of relieving the pressure on poor families and seeing that poor children received a proper infusion of moral virtue. These schools enjoyed a brief vogue in the United States in the 1820's. Around the same time, another English innovation, the Lancasterian, or monitorial, system, enjoyed enormous and rather more long-lived popularity in America. Later in the century, Horace Mann returned from Europe holding up the example of Prussian and Scottish schools; university reformers, too, argued the excellencies of German models. So the list goes. It was, after all, less than two decades ago that Sputnik prompted an enormous wave of admiration for the achievements of Russian education. Reformers, and Mr. Silberman is no exception, have not looked to foreign examples primarily to gain new ideas. Rather, they have sought there proof that an innovation to which they are already committed works. Reports of educational travelers have always told at least as much about the preoccupations and ideas of the travelers themselves as about the systems that they describe. In the case of Mr. Silberman, the English infant schools show, to his satisfaction, that fundamental educational reform can occur within a system of public schools. He also finds, within their type of informal education, confirmation of a pedagogical style that combines a freeing of the learner with an important guiding and controlling role for the teacher. It offers, he believes, an alternative to the American educational radicalism, which, in his unfair caricature, seeks a total abdication of adult responsibility combined with a total capitulation to the whims of children.

I do not care to question the desirability of informal education; I am willing, for the sake of argument, to grant its superiority to what goes on in the average American classroom. But I do wish to ask, again, about its larger purposes. What can we expect from the widespread introduction of informal education into American schools? Mr. Silberman discusses British schools in a fashion similar to the way he discusses American ones: in a social vacuum. He nowhere probes the connections between the schools and the social order in an attempt to find out if informal education is making any difference to the quality of British life. Nor do we learn from him precisely what the connection is between educational and social improvement. In fact, as he admits early in his book, since World War II there has been a phenomenal increase in educational achievements within America. Americans are a more educated, more thoroughly schooled people than ever before. Yet, few people would claim to discern much connection between that fact and any improvement in the quality or justice of American life.

At the conclusion of his book, Mr. Silberman claims that "we will not be able to create and maintain a humane society unless we create and maintain classrooms that are humane" (p. 524). This statement places him squarely in another tradition: those people who have seen in education a means to social reform. Presumably, he believes that effort and money spent on the introduction of informal education into American schools will precipitate an improvement in American society. The danger in this belief is that educational reform may be used, as it has been so often before, as a smokescreen or diversion from the serious social and economic reforms required by American society. This utilization of the schools as a substitute for social reform has been a characteristic American response to social problems for a very long time. Early in the nineteenth century, school reformers argued that education could solve the problems of crime, poverty, immorality, and inequality within an emerging urban and industrial society. Since that time, virtually every major social problem has found its way to the school, there to rest unsolved because education, quite simply, is powerless to solve it in the best of circumstances. Improving the schools has been a convenient way of avoiding the more difficult, contentious, and, to some, more ominous task of improving society.

Mr. Silberman's optimistic prediction that meaningful educational change can occur within existing school systems overlooks the connection between the structure of those systems and the educational outcomes that he deplores. However, two related features of those school systems have important consequences for the sort of learning that can go on within them and the objectives that they can reach; those features are their control—the powerlessness of the people whom they serve—and their form—bureaucracies. We often think of bureaucracy, or any other organizational form, as a disembodied, somewhat neutral shell. In fact, organizational form, as the history of bureaucracy reveals, reflects social values and social purposes. In education, bureaucracy became the dominant educational form by late in the nineteenth century because of a mixture of setting and priority. It was because men confronted particular organizational problems—mass schooling in an urban and industrial society—with particular priorities that they built bureaucracies. Those priorities—efficiency over responsiveness, order over participation, uniformity over cultural variety—reflected cultural values that became built into the very structure and functioning of school systems. Those systems still retain the shape given them in large cities by late in the nineteenth century, and they continue, consequently, to serve similar purposes.

The problem of control is related to the problem of bureaucracy. School reformers saw in centrally directed, professionally operated educational systems a way of reducing public control of education. They argued that earlier, more decentralized systems were hindered by partisan politics, nepotism, and the general ignorance of the people who made important decisions. The movement to centralize educational control coincided with attempts to centralize municipal government more generally and to transfer decision-making power to a small body of qualified, first citizens. Lurking behind this movement, of course, were a fear and distrust of ordinary people, in this case mainly immigrants. The centralization of city government, including schools, took place during a period of heavy immigration and of mounting nativist sentiment. Nativism, not infrequently, was sponsored by people leading the movement for municipal reform. Bureaucracy and centralized control have served as ways of keeping the common people from using government, including the schools, to express their own purposes.

The structure and control of education are issues that cannot be divorced from what happens within classrooms. That should be clear from their history. Introducing informal education into public educational systems without making other radical alterations will be—as was, for example, the project method—like moving around the furniture in a box. It is the walls of the box itself that must be torn down if education is to serve new purposes.

The argument that structural reform must precede a change in educational purpose and function raises the issue of community control. *Crisis in the Classroom* contains a long chapter on educational reform movements in the 1960's. That chapter does not mention the movement for community control or decentralization. Neither topic, strange to say, is mentioned elsewhere in Mr. Silberman's book. Yet, to many people surely, these movements are where the action is in school reform. One can only conclude that Mr. Silberman is committed to the structure of public education as it exists. The voucher system, performance contracting, radical decentralization: These are not [the] kinds of reforms he advocates or, even, cares to discuss. Insofar as one might gather from *Crisis in the Classroom*, the crisis at Ocean–Hill Brownsville never existed. Anyone unaware of the vitality of proposals for changing the control and funding of public education would leave Mr. Silberman's book without realizing that intelligent, informed, and sane people consider these radical measures to be live options. There are limits beyond which Mr. Silberman does not help or assist his reader to go.

In fact, Mr. Silberman's book rests comfortably within the long-standing style of elite reform that has marked American education since early in the nineteenth century. Consider, for example, his comments on the way in which informal education will come to American schools:

> In the United States . . . the impetus is likely to come from the outside [of the school system] more often than from within. It is crucial, therefore, that the most careful preparations be made before the changes are introduced. As we have seen, American parents are perfectly capable of understanding and accepting informal education if it is explained to them, and American teachers can adapt informal teaching styles with grace and enthusiasm if—but only if—they receive sufficient training and support." [p. 320]

As another instance, consider Mr. Silberman's admiration for the manner in which reform was brought about in Portland, Oregon. A group of people from Harvard developed a plan for an innovative high school and then looked around the country for a school in which they could put their idea into action. Portland allowed them to set up shop. The assumption underlying this sort of reform is that experts should decide what is best and then simply do it, though careful, perhaps, to mind their public relations. The people, one presumes, should be grateful.

This is how school reform has usually been carried out in America. Groups of influential people, considering themselves especially expert, have tried, often with success, to force educational change. Social policy and social change, it is assumed, issue from the top down. The problem is that this style of reform works badly. Innovations introduced in this way have not fared well; somehow, they have not met the goals set by their sponsors, who remain unable to account for their failure. The example par excellence is the public school system, founded and developed in precisely this manner. Mr. Silberman himself documents its continued failure, but he fails to draw the correct moral, which is this: Elite social and educational reform, like welfare bureaucracy, is bankrupt as social policy. At this point in history, any reform worthy of the name must begin with a redistribution of power and resources. That is the only way in which to change the patterns of control and inaccessible organizational structures that dominate American life. It is the only way in which to make education, and other social institutions as well, serve new purposes.

There is no doubt in my mind that, if we change the schools in the direction that Mr. Silberman suggests, they will become nicer places for children to be. This alone would be a great improvement. But if that is all we do, we shall fail to make education more equal, to eradicate the class and race biases that adhere in educational structures, or to affect the society that surrounds the school. To move on those fronts requires not only considering solutions that Mr. Silberman does not discuss but raising questions that he seems reluctant to ask. Mr. Silberman has tamed educational discontent. By co-opting instead of resisting it, he has removed its threat and, unfortunately, its promise. He has shown the comfortable way to educational radicalism; others undoubtedly will follow, happy that they can enlist in the cause of justice without sacrifice.